1997

# MORAL
# DEVELOPMENT

*A Compendium*

Series Editor
## BILL PUKA
*Rensselaer Institute*

A GARLAND SERIES

# SERIES CONTENTS

VOLUME

# 2

# FUNDAMENTAL RESEARCH IN MORAL DEVELOPMENT

Edited with introductions by
BILL PUKA

GARLAND PUBLISHING, Inc.
New York & London
1994

**Library of Congress Cataloging-in-Publication Data**

Moral development : a compendium / edited with introductions by Bill
Puka.
    p.   cm.
    Includes bibliographical references.
    Contents: v. 1. Defining perspectives in moral development — v.
2. Fundamental research in moral development — v. 3. Kohlberg's
original study of moral development — v. 4. The great justice
debate — v. 5. New research in moral development — v. 6. Caring
voices and women's moral frames — v. 7. Reaching out.
    ISBN 0–8153–1549–X (v. 2 : alk. paper).
    1. Moral development.   I. Puka, Bill.
BF723.M54M66   1994
155.2'5—dc20                                94–462
                                                                CIP

Printed on acid-free, 250-year-life paper
Manufactured in the United States of America

# CONTENTS

# Series Introduction

Moral development is an interdisciplinary field that researches moral common sense and interpersonal know-how. It investigates how children evolve a sense of right and wrong, good and bad, and how adults hone their abilities to handle ethical issues in daily life. This includes resolving value conflicts, fermenting trusting, cooperative, and tolerant relationships, and setting ethical goals. It focuses most on how we think about these ethical issues (using our cognitive competences) and how we act as a result.

These seven volumes are designed to function as a standard, comprehensive sourcebook. They focus on central concerns and controversies in moral development, such as the relation between moral socialization and development, moral judgment and action, and the effects of culture, class, or gender on moral orientation. They also focus on central research programs in the field, such as the enduring Kohlberg research on moral stages, Gilligan research on ethical caring and women's development, and related prosocial research on altruism.

The studies contained here were compiled from the "wish lists" of researchers and educators in the field. These are the publications cited as most important (and, often, least available) for effective teaching and research training and for conveying the field to others. Unfortunately, the most crucial studies and essays in moral development are widely scattered across hard-to-find (sometimes out-of-print) volumes. Compiling them for a course is difficult and costly. This compendium eases these problems by gathering needed sources in one place, for a single charge. Regrettably, rising reprint fees frustrated plans to include *all* needed resources here, halving the original contents of these volumes and requiring torturous excising decisions. Even so, compared to other collections, this series approaches a true "handbook" of moral development, providing key sources on central issues rather than "further essays" on specialized topics.

A major aim of this series is to represent moral development accurately to related fields. Controversies in moral development have sparked lively interest in the disciplines of philosophy, education, sociology and anthropology, literary criticism, political science, gender and cultural studies, critical legal studies, criminology and corrections, and peace studies. Unfortunately, members of these fields were often introduced to moral development through the highly theoretical musings of Lawrence Kohlberg, Carol Gilligan, or Jean Piaget—or by highly theoretical commentaries on them. Jumping into the fray over gender or culture bias in stage theory, theorists in the humanities show virtually no familiarity with the empirical research that gave rise to it. Indeed, many commentators seem unaware that these controversies arise in a distinct research field and are context-dependent.

This compendium displays moral development as a social science, generating research findings in cognitive developmental, and social psychology. (Students are invited to recognize and approach the field as such.) Theory is heavily involved in this research—helping define the fundamental notions of "moral" and "development," for example. But even when philosophically or ethically cast, it remains psychological or social scientific theory. It utilizes but does not engage in moral philosophy per se. Otherwise, it is not moral development theory, but meta-theory. (Several extensively criticized Kohlberg articles on justice are meta-theory.) The confusion of these types and levels of theory has been a source of pervasive confusion in the field. The mistaken assessment of psychological theory by moral-philosophical standards has generated extremely damaging and misguided controversy in moral development. Other types of theory (moral, social, interpretive, anthropological) should be directed at moral development science, focusing on empirical research methods and their empirical interpretation. It should be theory of data, that is, not meta-theoretical reflection on the "amateur" philosophizing and hermeneutics interpolations of psychological researchers. (Likewise, social scientific research should not focus on the empirical generalizations of philosophers when trying to probe social reality or seek guidance in doing so from this theoretical discipline.) The bulk of entries in this compendium present the proper, empirically raw material for such "outside" theoretical enterprise.

To researchers, theorists, and students in related fields, this series extends an invitation to share our interest in the fascinating phenomena of moral development, and to share our findings thus far. Your help is welcomed also in refining our treacherously qualitative research methods and theories. In my dual disciplines of psychology and philosophy, I have found no more inspiring area of study. Alongside its somewhat dispassionate research orientation, this field carries on the ancient "cause" of its pre-scientific past. This is to show that human nature is naturally good—that the human psyche spontaneously unfolds in good will, cleaving toward fair-mindedness, compassion, and cooperative concern.

The first volume, *Defining Perspectives*, presents the major approaches to moral development and socialization in the words of chief proponents: Kohlberg, Bandura, Aronfreed, Mischel, Eysenck, and Perry. (Piaget is discussed in detail.) This first volume is required reading for those needing to orient to this field or regain orientation. It is crucial for clarifying the relations and differences between moral development and socialization that define research.

The second volume, *Fundamental Research*, compiles the classic research studies on moral levels and stages of development. These studies expose the crucial relation of role-taking and social perspective to moral judgment and of moral judgment to action. They also divine the important role of moral self-identity (viewing oneself as morally interested) in moral motivation.

The third volume contains *Kohlberg's Original Study*, his massive doctoral research project. The study, which has never before been published, sets the parameters for moral development research, theory, and controversy. (Major critical alternatives to Kohlberg's approach share far more in common with it than they diverge.) Here the reader sees "how it all started," glimpsing the sweep of Kohlberg's aspiration: to uncover the chief adaptation of humankind, the evolving systems of reasoning and meaning-making that, even in children, guide effective choice and action. Most major Kohlberg critiques fault features of this original study, especially in the all-male, all-white, all-American cast of his research sample. (Why look here for traits that characterize all humans in all cultures through all time?) It is worth checking these criticisms against the text, in context, as depictions of unpublished work often blur into hearsay. It is also worth viewing this study through the massive reanalysis of its data (Colby, Kohlberg, et al.) and the full mass of Kohlberg research that shaped stage theory. Both are liberally sampled in Volume Five.

*The Great Justice Debate,* the fourth volume, gathers the broad range of criticisms leveled at moral stage theory. It takes up the range of "bias charges" in developmental research—bias by gender, social class, culture, political ideology, and partisan intellectual persuasion. Chief among these reputed biases is the equation of moral competence and development with justice and rights. Here key features of compassion and benevolence seem overlooked or underrated. Here a seemingly male standard of ethical preference downplays women's sensibilities and skills. Responses to these charges appear here as well.

Volume Five, *New Research*, focuses on cross-cultural research in moral development. Studies in India, Turkey, Israel,
Korea, Poland, and China are included. While interesting in itself,
such research also supports the generalizability of moral stages,
challenged above. Indeed, Volume Five attempts to reconceive or
re-start the central research program of moral development from
the inception of its matured research methods and statistically
well-validated findings. From this point research is more data-
based than theory-driven. It can address criticism with hard
evidence. Regarding controversy in moral development, Volumes
Four and Five go together as challenge and retort.

Volume Six, *Caring Voices*, is devoted to the popular "different
voice" hypothesis. This hypothesis posits a distinct ethical orientation of caring relationship, naturally preferred by women, that
complements justice. Compiled here is the main record of Gilligan's
(and colleagues') research, including recent experiments with
"narrative" research method. The significant critical literature on
care is well-represented as well, with responses. While Gilligan's
empirical research program is more formative than Kohlberg's,
her interpretive observations have influenced several fields, especially in feminist studies. Few research sources have more commonsense significance and "consciousness-raising" potential. The student reader may find Gilligan's approach the most personally
relevant and useful in moral development.

*Reaching Out*, the final volume, extends moral development
concerns to "prosocial" research on altruism. Altruistic helping
behavior bears close relation to caring and to certain ideals of
liberal justice. This volume emphasizes the role of emotions in
helping (and not helping), focusing on empathic distress, forgive-
ness, and guilt. It also looks at early friendship and family influences. Moral emotions are related to ethical virtues here, which
are considered alongside the "vices" of apathy and learned help-
lessness. Leading researchers are included such as Hoffman,
Eisenberg, Batson, and Staub.

# INTRODUCTION

This volume provides the empirical basis for the most crucial tenets of moral development theory, especially Kohlberg's theory.

Included here are crucial studies by Rest (on the limitations and interrelation of moral stages), Selman (on social role-taking), Blatt (on developmental rates and their amenability to stimulation), Candee, and Krebs (on the relation of moral judgment to action). Blasi's comprehensive review of judgment-action research is included with his research on how moral self-identity bridges the judgment-action gap. The interesting relation between moral and religious development is also traced (Fowler and Oser), modeling potential applications of moral development to related areas.

Studies of "inherent moral development" are best assessed relative to environmentalist or socialization alternatives. Thus social-learning attempts to explain stage development are presented here (Denney and Duffy) with investigations of situational influences on development. For closer contrast, Hogan's developmental alternative to the Kohlberg-Piaget model is recalled. "Heretical" Piaget-Kohlberg research is cited by Damon (on early childhood development) and Turiel and Nucci (on conventional morality). Studying children significantly younger than Kohlberg's original research subjects, Damon developed a more multifaceted psychology of moral development and motivation, focusing on authority and distributive justice. By not prejudging conventional, or personally relative ethics, Turiel and Nucci discovered a developmental basis for their prominence in daily life. Indeed, these researchers uphold separate and legitimate tracks of such development that are not supplanted, but sustain alongside principled morality. Including Likona's survey of distinctly Piagetian research helps hold the line against Kohlberg revisionism and dominance. Gibbs and Youniss and Damon (in Volume Five) legitimate this effort, preferring Piagetian accounts of certain moral phenomena over Kohlberg's.

*Journal of Moral Education* Vol 4, No 2, pp 129-161
© Pemberton Publishing Company Ltd, 1975

MOSHE M. BLATT and LAWRENCE KOHLBERG

# The Effects of Classroom Moral Discussion upon Children's Level of Moral Judgment

Abstract:

An experiment is reported on the effects of a moral education programme in schools. Children were pretested on Kohlberg's index of level of moral thinking. The experimental group was then given twelve hours of discussion of moral problems other than those used in Kohlberg's test spread over twelve weeks. Subsequent testing showed that the experimental group had had tended to move towards a higher level of thinking when compared with controls.

Key Words:

Discussion of moral problems. Kohlberg. Moral thinking.

This paper describes an experiment in classroom moral education and reports its results. Such research reports upon programmes of moral education have been extremely rare since the 1930's. The 1920's and 1930's witnessed a great deal of practical and research interest in moral or character education in the public schools and in church groups (Hartshorne and May, 1928; Jones, 1936). During this period, moral education was conceived of as explanation of the conventional code, exhortation to follow the code, and the planning of group or individual activities which would manifest virtue or good works in terms of this code (Jones, 1936). Research evalution of the results of moral education classes was based on tests of increase of moral knowledge (verbal espousal of the conventional code) and increase in honesty or service as experimentally measured. The results of research evaluation were extremely disappointing. Most character education classes led to no significant changes in experimental tests of moral behaviour (Hartshorne and May, 1928-1930), though some led to slight changes in measured honesty (Jones, 1936). Slight changes in moral knowledge were not paralleled by changes in moral behaviour. These disappointing research results, fitting with liberal opposition to verbal indoctrination and to confusions of church and state in moral education (Kohlberg, 1967), led to a marked decline in moral education programmes.

On the basis of recent research findings (Kohlberg (1966, 1970), Kohlberg and Turiel (1971)), Kohlberg (1974) has elaborated an approach to moral education that might be free of many of the limitations of earlier approaches. The approach is centred on cross-cultural and longitudinal research findings indicating that moral judgment develops through the following culturally universal invariant sequence of stages.

Stage 1: *Obedience and punishment orientation.* Egocentric deference to superior power, prestige. Avoidance of punishment and of acts labelled ' bad '.

Offprints may be obtained from Dr Moshe Blatt, c/o Professor Kohlberg, Department of Education, Harvard University.

Stage 2: *Naive instrumental hedonism.* Right action is that instrumentally satisfying the self's need and occasionally other's. Awareness of relativism of value of each actor's needs and perspective. Naive egalitarianism and orientation to exchange and reciprocity.

Stage 3: *Interpersonal concordance or ' good boy' orientation.* Orientation to approval and to pleasing and helping others. Conformity to stereotypical images of majority or natural role behaviour, and judgment by intentions.

Stage 4: *Authority and social order orientation.* Maintaining the given social order for its own sake. Regard for earned expectations of others.

Stage 5: *Contractual legalistic orientation.* Recognition of an arbitrary element or starting point in rules or expectations for the sake of agreement. Duty defined in terms of contract, general avoidance of violation of the will or rights of others, and majority will and welfare.

Stage 6: *Universal ethical principle orientation.* Orientation not only to actually ordained social rules but to principles involving appeal to logical universality and consistency. These principles are primarily principles of justice, of reciprocity and equality of human action, of universal respect for human rights and for human personality.

These findings on moral judgment have been supported by a series of studies relating moral judgment to moral action. a variety of naturalistic and experimental studies have demonstrated clear-cut relationships between moral judgment and moral action in the areas of honesty, non-delinquency, refusal to violate the rights of others, and student activism. As an example, Krebs (see Kohlberg, in preparation) administered moral judgment interviews and a battery of four Hartshorne and May experimental tests of cheating to 120 junior high school subjects. He found that 73 per cent of the preconventional subjects cheated on one or more of the tests, that 66 per cent of the conventional subjects cheated, while only 20 per cent of the principled subjects cheated. Assuming that moral development passes through a natural sequence of stages, the approach defines the aim of moral education as the stimulation of the next step of development rather than indoctrination into the fixed conventions of the school, the church, or the nation. It assumes that movement to the next step of development rests not only on exposure to the next level of thought, but to experiences of conflict in the application of the child's current level of thought to problematic situations. In contrast to conventional moral education, then, the approach stresses:

1. Arousal of genuine moral conflict, uncertainty, and disagreement about genuinely problematic situations. (In contrast, conventional moral education has stressed adult ' right answers,' and reinforcement of the belief that virtue always is rewarded.)

2. The presentation of modes of thought one stage above the child's own. (In contrast, conventional moral education tends to shift between appeals to adult abstractions far above the child's level and appeals to punishment and prud_ence liable to rejection because they are below the child's level.)

These two principles are based on a series of experimental findings by Turiel and his colleagues using our moral measures (see Kohlberg, in preparation). The first principle may be stated as saying that verbal moral arguments or judgments are only assimilated into the child's thinking if they are one level above the child's own. Turiel divided sixth-grade children at varying stages of development into three experimental groups. One group received brief role-playing experiences with an adult verbalizing at one stage above the child's own, a second group was exposed to role-playing messages two stages above the child's own, and a third group received messages one stage below the child's own. The children exposed to messages one stage above their own assimilated more of the messages than did either of the other groups. When asked on a post-test to present their own advice on the moral situations, the children exposed to the stage above used more thinking at the stage to which they were exposed than did the other two groups. Subsequent studies demonstrated that this effect was due to rejection of lower level messages (which were comprehended) and to noncomprehension of the two-stage up messages (which were linked).

The second principle may be stated as saying that higher stage reasoning is assimilated by the child only if it arouses cognitive conflict in the child. As an example, Turiel found that moral reasoning at a higher stage than the child's own led to increased usage of moral thinking at the next stage up only if it disagreed with, or introduced uncertainty into, the child's own decision on moral dilemmas.

While the experimental studies of Turiel report statistically significant upward change by exposure to moral reasoning at the next stage up under appropriate conditions, the amount of such change is extremely limited. The present set of studies are the first to explore moral judgment change by applying developmental principles to a programme of moral education, in which cognitive conflict and exposure to higher stages of reasoning occurs in the context of continuing and intense moral discussion between peers in a classroom setting.

The present series of studies, then, explored the effects of guided peer discussions of moral conflicts upon junior and senior high school children's moral reasoning. The essential rationale was to expose the children to cognitive conflict about moral reasoning, to the awareness of different moral points of view, and to expose the children to judgments one stage above their own; by encouraging children at adjacent stages to argue and discuss until some change of the lower-stage children took place.

The experimental education studies reported here were not only designed to produce moral change by developmental principles, but to maximize the long range beneficial effects of such change. Conventional measures of moral change such as changes on behaviour and attitudinal measures of honesty or conscience have little predictive validity. Honesty measures administered longitudinally correlate very little with the same measures given a year later, and increases in honesty due to character education intervention wash out in a year in comparison with control groups (Jones, 1936). In contrast, moral judgment maturity in junior high and high school predicts well to adult moral maturity. This predictability increases in pre-adolescence. At age ten, moral maturity predicts poorly to adulthood whereas at thirteen it predicts reasonably well. This suggests, following Bloom's (1964) argument, that pre-adolescence is a favoured or 'critical' period for intervention into moral development. During the period from age ten to fourteen, children are typically moving from pre-conventional (Stage 1 and 2) to conventional (Stage 3 and 4) morality. A developmental intervention would aid those lagging in such a movement to take this next step. Without such aid some might be expected to stabilize at the pre-conventional level, as do most adolescent delinquents. Accordingly, our first study was devoted to intervention at the pre-adolescent (age twelve) level. Our second study replicated the pre-adolescent intervention with more representative classrooms and explored the effects of intervention at the adolescent or late high school level as well. Both studies involved one year follow-ups to provide a preliminary assessment of the long-range effectiveness of the intervention.

Our assessment of the moral discussion programme was focused upon change in stage of moral reasoning, since moral reasoning was the focus of the moral discussion programme. Since a comprehensive approach to moral education must attend to moral action as well as moral judgment, we decided to also include some Hartshorne and May experimental honesty measures in our assessment design.

Our research is presented as two studies. The first study was a pilot study of a moral discussion programme with a group of twelve children aged 11-12 in an upper middle-class Jewish Sunday school. The second study was a systematic replication in the public schools with four groups varying in age and social class, and with matched controls.

### Study 1 — A Pilot Classroom Discussion Programme in a Jewish Sunday School

Our first study of the effects of moral discussion was a pilot study, but is reported in depth for two reasons. First, all the basic findings in the study were replicated in Study 2. Second, the data analysis in Study 1 was conducted with more depth with regard to qualitative and quantitative analysis. As Kohlberg has argued, the validity of tests of theory rests not on group statistics based on large numbers of subjects, but on replication of expected pattern in each individual subject, where these replications cover wide variation of test and cultural setting. Study 1 is, in a sense, a single case study of one classroom intervention by one teacher which ' worked '. This case study of a classroom is replicated in Study 2 with four more classrooms taught by the same experimenter. The fact that the intervention ' worked ' in a replicable way is less a test of moral development theory than it is a test of whether the particular experimenter had some reliable impact on classroom groups. Moral development theory enters in the analysis of results in terms of individual children's patterns of change, given such impact. As an example, the theory claims that if a teacher has an impact upon structure of moral reasoning, it will be reflected in movement to the next stage up, *in each case*. In Study 1, we report pattern data on each case; pattern data is reported in more summary form in Study 2.

### Method
Subjects and Design:

The moral education programme took place in a Reform Jewish Sunday school class which the author taught composed of thirty children aged 11-12 and coming from professional or academic families. Of the thirty children, thirteen were randomly selected for pretesting. Eleven of the thirteen children were available for post-testing and ten for follow-up testing one year after the original post-test. Six of the eleven children were boys, five were girls.

The control groups used in the study were those used as controls in Turiel's experiments. There were three such control groups, all of the same age and social class as the experimental group. The second Turiel control group was Jewish like our experimental group, the remaining two groups were Christian. All three control groups were composed of children at the same moral stages found in our experimental group (Stages 2, 3, and 4). There were twelve children in the first control group, nine in the second, and twelve in the third. All control groups received pretests and post-tests spaced by about one month, as had our experimental group. The first control group (Control 1) taken from Turiel's first experiment (see Kohlberg, in preparation) was our basic pre-post control. The second control group (Control 2), taken from Turiel's second experiment, was added as a control for our follow-up study because it had a one-year follow-up test as well as a post-test. The third group (Control 3), was the experimental group in Turiel's first study, which was exposed to about 40 minutes of adult advice at one stage above the child's own. This group was added to determine whether our classroom change was a larger change than that obtained by brief passive exposures to higher level thinking.

Classroom Procedure:

Immediately after pretesting, the teaching programme began. The programme lasted for twelve weeks, a total of twelve hours of discussion. The discussions focused upon a series of moral conflict situations different from those employed in the Kohlberg moral judgment test used as the pretest.

After presenting a conflict situation, the children were asked to supply the possible ways of resolving it. These suggestions were noted on the blackboard. The children were then asked to elaborate the consequences of each solution for the individuals involved. In examining these consequences, the examiner attempted to point out psychological and social dimensions of the experiences involved. Next, children were asked to specify the standard or hierarchy of values implicit in each of the solutions, followed by a discussion of each of these moral standards or values. The writer then attempted to stimulate controversy by introducing controversial questions and issues that should be dealt with. He tried to establish an atmosphere in which there was protection of freedom of expression and in which understanding of alternative views was encouraged. This involved drawing a clear line between understanding someone's point of view and agreeing with it and clarifying the issues of disagreement.

As the pretest indicated, there was a wide range of moral judgment levels (Stages 1 through 4) used by the children. These differences between the children resulted in spontaneous arguments as to these standards and their application to the conflict situations. As these arguments developed, the examiner would take the ' solution ' proposed by a child who was one stage above the majority of the children discussing the dilemma and clarify and support that child's argument. The experimenter elaborated this solution until he felt that the children understood its logic and seemed convinced that its logic was reasonable or fair. The experimenter made it a point to leave as much of the argument to the children as possible; he stepped in to summarize the discussion, to clarify, add to the argument and occasionally present a point of view, himself. In addition, he tried to encourage higher level children to point out why the stages below were incomplete or inadequate. When the experimenter felt that the higher stage children's attempts to point out the weakness of the lower stage arguments or the validity of their own arguments were inadequate, the experimenter would take over and try to present a more convincing argument.

At the point at which the experimenter felt that there was a consensus (say, on Stage 3) among the children, he would present a new situation in which he followed the same procedure but supported an approach which was characteristic of thinking one stage above the previous majority consensus (Stage 4).

In summary, then, the procedure was based on the assumption that higher stage subjects would influence lower stage subjects more than the reverse in a free discussion. This 'natural' tendency was reinforced by the experimenter's side-taking arguments. The procedure also assumed that arguments one stage up would be most effective. This assumption led to supporting progressively higher levels of argument advanced by the children, eg, initial support for Stage 3 subjects and later support for Stage 4 subjects.

Curriculum Content and Sequence:

The only prepared curriculum materials used in the study were a set of ' open ' moral dilemmas designed to arouse genuine conflict or uncertainty as to moral reasoning and choice. Open dilemmas, like the Kohlberg test dilemmas, are ones on which there is no clear agreed upon ' morally correct ' choice. ' Should you steal a drug to save your wife? ' This is an open dilemma. ' Should you steal a baseball because you want it for a game? ' is a closed dilemma, useless for developmental discussion. Some of the conflict situations used were biblical, some non-biblical. The first situation (Genesis, Chapter 13) describes the conflict between Abraham and Lot. This situation was used to point out a conflict in which a stronger and more powerful figure did not impose his will on a less powerful one, and did not pursue selfish and hedonistic goals with regard to material goods. The experimenter used this situation to expose the class to Stage 3 reasoning (orientation to approval and to pleasing and helping others).

In the second situation (Genesis, Chapter 14: 1-23), Abraham contributes to saving the life of Lot and others and does not want to be rewarded for it. In this situation the experimenter intended to explore the value of human life in general and contrast this with the value of property. In addition, the experimenter stimulated discussion and exploration of the issue of moral motivation and reward, particularly that of Abraham. A third non-biblical situation was made up for the classroom programme, as follows:

> In a working family of six people the oldest son graduated from high school and was accepted to a college with a partial scholarship. Just before he was ready to go, his father became ill and was hospitalized. The family did not have means for support, unless the oldest son postponed going to college (which would possibly mean losing his partial scholarship) and went to work to support his family until the father was able to work.
> What should the boy do?

In this situation the experimenter continued to uphold and support Stage 3 arguments.

In a fourth situation (Genesis, Chapter 22: 1-19), Abraham offers Isaac for sacrifice. At this point the experimenter introduced and upheld Kohlberg's Stage 4 mentality (authority and social order maintaining orientation) in its application to a religious or divine authority, defining duties based on maintaining a socio-religious order for its own sake, and upon maintaining earned expectations of others. In exploring this situation the experimenter led the class to reconsider the previous three situations. This time the experimenter began to support and uphold the children who argued on Stage 4.

The fifth situation (Genesis, Chapter 37) deals with the episode in which Joseph was sold into slavery by his brothers. This situation was chosen by the experimenter to introduce Stage 5 issues of ' rights '. The questions were raised, ' Did the father have the right to prefer and love one child more than the others? ' ' If so, did he have the right to express openly such a preference? ' ' Did the brothers have the right to be angry, and did this " right " justify their actions? '

Following this discussion of rights, the experimenter introduced the general issue, ' How do we know what is " right "? ' Here the experimenter proposed that, ' one possible way of resolving disagreement about what is right is based on social contract — that what is right is what the members in a democratic society freely agree upon '. Such a view reflects Stage 5 contractual legalistic orientation (recognition of an arbitrary element or starting point in rules or expectations for the sake of agreement; general avoidance of violation of the will or rights of others). In this context, traffic laws and the rights of property were examined, and a re-examination of the penal system was begun. In the last session the experimenter introduced some ideas of Kohlberg's Stage 6 (orientation to universal ethical principles) presenting situations of obedience to law in Nazi Germany and obedience to discriminatory laws in the South at present and during the slavery period. Discussion centred around the issue of an act being morally right and legally wrong, focusing upon the notion of moral principles of ' moral law ' as distinct from legal law.

Pretest of Moral Judgment:
During the first meeting the experimenter interviewed each child individually, using Kohlberg's moral judgment Situations I, III, IV and VIII.

Post-Test of Moral Judgment:
The post-test consisted of the original four situations administered to the children on the pretest. In addition, two new situations, II and VII were added. The post-testing was done by two people, the experimenter (Blatt) and Kohlberg. As in the pretest, the entire class took the same paper and pencil cheating test.

Follow-Up Testing of Moral Judgment:
One year after the post-test, the children were readministered the four pretest situations.

Scoring Moral Judgment:
For each of the hypothetical situations Kohlberg (1958, 1970) has formulated a detailed ' sentence coding guide ' constructed on the basis of responses given by a large number of subjects. A subject's responses to a given situation are divided in

' thought-content ' units roughly corresponding to sentences. Each unit is then classified according to aspect and stage. A profile of each subject was formed from the percentage of statements given at each stage as determined by the coding guide. In addition to classifying the subject in terms of the stage most used, this profile of per cent usage of each stage (1-6) yields a moral maturity score (MMS). The MMS is the sum of the products of the percentages in a ' profile ' multiplied by ordinal value or number of the stage. The maximum MMS is 600 (100 per cent Stage 6), the minimum is 100 (100 per cent Stage 1).

In addition to being coded by sentences, each story was globally rated by story, ie, assigned a stage score according to a global rating manual. The rating assigns either a pure stage or a mixture of a major and a minor stage to each story. On each story three points are assigned. If a mixed orientation is found, two points are assigned to the dominant stage and one point to the minor stage. Points for each stage are added across situations, and percentaged, yielding profiles and MMS scores as in the sentence method.

Moral Judgment Scoring Reliability:

In the present study a rater scored blind all protocols on both global and sentence scores. A second rater also scored blind all protocols by global rating only.

Because published data on reliability is scarce, we present the global rating reliability coefficients between raters in detail in Table 1.

TABLE 1

Interjudge Agreement, Global Rating Method, Study 1

A.  Percentage Agreement on Major Code of each Child at each Testing across Stories

|  | Pretest | Post-Test | Follow-Up | Total |
|---|---|---|---|---|
| Same Stage | 80 | 70 | 73 | 73 |
| One Stage Off | 13 | 16 | 28 | 19 |
| Two Stages Off | 7 | 11 |  | 6 |
| Three Stages Off |  | 3 |  | 1 |

B.  Percentage Agreement on Major Code of Response to each Story

|  | III | IV | VIII | I | VI |
|---|---|---|---|---|---|
| Same Stage | 77 | 68 | 69 | 78 | 40 |
| One Stage Off | 23 | 23 | 21 | 7 | 60 |
| Two Stages Off |  | 8 | 7 | 15 |  |
| Three Stages Off |  |  | 13 |  |  |

C.  Correlations Between Judges' Global Ratings of Uses of each Stage

| Stages: | 1 | 2 | 3 | 4 | 5 | 6 | M.M.S. |
|---|---|---|---|---|---|---|---|
| Interjudge  r: | .86 | .84 | .76 | .74 | .26[1] | .83 | .89 |

[1] The low correlation between judges on Stage 5 is caused by a single ' deviant ' case, since only four of the 33 cases had any score on the stage at all.

The correlation coefficients of agreement in Table 1 are similar (except for Stage 5 scores) to those reported elsewhere, as are the percentage agreement scores.

Pretests and Post-Tests of Moral Behaviour:

Previous to the moral judgment interview, the entire class simultaneously took three Hartshorne and May (1928) paper and pencil cheating tests, which are administered as ' Coordination Tests '. These three tests were the ' Squares ' test,

'Circle' test and 'Mazes' test. Copies of these tests and instructions used are to be found in Lehrer (1967) and Krebs (1967). The tests were readministered after the last discussion session.

## Results
### Amount of Change:

The major findings are that the classroom experience led to a significant increase in moral judgment maturity and that the increase was still evident one year later, in contrast to changes in the control groups. The overall findings with regard to moral maturity are presented in Table 2.

TABLE 2

Moral Maturity Scores of Experimental and Control Groups on
Pretest and Post-Test — Study 1

|  | Experimental | | Control 1 | | Control 2 | | Control 3 | |
|---|---|---|---|---|---|---|---|---|
|  | Glob | Sent | Glob | Sent | Glob | Sent | Glob | Sent |
| Pretest | 238 | 251 | | | 285 | 288 | | |
| Post-Test | 304 | 314 | | | 289 | 271 | | |
| New Stories | 333 | 278 | | | — | — | | |
| Year Follow-Up | 293 | 282 | | | 263 | 267 | | |
| Pre to Post Change | 66 | 63 | 06 | 08 | 04 | −17 | 05 | −12 |
| Post to Follow-Up Change | −11 | −31 | | | −26 | −08 | | |

As Table 2 indicates, the mean increase in moral maturity scores of the classroom groups from Pretest to Post-Test (on the stories used in both tests) was 66 by the global rating method, and 63 by the sentence method.[1] (A mean increase in moral maturity score of 100 would indicate a one stage upward movement.) This change was statistically significant (t = 3.8, p <.01). In contrast to the increase of 66 points by the classroom group, the various measures of control group change on moral maturity score from pretest to post-test ranged from − 17 to + 08, none of these changes being statistically significant.

Expressed in more qualitative terms, 63 per cent of the experimental children moved up one stage or slightly more (in modal stage), 9 per cent moved up half a stage (to a mixture of their pretest stage and the next higher and only 28 per cent remained at the same stage on the post-test. (This patterning of change is analyzed further in the next section.) In contrast, only 5 per cent (one of 21) of the control subjects showed a one stage change of dominant stage and a moral maturity increase of more than 50.

Expressed in still different terms, 38 per cent of the thinking of the children post-test was at a higher level than their thinking in the pretest (or 30 per cent if the sentence coding method is considered).[2] In contrast, the percent of thinking

[1] The tables present classroom results by global and sentence methods which compound differences in method with differences in rater. The reported global scores are those of one rater, the sentence scores those of the other.

[2] This estimate is based on examining increases in each subject's usage of each stage above his modal level (as defined on the pretest). If a Stage 3 subject used 10 per cent Stage 4 and 5 per cent Stage 5 thinking on pretest and used 30 per cent Stage 4 and 10 per cent Stage 5 thinking on post-test, the amount of higher level thinking he engaged in on post-test would be 25 per cent. A percentage increase in higher thinking implies, of necessity, a parallel drop in lower thinking.

at a higher level on post-test in Control 1 was 4 per cent (1 per cent by the sentence method), 17 per cent in Control 2 (2 per cent by the sentence method), and 5 per cent in Control 3 (on both measures).

On one year follow-up, the post-test results are essentially unchanged. The experimental group has declined slightly but non-significantly in moral maturity scores ( – 11 on the global scores, – 31 on the sentence score), but so has the control group (which dropped – 26 on the global rating and – 08 on the sentence ratings).

The results indicate that an educational programme was able to stimulate or ' speed up ' natural developmental trends in moral judgment. Furthermore, the stimulation of development which occurred was not an artificial acceleration followed by a plateau. While the classroom group as a whole made no gains from post-test to follow-up, neither did the controls. In other words, the control group showed no tendency to catch up to the experimental children during the follow-up.

It is interesting to note that not only did the controls fail to catch up with the experimental group in the year follow-up, but the children who failed to change in the experimental group also failed to catch up on the follow-up.

A correlational analysis of moral maturity scores clarifies this point. Pretest level did not predict very well to post-test level (r = .65), while post-test level did predict well to follow-up status (r = .84). This high correlation indicates that there was little catch up by the non-changers in the experiment to disturb the order of maturity on post-test. The four experimental subjects who showed no change in the experimental period (ie, changed less than 50 MMS points) also showed no change from post-test to follow-up.

Finally, Table 2 not only indicates that the post-test gains of the classroom group are essentially stable over time, but also indicates that they generalize to new verbal situations. While none of the stories used in the pretest was discussed in class, it is possible that they might have been informally discussed by the children or consciously related to the class discussion. Performance on the two new stories first used in the post-test is not open to this interpretation. Table 2 indicates that post-test performance on the new stories is at about the same level as post-test performance on the retest stories.

In summary, we may conclude that this particular experimental class had a genuine effect upon the average moral judgment maturity of its members still manifested one year later. Further consideration of the experimental replicability of the developmental effect is presented in Study 2.

Moral Behaviour Change:

Although naturalistic studies indicated a correlation between moral judgment maturity and experimental honesty, the increase in moral judgment maturity in the class was not reflected in an increase in experimental's honesty, the amount of cheating on the pretest and the post-test was essentially the same. Those who cheated on the pretest cheated on the post-test, while those who resisted cheating on the pretest resisted on the post-test (with one exception). Interpretation of this negative finding is presented in its replication in Study 2. The remainder of our findings and interpretations of Study 1 are devoted to the question of the meaning of the experimental effect for developmental theory as this relates to the pattern rather than the amount of change in the experimental group.

Pattern of Change:

We have so far considered only the overall moral maturity score. The actual pattern of usage of each stage of thinking by the classroom group at each testing is presented in Table 3.

TABLE 3

Usage of each Stage of Thought by the Classroom Group at Three Testings (Global Method[1]) — Study 1

| Stage: | 1 | 2 | 3 | 4 | 5 | 6 |
|---|---|---|---|---|---|---|
| Pretest | 14 | 47 | 25 | 14 | 00 | 00 |
| Post-Test | 08 | 23 | 27 | 39 | 01 | 02 |
| Follow-Up | 14 | 22 | 30 | 28 | 02 | 03 |
| Change | | | | | | |
| Pre to Post | −06 | −24 | 02 | 25 | 01 | 02 |

[1] The parallel percentages by the sentence scoring method were all within 5 per cent of the corresponding global scores reported here.

Table 3 indicates a significant decline (− 24 per cent or − 12 per cent) in Stage 2 usage and a significant increase (+ 20 per cent or + 25 per cent) in Stage 4 thinking after the classroom experience (t = 2.5, p <.05 for both Stage 2 and Stage 4 changes on global ratings). No significant changes occurred from post-test to follow-up.

The results of Table 3 are open to two interpretations. The first is that most change was a change of Stage 2 children to Stage 4, a two stage up change. The alternative interpretation is that children's Stage 2 thinking changed to Stage 3 and Stage 3 thinking changed to Stage 4. To examine this issue, Table 4 presents change scores relative to the child's own moral stage.

TABLE 4

Percent Stage Change in Experimental and Control Groups Defined in Reference to Child's Original Modal Level — Study 1 (Global Method[1])

| Stage Relative to Subject's Modal Stage: | −2 | −1 | 0 | +1 | +2 |
|---|---|---|---|---|---|
| Experimental, Pre- to Post | −04 | −09 | −29 | 28 | 10 |
| Experimental, Pre- to Follow-Up | −06 | −09 | −23 | 23 | 08 |
| Control 2 Pre- to Post | −02 | −01 | −16 | +17 | 00 |
| Control 2 Pre- to Follow-Up | 09 | 04 | −20 | 02 | 04 |

[1] A similar pattern was found using the sentence method.

Table 4 indicates more changes to one stage up than to two stages up, an 18 per cent difference on the global measure. Expressed differently, the +1 increase (on the global measure) is statistically significant (t = 2.4, p <.05), the

*11*

+2 increase is not. This +1 increase is the 'normal' longitudinal pattern of change in a three-year interval between test and retest (Kramer, 1968).

TABLE 5

Stage Patterns of each Classroom S* at each
Test and Scores on Moral Interest and Conduct

| S | Pretest | Post-Test | Follow-Up | Cheated | Interest |
|---|---------|-----------|-----------|---------|----------|
| 1 | 2 | 2 (4) | 2 | no | low |
| 2 | 2 | 2 (1) | 1 (2) | yes | low |
| 3 | 2 (1) | 3 | 3 (2) | yes | medium |
| 4 | 2 | 2 (3) | 3 | yes | medium |
| 5 | 2 | 3 | 4 | no | high |
| 6 | 2 – 3 | 4 | 3 | no | high |
| 7 | 2 – 3 | 4 | 3 | yes | — |
| 8 | 2 – 3 | 4 (3) | 2 (1) | yes | — |
| 9 | 3 (2) | 4 | 4 | no | high |
| 10 | 3 | 4 (2) | — | — | — |
| 11 | 4 | 4 | 4 | no | high |

* S was considered a pure type if more than 50 per cent of his score was at a single stage no more than 33 per cent at another. He was considered a mixed type, eg, 3 (2), if his most used stage, eg, 3, was used less than 50 per cent and his next most used stage, eg, 2, was used more than 25 per cent.

As noted in the introduction to Study 1, the issue of pattern of movement is not one of group averages. Developmental theory holds that if a classroom process has an effect upon structure of reasoning, it will be reflected in movement to the next stage up *in each case*. Each deviation from the pattern must be plausibly accounted for, either in terms of measurement error or in the provisions of the theory. To consider the pattern issue, Table 5 presents the pretest, post-test and follow-up scores of each case. The cases are grouped as *non-changers* (four children who remained unchanged in modal stage from pretest to post-test), *developmental changers* (three children who moved up to the next stage) and *stage-skippers* (four children who moved up more than one stage). Three of the four 'stage-skippers' were mixed Stage 2-3 types at pretest who moved to Stage 4. The four 'stage-skippers' are an anomaly for developmental theory. The following interpretations of this anomaly are available:

   (a)  Interpretations consistent with developmental theory:

      (i)  The stage-skippers genuinely moved more than one stage, but in a developmental pattern, eg, they moved from Stage 2 to Stage 3 and then from Stage 3 to Stage 4, having been at Stage 3 at some period between the pretest and the post-test. This is a case of measurement error due to timing of the retests.

     (ii)  The stage-skippers learned some of the content of Stage 4 thinking through processes of verbal learning and imitation but did not really develop Stage 4 moral reasoning structure. As an example, they picked up phrases like 'moral law', 'God's law' used by Stage 4 subjects but did not really assimilate the underlying reasoning from the perspective of a generalized other or member of a sociomoral system. This is a case of measurement error due to inability to score for structure independent of content.

   (b)  Interpretation inconsistent with developmental theory:

*12*

(i) Social learning or didactic teaching and observational learning lead the stage-skippers to direct assimilation of a higher stage of reasoning without possession of the intervening stage-structure.

(ii) The stage-skippers, though showing a primary Stage 2 usage, had full comprehension of Stage 3 and Stage 4. Their stage of *production,* ie, their initial tendency to prefer Stage 2, and their final tendency to prefer Stage 4 were due to non-developmental social prestige or social learning factors, but their stage of *comprehension* was developmentally determined.

In deciding between these interpretations, we need to consider another major anomaly for developmental theory in the data of Table 5. In addition to evidence of stage-skipping, there is evidence of 'regression' or downward stage-change. According to developmental theory, true regression cannot occur except under conditions of organismic trauma damage or disorganization. In longitudinal work, downward movement of one-half stage or more (fifty or more moral maturity points) is taken to be an anomaly or 'regression' from the point of view of developmental theory, ie, it is a change not dismissed as measurement error.

In the previous section, we noted that an upward change of fifty or more moral maturity points could be interpreted as a change not due to measurement error, and that only one of the thirty-three Turiel controls showed such an upward change. In the present study, none of the thirty-three Turiel controls dropped fifty or more moral maturity points in the three-month test-retest interval. Neither did any of the experimental subjects drop fifty points in the period from pretest to post-test. The anomaly of 'regression' then occurred only in the follow-up period for the experimentals.

The two anomalies in Table 5 'stage-skipping' and 'regression' are systematically related. Three of the four children who regressed were in the Stage 2-3 group who advanced most from pretest to post-test. As Table 5 indicates, these three regressors 'skipped' Stage 3 stabilization to become Stage 4 at the post-test and then returned to Stage 3 or 2 in the follow-up. Tables 4 and 5, then, indicate that no classroom movement occurred in which +2 thought was assimilated and maintained without substantial prior usage of +1 thought. Where post-test +2 increase occurred at the expense of poorly stabilized +1 thought (in the pretest Stage 2-3 mixed types), these mixed types tended to 'regress' to a +1 level on follow-up. In contrast, where the class experience led to solid +1 increase, this movement could be built upon in subsequent development between post-test and follow-up. (As an example, Subject 5, a stabilized Stage 2 on pretest, moved to Stage 3 on the post-test and to Stage 4 on the follow-up).

The systematic relation of the two anomalies leads us, then, to interpret the apparent stage-skipping as measurement error. In other words, the content of +2 thought was assimilated without assimilation of its structure, and the scoring system did not allow adequate discrimination between content and structure. This interpretation is further examined and supported in the Study 2 replication.

A second major theoretical issue needs to be considered in relation to change pattern. This is the question of whether the classroom change represented the development of new higher stages absent at the pretest period, or merely the expansion of the next stage of thinking the child was already beginning to use. In recent studies Rest (Rest, Turiel and Kohlberg, 1969) has found that:

1. Assimilation of the +1 or +2 advice is contingent upon the capacity to comprehend that advice (as indicated by the ability to paraphrase it without distortion).
2. Comprehension of a higher level of advice is limited to those who spontaneously use that stage of advice (to the extent of at least 20 per cent of spontaneous responses to the pretest).
3. As implied by 1 and 2, only those already using 20 per cent or more of +1 reasoning showed significant increase in +1 usage after exposure to it.

The Rest findings suggest that simple passive exposure to the next stage up cannot lead to actual formation of a new stage. In contrast, Turiel reports some findings that exposure to cognitive conflict may lead some subjects to reorganize or generate new thinking at the next stage up. In the present study, it appeared that the experimental condition was effective more in active functions of the next step of reasoning rather than in expansion of already present +1 reasoning through passive exposure to new exemplifications of it.

Applied to our situation, the Rest findings on passive exposure lead to the expectation that the only children who could show a marked increase on +1 usage would be children who already showed some (20 per cent) +1 usage on pretest. In fact, this did not turn out to be the case. The +1 increase on the post-test of those showing some ($\geq$ 20 per cent) +1 usage on the pretest was 16 per cent (by global or 9 per cent by sentence methods) while the +1 increase on the post-test of those showing no (< 20 per cent) +1 pretest usage was 30 per cent (or 24 per cent by the sentence method). In summary, the classroom seemed to lead to the formation of a higher level of thought and not simply to its expansion.

Personal Characteristics of Changers:

We noted that only 63 per cent of the experimental subjects showed marked change due to the experimental treatment. One explanation for the finding of developmental change in some experimental subjects and not in others is that the changers were already transitional to the next stage. We have just discussed some findings inconsistent with this notion, eg, the findings that the changers were not already using some +1 thought on the pretests. Other characteristics of our changers are more compatible with the notion that they are transitional. Our Stage 4 experimental subjects failed to change. This is compatible with a variety of findings indicating that Stage 4 is an upper ceiling of development at age twelve and is therefore not amenable to experimental change.

Aside from status as transitional, a plausible condition for change is interest in, and attention to the discussion programme. To ascertain interest, the second post-test interviewer (Kohlberg) asked eight of the children what they thought of the programme and of the experimenter's teaching. Their responses could easily be classified into the following three levels of interest:

Low — Said nothing positive about the classes. When asked, 'Was the class more interesting than other Sunday school classes?' said, 'I don't know,' or

' No.'

*Medium* — Expressed ' polite ' or balanced approval or interest in the class. ' I liked it,' ' It was quite interesting,' ' It isn't that interesting all the time.' ' Some of the discussions are interesting, some are not.'

*High* — The key component of this response was ' challenge '. A typical response was, ' I liked the discussions because you really have to think very hard to solve them. I like that if we give him an answer, he gives another question.'

Children were also classified as to whether they changed little (less than 50 points in moral maturity scores), moderately (50-100 points) or markedly (over 100 points) from pretest to post-test. The results were that both of the two subjects showing moderate interest changed moderately, and that three of the four subjects showing high interest showed marked or high change, while the two children expressing low interest showed no change.

We do not know whether retrospective interest was itself an expression of the fact of having changed or whether it is an independent predictor of change. The association does increase confidence that developmental change relates to an active process of classroom involvement.

## Study 2 — Classroom Discussions in Public Junior High and High Schools

Study 2 was an extension and replication of the pilot study. A programme of classroom discussion was carried out by the writer with four public school class-rooms. These classrooms were chosen to systematically vary age (sixth grade and tenth grade) and to vary socio-economic status (lower middle-class versus lower-class) as associated with race (white versus black) in the community which was the site of the experiment. As noted earlier, the junior high school age was con-sidered as ' optimal period ' for a moral discussion programme, a notion supported by the results of Study 1. We wanted to determine whether a later period (tenth grade) would be of equal promise. With regard to socio-economic status and race, our white lower middle-class group represented what is often called the ' common man ' group in the sociological literature; our black lower-class group, confound-ing race or minority group status with socio-economic status, represented what is often called a ' disadvantaged ' group in the literature. Our selection of the ' dis-advantaged ' group was not based on the intention of studying racial differences in moral judgment. Rather, our intention was to assess the potential of a moral discussion programme with a group for whom purely verbal methods of education often seem ineffective, particularly if these methods are employed by teachers (like the writer) who represent the white middle-class. Our selection of the ' common man ' group was meant to obtain a different and representatively more numerous group than the upper-middle-class Jewish academic group used in Study 1.

In addition to extending the population base from that used in Study 1, more precise control groups were established. Two control groups for each experimental group were employed. The first control group spent its time in the usual class-room activities while moral discussion occurred for the experimentals. The second control group discussed the moral dilemmas used in the experimental groups under the supervision of their regular teacher, with little systematic teacher intervention, and with no effort by the teacher to use developmental principles. The aim of the study, then, was to determine the replicability and generality of the results of the first study, and to determine whether the results depended upon more than the sheer exposure of children to verbal moral dilemmas.

## Method

Design of Population:

One hundred and thirty-two subjects were chosen from a suburban Chicago school system. The subjects came from four schools, two predominantly black schools, and two predominantly white. The black children were generally from a lower-class background. The white children were mostly lower middle-class. For reference purposes, the groups will be labelled ' common man ' (white lower middle-class and upper lower-class) and ' disadvantaged ' (black upper lower-class and lower lower-class). Two grades were studied for each status group, sixth grade (age 11-12) and tenth grade (age 15-16). For reference purposes, these age-grade groups are labelled ' age 12 ' and ' age 16 '. For each age and status group, three conditions or groups were set up. The first, experimental group, *ExI*, engaged in moral discussion led by the writer using developmental principles. The second group, *ExII*, discussed the same moral dilemmas used in ExI, but without active leadership by an adult. The third group, *Control*, was the usual control group. There were, then, twelve class groups of eleven children each, representing all combinations of the following factors:

> Treatment: (a) ExI, (b) ExII, (c) Control
> Age: (d) 11-12, (e) 15-16
> Race: (f) white, (g) black

Within each group there were approximately equal numbers of boys and girls. Boys and girls within a single original classroom or home-room were randomly assigned to the ExI and ExII groups. Control children were obtained from another home-room group. At the younger age, both the common man and the disadvantaged control groups turned out to be significantly higher on IQ and academic achievement than their respective controls.

Classroom Procedures:

The basic procedures for running moral discussions in the ExI condition were similar to those discussed in Study 1. The following minor differences in procedures existed:

1. In Study 1, there were twelve weekly discussion sessions of more than one hour each; in Study 2, there were eighteen sessions held twice a week of forty-five minutes each.
2. In Study 1, Biblical and non-Biblical dilemmas were employed. No Biblical dilemmas were employed in Study 2. New dilemmas were written, and these were organized around the following issues corresponding to Kohlberg's (1972) issue-scoring system[3]:
   A. Law, Rules and their functions.

---

[3] These and additional dilemmas are obtainable at reproduction cost from Moral Education Corporation, Larsen Hall 301, Harvard University, Cambridge, Massachusetts 02138.

B. Issues of Conscience, motives and sanctions for action.

C. Family and parent-child relationships.

D. Authority and its relation to the individual.

E. Property issues and rights.

G. Punishment and justice in the relation of crime to punishment.

H. Value of Life.

I. Truth.

J. Love and sexual relationships.

To obtain some impression of the dilemmas and the actual classroom process, we present two classroom discussions of a dilemma as Appendix A.

The procedure for the ExII group differed from the ExI group in that it was mostly leaderless. In each classrom a child read the moral dilemma presented for discussion. A teacher from the permanent school staff was present in each room in accordance with school regulations but was instructed to remain out of the discussion as much as possible. This was done more easily and to a greater extent with the older groups. Observations in the younger ExII groups indicated that the teacher sometimes stepped in to give the child ' the right answer ', eg, ' stealing is always wrong '.

Pretest of Moral Judgment:

The same four dilemmas used in Study 1 were presented in an individual interview to all subjects by graduate students trained by the writer.

Post-Test of Moral Judgment:

As in Study 1, the original four pretest dilemmas were presented as well as two additional dilemmas new on post-test. The period from pretest to post-test was 10-12 weeks.

Follow-Up:

Retesting on the original four dilemmas was conducted a little more than one year after the post-test.

Scoring Moral Judgment:

The interviews were scored blind (no knowledge of individual or groups scored) by experienced scorers at Harvard. Scoring was based on the issue scoring procedure (Kohlberg, 1972). This procedure results in scores globally for each issue (issues) globally for each story (stories) and for issues on each story (cells). Results were similar for each of the measures so only the results by issues, the most reliable score, are reported.

Scoring Reliability Pretest and Post-Test of Moral Behaviour:

As is Study 1, three Hartshorne and May cheating tests were administered on pretest and post-test.

Results

Amount of Change due to Experimental Conditions:

The major findings are that, as in Study 1, the classroom experience led to a significant increase in moral judgment as compared to the control groups, and that this increase was still evident one year later. These results are presented in Table 6.

As Table 6 indicates, ExpI, the developmental moral discussion groups, increased an average of 34 points (one-third stage) in moral maturity from pretest to post-test, while the other two groups remained essentially unchanged. On one year follow-up, all the groups had increased about the same amount (about one-third of a stage), ie, the control groups showed no catch-up with the ExpI group.

In terms of amount of change, the average moral maturity increase of 34 points was less than the 66 point increase achieved in the classroom of Study 1. The mean increase in the four experimental classes of Study 2 ranged from 13 to 52. Amount of change was also less in terms of the percentage of experimental subjects moving up one full modal stage or more. While in Study 1, 63 per cent of the subjects showed such movement, in this study only 19 per cent of the subjects showed full one-stage-up movement. While the amount of change in the ExpI condition was less than in Study 1, the change was genuine.

### TABLE 6
#### Moral Maturity Scores of Experimental and Control Groups on Pretest and Post-Test — Study 2

|  | ExpI | ExpII | Control |
|---|---|---|---|
| Pretest | 241 (241)[1] | 243 (245) | 254 (262) |
| Post-Test | 275 (272) | 250 (256) | 239 (242) |
| Follow-Up | 305 | 293 | 279 |
| Pre-Post Change | +34 ( 31) | +07 ( 11) | −15 (−20) |
| Post-Follow-Up Change | ÷30 | ÷43 | 40 |

[1] Numbers in parentheses are the mean for the full original sample. Of the original sample of 132 subjects, 25 were lost on follow-up. The means for this group of 107 subjects are presented without parentheses.

Analyses of variance, summarized in Table 7, indicated that this differential effect of the ExpI condition was statistically significant.

Table 7 presents, in its second column, comparisons of change scores from pre-test to post-test for the various groups. The table indicates that the difference in change scores between the experimental and the control groups would occur by

### TABLE 7
#### Analysis of Variance and Covariance (IQ Controlled) of Moral Maturity Pretest and Change Scores — Study 2

| Source | d.f | Pretest F | | Pre-Post Change F | | Post-Follow-Up Change F |
|---|---|---|---|---|---|---|
| Exp Condition | 2 | .6 | | 8.6*** | (8.3***)[1] | .3 ( .4) |
| SES[2] | 1 | 7.0** | ( .6) | 3.0 | (1.1) | .5 ( .1) |
| Age | 1 | 57.7*** | (29.7***) | .1 | ( .0) | .2 ( .1) |
| Sex | 1 | .7 | ( 1.9) | .0 | ( .0) | .4 ( .4) |
| Condition X SES | 2 | 1.8 | ( .5) | .0 | ( .0) | .3 ( .1) |
| Condition X Age | 2 | 2.7 | ( .9) | .3 | ( .7) | .2 ( .8) |
| Condition X Sex | 1 | 1.0 | ( .8) | .2 | ( .7) | .4 ( .3) |
| SES X Age | 1 | 2.8 | ( .0) | 2.8 | (3.0) | 1.3 (1.6) |
| SES X Sex | 1 | .4 | ( 6 ) | 1.8 | (1.6) | .3 ( .2) |
| Age X Sex | 1 | 7.4** | ( 6.6**) | 5.5* | (5.6*) | .04( .08) |

Triple Interactions: none was significant.
* = p < .05
** = p < .01
*** = p < .001

[1] Values in parentheses are for the covariance analysis, IQ controlled.
[2] SES refers to socio-economic status, ' common man ' white versus ' disadvantaged ' black.

chance less than once in one thousand times.[4] It indicates that there is no significant difference between the groups in change from post-test to follow-up. Instead of representing these findings in terms of change scores, they can be represented in terms of differences between the groups at each time point. At the pretest, there were no significant differences between the experimental groups in moral maturity ($F = .1$). At both the post-test ($F = 5.3$, $p < .01$) and the follow-up time ($F = 3.6$, $p < .03$), the differences between experimental groups were significant (values reported are for the variance analysis, IQ controlled).

In summary, the results clearly indicate significant upward change in the ExpI moral discussion groups, compared to controls, change which was still evident one year later. This upward change is significant not only in comparison to the control group but to a group exposed to moral dilemmas but without developmentally guided moral discussion, the ExpII group. These spontaneous peer discussion groups did show some average increase in moral judgment from pretest to post-test, eleven points, and stood midway between the ExpI and control groups in terms of change. Such increase in the ExpII groups would be expected from various points of view including the developmental viewpoint which sees natural processes of peer discussion of moral conflicts as stimulating moral change.

TABLE 8

Patterns of Stage Usage of Status Sub-Groups on Pretest and on
Follow-Up — Study 2

| Stage | 1 | 2 | 3 | 4 | 5 | 6 | MMS |
|---|---|---|---|---|---|---|---|
| *Age 11 — First Test* | | | | | | | |
| Disadvantaged | 31 | 48 | 15 | 06 | 00 | 00 | 197 |
| Female | 40 | 43 | 10 | 07 | 00 | 00 | 185 |
| Male | 21 | 53 | 20 | 06 | 00 | 00 | 210 |
| Common Man | 21 | 40 | 29 | 10 | 00 | 00 | 227 |
| Female | 22 | 41 | 28 | 09 | 00 | 00 | 223 |
| Male | 21 | 39 | 30 | 11 | 00 | 00 | 230 |
| *Age 13 — Re-Test of Age 11 Two Years Later* | | | | | | | |
| Disadvantaged | 12 | 46 | 33 | 09 | 00 | 00 | 240 |
| Female | 10 | 48 | 34 | 08 | 00 | 00 | 240 |
| Male | 13 | 44 | 32 | 11 | 00 | 00 | 241 |
| Common Man | 06 | 31 | 43 | 20 | 00 | 00 | 279 |
| Female | 05 | 31 | 51 | 13 | 00 | 00 | 272 |
| Male | 06 | 30 | 35 | 28 | 00 | 00 | 287 |
| *Age 15 — First Test* | | | | | | | |
| Disadvantaged | 13 | 21 | 35 | 31 | 00 | 00 | 288 |
| Female | 06 | 19 | 39 | 35 | 00 | 00 | 303 |
| Male | 20 | 24 | 30 | 26 | 00 | 00 | 263 |
| Common Man | 09 | 17 | 33 | 41 | 00 | 00 | 308 |
| Female | 08 | 10 | 32 | 50 | 00 | 00 | 329 |
| Male | 10 | 25 | 33 | 31 | 01 | 00 | 286 |
| *Age 17 — Re-Test of Age 15, Two Years Later* | | | | | | | |
| Disadvantaged | 00 | 16 | 48 | 34 | 02 | 00 | 320 |
| Female | 00 | 20 | 45 | 31 | 04 | 00 | 320 |
| Male | 01 | 13 | 51 | 35 | 00 | 00 | 320 |
| Common Man | 01 | 07 | 41 | 42 | 09 | 00 | 351 |
| Female | 00 | 06 | 38 | 51 | 05 | 00 | 355 |
| Male | 02 | 08 | 44 | 33 | 13 | 00 | 347 |

[4] The conditions effect reported in Table 7 compares the three experimental groups with one another. An analysis comparing only the ExpI and control groups yielded similar results.

*19*

Group Differences in Pretest Moral Judgment:

The mean percent moral stage usage and moral maturity mean of the various sub-groups on pretest and on 18 month follow-up are presented in Table 8. Because of the relatively large number of subjects and the semi-longitudinal nature of the study, these figures are useful for reference purposes. The figures for the ' common man ' group at each age are comparable to those found in other studies. At age eleven this group is in transition to conventional morality; on retest at age thirteen, it is predominantly conventional. Continued movement to conventional morality, especially Stage 4, is evident through age seventeen. The disadvantaged group appears slightly slower in development with moral maturity on retest one and one-half years later, being comparable to that of the ' common man ' group of the same age at pretest.

These trends are indicated by the analysis of variance of pretest scores in Table 7. In addition to the expected age effect ($F = 57.7$), the socio-economic effect was also significant ($F = 7.0$). This effect disappears, however, if tested intelligence is controlled by covariance analysis ($F = .6$).[5]

Group and Classroom Differences in Response to the Programme:

The mean pretest to post-test change scores for each of the classroom groups are presented in Table 9. Considering first the ExpI classes, increases ranged from 13 to 52 moral maturity points, the latter being close to the gain of 66 moral maturity points found in the classrooms of Study 1. Gains did not relate in any simple way to the age or socio-economic status of the children. The younger disadvantaged and the older common man classes gained the most. This difference is reflected in a marginally significant interaction between SES and age in pre to post change ($F = 2.8$, $p < 10$). Rather than assuming such differences are due to some general interactive relation between age and social economic status, it seems more plausible to view them as due to the four classrooms as such, to the complex interactions among children and between the teacher and the class which determine the particular atmosphere of the four classrooms in the ExpI condition. The most important conclusion about classroom variation is that it was not related in a regular way to status or to age. There is no evidence of a limitation of the experimental moral discussion approach to the younger (or older) age or to more advantaged (or less advantaged) status.

TABLE 9

Mean Pre to Post Change in Moral Maturity in each Classroom Group

|                     | ExpI | ExpII | Control |
|---------------------|------|-------|---------|
| 11 Common Man       | 27   | 23    | −19     |
| 11 Disadvantaged    | 45   | 02    | −21     |
| 15 Common Man       | 52   | 35    | +08     |
| 15 Disadvantaged    | 13   | −06   | −11     |

[5] There is also a marginal sex X age interaction which disappears on retest. This may correspond to some studies reporting an advance by girls in early adolescence who are overtaken in late adolescence by boys. Its disappearance on retest (represented by marginally significant age X sex interaction on pre-post change), however, suggests some artifact since it is not a differential response to the discussion programme, but occurred in all conditions.

*20*

Turning to classroom variations in the ExpII condition, somewhat more regularity is apparent. In this condition, the children were left to discuss moral dilemmas among themselves without developmental teaching. Increases in this condition range from none ($-06$) to as much change (35 points) as occurred on the average for the ExpI groups. These variations may, again, have been due to classroom variations in atmosphere or to differential homeroom teacher structuring of the 'spontaneous' discussion. However, there was some consistent tendency for the spontaneous discussions to stimulate more change in the 'common man' classrooms than in the disadvantaged classrooms.[6]

The writer's observation of the ExpII classes suggested that the common man children showed more interest in, or ability to, engage in focused moral discussions under the ExpII conditions than did the disadvantaged children.

In summary, while there is considerable variation in effectiveness of ExpI moral discussion programme from one classroom to another, these variations appear not to be determined directly by the age or social status of the children involved. Variations in the effect of leaderless peer discussions are as marked from group to group as are variations in effectiveness of the developmentally directed group and appear to relate more directly to age and social status variations in interest and ability for verbal discussion than do the variations in the directed group.

Effects of the Programme on Cheating Behaviour:

As in Study 1, there was no positive effect of the moral discussion programme on resistance to cheating in the experimental tests. There was some increase in percentage of children cheating on the post-test over cheating on the pretest in all three conditions (18 per cent increase for ExpI, 15 per cent increase for ExpII, and 10 per cent increase for Controls). About half (47 per cent) of the children cheated on pretest, somewhat more (61 per cent) on post-test. Presumably the fact that cheating went apparently undetected on the pretest encouraged cheating on the post-test. In retrospect, experimental tests of honesty are not optional for detecting an influence of moral judgment change on behaviour. First, these measures are heavily determined by situational factors independent of moral orientation, as indicated by the systematic increase in cheating on post-test in all groups. Second, the relationship of moral judgment to cheating behaviour is most apparent in the disposition of principled (Stage 5 and 6) children to be consistently honest. Since only one child was scored as moving to the principled level through the intervention, it could not be expected that experimental increase in principled thinking would affect behaviour.

Pattern of Change:

We turn, now, to the results of most relevance to developmental theory, those as to whether the pattern of change in each condition was step-wise and sequential. The actual distribution of stage responses are presented in Table 10. Considering the ExpI group, as in Study 1 the main change from pretest to post-test is an 8 per cent decline in Stage 2 responses and a 10 per cent increase in Stage 4

---

[6] This tendency accounts for a marginal SES change effect as well as a marginal Age X SES X Condition interaction.

## TABLE 10
Percentage of Response at each Stage on Pretest, Post-Test
and Follow-Up in each Condition

| Stage | 1 | 2 | 3 | 4 | 5 |
|---|---|---|---|---|---|
| | | *Control* | | | |
| Pretest | .18 | .30 | .26 | .25 | .01 |
| Post-Test | .21 | .34 | .26 | .18 | .00 |
| Follow-Up | .06 | .28 | .43 | .20 | .00 |
| | | *ExpI* | | | |
| Pretest | .21 | .34 | .28 | .17 | .00 |
| Post-Test | .18 | .26 | .25 | .27 | .03 |
| Follow-Up | .06 | .24 | .40 | .25 | .05 |
| | | *ExpII* | | | |
| Pretest | .19 | .37 | .24 | .19 | .00 |
| Post-Test | .20 | .30 | .26 | .22 | .02 |
| Follow-Up | .05 | .25 | .40 | .29 | .01 |

## TABLE 11
**Pattern of Stage Change from Time 1 to Time 2 Control Group — Study 2**

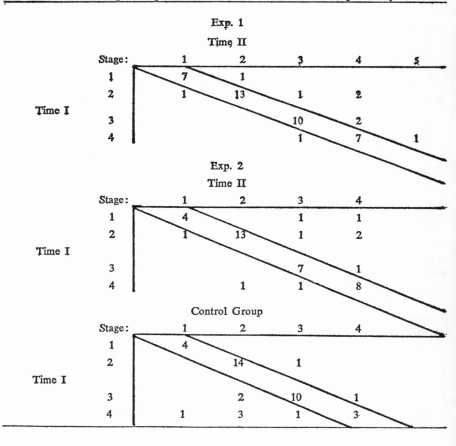

22

responses. The change in the ExpII condition is similar but less marked.

The issue raised, as in Study 1, is whether these changes are sequential, eg, whether those dropping in Stage 2 are moving to Stage 3 or whether they are skipping stages. The relevant data is presented in Table 11. The first table in Table 11 presents the number of subjects moving from one stage on pretest to another stage on post-test.[7] For example, there were eight subjects in ExpI condition who were Stage 1 on pretest, as indicated by the row marked Stage 1. Of these eight subjects, seven were still Stage 1 on post-test. These seven subjects are in the box indicated by the Stage 1 row (reading across) and the Stage 1 column (reading down). The remaining subject in the Stage 1 row (reading across), ie, who was Stage 1 on pretest, is Stage 2 on post-test. For the Stage 1 subjects, then, change in the ExpI condition was developmental. All Stage 1 subjects either stayed the same or moved to the next stage up. For the Stage 2 subjects, change was less orderly. One Stage 2 'regressed' to Stage 1, one moved to Stage 3, two moved to Stage 4. The diagonal lines in Table 11 denote the subjects who were unchanged from pretest to post-test. Thirty-seven or 80 per cent of the ExpI group were non-changers. The simplest prediction of developmental theory is that the remaining 20 per cent of the subjects who changed should move to the next stage. In fact, five of the nine changers (or of the seven upward changers) fall into this category. The remaining four cases are two Stage 2 'stage-skippers' to Stage 4, and two regressors. The pattern of stage-skipping from Stage 2 to Stage 4 was that found in Study 1, in which it was found that all 'skippers' 'regressed' to the next stage up on follow-up testing. Something similar appeared here. While only one of the two 'stage-skippers' was available for follow-up, he had 'regressed' from Stage 4 to Stage 3 on follow-up, just as was the case for the 'stage-skippers' in Study 1. The two 'regressors' had returned to their original higher stage on follow-up, so perhaps were cases of post-test scoring error.

Turning to the ExpII group, there are four 'stage-skippers' and two 'regressors' from pretest to post-test. Of these four 'stage-skippers', only one retained his post-test stage on follow-up, the others returning to their original position. As in the ExpI group, the cases of 'regression' appeared to be scoring error since neither of the two 'regressors' stayed at their regressed positions upon follow-up.

Turning finally to the control group, the two subjects who moved upward from pretest to post-test moved to the next stage up. There were seven 'regressors'. All of these cases of 'regression' represented scorer difficulty in distinguishing between a conventional Stage 4 orientation to rules in terms of society and order maintenance and a preconventional Stage 1 orientation to rules in terms of obedience and punishment. All 'regressors' were scored on pretest as Stage 4. Some of the regressors seemed correctly scored on pretest as Stage 4, were mis-scored on post-test as Stage 1, and were again correctly scored on follow-up as Stage 4. Others appeared to be over-scored on pretest as Stage 4, were correctly scored on post-test as Stage 1 or 2, and remained there on follow-up. It is

---

[7] In Study 1 we noted that a fifty point moral maturity score change was a fact of test-retest error. Subjects who did not change fifty points were classified as at the same stage on post-test. Those increasing or decreasing fifty points (ie, changers) were assigned to their dominant stage on post-test.

apparent that scoring error was particularly pronounced for the control group and helps account for the 'regression' effects also found in Turiel's retested control groups as reported in Study 1. The boredom of repeating responses to the same stories leads to more perfunctory responses for all groups but is most marked for non-motivated control groups. An orientation to rules elaborated as Stage 4 system-maintaining on pretest may appear to be a Stage 1 obedience labelling and trouble-avoiding orientation on retest.

In summary, there was no clear upward stage-skipping in the control group, some (5 per cent) in the ExpI group and more (10 per cent) in the ExpII group. Presumably the developmentally directed ExpI group stressed exposure to the next stage up whereas there was more 'random' modelling of higher stages in the free peer discussions. In any case, however, only one of the five stage-skippers from pretest to post-test (considering all groups together) retained his skipped stage on follow-up testing. In contrast, all subjects showing +1 change from pretest to post-test in any of the groups (ExpI, ExpII, Control) had either retained their advance or moved on to the next stage. With regard to 'regression' from pretest to post-test, this was lowest (5 per cent) in the ExpI group, next lowest (10 per cent) in the ExpII group, and highest (17 per cent) in the Control group. Almost all 'regressors' were initially scored Stage 4 on the pretest. This indicated scoring problems when 'law and rules' responses are not elaborated or probed in an interview. These problems were pronounced because of perfunctory responses to a repetitive post-test, especially in the Control group.

A final question about pattern of change raised in Study 1 is that of whether upward change was new thinking at a new stage or consolidation of thinking at the next stage up already being used by the student. In Study 1, we found that the +1 increase of those showing no (less than 20 per cent) +1 usage on pretest was greater than the increase in +1 usage of those already capable of comprehending and using some (> 20 per cent) +1 thought. Similar results were found in this study. ExpII subjects at each stage were divided into a group showing comprehension and usage of +1 thinking on pretest (> 20 per cent +1 usage) and a group showing no clear usage (< 20 per cent) of +1 thought. The group showing clear pretest usage of +1 thought showed no (4 per cent or less) clear increase in +1 thought on post-test. In contrast, the groups showing low pretest usage of +1 thought increased their +1 thinking on post-test. For various stages this ranged from 6 per cent (for Stage 4's increasing in Stage 5 usage) to 23 per cent (for Stage 3's increasing in Stage 4 usage). This suggests that the classroom discussions led to the actual formation of a higher stage of thought and not simply to the expansion of a capacity for higher thought already present.

## Conclusions and Discussion

We shall first discuss our findings with hope and then with caution. Hope is suggested by considering that while formal moral education has been a subject of thoughtful concern since the time of Socrates, the présent study is the first research report of a substantial and relatively enduring effect of a formal programme of moral education upon children. The differences between classroom change and change during a similar time period in control groups clearly indicates an effect not due to time, re-testing, or participating in an experiment. This classroom change was substantial and relatively enduring. It was substantial because a substantial proportion of the group moved the equivalent of almost one stage. It was relatively enduring because it was manifest on one-year follow-up. Furthermore, the change was replicated in five different classrooms varying in age and socio-economic and ethnic status. Since the studies reported, the writers have replicated the effect with a sixth suburban Boston classroom of high school seniors, yielding an average moral maturity increase of 43 (Dowell, 1971). Since this study was completed, similar levels of change through developmental discussion have been found in work with prisoners and with undergraduate students (Boyd, 1973).

Still more important, the change which occurred was primarily genuine stimulation of development rather than the verbal learning of moral cliches. The fact that much of the change induced was structural-developmental is indicated by the fact that while all children were exposed to the same stimuli, ie, moral judgments at all stages from Stage 2 to Stage 6, the actual changes in moral judgment which resulted were relative to the child's own stage and were usually to the next stage up — most movement by Stage 2's was to Stage 3; most movement by Stage 3's was to Stage 4. The exceptions were revealing and dramatic. Some Stage 2 (and one Stage 1) children displayed much Stage 4 thinking on the post-test, but they ' lost ' this thinking a year later and displayed an original stage or one-stage-up (eg, Stage 3) orientation on follow-up.

The findings and conclusions we have just summarized are encouraging for both practical and theoretical advance in the moral area. On a practical level, they imply that one of the most important areas for the improvement of public education is in the development of a rational approach to moral education. If brief periods of classroom discussion can have a substantial effect on moral development, a pervasive, enduring and psychologically sound concern for the school's influence upon moral development should have much deeper and more positive effects. Such a concern would pervade the curriculum areas of social studies, law education, philosophy, and sex education, rather than representing a new curriculum area. More deeply, it would affect the social atmosphere and justice structure of the school, in ways discussed elsewhere (Kohlberg and Turiel, 1971).

On a theoretical level, findings suggest that experimental studies of moral education can go far to help us understand the conditions for moral change. The present findings demonstrate the possibility of change, they do not yet indicate the optimal conditions for change from either a theoretical or a practical view. The limited evidence available, however, does suggest that the developmental teaching principles employed in this study lead to more change than is found in either free unstructured discussion of moral dilemmas or in didactic forms of legal or moral education.

With regard to unstructured moral disscussion, the difference between change in the developmentally structured ExpI classes and the changes in the spontaneous peer discussions of ExpII, indicate that the ExpI changes are more substantial than could be expected from sheer unfocused discussions of moral dilemmas. While our evidence is less conclusive, it also appears that our developmental approach to classroom discussion is more effective for stimulating development than didactic approaches. A more didactic approach, for instance, has been employed in an eight-month high school law course in which legal-moral dilemmas are used to develop knowledge of the law (Leary, 1972). Twenty students from three such classes were pretested and post-tested on moral judgment maturity. The moral maturity of students at post-test was the same (MMS = 273) as it was on pretest (MMS = 272) (Leary, 1972). This does not mean that developmental moral discussion is incompatible with didactic teaching about legal and moral philosophic concepts. Beginning efforts to combine the two approaches in a high school law course (Leary, 1972), a high school ethics course (Beck, Sullivan and Taylor, 1972), and an undergraduate ethics course (Boyd, 1972) are being made.

## References

Blatt, M. (1969). Studies on the effects of classroom discussion upon childrens' moral development. Unpublished doctoral dissertation.

Grim, P., Kohlberg, L., and White, S. (1968). Some relations between conscience and attentional processes. *J. Pers. Soc. Psychol.* **8**, 239-253.

Hartshorne, H., and May, M. A. (1928-30). *Studies in the nature of character:* vol. I, *Studies in deceit;* vol. II, *Studies in self-control;* vol. III, *Studies in the organization of character,* New York: Macmillan.

Jones, V. (1936). *Character and citizenship training in the public school,* Chicago: University of Chicago Press.

Kohlberg, L. (1958). The development of modes of moral thinking and choice in years ten to sixteen. Unpublished doctoral dissertation, University of Chicago.

Kohlberg, L. (1966). Moral education in the schools: a developmental view. in *School review* **74**, 1-30.

Kohlberg, L. (1964). The development of moral characters and moral ideology. in Hoffman, M., and Hoffman, L. *Review of child development research* vol. 1, New York: Russell Sage.

Kohlberg, L. (1969). Stages and sequence: the developmental approach to socialization. in D. Goslin (ed.) *Handbook of socialization theory and research,* Chicago: Rand McNally.

Kohlberg, L. (1967). Moral and religious education and the public schools, a developmental view. in T. Sizer (ed.) *Religious and public education,* Boston: Houghton, Mifflin.

Kohlberg, L. (1968). The child as a moral philosopher. in *Psychology today,* September.

Kohlberg, L. (in preparation). *Stages in the development of moral thought and action.* New York: Holt, Rinehart and Winston.

Kohlberg, L. (1969). Education for justice: a platonic view. in R. Mosher (ed.) *Moral education,* Cambridge: Harvard University Press.

Kohlberg, L. (in preparation). (ed.) *Recent research in moral development,* Holt, Rinehart and Winston.

Kohlberg, L. (1970). Moral stages as a basis for moral education. in Sullivan, E., and Rest, J. (ed.) *Moral education,* University of Toronto Press.

Krebs, R. (1967). Some relations between moral judgment attention and resistance to temptation. Unpublished doctoral dissertation, University of Chicago.

Rest, J. (1969). Preference for and comprehension of moral judgment. Published dissertation, University of Chicago.

Rest, J., Turiel, E., and Kohlberg, L. (1969). Level of moral development as a determinant of preference and comprehension of moral judgments made by others. *J. Person* (in press).

Turiel, E. (1966). An experimental analysis of developmental stages in child's moral judgment. in *J. Pers. Soc. Psychol.* **3**, 611-618.

Turiel, E. (1965). An experimental test of the sequentiality of developmental stages in the child's moral judgment. Unpublished doctoral dissertation, Yale University.

## APPENDIX A

### Examples of Class Discussions

*Dilemma:*

There was a case in court the other day about a man, Mr Jones, who had an accident in his house. His child, Mike, was wounded in the chest. He was bleeding heavily, his shoes and pants were soaked with blood. Mike was scared. He began screaming until he finally lost consciousness.

His parents were scared, too. His mother began screaming, crying. She thought her child was dying. The father no longer hesitated; he lifted Mike up, ran down the stairs and went outside in hopes of getting a cab and going to the hospital. He thought that getting a cab would be quicker than calling an ambulance. But, there were no cabs on the street and Mike's bleeding seemed worse.

Suddenly, Mike's father noticed a man parking his car. He ran up and asked the man to take him to the hospital. The man replied, ' Look, I have an appointment with a man about an important job. I really must be on time. I'd like to help you but I can't.' So Mr Jones said, ' Just give me the car.' The man said, ' Look, I don't know you. I don't trust you.' Mr Jones told Mrs Jones to hold Mike. She did. Then Mr Jones punched the man, beat him up, took his keys and drove away toward the hospital. The man got up from the street, called the police, and took them to the hospital. The police arrested Mr Jones for car theft and aggravated battery.

### Eleven-Year-Old — Common Man — 15th Session

Mr Blatt: What is the problem? Was the man legally wrong for refusing to drive Mr Jones and Mike to the hospital?

Student A: It's his car, he doesn't have to drive.

Mr B: Well, Mike was hurt. You said no, he's not legally responsible, because, why not?

Student A: Because it's his car.

Mr B: It's his car. It's his property, and he has the right of property and he can legally —

Student B: But a life is at stake.

Mr B: Okay. It's not so easy. Like here is property, but here is life, so the conflict here is between life, Mike's life, or that man's car.

Student B: But if Mike died, then that guy could be charged with murder, because, you know . . .

Student C: No, he couldn't. (Argument over whether he could or could not be charged with murder.)

Mr B: But do you people think this man has a right, a legal right, to refuse to give Mr Jones the car?

Student D: Does that man have children; he probably has to support a family, he's got a family, he can't just —

Student E: So? He can always find a job —

Mr B: The question is, do you think that the man who had the job, wouldn't he understand if you came up to him and said, ' Look, I was here, I wanted to be on time, but I saw this boy bleeding, and I wanted to help him out.' Don't you think he would understand? (Chorus of 'yes' and 'no'.)

Student F: No, because if you're supposed to go on the job —

Student G: You could make him show some proof.

Student F: Bring the kid there when he's well.

Mr B: All right. This man, who refused to give the car was not legally wrong. You couldn't take him to court. But do you think he was wrong in any way? (Chorus of 'yes'.)

Student B: He was just all wrong because if that kid died, I don't know what he'd be charged with, but he'd be charged with something. There's something, I don't know what it is, but there's something they could charge him with.

Mr B: I don't know if they could charge him legally, but you're right; there's something very wrong with that, because what is this man doing? Which is more important: property or life? (Chorus of 'life'.) Why? (Confused answers, on the principle that life is irreplaceable.) Life is something you can't replace, right? Everybody wants to live. Now this guy, what was he putting first, life or a job? What do you think is more important, losing a job and maybe getting another one, or saving a life? (Answers: 'saving a life.') Helping to save a life. But this guy refuses to help Mr Jones and Mike out, to take them to the hospital. What was he doing? He was putting his property before somebody else's life? (Answers: 'saving a life'.) Helping to save a life. But this guy you to lend me your car, I'll bring it back.' The guy said, 'No, I don't trust you.'

Student A: Well, he didn't know Mr Jones, maybe he didn't trust him.

Student D: What did he look like?

Student A: Yeah, I wouldn't trust nobody with my car.

Student H: Well, I would trust him if I knew him. (Confused comments about whether they would or would not trust somebody with their car.)

Student B: Would you care if you trust him or not?

Student E: Well, I wouldn't go so far as to beat him up and to take his car. He might still need it. (Conversation on beating up somebody.)

Mr B: So what you're saying is, this man's value, what he thought was most important was his property. His property was more important to him than somebody else's life. You said legally he was right. Right? (Agreements.) Can you say morally he was right? (Undistinguishable answers.) What do you mean by morally? Can somebody tell us what is meant by morally?

Student C: It's — there's not a law but —

Mr B: What kind of a law may be involved? It's not a legal law, although it may be, it doesn't have to be. What kind of law is it? What were you saying before, about your mother? What did she say?

Student B: God's law.

Mr B: God's law, what does it say about killing?

*28*

Student B:  Thou shalt not kill.

Students B
 and F:  God's law is moral law.

Mr B:  What do you mean?

Student B:  Cause this is the laws of this country and God has moral laws for every-body.

Mr B:  Oh, so what you're saying is — did you listen to what he's saying? Would you repeat what you said? It's very important.

Student B:  God's law is for everyone and there's different laws in different countries, so God's law, his moral laws are for everyone.

Student D:  God's laws include more people than laws down here, yes.

Mr B:  Now what you're saying is that God's laws are for all people regardless of where you live. And so, they're universal laws, right? They're for the whole universe, is what you're saying. All right. Now you said, from the legal point of view he was right, from a moral point of view he was wrong. He had a legal right to refuse his property but no moral right to do so. Now what about Mr Jones? Was Mr Jones justified from a legal point of view, in beating up the man and taking his car? (Chorus of ' no '.) Why not?

Student B:  Because there's a law that like, that guy's car, you know, he can say whatever he likes about it, he has a right to do what he wants with it, but with the moral law [Mr Jones] was doing pretty good.

Mr B:  He was doing right? Do you agree with him? He says that Mr Jones was doing right from a moral point of view.

Student B:  But it still went outside God's law, going against the law. Thou shalt not steal.

Mr B:  So what you're saying is —

Student D:  There's a problem. It's still stealing.

Student F:  Yes, he should have asked him. If the man said no, that should have been the answer.

Mr B:  Did he have a moral right to beat up the man and take his car? (Chorus of ' no '.) Why not?

Student F:  He didn't have no right to do it.

Student B:  There's another moral law . . .

Mr B:  Now, Mr Jones was brought before the judge. Should the judge consider the circumstances and let Mr Jones off free — (Chorus of ' yes ') or should he give him punishment and what punishment and why?

Student B:  I'd give him a week. (Argument in which the following is distinguishable: Mr B: ' Why would you give him ——? Student F: ' Yes, he didn't hurt the guy.' Student I: ' It still was a car theft.' Student F: ' He's got to get out and support his family again.')

Mr B:  What is the reason for punishment? Why do you think he needs to be punished? And, should he be punished for what he did or to teach him next time not to do something like that?

Student B:  Well, it [wouldn't] teach him to do that.

Student D:  No, he'll go out and do it again if you don't —

Student B: If your son was bleeding and you can't say if it happens again, if you're going to do the same thing.

Mr B: What did you — what were you about to say?

Student F: He couldn't help it; he couldn't stand there; by the time some help came he could have been dead.

Mr B: So what you're saying is, you wouldn't give him a big punishment?

Student D: I wouldn't give him one at all. Why not?

Student D: Look, he couldn't help it that much for saving a life. He couldn't just stand there and —

Mr B: What you're saying is to understand the situation he was in, the circumstance that he has a boy who was dying, his son was dying in his hands. And you would understand that he didn't steal to be greedy, he did it to save a life, and you'd understand this and you'd let him off because what he was doing, saving a life, was moral. Is that right? (Chorus of ' yes '.) Now about punishment — Why do we give punishment? Why do we punish criminals?

Student B: Like I said, so they won't do it again.

Mr B: Do you think that given the same situation, if he would get punishment, he'd do the same thing again? Well?

Student B: I think he would, too.

Student F: He'd probably go and be hysterical.

Mr B: Is it a matter of being hysterical or a matter of saving a life again?

Student B: He'd be out of his mind.

Mr B: He'd save a life again. Even if you were in your right mind — And therefore, punishing him would not really teach him a lesson, would it?

*Comment:*

The experimenter in the early portion of the transcript is endeavouring to get the students to sense a conflict between the legal and the moral. He endeavours to get students to see that the reasons which lead them to feel that the law is not the deciding element, reasons are general or moral, that they can relate to a more universal moral law, and involves the experimenter in attempting to translate the Stage 2 and Stage 3 thinking of the children into a Stage 4 level which is also compatible with Stage 5 reasoning and to develop a set of distinctions (moral versus legal, etc) in terms of which there is some possibility of consensus across levels. This pattern of teaching, effective with the Study 1 children, may have been oriented to too high a stage and too high a level of abstraction for this group.

### Fifteen-Year-Old — Disadvantaged — 15th Session

Mr Blatt: Would you have done that?

Student A: No. (Unclear.)

Mr B: One at a time. Go ahead, What?

Student A: He should have called the ambulance. He can't make nobody do something he don't want to do. (Inaudible rejoinder.)

Mr B: Was the man who refused to give Mr Jones the car, was he perfectly okay in what he did?

Student B: He could do anything he wanted to do with is own car. (Agreements.) And still, he could just go along. Or he could have helped the man if he wanted to, but only if he wanted to.

Mr B: All right. Mr Jones stole the car. Does Mr Jones have the legal right to beat up the man and take his car?

Student B: He doesn't have the legal right, no.

Mr B: No. Because this guy has a right to property and Mr Jones obviously has no right to hurt this guy. Now, what was involved on his side? What was Mr Jones' problem? (Chorus of 'the boy'.) And there was a case of life, right? (Chorus of 'right'.) This guy's right to property conflicts with this guy's right to life.

Student C: Yes, but the law doesn't say you can't steal unless somebody's life is involved. The law says you can't steal.

Mr B: So what you're saying is, according to the law it doesn't make any difference when you steal. Stealing is stealing, and wrong. Okay? (Chorus of 'right'.)

Student A: He was wrong to take the car.

Student C: You got to have a reason for what you steal.

Mr B: Suppose you steal when you're hungry. You steal food, you're hungry, you don't have any money.

Student A: That's against the law.

Student C: There a reason for it.

Student A: You get caught, I bet you get put in jail, don't you? Stealing a car, that's the same thing.

Student B: But this man had a real good reason for stealing the car.

Student A: What is a good reason for you doesn't have to be a good reason for somebody else.

Student B: If you were bleeding and your father was running around with you trying to get somebody to take you to the hospital and you know good and well that you want your father to hit that dude and take that car, wouldn't you?

Student A: No!

Student B: Yes, you would. You'd be laying there, bleeding to death, wouldn't you? You'd let your own self die?

Student A: But I'm saying that it's against the law. You took something that wasn't yours.

Mr B: All right, let me ask you, 'What is the purpose of the law?' (Two or three answer, 'To protect'.) To protect people and their property. In this case suppose you have here a person whose life is in danger. You say the function of the law is to protect the people. All right. Now, it has to protect life —

Student A: But what about the property part? What about the other person. He has to be protected, too.

Mr B: You're saying that it's not only this guy who has to be protected, it's also the other guy that has to be protected. Okay, but suppose this guy's right to property interferes with this guy's right to life. Is property and life the same?

Student A: That car may depend on that other man's life, too. He has to get a job. If he don't get it, he might die. You have to see what a person thinks is more valuable, a life or a car.

Mr B: So what you're saying is, circumstances don't make a difference. Stealing is stealing, no matter what. (Chorus of 'No'. Another chorus of 'Yes'.) Defend yourself.

Student A: I will not change my mind. Why should it make a difference? Tell me one good solid reason why it should. That's just like telling a doctor that he should take a man's life so he can save his best friend's life. Like his best friend needs a heart so he's going to go out and kill somebody.

Student D: It's wrong. I'd rather my friend died. Taking somebody else's heart to have his friend's life —

Mr B: But there you're depriving someone of life. You're saying that property equals life?

Student A: He had a good reason but that doesn't mean it's right.

Mr B: What kind of reason are you talking about? (Argument.)

Student E: A moral reason.

Student B: Legally it's wrong, morally it's right. (Argument.)

Student A: We are not arguing moral, we're arguing legal.

Mr B: I want you to consider both, moral and legal. All right. Mr Jones is brought before the judge. What punishment should Mr Jones get and why?

Student I: A fine, about a hundred dollars.

Mr B: All right, what's the purpose of punishment? What's the function of punishment?

Student A: So you won't do it again.

Mr B: All right, this is one. Any other reason?

Student A: To make the other person feel good.

Mr B: So what you're saying is — I don't understand why?

Student A: So, like, if somebody kills your child, or your mother, or father, or friend, and they get punished it'll make you feel better, maybe.

Mr B: Okay, so what you're saying is that we —

Student A: Satisfy the man.

Mr B: Satisfy the man, and we have a good reason. To prevent others —

Student A: Protecting people's rights.

In this class, the discussion centres around Student A's position that taking the car was unjustified. Student A's position is a mixture of Stage 1 (It's still stealing, I'll bet you get put in jail) and Stage 2 (You can't make somebody do something he don't want to do). His view is that apart from law and punishment everything is arbitrary (in a Stage 2 sense). 'What is a good reason for you doesn't have to be a good reason for someone else,' 'You have to see what a person thinks is more valuable, a life or a car.' The teacher as well as the other students attempt to convince him that there are good reasons independent of the law which may be formulated at a Stage 2 or 3 level, and that you should think of the ' morally right ' and of ' good reasons ' as well as the legally right. The teacher's purpose and structuring is similar to that in the first session, but there is a sustained spontaneous dialogue. Student A, though unwilling to shift the content of his choice seems to move toward accepting the notion that there are good reasons, though he insists, ' We are not arguing moral, we are arguing legal.'

# The hierarchical nature of moral judgment: A study of patterns of comprehension and preference of moral stages[1]

James R. Rest, *University of Minnesota*

Kohlberg (1958, 1969) has characterized the development of moral judgment in terms of a typology of six stages. Each stage is defined as a distinctive orientation to moral problems, and it is claimed that the six stages represent an invariant, universal developmental sequence. Each succeeding stage is said to be an advance over the preceding stage in being a more differentiated and integrated structure. In other words, the stages are said to be *hierarchically* related: a new stage does not simply replace a previous stage, nor is it added to it, but rather the new stage is a transformation of elements of the old along with new elements into a new emergent structure.

One of the main implications of a stage hierarchy is that a higher stage is more complex than a lower stage and that a higher stage logically presupposes the simpler lower stage. If logical complexity is parallel to psychological difficulty, then it follows that Kohlberg's stages are increasingly more difficult to comprehend, and that understanding or attainment of a more advanced stage presupposes attainment of the simpler, less advanced stages —i.e., that the stages form a Guttman scale of comprehension. Empirical demonstration is important because it would support the theory for why the stages are naturally ordered as they are and why there is not "skipping around." The theory is namely that the lower stages are easier and hence are possible responses for a subject before the more difficult stages.

1. This research was supported by NICHD Grant HD 02469 to Dr. Lawrence Kohlberg. It was based on a thesis submitted to the Department of Psychology, University of Chicago in partial fulfillment of the requirements for the Ph.D. degree. I wish to thank Dr. Kohlberg for his help and encouragement and Dr. Keith Moore for help with scoring reliability. Author's address: 330 Burton Hall, Department of Psychological Foundations, University of Minnesota, Minneapolis, Minnesota 55455.

The usual method of stage assessment is to present to a subject a hypothetical moral dilemma, ask the subject to tell what he would do in the situation, and ask for reasons for his choice of action. A scorer then classifies the reasoning according to established scoring guides (Kohlberg, 1958). Evidence that Kohlberg's stages depict a natural sequence of development comes from observations that older subjects manifest higher stage characteristics (c.f. Kohlberg, 1958), that over time subjects naturally tend to change "upwards" (c.f. Kohlberg & Kramer, 1969), and that when change is induced it tends to be to the next highest stage (c.f. Turiel, 1969). Now whereas this method of stage assessment and this kind of evidence (change for the higher stage) provide support for the sequentiality of Kohlberg's stages, they do not provide direct evidence for the hierarchical nature of the stages.

In studies of moral judgment, it is usually assumed that a subject's moral judgments are produced at the highest stage he is capable of. Also it is usually assumed that when a subject later produces moral judgments at a higher stage, that the change represents the acquisition of new capacities. It is possible, however, that a subject might not produce moral judgments at the highest stage of which he is capable. And it is possible that changes of stage levels over time do not represent changes in capacity, but rather shifts in preferences for certain kinds of moral judgments. Therefore, to claim that any set of stages comprise a hierarchical order, more evidence is necessary than observing a natural sequence in changes over time. The sequence of stages observed in natural development has to be shown to be an order of increasing difficulty, and it must be shown that subjects prefer to produce or use the highest stage of which they are capable. Consequently what is needed operationally is: (a) a *capacity* measure of stages of thinking which takes inventory of all the stages of thinking which are possible for the subject (whereas in Kohlberg's usual method of stage assessment, there is evidence only of the capacity to think at stages which the subject personally endorses and is spontaneously producing); and (b) a method of assessing the subject's *preference* for the various stages of thinking which is independent of capacity measures and independent of spontaneous productions.

Kohlberg has described the characteristics of moral judgment at the six stages of development and has begun the theoretical account of how each succeeding stage elaborates, extends, and further differentiates the cognitive structure of the earlier stage. By this theoretical account, each succeeding stage is a more adequate and complex framework for making moral decisions— hence Kohlberg's theoretical discussions of the stages make it very plausible that his stages are hierarchical. The purpose of the present study is to test empirically this theoretical scheme by examining patterns of comprehension capacity and preference of the stages. The logic of the study is similar to studies in psycholinquistics which test whether psychological difficulty is predictable from a particular theoretical scheme of syntactic complexity (c.f. Fodor & Garett, 1966), and studies of Piagetian stages (c.f. Flavell & Wohlwill, 1969, pp. 96–98; see also Rest, 1969b). If it were shown that Kohlberg's stages did not form an order of psychological difficulty, the hierarchical nature of his stages, or his particular analysis of the salient developmental characteristics, or both, would be questionable.

Note that a measure of general cognitive capacity such as I.Q. scores would be inappropriate for the purposes of the present study. Because we want to test the relative psychological difficulty of Kohlberg's stages, we must use materials specifically designed to vary his stage characteristics. Knowing where someone is in the I.Q. distribution does not tell us what modes of moral thinking he can or cannot use, nor can I.Q. scores tell us directly which stage is more difficult than another stage. Therefore using I.Q. measures would be just as senseless in the present study as using I.Q. scores to test a specific theoretical scheme of syntactic complexity or for testing the relative complexity of Piagetian stages. Furthermore, Kohlberg (1969, p. 391) reports that I.Q. scores have only moderate correlations with his moral judgment measures, that for some stages the correspondence is negligible, and that the relationship seems to be curvilinear rather than linear. Therefore correlation of I.Q. with moral judgment does not have the linearity to explain the sequencing of the stages.

Many theories besides the cognitive-developmental theory would make the general prediction that more complex forms of responding are more psychologically difficult. That, however, is not the point of the present study. This study aims to test whether Kohlberg's specific characterizations of the natural sequence of moral judgment development—which describes actual subjects in cross-sectional and longitudinal studies—does in fact constitute an order of increasing psychological difficulty. Only cognitive developmental theorists (notably Piaget and Kohlberg) have attempted to describe the course of moral judgment development and have attempted to account theoretically for the predicted changes over time in terms of increasing cognitive complexity. Other theories have emphasized variables such as reinforcement, modelling opportunities, or vicissitudes of libido to account for changes in moral judgment and have not given any specification as to what increasing complexity in moral judgment would be like. This study tests the cognitive complexity dimension of Kohlberg's specific stage characterizations, and this has bearing on the feasibility of explaining developmental change in terms of increasing cognitive complexity.

An earlier study (Rest, Turiel & Kohlberg, 1969) provided evidence that Kohlberg's stages comprise an order of difficulty of comprehension. The present study reports more definitive evidence, and while its design and method use a similar strategy, the present study avoided some weaknesses (see Discussion). Prototypic statements were prepared for each of the six stages as stimulus material. The subjects discussed those statements and these discussions were scored for understanding of that stage's thinking. This gave a measure of comprehension for every stage for each subject. Previous to obtaining this measure of comprehension, subjects had been given Kohlberg's usual moral judgment interview and scored in the usual way so as to determine the subject's predominant stage (his "own" stage). Third, in addition to discussing the prototypic statements from which were derived measures of comprehension, the subjects were also asked to indicate their preference for the statements, and hence indirectly, their preference for each stage of thinking.

The first hypothesis of the present study was that statements at stages above the subject's own stage are increasingly more difficult to comprehend, and that statements at levels below are comprehended even though the subject does not spontaneously use these levels. The postulation of hierarchical order of stages implies that the more advanced stages are more adequate ways of making moral judgments. Therefore if a subject understands the underlying structure of prototypic statements, he should recognize the greater adequacy of the higher stage statement and express a preference for it. And so the second hypothesis was that insofar as the subjects comprehend various stages of thinking, they tend to prefer the highest comprehended. The third hypothesis of the study was that there should be a match between the subject's spontaneous stage on the "pretest" interview and the highest stage that was comprehended of prototypic statements.

## METHOD

### Subjects

The 47 subjects of the study (except 5)[2] came from the 12th grade in a middle-class suburb of Chicago. The subjects volunteered for the study and were interviewed for the most part during free periods in school.

### Procedure and design

The first step was to "pretest" subjects for their own spontaneous moral orientation, using Kohlberg's moral judgment interview (1958). This involves presenting hypothetical moral stories to the subject, such as the "Heinz Story" (Kohlberg's Situation III) (see below), and scoring the responses for stage according to Kohlberg's guides.

In Europe, a woman was near death from a very bad disease, a special kind of cancer. There was one drug that the doctors thought might save her. It was a form of radium that a druggist in the same town had recently discovered. The drug was expensive to make, but the druggist was charging ten times what the drug cost him to make. He paid $200 for the radium and charged $2,000 for a small dose of the drug. The sick woman's husband, Heinz, went to everyone he knew to borrow the money, but he could only get together about $1,000 which is half of what it cost. He told the druggist that his wife was dying, and asked him to sell it cheaper or let him pay later. But the druggist said, "No, I discovered the drug and

2. The other five subjects had been identified in another study as high stage subjects and were added to bolster the number of subjects in those categories.

I'm going to make money from it." So Heinz got desperate and broke into the man's store to steal the drug for his wife.
Should the husband have done that? Why?

Each subject's interview is depicted in terms of the proportion of his responses scored at each stage; the subject's predominant stage of usage is his "own" stage. Table 1 shows that our sample of subjects were spread out over the six stages.

*Table 1.* Subjects' moral orientation on pretest.

| Groups | Predominantly used Stage | | | | | | |
|---|---|---|---|---|---|---|---|
| | 1 | 2 | 3 | 4 | 5 | 6 | Totals |
| Total number of subjects | 1 | 6 | 17 | 12 | 6 | 5 | 47 |
| No. of subjects receiving statements of Situation III | 1 | 2 | 9 | 5 | 3 | 4 | 24 |
| No. of subjects receiving statements of Situation VI | 0 | 4 | 8 | 7 | 3 | 1 | 23 |

In the second phase of the procedure a set of prepared statements was used. Following is a design summary of considerations that went into making up the statements.

1. For the set of statements to one situation, the same five aspects were used for all stages. Hence any differences between subject's comprehension of statements could be attributed to differences in stage and not to differences in aspect.

2. For each stage and aspect, one statement was written advocating one course of action and a second statement written advocating the opposite course of action. Hence the exemplification of a stage-aspect feature was not confounded with specific actions.

3. The order of presenting the statements was counterbalanced. One-half of the subjects receive odd statements then even statements; the other half receive even then odd statements. Hence statements of one stage were not presented all at one time and the action alternatives (e.g., steal, or not steal) were alternated.

4. Scoring of subjects' responses to the statements was done for each statement separately and "blind" (i.e., without knowing whose response was being scored and without knowing how that subject had been scored on other statements).

One set of 60 statements used the Heinz Story as its background context (Situation III) and a second set of 60 statements used another of Kohlberg's stories as background (Situation VI).[3] As the

3. While the comprehension test used as background the same situations as

design summary indicates, the statements were balanced for ($a$) Stage, ($b$) Pro-con attitude, ($c$) and Substage aspect (e.g., "Motives and Circumstances in Judging Blame and Obligation"). The list below gives some samples of statements (Situation III background, aspect on "Motives and Circumstances").

### Six Stages of Orientation to Motives and Circumstances in Response to the Heinz Story

*Stage 1. Pro:* It isn't really bad to take it—he did ask to pay for it first. He wouldn't do any other damage or take anything else and the drug he'd take is only worth $200, he's not really taking a $2,000 drug.

*Stage 1. Con:* Heinz doesn't have any permission to take the drug. He can't just go and break into a store—maybe break through a window or break the door down. He'd be a bad criminal doing all that damage. That drug is worth a lot of money, and stealing anything so expensive would really be a big crime.

*Stage 2. Pro:* Heinz isn't really doing any harm to the druggist, and he can always pay him back. If he doesn't want to lose his wife, he should take the drug because it's the only thing that will work.

*Stage 2. Con:* The druggist isn't wrong or bad, he just wants to make a profit like everyone else. That's what you're in business for, to make money. Business is business.

*Stage 3. Pro:* Stealing is bad, but this is a bad situation. Heinz isn't doing wrong in trying to save his wife, he has no choice but to take the drug. He is only doing something that is natural for a good husband to do. You can't blame him for doing something out of love for his wife. You'd blame him if he didn't love his wife enough to save her.

*Stage 3. Con:* If Heinz's wife dies, he can't be blamed in these circumstances. You can't say he is a heartless husband just because he won't commit a crime. The druggist is the selfish and heartless one in this situation. Heinz tried to do everything he really could.

---

Kohlberg's usual spontaneous production task, this similarity is only a superficial one. The comprehension statements could have exemplified the stage characteristics with moral arguments abstracted from any particular situation or with other situations. The context of a specific situation was used so as to make the wording as concrete as possible. The crucial difference between the comprehension, preference, and spontaneous production tasks is not their situational context but the different kinds of responses which each requires.

*Stage 4. Pro:* The druggist is leading a wrong kind of life if he just lets somebody die. You can't let somebody die like that, so it's Heinz's duty to save her. But Heinz can't just go around breaking laws and let it go at that—he must pay the druggist back and he must take his punishment for stealing.

*Stage 4. Con:* It is a natural thing for Heinz to want to save his wife, but it's still always wrong to steal. You have to follow the rules regardless of how you feel or regardless of the special circumstances.

*Stage 5. Pro:* Before you say stealing is wrong, you've got to really think about this whole situation. Of course, the laws are quite clear about breaking into a store. And, even worse, Heinz would know there were no legal grounds for his actions. Yet, I can see why it would be reasonable for anybody in this kind of situation to steal the drug.

*Stage 5. Con:* I can see the good that would come from illegally taking the drug, but the ends don't justify the means. You can often find a good end behind illegal action. You can't say Heinz would be completely wrong to steal the drug, but even these circumstances don't make it right.

*Stage 6. Pro:* Where the choice must be made between disobeying a law and saving a human life, the higher principle of preserving life makes it morally right—not just understandable —to steal the drug.

*Stage 6. Con:* There are so many cases of cancer today that with any new drug cure, I'd assume that the drug would be scarce and that there wouldn't be enough to go around to everybody. The right course of action can only be the one which is consistent with Heinz's sense of justice to all people concerned. Heinz ought to act not according to his particular feelings to his wife, nor according to what is legal in this case, but according to what he conceives an ideally just person would do in this situation.

Subjects were presented statements one at a time (order counterbalanced, according to the design summary) and asked (*a*) to give equivalent recapitulations of the statement, (*b*) to state how the statement compared with their own ideas, (*c*) to evaluate or criticize the statements, (*d*) to rate each statement from 1 to 5 on how convincing or persuasive an argument it presented, and (*e*) to rank order the statements in terms of their comparative convincingness. Instructions to the subject were:

*41*

What reasons does the person give to back up his conclusion? How would you summarize his ideas? Restate the points that he is making.

How forceful or persuasive do you find the reasons in this statement (whether you yourself agree with the conclusion or not)? How would you rate it (1—very poor, 2—poor, 3—fair, 4—good, 5—very good)? What ideas do you agree with and disagree with?

What could you say against this statement? Even if you agree with it, what criticisms can you think up against the ideas he has, or the way he says them?

[Ranking instructions] Here are six statements that are talking about the same thing [Aspect on "Motives and Circumstances"] and all agree for the same course of action (steal the drug), but give different reasons [6 different stages]. Put the statement that is most convincing or forceful on top and the others in order underneath.

## Scoring and Reliability

The pretest interviews were scored in the usual way (Kohlberg, 1958). For comprehension scoring, a special guide was compiled which spells out the scoring criteria in detail (see Rest, 1969a). Table 6 gives some of our criteria for scoring as well as examples of answers judged "hits" or "misses."

*Stage 3*—Focus on actor's intentions rather than specific acts—Reciprocal role-taking makes it possible not only to consider the specific outward acts of a person but also to anticipate what are the person's inner goals and general dispositions. Since what is crucial to Stage 3 is that general positive relationships among people are maintained, a person's general inner disposition (his being a "good" person) is more important than isolated deviant acts. And deviant acts which are undertaken in behalf of personal relationships are excusable. In the Heinz story, our prototypic Stage 3 statements set Heinz's good intentions in contrast to a normally considered deviant action. Here is an exemplary statement:

> "Stealing is bad, but . . . Heinz isn't doing wrong in trying to save his wife. . . . He is only doing something that is natural for a good husband to do. You can't blame him for doing something out of love for his wife."

Here is a response that was scored a hit:

"Any good husband that wants to provide for his family and his wife what he should and out of goodness or out of his heart— he will do this, so you can't blame him for doing what he thought was right. . . ."

Here is an example of a response that was judged a miss—the recapitulation it gave of the prototypic statement showed no awareness of the focus on good intentions and seems to see Heinz's action as lacking thoughtful consideration:

"In this situation I guess his first impulse was to go and steal . . . I guess that was the only way he probably could do it. He didn't think twice before he did it."

*Stage 4*—The categorical and uniform character of law—Deviations and exceptions to law throw the whole system of shared expectations in doubt. If people no longer feel a categorical compulsion to comply with law or suspect that others lack respect for law, then there is no more common understanding about social order. Even if the actual behavior of people were not chaotic, Stage 4 realizes that without a common understanding there is chaos in men's minds about what to expect of each other. However, Stage 4 may not differentiate the chaos in men's minds from actual mass rioting. The following prototypic statement illustrates this (for Situation III):

"It is a nautral thing for Heinz to want to save his wife, but it's still always wrong to steal. You have to follow the rules regardless of how you feel or regardless of the special circumstances. Even if his wife is dying, it's still his duty as a citizen to obey the law. No one else is allowed to steal, why should he be? If everyone starts breaking the law in a jam, there'd be no civilization, just crime and violence."

Here is an example of a subject's recapitulation which was scored a hit:

"If Heinz was allowed to steal, then everyone would have to be allowed to steal, and our society would be one mass of crime and violence. . . . If our streets were filled with crime— I think they would be—everyone would live in fear. Heinz surely would not benefit from this. Since everyone is equal, the laws must apply equally to everyone; therefore, Heinz should not receive any special privileges."

An example of a miss on this idea is the following:

> "I don't know (what he's saying). . . . I really couldn't say. . . .
> I don't think everyone else should be brought into this—about
> stealing—it is just about him . . . it should be about him."

This subject apparently was looking at Heinz's deed as an isolated ,occurrence rather than seeing it as involving categorical social norms, binding on all, and as an issue of social order.

*Stage 5*—Maximizing welfare and the majority will—Stage 5's respect for the majority will is not deference of one individual to "something greater" or super-individual, but it is part of the package of accepting certain social obligations for the sake of being able to make important claims on others.

A Stage 5 prototype statement in Situation III read:

> "Heinz has to respect the general will of his society as it is
> set down in the law. The law represents the basis of how
> people have agreed to live with each other."

The connection between "general will of his society" and respect for law is evident in the following recapitulation judged a hit:

> "I think he meant that the majority of the people have set down
> laws to live by and because . . . this is how people have agreed
> to live with each other."

The following response was a miss because it did not seem to see the connection between legal-moral obligation and the interests and will of the constituent members of society:

> "Heinz doesn't have to respect the general rule of the society
> because it's a free nation. Heinz doesn't have to respect the
> majority—he has freedom of mind—he can love or hate it as
> much as he wants."

Another subject construed "respecting the general will" as the Stage 3 concern to be personally approved and admired by the others:

> "[He's saying] . . . people are more interested in what your
> neighbors are going to say about your new car . . . and what
> people are talking about. In our society today you are more
> interested in that the Joneses see you in Church. . . ."

A comprehension score for a given stage embodied in prototypic statements was based on the number of hits a subject got for the 10 statements at each stage.[4] For instance, if a subject got 9 hits out of 10 statements at Stage 2, then his comprehension score for Stage 2 was 90.

Reliability of the comprehension scoring was measured in several ways. First, a kind of "split half" reliability was assessed by comparing scorings for "pro" statements exemplifying a certain stage and aspect with its counterpart "con" statements. "Agreement" was defined in terms of scoring a subject with a hit on the statement (or not scoring a hit) both times. For the data from Situation III, agreement was 74 percent, and from Situation VI agreement was 72 percent.

Second, a coder scored and rescored the same set of 385 responses six months apart, scoring the second time "blind." There was 93 percent agreement on what responses were scorable. Of those judged scorable both times, the agreement in judging a response to a statement showing evidence of comprehension (or no evidence) was 86 percent. Considering the subject's comprehension scores for each stage (proportion of "hits" over 10 statements out of all his coded responses), the correlation of these scores over both scoring was .93.

Third, two different judges scored material from a different study but used the same statements and coding guides. After clarifying the rules for assignment, agreement on hits was 86 percent and 75 percent for misses.

Preference scores were obtained by having subjects give a rating for each statement—from 1 to 5, ranging from "very poor" to "very good." The sum of the ratings for the 10 statements of a stage gave a rating score for the stage. Also, subjects were asked to rank statements in order of preference, and similarly, the sum of ranks yielded a preference score for a stage. Hence there were two preference scores, completely independent of each other and based on two operations separated in time.

RESULTS

*Comprehension*

There were four major findings with regard to comprehension. The first is that a subject tends either to get nearly all hits for the statements of one stage or nearly all misses. In other words, comprehension of the various characteristics of a stage (independently defined and independently tested) tend to cluster together. Figure 1 shows the bimodal distribution of scores.

4. See Rest (1969a) for details on how the comprehension score for a stage was computed.

Since comprehension scores for a stage tend to be either very low or very high for a stage, this justifies dichotomizing the scores at the 50 percent point and justifies talking about the comprehension of a stage as a whole instead of talking about 60 separate items.

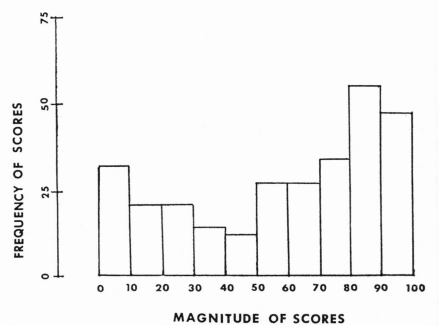

**MAGNITUDE OF SCORES**

*Figure 1.* Distribution of comprehension scores with regard to magnitude.

The second finding was that of cumulativity of comprehension scores for a subject—that is, if a subject showed high comprehension of a given stage, he showed high comprehension of all the preceding stages. This is indicated by the patterns presented in Table 2, patterns corresponding to the concept of a Guttman scale (Green, 1956).

The middle column of Table 2 (labelled "comprehension") lists for each subject the stages that were comprehended (i.e., scores for a stage above 50 percent). For instance, a subject who has a 5 listed in this column also has 4, 3, 2, and 1 listed. By this analysis, out of 47 subjects, 45 showed perfect cumulativity of

*Table 2.* Comprehension and preference patterns of individual subjects. Situation III

| Subject | PRETEST | | COMPREHEN-SION[c] | PREFERENCE | |
|---|---|---|---|---|---|
| | Predominant stage[a] | H.S.U. stage[b] | 1, 2, 3, 4, 5, 6 | Top rank[d] | Hi rate[e] 1, 2, 3, 4, 5, 6 |
| A | 1 | 2 | 1, 2 | – | 6 |
| B | 2 | 3 | 1, 2, 3 | 3 | 3,    5, 6 |
| C | 2 | 4 | 1, 2, 3 | – | |
| D | 3 | 3 | 1, 2, 3, 4 | – | 4, 5, 6 |
| E | 3 | 3 | 1, 2, 3, 4 | 6 | ND[f] |
| F | 3 | 3 | 1, 2, 3 | – | 2, 3, 4, 5, 6 |
| G | 3 | 3 | 1, 2, 3, 4 | 6 | 5, 6 |
| H | 3 | 4 | 1, 2, 3, 4 | 6 | 1,   3,   5, 6 |
| I | 3 | 4 | 1, 2, 3, 4 | 6 | 3, 4, 5, 6 |
| J | 3 | 4 | 1, 2, 3, 4 | – | 1, 2, 3, 4, 5, 6 |
| K | 3 | 4 | 1, 2, 3, 4 | – | 5, 6 |
| L | 3 | 5 | 1, 2, 3, 4 | ND | 3, 4, 5, 6 |
| M | 4 | 4 | 1, 2, 3, 4 | ND | 5 |
| N | 4 | 4 | 1, 2, 3, 4 | 5 | 4,   6 |
| O | 4 | 4 | 1, 2, 3, 4 | – | 3 |
| P | 4 | 4 | 1, 2, 3, 4, 5 | 5 | 5, 6 |
| Q | 4 | 5 | 1, 2, 3, 4, 5, 6 | 6 | 3, 4,   6 |
| R | 5 | 5 | 1, 2, 3, 4, 5 | 6 | 3, 4, 5, 6 |
| S | 5 | 5 | 1, 2, 3, 4, 5 | – | 4, 5, 6 |
| T | 5 | 6 | 1, 2, 3, 4, 5, 6 | 6 | 6 |
| U | 6 | 6 | 1, 2, 3, 4,    6 | 6 | ND |
| V | 6 | 6 | 1, 2, 3, 4, 5, 6 | 6 | |
| W | 6 | 6 | 1, 2, 3, 4, 5, 6 | 6 | 6 |
| X | 6 | 6 | 1, 2, 3, 4, 5, 6 | 6 | 6 |

comprehension, and the other 2 subjects missed only one earlier stage before their highest stage. Using Green's (1956) formula for scalogram analysis, the Reproducibility for Situation III's results was .993, with an Index of Consistency of .84, well over the .50 mark necessary for claiming scalability. The results for Situation VI were similar, with reproducibility of .993 and an Index of Consistency of .81. This is evidence that if a subject comprehends a stage, he also comprehends all the previous stages —that there is a cumulative order of difficulty to the stages.

Our third finding was that of a close relation of comprehension scores to the subject's own spontaneous stage of judgment in the pretest. Our hypothesis was that comprehension scores should

## Table 2 (continued)
### Situation VI

| Subject | PRETEST Predominant stage[a] | H.S.U. stage[b] | COMPREHENSION[c] 1, 2, 3, 4, 5, 6 | PREFERENCE Top rank[d] | Hi rate[e] 1, 2, 3, 4, 5, 6 |
|---|---|---|---|---|---|
| A | 2 | 2 | 1, 2̲ | 6 | 5, 6 |
| B | 2 | 4 | 1, 2̲ | – | |
| C | 2 | 2 | 1, 2̲, 3, 4 | – | 2, 4, 5 |
| D | 2 | 3 | 1, 2, 3 | ND[f] | 3 |
| E | 3 | 3 | 1, 2, 3, 4, 5 | ND | 6 |
| F | 3 | 3 | 1, 2, 3 | ND | 6 |
| G | 3 | 3 | 1, 2, 3, 4 | – | 2, 4, 6 |
| H | 3 | 3 | 1, 2̲, 3, 4 | ND | 4, 5 |
| I | 3 | 4 | 1, 2, 4 | – | 3, 4, 5, 6 |
| J | 3 | 4 | 1, 2, 3, 4̲ | – | 6 |
| K | 3 | 3 | 1, 2, 3, 4, 5, 6 | 6 | 2, 3, 4, 6 |
| L | 3 | 5 | 1, 2, 3, 4, 5̲ | 6 | ND |
| M | 4 | 4 | 1, 2, 3̲ | 6 | 2, 4, 6 |
| N | 4 | 4 | 1, 2, 3̲, 4 | 6 | |
| O | 4 | 4 | 1, 2, 3, 4̲ | 6 | 5 |
| P | 4 | 5 | 1, 2, 3, 4̲, 5 | ND | 2, 4, 6 |
| Q | 4 | 4 | 1, 2, 3, 4̲ | 4 | 4 |
| R | 4 | 5 | 1, 2, 3, 4̲, 5 | – | 2, 4, 5, 6 |
| S | 4 | 6 | 1, 2, 3, 4̲ | – | |
| T | 5 | 5 | 1, 2, 3, 4̲ | ND | 4, 5 |
| U | 5 | 5 | 1, 2, 3, 4 | – | |
| V | 5 | 6 | 1, 2̲, 3, 4 | 6 | 4, 6 |
| W | 6 | 6 | 1, 2, 3, 4̲, 5, 6 | 6 | 4, 5, 6 |

[a]Predominant spontaneous stage of usage in pretest.
[b]Highest substantially used stage on pretest (at least 20 percent).
[c]Stages with comprehension score of at least 50 percent. Underlined stage is most preferred (by ranking) of those comprehended.
[d]Stage which was ranked on top in at least 3 out of 5 rankings.
[e]Stages with at least 5 out of 10 statements rated good or very good.
[f]ND signifies "no data."

be high up to the subject's predominant test stage and then progressively decreased. This was found to be the case, as Table 3 shows in terms of averages instead of dichotomized data. Up to the subject's own predominant stage, average comprehension scores were high; then they began to fall increasingly as the statements were higher than the subject's level.

The same trend is evident if we look at the scores of individual subjects in Table 2 using the dichotomized data. Comparing a subject's predominant pretest stage in the first column

Table 3. Average comprehension scores.

| Situation | Statement's stage relative to subject's predominant pretest stage | | | | | | |
|---|---|---|---|---|---|---|---|
| | −3 | −2 | −1 | 0 | +1 | +2 | +3 |
| III (n = 24) | 88 | 85 | 76 | 76 | 53 | 19 | 12 |
| VI (n = 23) | 85 | 83 | 79 | 64 | 48 | 24 | 21 |
| III and VI | 87 | 84 | 77 | 71 | 51 | 22 | 17 |

(Pretest-Predominant Stage) with the stages comprehended in the third comprehension column, we see that almost all (43 out of 47) subjects comprehended all the stages up to their own predominant pretest stage. Almost half of the subjects (20 out of 47) also comprehended one stage beyond their predominant pretest stage. The fact that about half of the subjects have high comprehension scores up to their own predominant stage whereas the other half have high comprehension scores one stage beyond this indicates that the average comprehension score of the whole group of subjects of 51 percent at the +1 stage is due to the almost perfect comprehension of that stage by half the subjects (called "+1 comprehenders") and the failure of the remaining half (the "0" or own-stage "comprehenders") to comprehend +1 reasoning at all.

Our fourth finding was that the highest stages used on the pretest, rather than the predominant stage, was the best predictor of comprehension. On the pretest, as mentioned before, the spontaneous utterances of a subject were coded into stage categories, and the stage which had the predominant number of codes was called the subject's "own stage" or his pretest "predominant stage" (as the column is labelled in Table 2). All of the subject's responses are not scored at only one stage, however, and his use of stages higher than his own stage is of particular interest. Almost all of the subjects (84 percent) who showed on the pretest a substantial amount of codes at stages above their predominant stage also showed comprehension of statements above their predominant stage, whereas if a subject did not show substantial use of stages higher than his predominant stage there was only 30 percent probability of his comprehending statements higher than his predominant stage. In Table 2, this match can be seen by comparing column 2 (Pretest-H.S.U. Stage) with column 3, Comprehension. The table indicates that if a subject's predominant stage on the pretest was Stage 3 but he also used a substantial amount of Stage 4, chances are that he would comprehend Stages 1, 2, 3 and 4 statements. (For this study 20 percent or more usage of a stage was defined a "substantial" amount). Therefore we found that subjects tend to produce spontaneously a substantial amount of the highest stage

*Table 4.* Comprehension as a function of stage of statement and subject's highest stage of substantial use.

### Situation III

| Subject's stage | Stage of statement | | | | | |
|---|---|---|---|---|---|---|
|  | 1 | 2 | 3 | 4 | 5 | 6 |
| 6 (n = 5) | 90 | 93 | 83 | 87 | 64 | 74 |
| 5 (n = 4) | 82 | 98 | 84 | 72 | 64 | 33 |
| 4 (n = 9) | 84 | 81 | 85 | 59 | 20 | 7 |
| 3 (n = 5) | 74 | 79 | 77 | 53 | 17 | 3 |
| 2 (n = 1) | 92 | 50 | 25 | 30 | 0 | 0 |

### Situation VI

| Subject's stage | Stage of statement | | | | | |
|---|---|---|---|---|---|---|
|  | 1 | 2 | 3 | 4 | 5 | 6 |
| 6 (n = 3) | 84 | 68 | 73 | 70 | 36 | 50 |
| 5 (n = 5) | 88 | 81 | 83 | 76 | 62 | 22 |
| 4 (n = 7) | 93 | 72 | 54 | 52 | 34 | 14 |
| 3 (n = 6) | 91 | 80 | 74 | 62 | 24 | 25 |
| 2 (n = 2) | 86 | 73 | 36 | 29 | 9 | 0 |

that they comprehend, although the predominance of spontaneous productions is often lower.

Table 4 shows how a subject's highest substantially used stage on the pretest predicts to comprehending a statement at each stage. The jagged line demarcates statements at stages above and below the subject's highest substantially used stage on the pretest. The table shows that generally above the jagged line the probability is high that a subject comprehended a statement, and the converse below.

*Preference*

There were two major preference findings. The first finding supported our hypothesis that insofar as subjects comprehend various stages of thinking, they tend to prefer the highest comprehended. The data relevant to this hypothesis is given in Table 2, column 3 (comprehension) which lists all the stages comprehended by each subject. Among these possibilities, the stage with the most preferred rankings is underlined. The table shows that for 80 percent of the subjects, the highest stage of those comprehended was most preferred. Thus the preference hypothesis of the study was confirmed in regard to preference comparisons among comprehended stages. It is notable that the subject's own predominant stage on the pretest did not predict his preference; that there was no special investment in one's own predominant stage.

The second preference finding concerns preference among all statements whether the subject comprehended it or not. The finding was that virtually all subjects tended to prefer the highest stage statements in their developmental order—that is, preferring Stage 6 most, Stage 5 next, and so on.

Table 5 below, shows the average ranks for the statements of each stage and bears out this generalization with few exceptions. The averages for subjects grouped by pretest stage also generally tended to show increasing preference in the order of the developmental order within each grouping. And the averaged preference trends from the rating data were similar to the ranking data.

The last two columns of Table 2 give the preference patterns of individual subjects. It was found that out of 38 subjects

*51*

Table 5. Average rank of statements.

|  | Stage of statement | | | | | |
| --- | --- | --- | --- | --- | --- | --- |
|  | 1 | 2 | 3 | 4 | 5 | 6 |
| Situation III | 5.0 | 4.4 | 3.6 | 3.2 | 2.8 | 2.0 |
| Situation VI | 5.2 | 3.6 | 3.8 | 3.0 | 3.2 | 2.2 |

for whom there was complete ranking data, 61 percent showed consistent top preferences (that is, out of the 5 rankings, they ranked the statements of one stage on top at least 3 times.) Of those that did show a consistent preference, 83 percent preferred Stage 6 statements. Subjects who preferred Stage 6 statements came from every possible stage.

The findings were similar for the rating preference patterns. Of the subjects who rated at least 5 out of the 10 statements of a stage as good or very good, 30 subjects rated Stage 6 statements as good, 21 subjects rated Stage 5 as good, 21 subjects rated Stage 4 as good, 12 so rated Stage 3 statements, 8 so rated Stage 2 statements, and 2 so rated Stage 1 statements. Good ratings for a stage were roughly cumulative, that is, those subjects who rated low stages as good, tended also to rate all the higher stages as good. Again, the trend was to prefer Stage 6 statements regardless of comprehension or use of Stage 6, and the order of preference of the stages tended to be increasing as the developmental order advances.

The significance of the preference trends are only partially clear. If a subject gives evidence of understanding statements in their stage distinctive way, it is reasonable to interpret preference for one statement over another as that the subject is judging one stage's thinking as more adequate than the other. By this interpretation, this study supports the claim that subjects reject their "old," too simplistic ways of thinking. But if a subject gives no evidence of understanding a statement in its intended stage-distinctive way, it is problematic to make inferences about how the subject is judging the intended stage's structural adequacy. There are insufficient grounds in this analysis, for instance, to conclude that subjects are choosing Stage 6 statements for their Stage 6 reasons. Nevertheless it has been demonstrated that the trend of increasing preference is counter to the ease of comprehension—i.e., the increasing difficulty of statements does not make them less preferable. Also it seems safe to say that subjects reject the statements of stages that they have themselves already passed through.

### DISCUSSION AND CONCLUSIONS

The present study's finding of a cumulative order of difficulty supports the claim that each succeeding stage is more cognitively differentiated and integrated than the preceding one, and its finding of an order of preference is consistent with the claim that each succeeding stage is more conceptually adequate. The increasing difficulty of the stages sets upper limits on what kinds of moral judgments are conceptually possible for a subject, and preference for greater structural adequacy sets lower limits on what kinds of moral judgments the subject would be satisfied with. Thus the two factors—comprehension and preference—largely account for the developmental stage at which a subject is actually producing moral judgments and for the stage of judgment presented to him which he will assimilate.

This study's results are in substantial agreement with a previous study using a different method and sample (Rest, Turiel, & Kohlberg, 1969). This previous study found an order of increased difficulty of comprehension for statements one stage below, one stage above and two stages above subject's own. The present study examined comprehension of all stages lower than the subject's own (not just the one below) and determined that essentially all subjects are able to comprehend all stages below their own. With regard to comprehension of stages higher than the subject's own the present study adds the following new findings: (a) some subjects can "thoroughly" comprehend thinking above their predominant spontaneous level (this comprehension is not just fragmentary but involves getting a majority of hits on the statements at the +1 level); (b) the subjects with this ability to comprehend statements above one's predominant stage are those showing spontaneous use (at least 20 percent) of higher level thinking—other subjects do not comprehend stages any higher than their own; and (c) usually when subjects spontaneously use a stage higher than their own, it is the next above, so that where comprehension of a higher stage occurs, it is usually comprehension of the stage above.

With regard to preference, the Rest, Turiel and Kohlberg (1969) study had found that subjects tend to reject statements at stages lower than their own stage. It did not clearly determine whether subjects preferred +1 or +2 statements to one another or either to statements at their own stage (which were not presented). The present study indicates that subject's preference for statements does not tend towards their own spontaneous predominant stage, but tends to be for statements at least as high as they can comprehend and possibly even for stages higher than this. There is no particular preference for either one's own stage or to the next stage towards which one is moving; there is an ordered preference for the highest stage one can comprehend, regardless of one's own spontaneous stage.

As has been stated, the trends for ordered preference of higher stages which are not comprehended is ambiguous in meaning. One hypothesis about why subjects prefer uncomprehended high-stage statements is that subjects may not understand the statements, but the complexity and abstractness of the statements make them sufficiently ambiguous so that subjects may "project" some of their own ideas into the statements but see them expressed in words which are difficult to challenge or refute. Some subjects said that they liked the Stage 6 statements because that's what they said (although they were scored as neither using nor comprehending Stage 6). This suggests the interpretation that the subjects sensed an order of abstractness and complexity without understanding the abstract ideas themselves, and felt an abstract answer was more appropriate to the test-taking situation.

A rival hypothesis of this preference finding is that subjects really do understand the Stage 6 thinking in the statements, but only intuitively and faintly and cannot express it or give evidence of understanding it by our test of comprehension. This hypothesis derives from the view that even at early stages of development children are discriminating about the character of even the higher forms of justice (Kohlberg, 1968). Some support for this hypothesis comes from the fact that in the five ranking trials, subjects were fairly consistently choosing the Stage 6 statements and so they were discriminating something in the Stage 6 statements. Determination of which of these two alternative interpretations of our preference findings is correct would require a close analysis of what the subjects think they see in higher stage statements and why they say they like it.

From a cognitive developmental view, the tasks of spontaneous production, comprehension, and preference can be seen as "developmental decalage," in Piaget's terminology. According to this view, it is understandable why subjects should show comprehension of higher stages than that they predominantly use in the pretest. In the pretest, the subject has to make a construction of a situation "from scratch"—identify the relevant features, imagine the consequences of various courses of action, and integrate all of these considerations into a coherent justification of one course of action. The task of comprehending a prototypic statement is easier. All of this structuring has already been done for a subject. All the subject has to do in the comprehension task is to follow the points that the statement is making, and discuss them in an equivalent form. And so it is quite plausible that there will be some subjects who show some evidence of high level thinking spontaneously on the pretest, but who are not quite able to put a solution together at that high level by themselves without the help of the statements as models. When such a subject sees a solution in the statements he might then be able to follow the ideas after the statements have "spelled it out" for him. Thus some subjects can show full comprehension at stages which they were only able to partially produce. Comprehension of a stage higher than the subject's own is seldom if ever comprehension of something absent in spontaneous production, but comprehension of something already spontaneously present in the subject's own organization, whose extension is facilitated by the fact that the comprehension task is an easier test of usage than is the spontaneous production task.

Similarly, the preference task may be viewed as an even easier way of manifesting discrimination of high levels of thinking. In the preference task, not even the production of equivalent ideas is required. Therefore one could view the preference task as furnishing the earliest signs of the acquisition of new stages of thinking, and could see three tasks (preference, comprehension, and spontaneous production) as manifesting the acquisition of new stages of thinking at different points of consolidation.

Such an interpretation is quite different from other theoretical orientations which view preference or value judgments as a function of reinforcements, modeling, or libido, and not as a function of cognitive complexity and the subject's developmental stage. Other theories do not place importance on the individual's ability to appreciate cognitively the conceptual adequacy of moral judgments. Only cognitive developmental theory focuses on developments in a person's self-constructed conceptualizations of social-moral reality in order to explain changes in moral orientation over time. The present study has not just assumed that cognitive capacity is the crucial variable in spontaneous productions or stated preferences for arguments, but has demonstrated meaningful relationships among the three, and thus empirically supported these predictions from cognitive-developmental theory.

## SUMMARY

Comprehension of Kohlberg's stages of moral judgment was assessed by having subjects (47 high school seniors) recapitulate prototypic statements of each of the stages. A correct paraphrase of a statement was used as evidence that the subject could comprehend that stage's way of thinking. Preference for each stage was measured by having subjects rate and rank the prototypic statements. Comprehension of the statements ordered by stage was increasingly difficult and cumulative, forming a Guttman scale. About half of the subjects showed comprehension of statements as high as the stage that they predominantly produce on Kohlberg's usual free-response interview; about half showed comprehension 1 stage higher. Preference was for the higher stage statements. The comprehension and preference findings were interpreted as supporting the cognitive-developmental theory of a hierarchy of stages.

### REFERENCES

Flavell, J., & Wohlwill, J. Formal and functional aspects of cognitive development. In D. Elkind & S. Flavell (Eds.), *Studies in cognitive development.* New York: Oxford University Press, 1969, 67–120.

Fodor, J. & Garrett, M. Some reflections on competence and performance. In J. Lyons & R. J. Wales (Eds.), *Psycholinguistics papers*, 1966, 135–154.

Green, B. A. A method of scalogram analysis using summary statistics. *Psychometrika*, 1956, **21**, 79–88.

Kohlberg, L. The development of modes of moral thinking and choice in the years ten to sixteen. Unpublished doctoral dissertation, University of Chicago, 1958.

Kohlberg, L. Education for justice: A modern statement of the Platonic view. Ernest Burton Lecture on Moral Education, Harvard University, Cambridge, 1968.

Kohlberg, L. Stage and sequence: The cognitive-developmental approach to socialization. In D. A. Goslin (Ed.), *Handbook of socialization theory and research*. Chicago: Rand McNally, 1969.

Kohlberg, L., & Kramer, R. Continuities and discontinuities in childhood and adult moral development. *Human Development*, 1969, **12**, 93–120.

Rest, J. Hierarchies of comprehension and preference in a developmental stage model of moral thinking. Unpublished doctoral dissertation, University of Chicago, 1969a.

Rest, J. Looking for structure in moral judgment and language: The research strategy of the cognitive-development approach. Unpublished mimeographed paper, Harvard University, 1969b.

Rest, J., Turiel, E., & Kohlberg, L. Level of moral development as a determinant of preference and comprehension of moral judgments made by others. *Journal of Personality*, 1969, **37**, 225–252.

Turiel, E. Developmental processes in the child's moral thinking. In P. Mussen, J. Langer, and M. Covington (Eds.), *Trends and Issues in developmental psychology*. New York: Holt, Rinehart & Winston, 1969, 92–132.

*Manuscript received November 24, 1971.*

# Level of moral development as a determinant of preference and comprehension of moral judgments made by others[1]

James Rest, *University of Chicago,* Elliot Turiel, *Columbia University, and* Lawrence Kohlberg, *Harvard University*

According to certain developmental theories (Piaget, 1932; Kohlberg, 1963) the child passes through successive stages of moral judgment, each stage characterized by its particular mode of organizing the social and moral order. Kohlberg (1963) has postulated the following six stages of moral development:

*Stage 1:* Obedience and punishment orientation. Egocentric deference to superior power or prestige, or a trouble-avoiding set. Objective responsibility.

*Stage 2:* Naively egoistic orientation. Right action is that instrumentally satisfying the self's needs and occasionally others.' Awareness of relativism of value to each actor's needs and perspective. Naive egalitarianism and orientation to exchange and reciprocity.

*Stage 3:* Good boy orientation. Orientation to approval and to pleasing and helping others. Conformity to stereotypical images of majority or natural role behavior, and judgment by intentions.

*Stage 4:* Authority and social order maintaining orientation. Orientation to "doing duty" and to showing respect for authority and maintaining the given social order for its own sake. Regard for earned expectations of others.

*Stage 5:* Contractual legalistic orientation. Recognition of an arbitrary element or starting point in rules or expectations for the sake of agreement. Duty defined in terms of contract, general avoidance of violation of the will or rights of others, and majority will and welfare.

1. This research was supported by the Center for Urban Education and by N.I.C.H.D. Grant HD 02469 01 to the third author. Gary Kippel and Joan Lerner carried out the interviewing for the study and contributed a number of valuable suggestions to the design of the study.

*Stage* 6: Conscience or principle orientation. Orientation not only to actually ordained social rules but to principles of choice involving appeal to logical universality and consistency. Orientation to conscience as a directing agent and to mutual respect and trust.

Kohlberg views the six stages as forming an invariant developmental sequence in which attainment of an advanced stage is dependent on the attainment of each of the preceding stages. It is further assumed that a more advanced stage is not simply an addition to a less advanced stage, but represents a reorganization of less advanced levels. Evidence for these propositions comes from a variety of sources: age trends in various cultures and social classes supporting the ordering of the stages (Kohlberg, 1968); a Guttman "quasi-simplex" pattern in the correlations between the stages (Kohlberg, 1963); and longitudinal studies of individual development (Kohlberg, 1970). Experimental evidence comes from a study by Turiel (1966), which is the point of departure for the present research.

Turiel examined the postulation that Kohlberg's stages form an invariant sequence by testing the implication that movement to a moral stage differing from the child's own should be to the stage directly above the S's stage, rather than to any other stage. In Turiel's experiment, Ss were exposed to new moral reasoning in a treatment administered after Ss' stages had been determined in a pretest. One treatment group was exposed to moral judgments one stage above (+1) the S's stage; another group was exposed to thinking two stages above (+2); and the third group was exposed to thinking one stage below (−1). Turiel hypothesized that if the sequence of stages is invariant, Ss exposed to reasoning directly above their dominant stage would be influenced more than those exposed to stages further above their own. A second hypothesis was that if the acquisition of each stage is a reorganization of the preceding stages, and not simply an addition to them, then Ss should resist lower stages. Thus it was also expected that Ss exposed to a stage one above would be influenced more than Ss exposed to a stage one below.

Turiel's findings confirmed these two hypotheses since the group exposed to the stage one above assimilated more new thinking than either of the other two treatment groups (−1 and +2). This maximal posttest change for the +1 group was found both on the situations used in the treatment conditions and on pretest situations not used in the treatment exposure.

One purpose of the present study was to replicate Turiel's findings using a different experimental method. A second purpose was to attempt to isolate some of the developmental factors that might explain Turiel's results. More specifically, a developmental hierarchy implies that a subject's appreciation, comprehension, and assimilation of new modes of thought should be dependent on the relation between the level of his own mode and the level of the presented mode. Thus in the present study we were testing the following hypotheses:

1. Stages of thinking above S's predominant stage would be preferred to those below his stage if the Ss were asked to choose among them.

2. Stages of thinking above a S's predominant stage are increasingly more difficult for the S to understand than are the stages below his own level and hence cannot be correctly reproduced as readily as lower stages.

3. These two principles—preference for more advanced stages and increasing cognitive difficulty—interact such that subjects maximally accept into their own thinking moral reasoning one stage above their dominant stage. Hence, it was expected that Turiel's finding would be replicated: namely, that exposure to the stage one above the S's predominant stage would result in more assimilation than exposure to the stages two above or one below.

To study these hypotheses, Ss were presented with moral advice at stages one above, two above, and one below their own (as established by pretest). Then they were questioned to determine their preferences and comprehension of the advice. Ss were also asked to give their "own advice" on these situations.

## METHOD

### Subjects

This study used 11 male and 11 female fifth grade Ss between the ages of 10:6 and 12:3 as well as 12 male and 11 female eighth grade Ss between the ages of 13:4 and 14:6. All 45 Ss were obtained from a Catholic parochial school in the New York City area. The average I.Q. (as obtained from school administered tests, usually Otis) was 119, ranging from 95 to 150.[2]

## Design and Procedure

The procedure required two experimental sessions. In the first, the S's predominant stage was determined by a pretest interview. In the second session Ss were exposed to a series of moral arguments that were at three different stages in relation to the S's dominant stage: one below ($-1$), one above ($+1$), and two above ($+2$).

## Pretest Selection Interview

Each S was individually administered five hypothetical conflict situations from Kohlberg's (1958, 1968) moral judgment interview. A S's responses were scored (as described below) and the stage with the predominant number of responses determined the S's stage.

## Exposure Condition

Then in the second session Ss were given two booklets (one for each of two conflict situations) each composed of four parts.

1. The first part of each booklet contained a conflict situation (Situation II in one booklet and Situation III in the other) from the Kohlberg interview. These two situations had not been used in the pretest. As an example, Situation III is as follows:

In Europe a woman was near death from a special kind of cancer. There was one drug that the doctors thought might save her. It was a form of radium that a druggist in the same town had recently discovered. The drug was expensive to make, but the druggist was charging ten times what the drug cost him to make. He paid $200. for the radium and charged $2,000. for a small dose of the drug. The sick woman's husband, Heinz, went to everyone he knew to borrow the money, but he could only get together about $1,000, which is half of what it cost. He told the druggist that his wife was dying and asked him to sell it cheaper or let him pay later.

2. Children in each stage group were roughly equated for age and I.Q. as follows:

|         | N  | I.Q. | Percentage in younger (5th) grade |
|---------|----|------|-----------------------------------|
| Stage 1 | 4  | 120  | 75                                |
| Stage 2 | 9  | 114  | 58                                |
| Stage 3 | 17 | 119  | 35                                |
| Stage 4 | 12 | 124  | 42                                |

But the druggist said, "No, I discovered the drug and I'm going to make money from it."

Heinz is not sure about what he should do in this difficult situation. He doesn't know if it is right for a husband in his situation to steal the drug for his wife. So Heinz went to some of his friends and asked them for advice. Listed on the next page are the names of the six friends Heinz went to and next to each name you will find the advice given by that friend.

2. The second part of the booklet contained six sets of "advice" as possible solutions to the conflict. Two sets of advice were one stage below ($-1$) the $S$'s predominant stage, two sets were one above ($+1$), and two sets were two stages above ($+2$). (Stage one Ss could not be given statements at the stage below and instead were given statements at their own stage.) The two sets at any given stage advocated opposing courses of action. Examples of two stage 3 sets of advice are as follows:

*Bruce.* You should steal the drug in this case. It isn't really right to steal but no one would blame you for doing it. Any man should love his wife enough to do that. The person who should really be blamed is that druggist who was just being mean and greedy. Considering what he is doing, it isn't so bad to get the drug to save your wife's life.

*David.* You really should not steal the drug. There must be some better way of getting it. You could get help from someone. Or else you could talk the druggist into letting you pay later. The druggist is trying to support his family so he should get some profit from his business. Maybe the druggist should sell it for less, but that still doesn't mean you should just steal it.

The expressions in the statements were derived from Kohlberg's (1958) coding forms, which are based on actual responses of Ss (with some balancing of language difficulty and style) and are similar to those used in the Turiel (1966) treatment conditions.

3. The third part of the booklet had the following set of questions aimed at eliciting $S$'s preference and understanding of the presented advice:

(1) and (2). Would you choose the two friends whom you think have given the best advice? Can you say why you have chosen these?

(3) and (4). Now choose the two friends whom you think have given the worst advice. Why did you pick these?

(5). Which friend do you think gave the smartest advice? Why?

(6). Which friend do you think gave the advice that reflects the "most good"? Why?

(7). Which one of the friends do you think is the smartest person? Why?

(8). Which one of the friends do you think is the "most good" person? Why?

(9). Which friend gave the advice that makes the most sense to you? Why?

4. Finally the following question asked for S's own advice on the situation at issue:

Suppose you were one of Heinz's friends and he came to you for advice. What would you tell him to do?

Situation III had an additional question aimed at assessing the S's recall of the statements:

Now we would like to know what you remember about the advice that was given to Heinz by his friends. Please list below as much of that advice as you can recall.

The Ss were grouped according to their predominant stage and the appropriate booklet was used with each group. A proctor read through parts one and two of the booklet with the subjects to make sure that there was no difficulty in reading the material. Ss could refer back to the original statements when answering all questions except those asking for their own advice, and for recall of advice.

The S's reasons for favoring a statement, which usually restated or recapitulated part of the original statement, could be scored for stage level. In addition, the responses to the "own advice" and recall questions were scored for stage level.

*Scoring Methods*

Kohlberg (1958) has formulated a scoring system that contains coding guides for each of the hypothetical Situations. A S's responses to a given Situation are divided into "thought-content" units classifiable according to stage. Ss are classified as being at the stage they use most. Each S, however, also has a "profile" of percentage usage of statements at each stage.

The interjudge reliability on Kohlberg's coding system has been found to be .94 (Turiel, 1966). In the present study interjudge reliability for coding the recapitulations and discussions of advice was

Table 1. Percentage choice of advice at difference levels for two Situations (II and III).

| S's stage | Stage level of advice | Best −1 | Best +1 | Best +2 | Smart −1 | Smart +1 | Smart +2 | Good −1 | Good +1 | Good +2 | General preference[a] −1 | General preference[a] +1 | General preference[a] +2 | Worst −1 | Worst +1 | Worst +2 |
|---|---|---|---|---|---|---|---|---|---|---|---|---|---|---|---|---|
| 1 | II | 00[b] | 25 | 75 | 00[b] | 00 | 100 | 00[b] | 13 | 88 | 00[b] | 11 | 89 | 63[b] | 38 | 00 |
|   | III | 38[b] | 25 | 38 | 45[b] | 09 | 45 | 14[b] | 14 | 71 | 35[b] | 15 | 50 | 38[b] | 38 | 25 |
| 2 | II | 00 | 58 | 42 | 03 | 60 | 37 | 25 | 50 | 25 | 08 | 57 | 35 | 54 | 29 | 17 |
|   | III | 04 | 50 | 46 | 08 | 67 | 25 | 13 | 50 | 38 | 08 | 57 | 35 | 67 | 08 | 25 |
| 3 | II | 06 | 50 | 44 | 06 | 57 | 37 | 15 | 41 | 44 | 08 | 50 | 41 | 56 | 18 | 26 |
|   | III | 06 | 44 | 50 | 02 | 45 | 53 | 18 | 50 | 32 | 08 | 46 | 46 | 50 | 21 | 29 |
| 4 | II | 33 | 46 | 21 | 31 | 46 | 23 | 38 | 42 | 21 | 34 | 45 | 22 | 42 | 25 | 33 |
|   | III | 21 | 29 | 50 | 14 | 22 | 64 | 55 | 09 | 36 | 27 | 21 | 52 | 38 | 33 | 29 |
| Totals | | 12 | 44 | 44 | 11 | 46 | 43 | 24 | 39 | 37 | 15 | 43 | 42 | 51 | 23 | 26 |

[a] "General preference" includes data from all questions asking for best, smart, and good advice.
[b] Stage 1 subjects had no −1 choice and the same stage statements were substituted.

65

assessed. On samples from both Situations II and III, there was 71 per cent agreement in assigning sentences to a moral stage with only 15 per cent of the scoring having a discrepancy of more than one stage. The scoring agreement was fairly constant at each stage and in both Situations.

## Major Findings: Results and Discussion

Our first hypothesis, that a subject will prefer statements at a stage above his own, implies that when the subject states a preference from among −1, +1, and +2 advice, he rejects the −1 advice more than either of the other two. The relevant data are presented in Table 1, which summarizes the nine preference questions under the four headings: "Best," "Worst," "Smart," and "Good."

The percentages in Table 1 represent the relative frequencies that −1, +1, or +2 advice was picked as a preference. The choices for the two situations are represented separately and subjects are grouped according to their dominant stage. The totals at the bottom of the table are the percentages of all the subjects in both situations choosing the −1, +1, or +2 advice. The totals under "general preference" sum the "Best," "Smart," and "Good" columns.

As Table 1 shows, to every positive question, whether the preference was stated in terms of "Best," "Smart," or "Good," subjects tended to choose the advice of the stages higher than their dominant stage. On the other hand, subjects tended to pick the advice of the stage below their stage as the "Worst advice." This trend is true for children at each stage, including Stage 1 subjects who were given their own stage advice as a substitute for the −1 advice.

This tendency to prefer the two higher stages over the stage below the S's own is statistically significant. If preference for each stage were solely a matter of chance, the probability of subjects choosing the stage below would be 1 out of 3. The probability of deviations from this expectancy can be calculated using the Normal Approximation of the Binomial Distribution.[3] The

3. This test is based on summing a number of nonindependent choice responses made by the same Ss, which inflates the N used in the test. Tests of single choices (e.g., the one smartest piece of advice), however, also yield significant results. In general, conviction as to the reliability of the results of this study

Table 2. Percentage of recapitulations of advice at each stage relative to S's own stage.

| Stage of the advice recapitulated | Stage of S's recapitulation | | | | | | |
|---|---|---|---|---|---|---|---|
| | —3 | —2 | —1 | 0 | +1 | +2 | +3 |
| —1 as "preferred advice" | 06 | 03 | 64[a] | 14 | 11 | 02 | 00 |
| —1 as "worst advice" | 02 | 06 | 79 | 11 | 02 | 00 | 00 |
| +1 as "preferred advice" | 03 | 05 | 27 | 18 | 43 | 03 | 00 |
| +1 as "worst advice" | 04 | 06 | 34 | 16 | 36 | 04 | 00 |
| +2 as "preferred advice" | 02 | 07 | 18 | 19 | 26 | 28 | 00 |
| +2 as "worst advice" | 05 | 05 | 57 | 05 | 00 | 30 | 00 |
| Stage of advice recalled | 05 | 08 | 38 | 15 | 25 | 09 | 00 |

[a]Underlined figures are "correct" recapitulations of the original statements of advice.

probabilities of subjects preferring —1 advice at less than expectancy and choosing it as "bad advice" at more than expectancy were all less than .01.

The second hypothesis, that thinking at stages above the predominant stage is more difficult to comprehend than thinking below, was examined by coding the stage level of Ss' attempts at recapitulating the advice statements (Table 2).

Table 2 shows that the accuracy of the recapitulations (i.e., the percentage of recapitulations at the stage of the original advice) decreased as the stage level increased. Ss preferring a —1 statement recapitulated it correctly 64 per cent of the time; Ss preferring the +1 statement recapitulated it correctly 43 per cent of the time; whereas Ss preferring the +2 statement recapitulated it correctly only 28 per cent of the time. The difference in accuracy in the —1, +1, and +2 recapitulations is highly significant. From the Chi-square "goodness of fit" test, the probability of such differences in accuracy occurring if the null hypothesis were true would be less than .001.[4]

rests on the consistency of pattern of the findings, rather than upon the statistical significance of any single finding. As Table 1 indicates, preference for the higher level is found for each story situation and for every form of preference questioned (best, smartest, worst, etc.).

4. In reporting the data in terms of stages below and above the subject's assigned stage, i.e., using the categories —3, —2, —1, 0, +1, +2, +3, there is the complication that no lower stages exist for Stage 1 subjects, and there are no —2 or —3 categories possible for Stage 2 subjects. Analyses were done to ascertain how much the overall picture is affected by this bias in using these categories to report the data (see Rest, 1967). All the data from Stage 1 sub-

Further evidence of a hierarchy of comprehension of state-ments at various levels is contained in responses to the instruc-tion, "Recall as much as possible of the various sets of advice," for Situation III. These results, also presented in Table 2, show more −1 advice recalled than any other, with a steady decline in amount of correct recall as the relative stage of advice becomes higher. The "inaccurate" columns of Table 2 (those which do not match the actual stage of the advice recapitulated) show another trend that supports the notion of a hierarchy of com-prehension: there is a general tendency to distort advice to either the S's own level ("O") or the −1 level. There is a particularly strong tendency to distort disliked advice to the −1 level. At every stage of advice, disliked advice is more likely to be assim-ilated to the −1 level than is preferred advice. As we discuss in more detail later, this tendency is particularly striking with ad-vice that is difficult (e.g., +2).

Kohlberg's assumption of developmental hierarchy suggests that the increased order of difficulty in comprehension should be an individual as well as a group trend. To examine this assump-tion, a scalogram (Guttman, 1950) analysis was made of re-sponses to each of the two situations, as indicated in Table 3. For this analysis a pass was assigned for comprehension of state-ments in a given situation at a given level if at least one state-ment at that level was correctly recapitulated. While the num-ber of items and Ss is too small for a statistical evaluation of reproducibility, Table 3 indicates a general fit to a cumulative pattern, i.e., to a pattern in which all Ss who comprehend a high-er level comprehend each of the lower levels, with the reverse not being true. Of the scoreable cases only 12 per cent on Sit-uation II and only 27 per cent on Situation III fail to fit such a cumulative pattern. Furthermore, recall, as well as recapit-ulation, fits the same cumulative pattern. Regardless of what ad-

jects were eliminated since they could not contribute to any minus category. Also, all responses scored at −3, −2, or +3 levels were eliminated since all subjects could not contribute to these categories. Comparison of this data with the corresponding preference rows in Table 2 showed that the overall picture is very much the same. As noted in the previous footnote, use of the Chi-square test inflates the N by pooling non-independent responses by the same individual. Even with a sharply reduced N, the results would be significant. Data indicating that the trends are true for each individual, as well as for the group, are presented subsequently.

*Table 3.* Cumulative scale-types in comprehension and recall.

| Scale-types | Correct statements | | | Frequency of scale-type | | |
|---|---|---|---|---|---|---|
| | −1 | +1 | +2 | Situation II | Situation III | Recall |
| C | + | + | + | 7 | 6 | 8 |
| B | + | + | − | 8 | 9 | 19 |
| A | + | − | − | 8 | 7 | 13 |
| A' | − | − | − | 2 | 2 | 2 |
| Non-scale-types | | | | 3 | 9 | 3 |
| Incomplete information | | | | 17 | 12 | — |

vice was liked or assimilated into "own advice," those Ss recalling higher advice recalled all lower levels, but the reverse was not true (i.e., only 3 out of 45 cases were exceptions to this trend).

In summary, it was found that accuracy of recapitulation declined as the stage of the statement was more advanced, that the increasing inaccuracy of more advanced thought was an individual trend as well as a group trend, and that these trends in recapitulation corresponded to trends in recall. These findings indicate that the thinking above the subject's predominant stage is more difficult to comprehend than the thinking below.

We shall now consider the hypothesis that the two trends just discussed—preference and comprehension—combine to produce more assimilation of +1 thinking than −1 or +2 thinking. One way of assessing amount of assimilation is to compare stage usage in the pretest interview with stage usage in the S's own advice. The distribution of pretest responses of the Ss in this study, pre-

*Table 4.* Distributions of stage usage in pretest, own advice and recall.

| | Stage of responses relative to Ss' assigned stages | | | | | | |
|---|---|---|---|---|---|---|---|
| | −3 | −2 | −1 | 0 | +1 | +2 | +3 |
| Profile of usage in pretest interview (base line of expected stage usage) | 04 | 10 | 18 | 46 | 15 | 06 | 01 |
| Stage usage in own advice minus pretest profile | −01 | −03 | +08 | −20 | +16 | +01 | −01 |
| Stage usage in own advice minus Turiel controls | 00 | −02 | +01 | −14 | +18 | −02 | −01 |
| Stage usage in recall minus pretest profile | +01 | −02 | +20 | −31 | +10 | +03 | −01 |

sented in Table 4, may be used to estimate the stage distribution for Situations II and III if the Ss had responded to these situations without presentation of advice. Therefore, the effects of the experimental conditions (Ss being exposed to −1, +1, +2 thinking) can be assessed by using the pretest profile as a base line of comparison. Subtracting the pretest profile percentages from the respective "own advice" percentages yields the distribution presented in Table 4.

Table 4 shows a definite increase of +1 usage in "own advice" over that expected from the pretest, while there is no increase in +2 usage and only a small increase in −1 usage.[5] This "increase-over pretest" estimate of assimilation is based on the assumption that the Ss' natural stage on the advice Situations (II and III) is represented by their stage scores on the six pretest situations. Another base line of comparison for estimating assimilation is provided by the stage scores on the two advice Situations for subjects in Turiel's (1966) control group. Subjects in the present study and in Turiel's group had comparable pretest profiles. The subtraction of the Turiel control Ss' percentages from the "own advice" percentages (Table 4) shows an increase in +1 usage and no assimilation of −1 or +2 advice. Either method of estimating assimilation yields the same results as those of the Turiel (1966) study: most assimiliation of +1 thinking, less of −1 thinking, least of +2 thinking. Table 4 also clearly indicates that less assimilation of −1 advice is not a result of differential short-term forgetting of this advice. Subjects were able to recall −1 statements more than statements at the other levels; but the "own advice" data show that subjects did not use the −1 level and did use the +1 level—a finding consistent with their stated preference for +1 over −1 advice.

While −1 statements were not used as "own advice," even though they are understood, the failure of +2 advice to influence "own advice" is a function of unavailability. Table 1 indicated that Ss liked +2 statements as well as +1 statements, but Table 2 indicated they were only about half as likely to recapitulate +2 correctly (26 per cent correct recapitulation as opposed to 46

5. The Chi-square statistic for "goodness of fit" of the three change scores was used, taking the average of the three scores as the "expected" value. The probability of obtaining these differences by chance is less than .01 ($\chi^2 = 13.6$).

per cent). When +2 advice was preferred, it was as likely to be recapitulated in +1 terms as in +2 terms. By the time Ss gave "recall" responses (Table 2), they gave essentially no more +2 responses (9 per cent) than would be expected from the pretest or control group profiles. This lack of accurate recapitulation and recall of preferred +2 advice is consistent with the little use of +2 concepts in "own advice."

In summary, the results indicate that: (a) children prefer concepts that are above their predominant stage (whether one or two stages up) to concepts that are below, (b) children find thinking two stages above their own more difficult to comprehend than thinking one stage above, and thinking one stage above more difficult than thinking one stage below, and accordingly, (c) children assimilate thinking that is directly above their own stage more readily than thinking that is either one stage below or two stages above their own. The last finding substantiates Turiel's (1966) findings and supports Kohlberg's contention (1963, 1970) that his developmental stages form an invariant sequence. The two preceding findings may be considered in explaining the last finding. The greater assimilation of +1 thought is the joint result of preference for a higher over a lower stage and of increased difficulty of comprehending a higher than a lower stage. It was shown that the greater assimilation of +1 than −1 advice was due to the preference factor, not the comprehension factor, since the lower-level thinking was accessible to recapitulation and recall. (When asked to recall advice, more −1 thinking was reproduced than thinking at either of the two other stages.) In contrast, the fact that children more readily assimilate +1 than +2 material is to be explained in terms of a comprehension rather than a preference factor. (Only 28 per cent of the +2 advice chosen as preferred was recapitulated at its own level.)

The quantitative findings summarized may be further clarified by means of a qualitative analysis. This analysis indicated that the failure to like and assimilate lower-level advice was due to a rejection of its structural-developmental characteristics. While this almost always held true for children's rejections of lower-level (−1) advice, their rejection of higher level advice was almost never based on rejection of its structural characteristics, but was due to other reasons.

The fact that lower-level statements were comprehended, but not assimilated into the child's self-accepted belief system because of an active rejection of the structural components, was clearly documented in children's reasons for considering lower-stage responses to be "bad advice." Stage 2 (instrumental need and exchange orientation) Ss tend to reject Stage 1 (punishment and obedience orientation) advice because it is fearful and instrumentally irrational. One Stage 2 S justified his choice of two Stage 1 statements as "worst advice" as follows: "Albert says that you should tell so that you can keep out of trouble with his father. It is not right to fear your father. Robert says that you should not tell because if you do Joe will beat you up. He is putting wrong things into Alex's mind by telling him that his brother will beat him up." It is apparent that this S grasped the general orientation of Stage 1 thinking and explicitly rejected it. This S said of the Stage 1 "adviser" in another place, "He is a type of very timid man who knows no evil."

While Stage 2 Ss tend to reject Stage 1 advice because it is fearful and foolish, Stage 3 (empathy- and approval-oriented) subjects tend to reject Stage 2 advice (based on exchange and instrumental needs) because it is egoistical and ignores moral feelings. One Stage 3 S rejected Stage 2 advice (to keep quiet for a brother because one might want a favor from him one day) by saying, "I don't like the idea that 'if you do this, then I'll do that.' You should not make a decision because you'll be paid off." Another Stage 3 S said the Stage 2 advice was bad advice "because it is making him think just of himself and that's not right." Stage 4 (rules- and authority-oriented) Ss, in turn, tend to reject Stage 3 advice because it is based on personal feelings and relationships rather than upon moral rules. A Stage 4 S justified his rejection of Stage 3 advice (to keep quiet about the brother) as follows: "It's stupid not to do right because you're afraid of losing your brother's friendship or because you're afraid of what your father might think."

We have said that the rejection of lower-level advice is based on rejection of understood structural-developmental characteristics. In contrast, rejection of higher-level advice is almost never based on a correct apprehension of the developmental-structural characteristics of the advice. In some cases the advice was rejected for nonstructural reasons, such as the content of the act recommended, or the claim that the advice was factually incorrect. When higher-level advice was rejected for structural reasons, its structural components were misinterpreted as being at a stage below the S's own. Table 2 indicated that +2 advice was especially vulnerable in this regard, with 57 per cent of all +2 statements considered "bad advice" being misinterpreted as at the −1 level and another 10 per cent at still lower (−2 and −3) levels. The table also indicated that some +1 advice was rejected on the same basis, with 44 per cent of the +1 statements considered "bad advice" being interpreted as above the S's own level. As an example of this mode of rejection, a Stage 4 subject misinterpreted Stage 6 advice based on considerations of maintaining a trust as being a Stage 3 concern about disapproval. He therefore rejected it because, "you should think about doing right and not about what the brother or father think about you" (i.e., about the brother's feeling a trust had been violated).

Another reason for rejection of higher-level advice was said to be due to noncomprehension of structure and rejection of content (the act recommended) without rejection of structure. As an example, a Stage 4 S who chose as "smartest" the Stage 6 advice to steal the drug because of the moral value of human life went on to say, "Jean was smart to say you would be morally right to steal but it's still wrong, so don't." This child seems aware of the lofty rings of the words "morally right" but for her the real determiner of right is the law concerning stealing and her total reaction is based on the resulting content considerations. Rejection of higher-level advice was also based on disputing pragmatic details of the situation without explicit recognition of the value principles raised by such advice.

Our qualitative analysis also indicated that the limited assimilation of preferred higher-level advice involved not only a lack of comprehension, but also a reinterpretation of the advice at the subject's own level. We noted that +2 advice was liked as well as +1 advice, especially if it agreed in content with the child's choice. However, about as much preferred +2 advice was interpreted at the child's own level (19 per cent) or at the one above (26 per cent), as was interpreted at the message's actual level (28 per cent). An example of this active downward misinterpretation of +2 advice may be cited. On Situation III, a Stage 2 child picked a Stage 4 statement as "smartest advice." This preference was made partly because the S agreed with the content of the advice chosen (don't steal) since she did not also pick a Stage 4 statement advising stealing. The statement approved was: "Even though you are desperate it is still wrong to steal. The druggist is wrong—he should let you have it for less, but two wrongs don't make a right. The druggist does have a right to the drug since he worked hard to invent it. You are going against the druggist's rights if you steal it like that." The Stage 2 S justified this advice by saying: "Karen gave the smartest advice because she was thinking that if Hilda would steal the drug it wouldn't help her any. If she waited, the druggist might sell it for less." Here the S has completely missed the issues of rights and of categorical rightness of wrongness in the advice and has assimilated it to purely pragmatic Stage 2 considerations. The high-sounding terminology of the Stage 4 statement may have reinforced the child's preference but it has not been assimilated into her way of thinking about it.

The import of these rather complicated findings may be clarified if we consider their implications for the processes of response by citizens to moral messages of social leaders. It has been found that almost any statement by social leaders concerning issues of sociomoral import is reliably codeable in terms of the moral stages of sentences in it, e.g., Adolf Eichmann's self-justifications (Stages 1 and 2), Martin Luther King's "Letter from a Birmingham Jail" (Stage 6), Stokely Carmichael's Black Power utterances (Stage 2), Berkeley students' justifications of participation in the "free speech" sit-in (Kohlberg, 1967; Haan, Smith, & Block, 1969). The "official morality" of the United States, as represented by the language of the Constitution, of the Supreme Court, of most presidential utterances, and of voluntary organizations (like the APA) is a morality of principle (Stage 6), and especially a morality of social contract and of law-based individual rights (Stage 5).[6] The majority of adults in the American society, however, most heavily use conventional (Stages 3 and 4) levels of moral judgment (Kohlberg, 1968). The findings of the present study help to

6. Brief descriptions of the moral stages are found in the introduction to this paper. For more complete discussion of the stages see Kohlberg (1963, 1968).

explain this discrepancy. In addition to suggesting that preference for (and assimilation of) moral messages may be heavily determined by their developmental level relative to that of their audience, the present study suggests that this level may effectively be somewhat higher than that of the audience. As an example, a finding of a majority of student Republicans at Stage 4 (Haan, Smith, & Block, 1969) is not inconsistent with a "Republican" veneration of the Constitution, a document phrased primarily in the social contract language of Stage 5, or a veneration of Eisenhower, whose public utterances were usually at the same stage.

While the findings of the present study help explain the trend for leadership in a society to be expressed at a level higher than that of most of its citizens, it also suggests that higher-level statements may elicit approval with a distorted comprehension and assimilation of the higher-level message. The actual effect of the higher-level message may be to elicit a positive attitude toward the content of the action endorsed, rather than to communicate the structural level of thought and judgment on which the endorsement of policy is based.

SOME UNPREDICTED FINDINGS AND THEIR IMPLICATIONS

Within the context of the concept of developmental stage, the findings just reported are noncontroversial. It is hard to question the notion that individuals assimilate material at the level to which they are moving (+1), in comparison to material beneath them (−1) or material they fail to comprehend (most +2). The question still remains whether the individual's preference and assimilation of new material is oriented to his own level or to the highest level he can comprehend. Piaget's "equilibration" conception of developmental stage (Turiel, 1969) holds that an individual's own stage is an equilibrated structure to which new stimulation is assimilated. It is implied by this view that under ordinary conditions the individual most prefers the use of this stage. His next preference should be for the +1 stage, which he should attempt to use instead of his own under conditions of disequilibrium, i.e., in problems where own-stage thinking breaks down or is self-contradictory. However, the equilibration view is not explicit on preference and assimilation of statements made by others.

An alternate "Platonic level" notion (Kohlberg, 1969) holds that the individual intuitively appreciates a developmental hierarchy and will prefer a higher-level statement over a lower-level regardless of his own place in the hierarchy, as long as he is capable of recognizing the difference between one level and the next. The Platonic view suggests first that the individual may be able to prefer and comprehend material one or two stages above his own, even though he cannot spontaneously produce such material and hence is not at that stage himself. Second, the view implies that the individual will prefer the highest level which he can at all comprehend, rather than preferring his own level or the one above it. An analogy from the realm of aesthetics may clarify the Platonic view. An individual's aesthetic productions may be at the level of "Chopsticks" on the piano, or a third-grader's drawings. Yet his comprehension of art may be at the level of Bach or Picasso, i.e., at a far higher level of formal organization than anything he can produce, and he may prefer this level to levels which he can himself produce. We term the view "Platonic" because it assumes that the developmental order exists in passive intuition, as well as in the active reorganization of mentality in ontogenesis. In addition, it is Platonic in supposing that there may be a latent higher-level structure in the child who displays no active or spontaneous expression of this structure, but who will display it under certain eliciting conditions of partial exposure to it (as Meno's slave was supposed to have the structure of geometric intuition in himself prior to Socrates' elicitation of it).

The first implication of the Platonic view is that the individual should prefer +2 thinking to +1 thinking if he comprehends the +2 thinking at all, and he should prefer +1 thinking over his own level (at least under conditions when he need not engage in self-defensive operations). On the basis of the equilibration hypothesis, one might make the alternate prediction that the individual would prefer his own stage and the one above. The preference data which indicated equal choice of +1 and +2 advice for our Ss as a total group (Table 1) are ambiguous in their implications for this hypothesis. Table 2 indicated that when +2 advice was preferred, it was often (45 per cent of the time) interpreted as at the S's own level or at the one above.

*Table 5.* Accuracy of recapitulation and preferences of A, B, & C groups.

| | Group A | | | Group B | | | Group C | | |
|---|---|---|---|---|---|---|---|---|---|
| | $-1^a$ | $+1$ | $+2$ | $-1$ | $+1$ | $+2$ | $-1$ | $+1$ | $+2$ |
| Percentage accuracy of recapitulation | | | | | | | | | |
| Situation II | .82 | .20 | .05 | .73 | .70 | .23 | .79 | .45 | .72 |
| Situation III | .72 | .23 | .08 | .50 | .70 | .27 | .69 | .57 | .80 |
| Situations II & III combined | .77 | .21 | .06 | .57 | .70 | .26 | .76 | .47 | .74 |
| Preferences | | | | | | | | | |
| Situation II | .20 | .40 | .40 | .06 | .63 | .31 | .06 | .22 | .71 |
| Situation III | .20 | .39 | .41 | .05 | .62 | .32 | .10 | .19 | .71 |
| Situations II & III combined | .20 | .39 | .41 | .06 | .63 | .32 | .07 | .21 | ,71 |

*Stage 1 Ss had no—1 advice and their responses to Stage 1 advice are substituted.

Presumably, then, most choices of $+2$ advice were based on a recognition that it was above the $-1$ advice, without an actual recognition of the characteristics of $+2$ thinking. This interpretation seems supported by the fact that $+2$ statements were chosen as worst advice and correctly interpreted 30 per cent of the time, whereas they were never chosen as worst advice if given a $+1$ interpretation (Table 1).

A test of the Platonic view requires a separation of the total group of Ss into groups differentiated on the basis of comprehension of advice at various levels. Ss were assigned to hierarchical comprehension groups as already indicated in Table 3. Group A understood only $-1$ advice, Group B understood both $-1$ and $+1$ advice, and Group C understood all three types of advice.[7] The Platonic interpretation implies that Group C subjects comprehended both $+2$ and $+1$ advice, and preferred the $+2$ advice to the $+1$ advice for structural reasons.

This Platonic interpretation can be best considered by inspec-

7. In order to define comprehension groups independent of assimilation (on "own advice"), the groups were rescored to exclude "own advice" responses in their definition. After this exclusion, there were so many cases of incomplete information on comprehension that Ss were assigned to the highest level at which they had two correct responses rather than by the cumulative scale procedure. This redefinition of assignment criteria for the comprehension groups still maintains their essential cumulative-order relations, however. Table 5 indicates that the redefined Group A shows a high rate of accuracy of comprehension only for $-1$, Group B only for $-1$ and $+1$, and Group C for all three levels of advice.

Table 6. Percentage level usage in own advice and pretest interview by A, B, & C groupings.

| | Group A | | | | | | | Group B | | | | | | | Group C | | | | | | |
|---|---|---|---|---|---|---|---|---|---|---|---|---|---|---|---|---|---|---|---|---|---|
| | −3 | −2 | −1 | 0 | +1 | +2 | +3 | −3 | −2 | −1 | 0 | +1 | +2 | +3 | −3 | −2 | −1 | 0 | +1 | +2 | +3 |
| **Own advice** | | | | | | | | | | | | | | | | | | | | | |
| Situation II | 02 | 05 | 35 | 35 | 19 | 04 | 00 | 00 | 00 | 24 | 21 | 56 | 00 | 00 | 00 | 00 | 00 | 57 | 07 | 36 | 00 |
| Situation III | 11 | 08 | 33 | 25 | 19 | 04 | 00 | 00 | 18 | 12 | 03 | 62 | 06 | 00 | 00 | 00 | 00 | 13 | 50 | 38 | 00 |
| Situations II & III combined | 06 | 07 | 34 | 30 | 19 | 04 | 00 | 00 | 12 | 16 | 09 | 60 | 04 | 00 | 00 | 00 | 00 | 47 | 17 | 36 | 00 |
| **Pretest interview** | | | | | | | | | | | | | | | | | | | | | |
| Situation II | | | 18 | 45 | 14 | 07 | 01 | 00 | 05 | 17 | 49 | 25 | 03 | 01 | 04 | 13 | 20 | 43 | 14 | 03 | 03 |
| Situation III | | | 18 | 45 | 14 | 06 | 01 | 01 | 10 | 20 | 45 | 19 | 04 | 01 | 00 | 00 | 00 | 42 | 25 | 11 | 22 |
| Situations II & III combined | | | 18 | 45 | 14 | 07 | 01 | 01 | 09 | 19 | 46 | 20 | 04 | 01 | 04 | 11 | 18 | 43 | 16 | 04 | 06 |
| **Assimilation effect** | | | | | | | | | | | | | | | | | | | | | |
| Situation II | | | 17 | | 05 | −03 | | | | 07 | | 31 | −03 | | | | −20 | | −07 | 33 | |
| Situation III | | | 15 | | 05 | −02 | | | | −08 | | 43 | 02 | | | | 00 | | 25 | 27 | |
| Situations II & III combined | | | 16 | | 05 | −03 | | | | −03 | | 40 | 00 | | | | −18 | | 01 | 32 | |
| **Recall situation III** | | | | | | | | | | | | | | | | | | | | | |
| Percentage | 13 | 07 | 45 | 11 | 20 | 04 | 00 | 00 | 08 | 35 | 15 | 29 | 13 | 00 | 10 | 00 | 25 | 00 | 40 | 25 | 00 |
| Mean N | .48 | .25 | 1.58 | .38 | .71 | .13 | .00 | .00 | .34 | 1.47 | .66 | 1.22 | .56 | .00 | .33 | .83 | .83 | .00 | 1.33 | .83 | .00 |

tion of Tables 5 and 6. Table 5 indicates that Group C, the only group comprehending all the stages, preferred +2 advice over +1 and −1 advice. In contrast, Group B (understands +1 but not +2) preferred +1 over +2 statements, while Group A did not show differential preference between the two higher levels. Although Group A showed the highest preference of any group for the −1 statements, it is interesting that they still showed more preference for +1 and +2 statements. Thus it appears that each group prefers at least the highest level it can comprehend. Given preference for the highest level comprehended, we must next consider whether this level is maximally assimilated into "own advice." Table 6 indicates that Group A did not assimilate any higher level advice, that Group B only assimilated +1 advice, and that Group C assimilated both +1 and +2 advice, with considerably greater assimilation of the +2 than the +1 advice. Thus, the first implication of the Platonic view (preference and assimilation of the highest level comprehended) receives considerable, though tentative, support from the data.

The Platonic view further implies an orderly progression from latent appreciation of a higher-level structure to its active expression. In Piaget's (1947) terminology, there is a passive-active "horizontal decalage" in moral judgment as well as a "vertical decalage" of stages. Studies in the development of grammar will illustrate the meaning of this concept (Fraser, Bellugi, & Brown, 1963; Lovell & Dixon, 1967). These studies indicate a vertical order of difficulty in the development of various grammatical contrasts. In these studies, most Ss differentiated location of a noun as subject and as object, fewer differentiated singular and plural, and few differentiated location of a direct and indirect object. Orthogonal to this vertical hierarchy is a second order of difficulty such that any grammatical contrast is most easily imitated, less easily comprehended (paired with appropriate pictured scenes), and still less easily produced (used in describing pictured scenes). Every child showed this horizontal decalage for each grammatical contrast. Therefore, children's developmental status must be defined by location in both orders. Neither three-year-old nor six-year-old children produce the indirect/ direct object contrasts, but many six-year-olds can imitate the contrast and some can comprehend it. In moral development, the analogous vertical hierarchy is the order of stages; the horizontal hierarchy is the order of preference, comprehension, assimilation, and spontaneous usage of any given stage of thought. Children should prefer and comprehend a higher mode of thinking in advance of their capacity to assimilate it and assimilate it in advance of their capacity to use it spontaneously in new situations.

The existence of a horizontal decalage in orientation to higher-level moral statements is indicated by a comparison of assimilation and pretest usage (contained in Table 4) with data on preference and comprehension (contained in Tables 1 and 2). Ss showed a relatively high degree of preference (43 per cent) and comprehension (43 per cent) of +1 advice. They showed a lower degree of recall (25 per cent) and assimilation (31 per cent of "own advice," 16 per cent above pretest expectancy) of this advice. Spontaneous pretest usage of +1 thought was still lower (15 per cent). A similar decalage existed for +2 advice: a high level of preference (42 per cent), a lower level of comprehension (29 per cent), and a still lower level of recall (9 per cent), assimilation (7 per cent usage in "own advice," 1 per cent above pretest expectancy) and spontaneous usage (6 per cent).

The horizontal order of difficulty just described at the group level was also found at the individual level. We have already noted that individuals could be assigned to one of three hierarchical comprehension groups. Tables 5 and 6 indicate that the horizontal decalage holds for these subgroups as well as for the sample as a whole. Group C comprehends and prefers +2 advice quite highly (comprehension 74 per cent, preference 71 per cent), recalls (25 per cent) and assimilates +2 advice less well (36 per cent of own advice, 32 per cent over pretest expectancy) and shows least spontaneous pretest usage of it (4 per cent). Similarly, Group B comprehends and prefers +1 advice quite highly (70 per cent comprehension, 63 per cent preference), recalls (29 per cent) and assimilates +1 advice less well (60 per cent of "own advice," 40 per cent above pretest expectancy), and shows least spontaneous pretest usage of it (20 per cent). Group A, which comprehends the +1 advice least, still comprehends and prefers it more than it assimilates or spontaneously uses it.

The Platonic view we have just outlined receives considerable support from our data. However, this evidence need not be seen as contradictory to the notion of equilibration. Rather, in our view, the two positions may be considered complementary in that they refer to somewhat different, although related, processes. Plato held that an inherited hierarchy of mental structures exists latently. (Socrates was supposedly able to elicit inborn geometric knowledge from Meno's slave.) It is not our belief that the moral structures are inherited, but rather, result from a self-constructive process of organism-environment interaction (Kohlberg, 1970; Turiel, 1969). However, important aspects of the Platonic view, supported by evidence from this study, can be integrated with the equilibration hypothesis of step-by-step change. It appears that there exists an intuitive "knowledge" of a range of the developmental hierarchy such that the individual can appreciate, comprehend, and to some extent, assimilate levels of thinking that are beyond his own level of functioning. On the other hand, the equilibration view seems to be applicable to the process of change in spontaneous usage of moral structures. An individual may change from reliance on a given structure to the next stage, when his present stage is experienced as functionally inadequate. Thus we are suggesting that appreciation and comprehension is "Platonic," insofar as there is a passive intuition of a wide range of the hierarchy, while change in spontaneous usage encompasses a narrower range of the hierarchy.

It is clear that in most areas of thought, the ability to appreciate and comprehend higher-level material outstrips the ability to function spontaneously at that level. For instance, structurally advanced moral philosophy can be understood by individuals who are not, themselves, able to produce it or apply it in problem situations. For production of a higher level, a reorganization from the previous level to the next one must occur: a process which may differ from that of intuitive comprehension.

The Platonic interpretation has additional implications for the process of developmental change in moral judgment. The existence of an order of comprehension and preference for moral concepts which is independent of spontaneous usage of these concepts may represent an important basis for the assessment of future moral learning or development. As stated by Vygotsky (1962, p. 103):

Having found that the mental age of two children was, let us say, eight, we gave each of them harder problems than he could manage on his own and provided some slight assistance: The first step in a solution, a leading question, or some other form of help. We discovered that one child could, in co-operation, solve problems designed for twelve-year-olds, while the other could not go beyond problems intended for nine-year-olds. The discrepancy between a child's actual mental age and the level he reaches in solving problems with assistance indicates the zone is four for the first child and one for the second. Experience has shown that the child with the larger zone of proximal development will do much better in school.

It may be, then, that the individual's membership in one of our comprehension groups is an important clue to his "zone of proximal development," i.e., that the child in a more advanced comprehension group has a greater readiness for upward movement than the child in a lower comprehension group.

Because of the potential theoretical and educational importance of discriminating between children at the same moral stage but of different comprehension subtypes (or in "different zones of proximal development") we went on to analyze some of the characteristics of children in the comprehension subgroups. In discussing these analyses, we may first summarize some of the factors which do not determine differences in comprehension. First, differences in comprehension are not arbitrary. Children do not fall into Group C simply because they happen to like and understand one or two pieces of +2 advice on the basis of appealing and comprehensible content[8] (Rest, 1967). Second, differences in comprehension are not due to slight differences in spontaneous usage of stages above the child's major stage, since the pretest profiles of the various comprehension groups were identical (Table 6). Third, differences in comprehension are not

8. This interpretation may be ruled out first because there was considerable, though far from complete, situational consistency in the individual's comprehension type. (About 50 per cent of the Ss were classified in the same comprehension group on the two situations and about 90 per cent had a discrepancy of not more than one scale point, where three was the highest possible discrepancy.) Second, it may be ruled out because of evidence of scaleability, i.e., the ability of Ss in Group C to comprehend the nonpreferred +1 and −1 advice as well as the preferred +2 advice.

due to general differences in motivation or verbal and mnemonic skills. If this were the case, one would expect the groups to differ in absolute score (or mental age) on the verbal I.Q. test (Otis). No differences were found, however, between the comprehension groups on mental age, I.Q., or chronological age[9] (Rest, 1967).

The major factors in our data which do differentiate our comprehension groups are suggested by the equilibration theory elaborated elsewhere (Turiel, 1969). First, this theory suggests, and a variety of evidence indicates, that the "hard-boiled" or differentiated stages (Stages 2 and 4) are more stable than the diffuse conforming stages (Stages 1 and 3). Second, equilibration theory suggests two "opposite" restrictions on upward movement. The first is that the child may have just moved into a given stage and is in a process of stabilizing at that stage. The second is that the child may have fixated at a given stage, i.e., particular factors in his personality or situation may have led him to harden at the stage or ward off conflicting stimulation.

The data presented in Table 7 indicate that all these factors influence membership in a comprehension group. First, we may note that Ss least comprehending of higher stages (Group A) tend to be in Stages 2 and 4, the more stable stages. Whereas only about 50 per cent of the subjects in Stages 1 and 3 fall in Group A, about 75 per cent of the subjects in Stages 2 and 4 are in this group. Second, an examination of Table 7 shows an Age x Stage interaction expected from equilibration theory. The older Ss in Stages 3 and 4 are less likely to be in the low comprehension group (A) than the younger Ss in these stages. It would seem that the younger Stage 3 and 4 Ss have just attained, and are stabilizing, their modal stage and thus are at the limit of their upward capacity, while the older Ss have a greater sensitivity to still higher stages of thought. Table 7 also shows that older Ss at the lower stages seem more likely (Stage 1), or as likely (Stage 2), to be in the lowest comprehension group as the younger Ss. Thus, it can be seen that the tendency

9. Another line of evidence also indicates that the comprehension groups represented differential sets toward comprehending or assimilating higher moral stages rather than mere differences in verbal accuracy. Group C not only correctly reproduced more +2 advice, but also was more likely than the other groups to interpret incorrectly +1 or −1 advice as at the +2 level. Similarly, Group B incorrectly, as well as correctly, recapitulated more advice at the +1 level (Rest, 1967).

*Table 7.* Percentage of subjects of A, B, C groups in stage-age breakdown.

|  | A | | B | | C | | Number of Ss in stage | |
|---|---|---|---|---|---|---|---|---|
|  | Sit II | Sit III | Sit II | Sit III | Sit II | Sit III | Sit II | Sit III |
| **Stage 1** | | | | | | | | |
| 5th grade | 33 | 33 | 00 | 00 | 67 | 67 | 3 | 3 |
| 8th grade | 100 | 100 | 00 | 00 | 00 | 00 | 1 | 1 |
| Total | 50 | 50 | 00 | 00 | 50 | 50 | | |
| **Stage 2** | | | | | | | | |
| 5th grade | 75 | 50 | 25 | 50 | 00 | 00 | 8 | 8 |
| 8th grade | 75 | 50 | 25 | 50 | 00 | 00 | 4 | 4 |
| Total | 75 | 50 | 25 | 50 | 00 | 00 | | |
| **Stage 3** | | | | | | | | |
| 5th grade | 67 | 50 | 33 | 50 | 00 | 00 | 6 | 6 |
| 8th grade | 45 | 37 | 09 | 64 | 45 | 00 | 11 | 11 |
| Total | 53 | 41 | 18 | 53 | 23 | 00 | | |
| **Stage 4** | | | | | | | | |
| 5th grade | 80 | 80 | 00 | 20 | 20 | 00 | 5 | 5 |
| 8th grade | 71 | 83 | 14 | 00 | 14 | 17 | 7 | 6 |
| Total | 75 | 82 | 08 | 09 | 17 | 09 | | |

for older higher-stage children to be in a higher comprehension group is reversed for older subjects at the two lowest stages. Presumably, these older low-stage subjects have become fixated or crystallized at the lower stages, and over the years have become insensitized or rejecting of possibilities for change or further development.[10]

In summary, then, the individual's capacity to understand, appreciate, and assimilate higher stages of moral thought is a characteristic distinguishable from his spontaneous stage and it represents the individual's openness to modes of thought which

10. The interpretations just advanced assume that relations between pretest stage and comprehension type are not due to a "regression to the mean" effect such that measurement error led high comprehenders to receive low scores on the first test (pretest) and then higher scores on the second (comprehension) test. This interpretation seems ruled out by the findings of pairings between Stages 1 and 3 and between 2 and 4 and by the age × stage interaction (Rest, 1967). The interpretation also assumes that comprehension groups are related to a subject's stage and are not simply an artifact of his stage-placement. To check this assumption, the patterns of comprehension, preference, and assimilation reported for the comprehension groups as a whole (Tables 5 and 6) were examined for the comprehension groups within each stage (Rest, 1967). At each stage the characteristic differences between comprehension types were similar to those reported for the groups as wholes.

have a natural hierarchical relationship to one another. We suggested that these individual differences in what Vygotsky termed "the zone of proximal development," distinct from the child's spontaneous level, might be an important predictor of future learning or development. At the close of the previous section, in discussing social leadership, we suggested that individuals may positively evaluate leaders emitting messages above their own level, but only assimilate higher-stage messages if they were one stage above the individual's own stage. Utilizing the concept of a "zone of proximal development," we suggest that some people can comprehend and appreciate leadership two levels above their own, some one level above their own, and others only their own level. As an example, Haan, Smith, & Block (1969) found a group of Stage 2 Berkeley students active in the civil rights movement and another group active in the Ayn Rand "objectivist" movement. The latter movement offers Stage 2 leadership statements, the former offers a breadth of leadership statements ranging from Stage 2 (Black Power) to Stage 6 (universal human rights). The type of leadership sought by students may be a function of their "zone of proximal development."

## SUMMARY

On the basis of Kohlberg's developmental hierarchy of moral judgment, it was hypothesized that modes of moral thought above an individual's own stage would be preferred to modes below, and that modes of thinking above are increasingly more difficult to comprehend than stages below. After determining each subject's dominant moral stage in a pretest, the subjects were presented with a series of moral statements corresponding to the stages one below, one above, and two above their own. Measures of preference, comprehension, and assimilation of these statements were then obtained. It was found that children generally prefer concepts above their own stage to concepts below. Thinking two stages above was more difficult for subjects to comprehend than thinking one stage above, which in turn was more difficult than thinking one stage below. Further analyses showed that assimilation effects were a function of both the S's preference and the highest level of thinking comprehended. The results were also discussed in relation to social leadership and developmental change.

REFERENCES

Fraser, C., Bellugi, U., & Brown, R. Control of grammar in imitation, comprehension and production. *J. verb. Learn. verb. Behavior*, 1963, **2**, 121-135.

Guttman, L. The basis for scalogram analysis. In S. A. Stoufer et al., *Measurement and prediction*. Princeton: Princeton Univer. Press, 1950. Pp. 60-90.

Haan, Norma, Smith, M. B., & Block, Jean. The moral reasoning of young adults, political-social behavior, family background and personality correlates. *J. pers. soc. Psychol.*, 1969, in press.

Kohlberg, L. The development of modes of moral thinking and choice in the years ten to sixteen. Unpublished doctoral dissertation, Univ. of Chicago, 1958.

Kohlberg, L. The development of children's orientations toward a moral order: 1. Sequence in the development of moral thought. *Vita Humana*, 1963, **6**, 11-33.

Kohlberg, L. Moral education, religious education, and the public schools: A developmental view. In T. Sizer (Ed.), *The role of religion in public education*. Boston: Houghton Mifflin, 1967.

Kohlberg, L. Education for justice, a modern statement of the Platonic view. In R. Mosher (Ed.), *Moral education*. Cambridge, Mass.: Harvard Univer. Press, 1969.

Kohlberg, L. *Moral development*, 1970, book in preparation.

Lovell, K., & Dixon, E. M. The growth of the control of grammar in imitation, comprehension and production. *J. Child Psychol. Psychiat.*, 1967, **8**, 31-39.

Piaget, J. *The moral judgment of the child*. Glencoe, Ill.: Free Press, 1948 (originally published 1932).

Piaget, J. *The psychology of intelligence*. New York: Harcourt, Brace, 1950 (originally published 1947).

Rest, J. Level of moral development as a determinant of preference and comprehension of moral judgments made by others. Unpublished minor research paper, Univer. of Chicago, 1967.

Rest, J. Sequence in preference and comprehension of moral judgment. Unpublished doctoral dissertation, Univer. of Chicago, 1968.

Turiel, E. An experimental test of the sequentiality of developmental stages in the child's moral judgments. *J. pers. soc. Psychol.*, 1966, **3**, 611-618.

Turiel, E. Developmental processes in children's moral thinking. In P. Mussen, J. Langer, and M. Covington (Eds.), *New directions in developmental psychology*. New York: Holt, Rinehart & Winston, 1969.

Vygotsky, L. S. *Thought and speech*. Cambridge, Mass.: M.I.T. Press, 1962.

*Manuscript received March 25, 1968.*

The cost of pages beyond twenty has been borne by the authors.

# THE RELATION OF ROLE TAKING TO THE DEVELOPMENT OF MORAL JUDGMENT IN CHILDREN

ROBERT L. SELMAN

Boston University

SELMAN, ROBERT L. The Relation of Role Taking to the Development of Moral Judgment in Children. CHILD DEVELOPMENT, 1971, 42, 79–91. *In order to explore the relationship in middle childhood between two social-cognitive processes, role-taking ability and moral reasoning, 60 middle-class children (10 boys and 10 girls each at ages 8, 9, and 10) were administered Kohlberg's (1963) moral-judgment measure, two role-taking tasks, and the Peabody Picture Vocabulary Test, a conventional measure of intelligence. Results indicated that at this age range, with intelligence controlled, the development of reciprocal role-taking skills related to the development of conventional moral judgment. Results of a reexamination 1 year later of 10 subjects whose role-taking and moral-judgment levels were low in the original study supported the hypothesis that the development of the ability to understand the reciprocal nature of interpersonal relations is a necessary but not sufficient condition for the development of conventional moral thought.*

## INTRODUCTION

This paper will report two studies whose purpose was to explore the relationship in middle childhood between two developing age-related social-cognitive processes: the ability of the child to take the role

This research was supported in part by National Institute of Mental Health grant MH 10226-04 and in part by a Boston University dissertation fellowship. The author would like to express his appreciation to Dr. Freda Rebelsky and Dr. Lawrence Kohlberg for their suggestions and encouragement and to Mrs. Anne P. Selman and Miss Judy Green for assistance in data collection. Author's address: Harvard University, Graduate School of Education, Larsen Hall, Appian Way, Cambridge, Massachusetts 02138.

of another and his ability to make qualitatively higher-level moral judgments.

Role taking as defined by Flavell (1968) in his recently published studies of this skill is the ability to understand the interaction between the self and another as seen through the other's eyes. This definition implies an ability to make specific inferences about another's capabilities, attributes, expectations, feelings, and potential reactions. These aspects make more explicit the social-interpersonal component of role taking. Its cognitive component can be seen more clearly in the necessity to attend to, shift, balance, and evaluate both perceptual and cognitive social-object input. Development of reciprocal role-taking ability implies an increasingly accurate perception of what another will do in a given situation, and specifically of how one's own actions will affect the attitude of another toward oneself.

The development of morality in children has been studied in a variety of ways. Parental practices, childhood antecedents, and transgression reactions have been examined in relation to morality variables such as guilt, confession, or resistance to temptation (Aronfreed 1968; Hoffman 1963; Rau 1963; Rebelsky, Allinsmith, & Grinder 1963). Piaget ([1932] 1965) and Kohlberg (1963) have each focused on the judgmental aspects of moral development, that is, how children think about moral issues rather than how they might specifically act. Both researchers report that the child's moral thought processes are qualitatively different from the adult's and that mature moral judgment develops through an invariant sequence of stages, each stage being a reorganization of, rather than a mere addition to, the previous stage. Kohlberg has found empirical support for such a series of stages. The following is a synopsis of Kohlberg's (1969) six stages.

*Preconventional Level*

*Stage 1:* Obedience and punishment orientation. Egocentric deference to superior power or prestige, or a trouble-avoiding set. Objective responsibility.

*Stage 2:* Naïvely egoistic orientation. Right action is that instrumentally satisfying the self's needs and occasionally another's. Awareness of relativism of value to each actor's needs and perspective. Naïve egalitarianism and orientation to exchange and reciprocity.

*Conventional Level*

*Stage 3:* Good-boy orientation. Orientation to approval and to pleasing and helping others. Conformity to stereotypical images of majority or natural role behavior, and judgment by intentions.

*Stage 4:* Authority and social-order-maintaining orientation. Orientation to "doing duty" and to showing respect for authority and maintaining the given social order for its own sake. Regard for earned expectations of others.

*Principled Level*

*Stage 5:* Contractual legalistic orientation. Recognition of an arbitrary element or starting point in rules or expectations for the sake of agreement. Duty defined in terms of

80

contract, general avoidance of violation of the will or rights of others, and majority will and welfare.

*Stage 6:* Conscience or principle orientation. Orientation not only to actually ordained social rules but to principles of choice involving appeal to logical universality and consistency. Orientation to conscience as a directing agent and to mutual respect and trust.

Kohlberg strongly emphasizes the general hypothesis that higher levels of moral thought require the ability to take the role of another. According to his theory, the cognitive characteristics of the conventional level of morality, which usually replaces the less structured preconventional level of morality at some time between ages 9 and 13, are: moral stereotyping, empathic moral definition, sensitivity to and self-guidance by anticipated approval or disapproval of others, and identification with authority and its goals. All of these characteristics imply that conventional morality is based in large part on role taking, or taking the perspective of other people.

Flavell's (1968) role-taking data show developmental reorganizations in this process (as operationalized) between the ages of 8 and 10. Children within this limited age range seem to develop toward a progressively less egocentric view and toward a progressively greater ability to use role-taking skills instrumentally in solving interactional problems. Similarly, Kohlberg's (1963) data indicate that, although the moral-judgment process continues to develop into adolescence and early adulthood, children in middle childhood reorganize their moral cognitive structure from a naïve hedonistic view to a more conventional "adult-like" form. The present studies were undertaken to test the hypothesis that in the middle-childhood period of 8 to 10, the development of the ability to understand reciprocal social perspectives (role-taking ability) is a necessary condition for the development of higher levels of moral judgment.

## STUDY 1

*Method*

*Subjects.*—The Ss were 60 middle-class children attending a suburban summer day camp. There were 20 8-, 9-, and 10-year-olds. Each of the three age groups consisted of 10 boys and 10 girls. Occupational and educational levels of parents were ascertained to control for homogeneity of social class; children with histories of emotional disturbances were excluded from the sample.

*Procedures.*—Subjects were administered two role-taking tasks (RTT 1 and RTT 2), Kohlberg's Moral Judgment Scale (MJS), and the Peabody Picture Vocabulary Test (PPVT), a measure of conven-

81

tional intelligence. Subjects were tested in same-sex pairs, a random half of the Ss receiving the MJS first (administered by E1, a female research assistant) and half of the Ss receiving the role-taking tasks (RTTs) and PPVT first (administered by E2, the author). The area of testing of E2 was about 50 feet distant from E1's, out of the range of hearing but not out of sight. This was made necessary by the nature of the administration of the RTTs, which required reference to a third person, in this case, S's partner. To facilitate the procedure, both sets of tasks were devised to take approximately the same length of time to administer (20 to 30 minutes). Upon completing one set of tasks, Ss were set to the other E to do the remaining set of tasks.

Instruments.—Scores on the RTTs reflected qualitative differences in ability to shift social perspective. The two RTTs were devised by Flavell and his collaborators (1968), but the scoring procedures were somewhat modified for the present study.

In RTT 1, E showed S two boxes; on one box there was printed "10¢" and on the other "5¢." Within each box was the appropriate amount of money, a dime and a nickel, respectively. The S was told that in a few minutes his partner, O, was going to come over and choose one box and take the money from it. The S's task was to remove the money from either the dime or the nickel box, whichever one he expected O would choose, and thereby to trick O. The important thing for S to remember, E pointed out, was that O knew that S was going to try to trick him. Thus, S's task was to predict which box O, with knowledge of S's intentions, would choose. After he removed the money from the box, S was asked why he thought O would choose the box from which S removed the money.

Subject's responses were analyzed and scored at one of three catagories, reflecting three assumed a priori levels of role-taking ability. A score of 1 was assigned to children's choices which indicated a lack of realization that in this particular game an understanding of another person's motives was relevant and important to one's own choice. The protocols in this category consisted of Ss who could not or would not attribute a choice to O or Ss who could offer no rationale for the choice they felt O would make.

A child's response was categorized at level 2 if the child showed the awareness that there was a motive behind a choice but did not indicate that he was aware of the fact that O might also be cognizant of motives. In fact, category 2 reflects S's attribution to O of cognitions related only to the game material and S's failure to account for the possibility that O and S are in a situation in which O should try to take S's motives into account and vice versa.

Category 3 indicates the highest level of role taking scored for this task and was given to Ss who indicated an awareness that O knew

82

90

that one choice and certain advantages (monetary) over the other, that this might influence $O$'s choice, and that this in turn had implications for the choice that $S$ was to make. It should be stressed that success here implies that the child has an understanding of the reciprocal functioning of a role-taking process; even as $S$ makes his decision on the basis of his imputing thoughts and actions to $O$, so he sees $O$ as imputing similar thoughts and actions to him. For example, a $S$ who notes, "He will think I will take the dime box and so he will switch to the nickel, so maybe I better take the nickel box," was scored here. Any $S$ who continued this reasoning ad infinitum was also scored in category 3.

In RTT 2, $E$ placed before $S$ an ordered series of seven pictures showing a story of a boy being chased by a dog, running down a street, and climbing a tree to eat an apple as the dog trots away, and asked him to tell an appropriate story about the pictures. This part of the task is straightforward, and the telling was completed successfully by all $S$s. Then three specific cards were removed from the series, and $S$ was asked to tell the story as $O$ would tell it if he were to then come over to the test area and look at the four cards. Removing the three cards eliminated the fear of dog motive for climbing the tree. The remaining four cards show a boy first walking and then running to an apple tree, climbing it, and eating an apple. There is still a dog in the last picture, but it does not relate to the motivational theme of the four-card story. To tap specifically the way the child dealt with this change of set, he was asked, after telling this new story, why $O$ would think the boy climbed the tree and also what $O$ would think the dog is doing in the last picture.

As in RTT 1, a categorical system of scoring reflecting qualitative differences in the role-taking skill necessary for each task was devised. Category 1 classifications were made for those $S$s who could not perform any transformation of the original story. In both accounts, the angry dog remained the spontaneously explained motivational force behind the boy's climbing the tree.

Category 2 reflected the ability of $S$ to tell a straightforward, four-card, perceptually correct story but the inability to maintain this perceptual image presentation upon being asked the motivational conditions of the four-picture story. For example, upon being asked to tell the story as $O$ would see it, $S$ responds, "He walks with a stick; he runs down the street; he climbs a tree and eats an apple." However, when asked why the boy climbed the tree, he responds, "To get away from the dog."

Category 3 is the highest level of role-taking skill measured by this task. Here the child successfully told the four-card story that $O$ would tell, suppressing the original seven-card motivational scheme. Upon being questioned, $S$ indicated that he understood the nature of this task, that is, that $O$ did not have information available earlier to $S$ and that lack of this information would influence the way $O$ would tell

**83**

this story. As in RTT 1, this level of role-taking skill was taken as indicative of an understanding of the reciprocity of alternative viewpoints.

Kohlberg's measuring technique for the assessment of each child's developmental level of moral judgment (MJS) was administered by *E1*. A complete explanation of administration and scoring, as well as empirical evidence for the sequential development of stages, can be found elsewhere (Kohlberg 1963).

A typed, coded transcription was made from each child's tape-recorded moral-judgment interviews and scored blind by *E2*. A research assistant trained in this scoring system scored 10 random protocols, and these scores were compared with those of *E2*. There was 90 percent agreement between judges for assigning levels of moral judgment. Each *S* was scored on the basis of his responses to questions about morally right actions in stories with conflicting yet culturally acceptable solutions. As previously found for samples at our age range, scores fell into the lower two of three possible levels of moral-judgment development. Each level is subdivided into two stages. Level 1, the level of preconventional morality, consists of stage 1, that of an orientation of punishment and obedience, and stage 2, that of naïve instrumental hedonism. Level 2, conventional morality as reflected in social conforming thought, consists of stage 3, that of the morality of good relations and approval of others, and stage 4, the morality of authority maintenance.

## RESULTS

Because both the moral-judgment and the role-taking scores yield limited categorically ordered data, a $\chi^2$ analysis of association of MJS and RTTs 1 and 2 was performed. This procedure was followed as well in looking at the relation of the RTTs to one another and in looking at the significance of association of both RTT scores and MJS scores to the external variables of sex, age, and intelligence. (This nonparametric approach presented a statistical limitation; it was not possible to directly partial out the effects of the continuous external variables of age and intelligence upon the two main variables under investigation. However, as will be seen, one way which was decided upon was to trichotomize external variables according to ranked scores, examine the relationship between RTTs and MJS at each level of age or of the intelligence measure, and draw some conclusions about the various interactions.)

*Role-taking tasks.*—The relation between RTTs was examined by means of a $\chi^2$ analysis of the association among the three RTT categories. Although the association between RTTs 1 and 2 was significant ($\chi^2 = 18.055$, 4 *df*, $p < .01$), the three categorical scoring levels for each task were apparently not of equivalent difficulty across both tasks. For

84

example, 30 *S*s scored at category 3 for RTT 2, whereas only 23 *S*s scored at this highest level for RTT 1. Subjects were in general slightly less successful in exhibiting the role-taking skills necessary for success on RTT 1 than those necessary for success on RTT 2; logically, RTT 2 appears to have been an easier task. In examining their relation to MJS levels, RTT scores were dichotomized between categories 2 and 3, based on the assumption that this dichotomy represented the distinction between reciprocal (category 3) and nonreciprocal (categories 1 and 2) role-taking skills. However, it is likely that category 3 of RTT 2 is not as operationally sound a measure of reciprocal role taking as is this category in RTT 1. It is less clear that RTT 2 requires for success, as part of *S*'s role taking, that he see, in taking *O*'s role, *O*'s reciprocal taking of *S*'s role as well. For this reason, each RTT measure was examined separately in relation to the MJS scores as well as in relation to the external variables of age, sex, and intelligence.

*Relation of RTTs to MJS.*—There was a significant association between each of the two main MJS levels (preconventional and conventional) and the two main RTT levels (nonreciprocal and reciprocal) for both RTT 1 ($\chi^2 = 18.921$, 1 *df*, $p < .01$) and RTT 2 ($\chi^2 = 13.203$, 1 *df*, $p < .01$). Initially, the relation of the RTTs to the MJS was examined across each of the four stages of moral development as well as across the two subsuming levels. For both MJS stages 1 and 2, RTT scores, on the whole, were at nonreciprocal RTT categories 1 or 2. The opposite was true for MJS stages 3 and 4; the great majority of RTT scores were at the reciprocal category 3 (see table 1). Given this natural dichotomy of RTT level scores between the two higher and two lower stages of moral development, the results have been presented only for the MJS levels (conventional vs. preconventional) which incorporate these four stages.

*Relation of RTTs and MJS to external variables.*—In order to ex-

TABLE 1

RELATION OF RTT LEVELS TO MJS LEVELS AND STAGES

| | MJS | | | | | |
| | Preconventional | | | Conventional | | |
| | Stage 1 | Stage 2 | Level 1 | Stage 3 | Stage 4 | Level 2 |
|---|---|---|---|---|---|---|
| RTT 1: | | | | | | |
| Nonreciprocal... | 16 | 13 | 29 | 5 | 3 | 8 |
| Reciprocal...... | 2 | 2 | 4 | 11 | 8 | 19 |
| RTT 2: | | | | | | |
| Nonreciprocal... | 13 | 11 | 24 | 3 | 3 | 6 |
| Reciprocal...... | 5 | 4 | 9 | 13 | 8 | 21 |

85

amine the relation of each RTT task to age and sex, contingency tables were formed (three RTT categories by either the three age levels [8, 9, and 10] or by sex) and $\chi^2$ analyses were performed. The relation of RTTs and PPVT IQs was examined in the same manner, using ranked PPVT scores trichotomized. As indicated in table 2, $\chi^2$ analyses revealed a significant level of association between each RTT and age and intelligence but no significant relation between RTTs and sex. Point-biserial correlations were also performed; correlations of RTTs 1 and 2 with the PPVT IQ scores were .64 and .66, respectively. Similarly, $\chi^2$ analyses also indicated that MJS (two levels) did not relate significantly to age, sex, or intelligence. There was, in general, a heterogeneity of moral-judgment-stage usage at each age level, with a trend toward higher-stage usage associated with increased age. The modal stage of moral-judgment usage was stage 2. There was a positive point-biserial correlation of .29 between MJS and the PPVT, but this did not reach significance.

The fact that there was a high positive correlation between the PPVT and the RTTs but only a low positive correlation between this IQ measure and the MJS indicated that any high covariations of MJS and RTTs 1 and 2 would not be simply a function of a general-intelligence factor.

In order to assess the relation between RTTs and MJS scores as affected by mental-age patterns, Ss were ranked according to their raw PPVT scores and on this basis placed into low, middle, or high mental-age-range groups, 20 Ss per group. The relation between each RTT and MJS for each mental-age-level group was examined separately by $\chi^2$. Role-taking-task categories 1 and 2 were combined as previously

TABLE 2

SUMMARY OF $\chi^2$ ANALYSES: ASSOCIATION OF EXTERNAL VARIABLES (AGE, SEX, IQ)
WITH RTT CATEGORIES AND MJS LEVELS

| External Variable | Mean of External Variable | Standard Deviation | RTT 1 | RTT 2 | MJS |
|---|---|---|---|---|---|
| Age: (8, 9, and 10 years).. | 113.00 (months) | 9.022 (months) | 9.49* (4 df) | 8.40* (4 df) | 1.21 (2 df) |
| Intelligence: (low, medium, and high).............. | 113.25 (PPVT) | 13.79 (IQ points) | 14.82** (4 df) | 17.20** (4 df) | 3.63 (2 df) |
| Sex.................. | ... | ... | 0.906 (2 df) | 0.267 (2 df) | 0.606 (1 df) |

* $p < .05$.      ** $p < .01$.

86

and designated as nonreciprocal RTT, and RTT category 3 was designated as reciprocal RTT. Thus, for both RTTs 1 and 2, a two-by-two contingency table was formed comparing nonreciprocal and reciprocal RTTs with conventional (stages 3 and 4) and preconventional (stages 1 and 2) levels of MJS (see table 3).

Similar results were forthcoming for each RTT's relation to MJS over the three levels of mental age. There was no significance between RTTs and MJS for either the lower or the upper groups ranked by raw PPVT scores. However, the association between the MJS and both RTTs 1 and 2 in the middle mental-age range was significant (see table 3).

The relation of each RTT to MJS over each of the three chronological age levels (8, 9, and 10), that is, with chronological age partialed out, was found to be significant (see table 4).

TABLE 3

SUMMARY OF $\chi^2$ ANALYSES: ASSOCIATION BETWEEN MJS AND RTTs AT EACH OF THREE MENTAL-AGE LEVELS

| VARIABLES ASSOCIATED | MENTAL-AGE LEVEL (GROUPS TRICHOTOMIZED ON BASIS OF RANKED PPVT SCORES) | | | |
|---|---|---|---|---|
| | Low | Medium | High | SUM OF $\chi^2$ |
| MJS-RTT 1[a] | 1.06 | 4.98* | 1.99 | 8.03* |
| | (1 df) | (1 df) | (1 df) | (3 df) |
| MJS-RTT 2[a] | 0.94 | 8.10** | 1.07 | 9.10* |
| | (1 df) | (1 df) | (1 df) | (3 df) |

[a] For RTTs: levels 1 and 2, nonreciprocal RTT; level 3, reciprocal RTT.
* $p < .05$.        ** $p < .01$.

TABLE 4

SUMMARY OF $\chi^2$ ANALYSES: ASSOCIATION BETWEEN MJS AND RTTs AT EACH OF THREE CHRONOLOGICAL AGE LEVELS

| VARIABLES ASSOCIATED | AGE LEVEL (YEARS) | | | |
|---|---|---|---|---|
| | 8 | 9 | 10 | SUM OF $\chi^2$ |
| MJS-RTT 1[a] | 4.12* | 5.49* | 0.288 | 9.89* |
| | (1 df) | (1 df) | (1 df) | (3 df) |
| MJS-RTT 2[a] | 5.93* | 0.202 | 8.57** | 14.70** |
| | (1 df) | (1 df) | (1 df) | (3 df) |

[a] For RTTs: levels 1 and 2, nonreciprocal RTT; level 3, reciprocal RTT.
* $p < .05$.        ** $p < .01$.

87

*Discussion*

The significant relation of the role-taking tasks to the moral-judgment measure at each age level and with intelligence statistically controlled supports the hypothesis that, in middle childhood, the greater ability to take another's perspective is related to higher levels of moral judgment. Beyond this general conclusion, it should be noted that the major shift in the relation between role-taking and moral-judgment level seems to occur on the one hand between role-taking categories 2 and 3, that is, between nonreciprocal and reciprocal role-taking ability, and on the other hand between the two moral-judgment levels (preconventional and conventional) rather than stepwise across four stages (see table 1). Generally, when judging situations involving moral conflicts, nonreciprocal role takers tended to use preconventional moral thought and reciprocal role takers tended to use conventional moral reasoning when confronted with moral issues. This supports the suggestion that the child's reorganization to a conventional level of morality is due in part to an increase in reciprocal role-taking skills, although it in no way proves it; the associations are correlational and not causal.

The second point to be discussed involves the interaction between conventional measure of intelligence discussed in terms of mental-age scores and the experimentally measured relationship of moral and role-taking development. It will be recalled that only at the middle mental-age range did there occur the predicted relationship: those who scored at the reciprocal role-taking level (category 3) scored at the conventional level of moral judgment, and those who scored at the nonreciprocal role-taking level (categories 1 and 2) scored at the preconventional moral-judgment level. (It should be noted in the discussion of the three mental-age levels as high, middle, and low that these are relative terms, appropriate only to our sample. Our middle group, for example, is at an IQ range of 109–120, fairly high in comparison to the general population. The average mental age of the sample was about 10 years.) In the low mental-age group, Ss scored low on both role-taking and moral-judgment measures. The reverse was true for those at the upper mental-age levels.

This interesting relation of role-taking ability to moral thought level over the three mental-age levels suggests that children of a mental age of approximately 10 are beginning to utilize newly developed reciprocal role-taking skills in making conventional moral judgments. Children at a higher mental age probably developed this skill at an earlier chronological age, and the children at lower mental ages will most likely do so at a later age.

On the basis of these results, the Flavell (1968) data on reciprocal role taking (that it is generally attained by age 11–12 by all Ss), and

Kohlberg's (1969) data on conventional moral judgment (that it is generally attained by age 13), it follows that the time period during which one chooses to examine the codevelopment of these two processes is critical. It is illogical to anticipate finding a close relationship between role taking and moral judgments at any and all ages. By age 13, a ceiling effect appears in the relationship in that most $S$s attain the higher level on both variables. (This is not to imply that moral development does not continue or even that role taking operationalized differently might not continue to develop as well.)

## STUDY 2

In study 1, the significant relation of the RTTs to the MJS supported the general hypothesis that, in middle childhood, greater ability to shift perspective is related to higher levels of moral judgment. Study 2 was essentially a follow-up of study 1 and will not be reported in great detail here.

The results of study 1 give little clew as to whether the two processes under examination develop simultaneously and with a high degree of interdependence or whether the development of one process precedes in time or is in some way antecedently related to the other.

The hypothesis, then, of study 2 was that, in order to obtain a conventional level of moral judgment, it was necessary to be able to understand the reciprocal nature of interpersonal relations and to see that one's own actions can affect the way another person reacts in a social situation. The reexamination of $S$s who the previous year had scored low on both variables (i.e., who both were at level 1 [preconventional] on the MJS and were at either category 1 or category 2 on both RTTs) could clarify the order of development of these variables. If $S$s tended either to simultaneously increase levels on both variables or to remain the same level on both, this would support a strict *structure d'ensemble* conception of the temporal development of the two variables. On the other hand, if the level of measured ability on one variable increased without a concomitant increase in level on the other, this would argue for the systematic primacy of development of the increasing variable.

Ten $S$s, seven boys and three girls, all of whom had previously been categorized as low scorers on both the RTTs and MJS, were retested 1 year after the initial study (of the 22 $S$s falling into this category, only 10 could be located). The same instruments and procedures were employed as in the previous year (see Method section of Study 1).

Five $S$s, reached the reciprocal level in RTT 1, and six $S$s did so on RTT 2. On the other hand, only two $S$s obtained the conventional MJS level (level 2). Both of these $S$s concurrently obtained as well

89

the reciprocal level score (category 3) on both of the RTT measures. That is to say, no $S$ attained conventional moral judgment without reciprocal role taking; reciprocal role taking, however, was attained by $Ss$ without conventional moral judgments.

It should be noted that, evidently within this limited age range, the speed of the developmental timetable of these two processes across $Ss$ is not uniform, that is, that within 1 year, for example, some $Ss$' development of both processes is rapid while for others the pace is slower.

## CONCLUSION

Results of study 2 more clearly indicate that reciprocal role taking is a necessary condition for the development of conventional moral thought, in part by showing that it is empirically possible to obtain the level of role-taking reciprocity and still remain at a preconventional moral level.

From a cognitive developmental viewpoint, there is a theoretical position that helps to clarify the results. Level 2, and especially stage 3, of the moral development system is only achieved according to this theory when the child's conception of social-moral interaction is constructed so as to focus upon the consequences of dyadic interaction, especially the effect of one's actions on another's subsequent reactions. It would seem that the reciprocity evidenced by category 3 role taking is a necessary component of such a world viewpoint. Although both stages 1 and 2 of moral development (obedience orientation and instrumental hedonistic orientation) entail the use of role-taking skills, these skills are of a less integrated, stable, and permanent nature than the reciprocal role-taking skills used at the conventional level of moral thought. At the preconventional moral level, and especially stage 2, the child's moral conceptions are characteristically *quid pro quo*. The reciprocity involved here is less differentiated in that moral judgments at this level do not consider justifications based on mutual understanding of different views, but is instead a reciprocity of equal exchange.

By contrast, at moral stage 3, the child "naturally" places a strong emphasis upon the interpersonal aspects of the moral situation. His concern shifts from what will happen to him to what others think of him. The concurrent or preceding developments in a child's reciprocal role taking, that is, the realization that others are making judgments on the basis of his own actions and intentions as he is on the basis of his own cognizance of others' intentions and actions, are very clearly significant here.

Essentially, then, we have explored the restructurings of two social-cognitive processes, reciprocal role taking and moral reasoning, as they

90

allow for, mediate, stimulate, or coordinate with one another. Results of these studies support the suggestion that the child's reorganization to a conventional level of moral thought is due in part to the newly developed ability to deal with his own and others' perspectives in a reciprocal fashion.

## REFERENCES

Aronfreed, J. *Conduct and conscience: the socialization of internalized control over behavior.* New York: Academic, 1968.

Flavell, J. *The developmental psychology of Jean Piaget.* Princeton, N. J.: Van Nostrand, 1963.

Flavell, J. *The development of role-taking and communication skills in children.* New York: Wiley, 1968.

Hoffman, M. L. Childrearing practices and moral development: generalization from empirical research. *Child Development,* 1963, 34, 295-318.

Kohlberg, L. The development of modes of moral thinking and choice in the years ten to sixteen. Unpublished doctoral dissertation, University of Chicago, 1958.

Kohlberg, L. The development of children's orientation toward a moral order, I: Sequence in the development of moral thought. *Vita Humana,* 1963, 6, 11-33.

Kohlberg, L. Stage and sequence: the cognitive-developmental approach to socialization. In D. Goslin (Ed.), *Handbook of socialization: theory and research.* New York: Rand-McNally, 1969.

Piaget, J. *The moral judgment of the child.* 1932. Glencoe, Ill.: Free Press, 1965.

Rau, L. Conscience and identification. In R. R. Sears, L. Rau, & S. R. Alpert (Eds.), *Identification and child-rearing.* Stanford, Calif.: Stanford University Press, 1963.

Rebelsky, F. G.; Allinsmith, W. A.; & Grinder, R. Resistance to temptation and sex differences in children's use of fantasy confession. *Child Development,* 1963, 34, 955-962.

91

Journal of Personality and Social Psychology
1976, Vol. 34, No. 6, 1293-1301

# Structure and Choice in Moral Reasoning

## Dan Candee
### Harvard University

This study investigated the relationship between the structure of moral reasoning and specific moral choice. Subjects whose structural stage was determined by Kohlberg's Moral Judgment Interview were asked to resolve dilemmas involving the cases of Watergate and Lt. Calley. The consistent finding was that persons at each higher stage of moral structure more often made choices that were consistent with human rights and less often chose alternatives that were designed to maintain conventions or institutions. The gradual and consistent (monotonic) nature of this pattern suggests a model of cognitive development which emphasizes the role of individual concepts within the general stage structures.

Throughout the history of structuralism the issue of structure and choice has almost always been discussed in the context of distinguishing the two concepts. Piaget's original work began when he noticed that there was a consistency in children's reasoning about Binet IQ problems, though such consistency appeared to be absent from their solutions or choices. The methodological revolution occasioned by Piaget was to orient psychologists to the underlying form or structure of reasoning rather than final behavior or choice.

But why should we be interested in studying the structure of reasoning? It is because, ultimately, structure *is* related to choice. While any set of cognitive developmental stages is valid merely because it follows an invariant sequence, such stages would be of little interest if they did not lead to specific types of decisions. Piaget's discovery of formal operations as a set of structures would be of less interest were it not for the fact that having achieved formal operations an individual is able to solve multivariate problems that were unsolvable earlier. Likewise, in the social realm, we would be less interested in the structure of moral reasoning were it not for the prospect that the development of such reasoning leads one to make decisions that are more just.

The person who has most clearly articulated the structural nature of moral reasoning

is Kohlberg (1969, 1973). He has traced the development of moral structures through a series of six stages which, due to their logical interrelationships, form an invariant and culturally universal sequence. Moral structures are measured by having individuals reason about several moral dilemmas (cases in which two or more conventional values conflict). A typical dilemma involves a husband, Heinz, who must decide whether to steal a drug to save his dying wife after all reasonable attempts to obtain the drug have failed.

At each stage the dilemma is resolved using the principle which defines that stage. For example, a Stage 3 individual may respond, "Heinz should steal the drug because that is what any good, loving husband would do." Such reasoning (i.e., the subject's verbatim response) is considered surface reasoning or content. By analyzing a series of surface responses, it is possible to determine the basis on which an individual generally considers actions to be morally right or wrong. This basis is the underlying principle or structure. In the case of Stage 3 persons, the moral rightness of an act is determined by the degree to which it can commonly be expected to maintain harmony between people, a principle known as interpersonal concordance. Notice, however, that the structure of moral reasoning is defined independently of the resultant choice. Another individual, also at Stage 3, could use the same underlying structure to argue that Heinz should *not steal* the drug because he would cause *disharmony* between

Requests for reprints should be sent to Dan Candee, Center for Moral Education, Larsen Hall, Harvard University, Cambridge, Massachusetts 02138.

himself and the moral standards of his community.

Since structure and choice are conceptually independent, it had been thought that all arguments could be defended at any stage. However, the logic of Kohlberg's theory suggests that as the structure of moral reasoning develops, it leads to a single, most just conclusion. We have seen, for example, that Stage 3 reasoning could be used to defend opposing choices in the Heinz dilemma, depending on the reference group with which one wished to maintain harmony. As reasoning develops, its scope becomes more universal. By Stage 5 moral dilemmas are resolved with a consideration for human rights, rights which are seen as existing prior to and forming the basis of any human society. Thus, in the Heinz situation the structure of Stage 5 reasoning can lead to only one choice. Logically, it must advocate stealing the drug since the wife's right to life takes precedence over conventions protecting property. In this case the logic of the moral structure actually determines the nature of the moral choice.

The notion that form can determine choice also receives support from moral philosophy. Kohlberg (1973) takes the view that at the highest stage of development, all rational persons would, given the same information, come to the same conclusion in any moral dilemma. If morality is the just resolution of everyone's claim, there should be one solution to each situation that most equitably achieves this. A procedure suggested by Kohlberg (borrowed in part from Rawls, 1971) is to support only those claims that could be accepted were the actor given an equal chance of becoming any of the participants in the situation. Decisions made in this way are maximally protective of individual rights, since all rational persons would want to secure their own basic rights (life, liberty, etc.) before securing luxuries or conventions.

While a relationship between structure and choice seems likely, there has been no research designed specifically to test it. However, evidence collected in other studies involving the stages of moral reasoning is relevant here. These studies are of two types. Those that have treated moral judgment as a

continuous variable have found a linear correlation between higher stage reasoning and cluster of attitudes that have been called liberal (Fishkin, Keniston, & MacKinnon, 1973), libertarian (Rest, 1976), and nonexploitively permissive (Jurich & Jurich, 1974 The feature common to these clusters is tha individual rights are preferred over the main tenance of institutions, except where institu tions are themselves furthering rights.

Another type of study has measured mora judgment as a discrete variable. Most of these have been experiments in which person at different stages responded to the same situ ational conditions with different overt be haviors. The consistent results of these studie have been that subjects at the highest stag included in the sample (usually Stage 5) pe formed actions which were more consisten with the rights and welfare of other indi viduals, especially in situations where the en vironment provided either no incentive c actually punished one for doing so. Haan Smith, and Block (1968) showed that person who defended the principle of free speec despite imminent arrest were found largel among Stage 5 and 6 subjects, though to lesser extent among Stage 2 subjects as wel Jaquette (Note 1) found that Stage 5 sub jects were more likely than lower stage sub jects to aid a distress victim in the context ambiguous cues. Krebs (1967) found tha Stage 4 subjects more often refrained fron cheating even in the absence of an authorit than did subjects at Stage 2. Finally, conven tional persons (Stages 3 and 4) are less likel to engage in delinquent behavior than a those at the preconventional level (Stages and 2; Kohlberg & Freundlich, Note 2).

The major conclusion that can be draw from these studies is that an empirical rela tionship between structure and both att tudinal and behavioral choice exists. How ever, it is not clear whether the effect abrupt or continuous. Do Stage 5, and i some cases Stage 4, persons support choice based on rights, while lower stage persons d not, or do individuals at each higher stag endorse the choice consistent with rights in creasingly more often? Findings in line wit the abrupt position would support the view f development in which right answers are nown only by those who have apprenticed hrough the lower stages. On the other hand, ndings that support the continuous model rould suggest that the conclusions derived rom highest stage reasoning are *increasingly* erceived as more adequate as one develops.

In order to validate the existence of a relaionship between structure and choice in noral reasoning and to investigate its abrupt r continuous nature, subjects of known noral stage were asked to make choices in a umber of structured dilemmas. The dilemmas vere designed to pit a substantive or proedural right against some other concern. They involved the issues of Watergate [1] and .t. Calley, two well known instances of conicting moral concerns. It was hypothesized hat alternatives consistent with rights are ndorsed more often at Stage 5 than at lower tages. No prediction was made concerning he abrupt or continuous nature of the patern of response across the entire set of stages.

## METHOD

### Subjects

The sample consisted of 372 persons, predomiantly college students in a variety of locations. Although it was not possible to take either a truly andom or stratified sample, an effort was made to over the entire spectrum of institutions. Included vere 40 freshmen, 50 seniors, and 40 education gradate students at Harvard University; 20 freshmen nd 20 seniors at Boston State College; 25 freshmen nd 30 sophomores at Newton Junior College; and 2 juniors and seniors at St. Anselm's College (Manhester, New Hampshire). To add greater geographial distribution, 75 seniors at two Catholic prep chools in rural areas of Illinois and Michigan and 20 chool supervisors from the rural environs of Atanta, Georgia, and Richmond, Virginia, were also ncluded.

As a whole, the sample was distinguished by its ge (most subjects were 17 to 25 years old), region predominantly New England), and 1972 voting recrd (237 favored McGovern, 161 favored Nixon). ex was almost evenly distributed. To control for he possible effect of different subcultural milieus, the ata were analyzed separately by institutions as well s together.

### Measures

Each subject completed a written moral judgment nterview and a week later completed the Watergate-Calley questionnaire. The moral judgment interview s a semistructured measure which presents the subect with three dilemmas in story form (Should

Heinz steal the drug? Should Heinz be punished? Should a boy disobey his father who has broken a promise to him?). Each story is followed by a number of open-ended probe questions. Responses are classified according to one of five stages and an overall stage score derived. (Since Stage 6 is so rare it is not included in standard scoring.) Protocols were scored by the author using Kohlberg's standard manual (Kohlberg, Colby, Speicher-Dubin, & Lieberman, Note 3). A sample of 40 protocols was also scored by a second experienced scorer. Reliability to within half a stage was 95%. The convergent validity of the interview can be found in Kohlberg (1969).

The Watergate-Calley questionnaire consisted of 20 forced-choice questions which provided two and sometimes three response categories.[2] The questions presented situations in which a substantive or procedural right was in conflict with another concern (such as loyalty, sincerity, authority). The situations were chosen both for their public saliency and for the clearness with which they presented conflicting issues.[3] The questions relating to Lt. Calley were selected from items used by Kelman and Lawrence (1972). They were prefaced with an objective summary of the My Lai events.

To substantiate the claim that particular choices were most consistent with the concept of rights, six judges, none of whom were familiar with Kohlberg's theory, were asked to complete the questionnaire using the instructions in the next section. Three of the judges described themselves as conservatives on a scale of political ideology and had voted for Nixon, while the other three placed themselves in liberal categories and had favored McGovern. Both the ideology scale and the measure of candidate preference are described below (see Other Measures section). All judges showed at least 50% Stage 5 reasoning. The definition of rights embodied in the following instructions is based on philosophic discussions by Ross (1930), Frankena (1955), Hart (1955), Rawls (1971), and Nozick (1974).

### Instructions for Resolving Moral Situations

Following are the instructions given to the judges: "Below are a number of situations with alternative

---

[1] For a discussion of this study as it explains the Watergate events, see Candee (1975).

[2] Copies of the questionnaire are available from the author.

[3] The Watergate affair (1972–1974) involved a series of events stemming from the efforts of President Nixon and members of his reelection committee to cover up the committee's involvement in a number of illegal campaign practices including a break-in at the national headquarters of the Democratic Party. The Lt. Calley case occurred during the Vietnam War. It involved his being tried and convicted, in 1971, for the murder of 22 civilians in a village which had been suspected of Vietcong activity. Calley's main defense was that he was acting on orders previously given by his superiors.

answers. Choose your answer in accordance with the instructions. This is not necessarily a measure of your personal opinion. It is a measure of the implications of the instructions. The situations are taken from actual aspects of the Watergate and Lt. Calley affairs. Use your knowledge of these events to resolve ambiguities you may find in the questions."

*Judgment of right and wrong.* In deciding whether an actor is right or wrong, consider the human rights that are explicitly involved or that may be reasonably implied in the situation. The *basic* human rights include (a) life (protection from unwanted deprivation of life), (b) liberty (freedom of action, speech, association, belief, and freedom from unprovoked harm or intrusion), (c) procedural rights (fair trial, habeas corpus, equal consideration for a job, etc.), (d) political rights (vote, hold office), and (e) property. *Lesser* rights (including those sometimes known as special rights) involve rights derived from contracts, promises, family, and job relations.

1. If a claim to rights exists on one side of an issue and only the upholding of a convention or self-interest exists on the other, decide in favor of the side which protects rights.

2. If a claim to rights exists on both sides of an issue, decide in accordance with the order listed above. For example, life takes precedence over all other rights, while liberty prevails over all but life.

3. Consider the motives of the actor. Try to assess whether the actor's intent was to (a) protect basic rights or (b) protect an institution, convention, or self-interest. Use objective data, primarily the actor's publicly stated intention.

4. An action which violates lesser rights (see hierarchy above) is justified only if (a) it is performed for the publicly stated purpose of protecting more basic rights *and* (b) the action itself is reasonably related to those goals. To be reasonable an action must *either* (a) have a fair probability of being successful or (b) be virtually the only recourse available because either the more usual channels have failed or because basic rights would be jeopardized by the time such channels could be attempted.

5. Summary: If, on balance, an action was designed to protect basic rights (pursuant to the above qualifications), decide that the actor was right, not guilty, and so on. If, however, an action involved the violation of any rights without the justified attempt to protect more basic rights, consider the actor wrong, guilty, and so on.

*Duty.* Duties are correlative with rights. Therefore one's first duty is to insure the protection of basic rights, when they are immediately threatened. The order of duties follows the order of rights (see Judgment of right and wrong section above). In addition, there are certain other prima facie duties including the duty to treat all persons with human dignity, to be open and honest, to obey just institutions, and to act so as to increase the general welfare. These duties should be honored except in cases where they would actually compromise human rights.

*Principles of equality and universality.* Rights that are basic to human beings are to be applied universally (to everyone) and equally. This is particular pertinent in the case of criminal and procedur rights and duties. All persons must be prosecuted defended in a manner consistent with their alleg crime without respect to such morally irreleva criteria as power, status, race, sex, or creed.

*Responsibility.* An individual is considered r sponsible for his/her actions except in circumstanc where he/she could not reasonably have anticipate the actual outcome. This requires that the individu make a considerable and pointed effort to determi the nature and probable consequences of his/her ac It is the actor himself, armed with reasonab definite knowledge, who must ultimately decide t propriety of his own action.

The choices I expected on the basis of these in structions appear in Table 1. Reliability of the judg with this criterion was as follows: for 11 of the 2 items (Questions 1, 2, 4, 6, 7, 8, 9, 15, 16, 17, ar 19), agreement was 100%. For 6 other items (Ques tions 3, 5, 12, 13, 14, and 20), there was agreeme by five of the six judges. Of the remaining 3 item Question 10 showed equal 67% agreement amor both liberal and conservative judges, Question 18 r ceived 100% agreement among conservatives but on 33% among liberals, and Question 11 (dealing wi Daniel Ellsberg) received 100% agreement from li erals but 0% from conservatives. Thus, with on three exceptions, the foregoing instructions were su cessful in producing a reasonably nonpartisan con sensus on the implications of the concept of rights.

## Other Measures

In order to obtain a composite measure of eac subject's use of the rights alternatives, I constructe a Rights Index. This was the percentage of choic consistent with rights over the entire 20 question A general measure of political ideology was obtaine by having subjects rate themselves, relative to othe their own age, on a 9-point scale from highly con servative to radical. Candidate preference was simpl a self-report of the subject having favored Richar Nixon or George McGovern in the 1972 election. Sub jects who gave no choice were eliminated from tallie using that variable. An approximation of the effect different school milieus was obtained by ranking th schools according to academic entrance standards.

## RESULTS

The hypothesis of this study was strongl confirmed. There was a highly significar linear main effect of moral stage on the 20 question Rights Index. Means for Stages 2– were .48, .57, .70, and .86, respectivel $F(3, 356) = 59.37$, $p < .001$, linear trend $< .001$.

We can now interpret the data for the in dividual Watergate-Calley questions as pr sented in Table 1. A significant relationshi between moral structure and choice, as mea sured by chi-square, was found for 17 of the 20 questions. What is most important is that n each case the predominant pattern was nonotonic. That is, with only several exceptions found among the relatively few Stage 2 subjects, the percentage of persons endorsing the alternative consistent with rights was greater at each higher stage. A conservative measure of this association is Kendall's tau (rank correlation). In all cases for which chi-square was significant, tau was also. Of primary importance is the fact that in no case was the correlation negative. Among the 17 questions with significant chi-squares, there were no cases in which higher stage subjects

preferred the alternative less consistent with rights.

To help establish the validity of the results, the effect of moral structure on choice was compared with other variables which might also be expected to account for these findings. Since Watergate was a partisan political issue, the most likely competing variable would be one's candidate preference in the Watergate-tainted election of 1972. Accordingly, in Table 2, the results are presented separately for persons supporting Richard Nixon and those supporting his opponent, George McGovern. Although Nixon supporters tended to excuse both the Water-

TABLE 1

PERCENTAGE OF SUBJECTS CHOOSING RIGHTS ALTERNATIVES ON WATERGATE-CALLEY QUESTIONNAIRE

| Question | Moral stage | | | | $\chi^{2a}$ | tau |
|---|---|---|---|---|---|---|
| | 2 | 3 | 4 | 5 | | |
| 1. Do you approve or disapprove of Lt. Calley having been brought to trial? (Approve) | 0 | 45 | 78 | 89 | 36.29** | .43** |
| 2. Should American officers be convicted for war crimes ordered by their superiors? (Should) | 20 | 22 | 53 | 84 | 38.72** | .46** |
| 3. Do you consider Calley's actions: Right—what any good soldier would do under the circumstances; Wrong—but hard for him to know right from wrong; Wrong—clear violation of military code; Wrong—violation of morality regardless of military code? (Wrong—violation of morality) | 20 | 39 | 54 | 82 | 36.00** | .44** |
| 4. Do you consider Calley guilty or innocent of murder? (Guilty) | 60 | 40 | 66 | 97 | 27.86** | .38** |
| 5. E. Howard Hunt sincerely believed he was helping the country. Was he right to participate in the Watergate break-in? (No) | 64 | 64 | 75 | 89 | 13.92** | .17** |
| 6. Should money contributed for general use in the Nixon campaign have been given to the Watergate defendants to pay for their lawyers and feed their families? (Should not) | 66 | 65 | 82 | 87 | 18.22** | .20** |
| 7. Should the Watergate defendants have been allowed to conduct a public campaign to raise money for their defense? (Yes) | 46 | 33 | 53 | 88 | 53.97** | .36** |
| 8. Considering his duty as an officer in CRP (Committee to Reelect the President) should Magruder have admitted the burglars were hired by CRP or tried to cover up? (Admitted) | 40 | 53 | 77 | 94 | 46.43** | .36** |
| 9. Herbert Kalmbach asked his superior, "Is this a proper assignment and am I to go through with it?" He was told it was. If it later turns out that Kalmbach was collecting hush money, would you consider him responsible? (Yes) | 19 | 26 | 34 | 62 | 27.27* | .25* |
| 10. If the money was used as hush money, would you consider Kalmbach guilty of a crime? (Yes) | 19 | 33 | 40 | 54 | 12.08* | .18** |
| 11. Daniel Ellsberg stole top secret papers that belonged to the Pentagon because they contained information about the Vietnam War that he felt the public should know. Was Ellsberg right to steal the Pentagon Papers? (Yes) | 16 | 21 | 43 | 54 | 30.16** | .29** |

(table continued)

TABLE 1—(*continued*)

| Question | Moral stage 2 | 3 | 4 | 5 | $\chi^{2a}$ | tau |
|---|---|---|---|---|---|---|
| 12. Ellsberg stole the Pentagon Papers; Hunt and Liddy stole from Ellsberg's psychiatrist. Were the two crimes basically the same or different? (Different) | 20 | 36 | 64 | 83 | 28.55** | .44** |
| 13. If impeachment alone were held today, based on what you know at this time, would you be for or against impeachment? (For) | 41 | 65 | 84 | 98 | 43.93** | .33** |
| 14. If the President were already impeached and a vote were held today on removing him from office, would you be for or against removal? (For) | 30 | 60 | 78 | 96 | 43.18** | .34** |
| 15. John Caufield was the man who delivered the hush money to the Watergate burglars. Caufield knew the purpose of the money but had been told by John Dean that instructions to deliver the funds had come "from the Oval Office." Was Caufield right to have delivered the money? (No) | 60 | 83 | 85 | 100 | 7.87* | .11* |
| 16. Was it permissible to have a nurse take files from Ellsberg's psychiatrist to obtain more information on his theft of the Pentagon Papers? (No) | 69 | 89 | 94 | 98 | 20.35** | .12** |
| 17. John Ehrlichman stated that taking such files is common when investigating a political suspect. Was it permissible? (No) | 56 | 80 | 88 | 98 | 26.25** | .19** |
| 18. John Ehrlichman was in part responsible for preventing leaks of military secrets. Was he right to investigate Ellsberg concerning the Pentagon Papers? (Yes) | 92 | 86 | 79 | 85 | 3.17 | .04 |
| 19. Was Hunt and Liddy's break-in at Ellsberg's psychiatrist justified? (No) | 87 | 93 | 95 | 98 | 4.58 | .05 |
| 20. Was Ehrlichman, who had hired Hunt and Liddy, responsible for their exploits? (Yes) | 72 | 78 | 76 | 86 | 2.87 | .04 |
| $N^{b}$ Questions 1–4, 15 | (5) | (85) | (74) | (27) | | |
| $N$ Questions 5–14, 16–20 | (25) | (171) | (93) | (61) | | |

*Note.* Percentages are for choice consistent with rights. Moral stage defined as highest stage at which subject gave 25% of his/h responses on moral judgment interview. The wording of Questions 5, 6, 8, 9, 16–20 has been shortened for presentation here.
[a] The $df = 3$. For questions with more than two choices, those not consistent with rights were combined during analysis.
[b] The number of respondents varies slightly from question to question due to subject omissions, do not knows, and so on.
\* $p < .05$.
\*\* $p < .001$.

gate participants and Lt. Calley while Mc-Governites tended to condemn them, the pattern of choice by moral stage was the same *within* both camps. In the vast majority of cases there was greater support for the rights alternative among subjects at each higher stage within the same political group.

A similar analysis controlling for school was done for two of the larger subsamples. Within both the Harvard and Boston State groups, all questions followed the predicted pattern. No individual analysis was done for the other institutions.

An overall test of the effect of these competing variables on the pattern of content choices was obtained by using the 20-question Rights Index. The correlations of this index with moral stage, political ideology, 1972 can didate preference, and a dimension of schoo prestige is presented in Table 3. As can b seen, the relation of moral stage to the Right Index is greater than with any of the othe variables. When candidate preference, politi cal ideology, and school are entered first int a regression, the multiple correlation with th Rights Index is .57 ($R^2 = .32$), $F(3, 306) =$ 50.09, $p < .01$. However, the inclusion o moral stage increases the multiple correlatio to .70 ($R^2 = .49$), which is a highly signifi cant addition, $F(4, 305) = 76.62$, $p < .0$ Of course, when moral stage is entered firs into the regression, it absorbs nearly all th variance itself. The conclusion to be draw from these results is that the relationship be

TABLE 2

PERCENTAGE OF SUBJECTS CHOOSING RIGHTS ALTERNATIVE BY
MORAL STAGE AND CANDIDATE PREFERENCE

| | 1972 candidate preference | | | | | |
| | McGovern | | | Nixon | | |
| | Moral stage | | | Moral stage | | |
| Question | 3 | 4 | 5 | 3 | 4 | 5 |
|---|---|---|---|---|---|---|
| 1. Calley trial (Approve) | 51 | 91 | 95 | 26 | 59 | 71 |
| 2. Convict officers (Should) | 27 | 66 | 94 | 5 | 33 | 50 |
| 3. Calley's actions (Wrong—morality) | 44 | 66 | 85 | 15 | 33 | 71 |
| 4. Calley verdict (Guilty) | 44 | 79 | 100 | 28 | 42 | 86 |
| 5. Hunt (Wrong) | 66 | 75 | 88 | 63 | 78 | 91 |
| 6. General funds (Should not give) | 68 | 83 | 90 | 67 | 81 | 89 |
| 7. Public defense fund (Yes) | 34 | 55 | 89 | 36 | 48 | 80 |
| 8. Magruder (Admit hired) | 54 | 89 | 96 | 52 | 56 | 81 |
| 9. Kalmbach (Responsible) | 31 | 44 | 66 | 20 | 12 | 45 |
| 0. Kalmbach (Guilty) | 43 | 51 | 55 | 20 | 14 | 50 |
| 1. Ellsberg (Right to steal) | 37 | 57 | 62 | 5 | 22 | 10 |
| 2. Hunt, Ellsberg crimes (Different) | 58 | 55 | 88 | 33 | 80 | 67 |
| 3. Impeachment (For) | 86 | 96 | 97 | 40 | 64 | 100 |
| 4. Removal (For) | 91 | 94 | 95 | 24 | 46 | 83 |
| 5. Caufield (Wrong) | 85 | 89 | 100 | 73 | 76 | 100 |
| 6. Take Ellsberg's file (Wrong) | 97 | 94 | 100 | 80 | 93 | 91 |
| 7. Common excuse (Wrong) | 95 | 93 | 100 | 64 | 77 | 91 |
| | | | | | | |
| ʳᵃ Questions 1–4, 15 | (66) | (47) | (20) | (19) | (27) | (7) |
| ʳ Questions 5–14, 16–17 | (92) | (62) | (50) | (79) | (31) | (11) |

*Note.* Percentages are for choice consistent with rights. Moral stage defined as highest stage at which subject gave 25% of his/her
responses on moral judgment interview. The wording of questions has been shortened for presentation here. Only those questions
which were significant in Table 1 are presented here. Stage 2 subjects were eliminated from this table due to their infrequency.
ᵃ The number of respondents varies slightly from question to question due to subject omissions, do not knows, and so on.

ween moral stage and Watergate-Calley
choices is real and cannot be attributed to
other factors.

The tendency of higher stage persons to
choose the alternative consistent with rights
does not mean that, in fact, they share greater
consensus. Often, as in Questions 2, 8, 9, and
11, there was more actual agreement among
stage 3 persons of both political camps than
among those at Stage 5. At lower stages, persons are unaware of situational subtleties that
higher stage subjects find meaningful. For example, in the Kalmbach situation (Question

9), supplementary open-ended responses indicate that while Stage 3 subjects simply ex-
cused Kalmbach because he acted as a good
subordinate, Stage 5 subjects saw a complex
mix of dutiful behavior and one's ultimate responsibility to decide personally the propriety
of one's acts. Differences in the interpretation
of facts that were irrelevant at Stage 3 pro-
voked considerable disagreement at Stage 5.
However, the tendency of higher stage subjects from both political camps to see Kalmbach as increasingly more responsible suggests that the consensus at Stage 3 is unstable
and dissolves as individuals develop.

TABLE 3

INTERCORRELATIONS OF MORAL, POLITICAL,
AND EDUCATIONAL VARIABLES

| Variable | 1 | 2 | 3 | 4 | 5 |
|---|---|---|---|---|---|
| 1. Rights Index | — | .57 | .53 | .45 | .22 |
| 2. Moral development | | — | .27 | .29 | .25 |
| 3. Candidate preference | | | — | .55 | .28 |
| 4. Political ideology | | | | — | .23 |
| 5. School prestige | | | | | — |

*Note.* The $N = 372$. Numbers are product-moment
correlations.

DISCUSSION

The major result of this study was that persons at each higher stage of moral structure
more often made decisions in moral dilemmas
that were consistent with human rights and
less often chose alternatives which were designed to maintain conventions or institutions. These findings support the view that
moral structures are, at least partially, determinative of moral choice. Furthermore,

since the observed pattern was in all cases monotonic, there is empirical support for Kohlberg's claim that at the highest stage of reasoning all persons, given the same information, should reach the same answer. This is not to say that there was perfect agreement among Stage 5 individuals. Since disputes over information exist, there will never be consensus in the real world. Furthermore, even Stage 5 persons have not reached full development. However, the tendency at each higher stage to choose the answer consistent with rights more often, suggests the psychological validity of the philosophic claim that such answers are in a logical or objective sense right.

A process of decision making that accounts for these results rests on the assumption that nearly everyone sees the core of highest stage reasoning. For example, people at all stages recognize that life is more basic than either law or property as evidenced by the common response to Kohlberg's standard Heinz dilemma, "Property can be replaced but life cannot." In that story nearly everyone would like to save the woman's life. However, at lower stages factors which are irrelevant in terms of a philosophically valid moral decision may be given greater weight. A Stage 2 individual may want to justify helping the wife, but weigh the inconvenience of a lengthy trial, or even a jail term, equally if not greater. A Stage 3 person's altruism may be restrained because stealing is not consistent with being a good citizen. One aspect of development is that at each higher stage, an individual adopts, eliminates, and reorganizes concepts to increase the likelihood of coming to decisions which in some sense he or she knows to be right. In doing so the individual achieves structures that are more equilibrated both within themselves and with the outside world.

### Relation of Structure to Concepts

While the foregoing model accounts for the general relationship between structure and choice, it does not explain the mechanism by which structure and choice are related within each of the stages. That mechanism involves Piaget's (1970) definition of a structure as a whole or integrated system of elements which

is self-regulating in the sense that it provide the transformational rules by which any el ment in the structure can be generated fro any other without appealing to extrastru tural elements. As a transformational ru the principle of each moral stage defines set of equivalent concepts and imposes som limits on their substitutability. For exampl the principle of Stage 3, interpersonal co cordance, dictates that one can substitute an action which "a good citizen should do" a long as it is not based on conditions that wer rejected by development through Stage (physical power) or Stage 2 (blatant self-i terest). The monotonic nature of our resul suggests that the logical relation of rights conventions imposes more stringent conditior on concept substitutability at each highe stage. While "protecting rights" is but on of many "things a good citizen should do" a Stage 3 (others include being sincere, loya and dutiful), it is logically paramount a Stage 5. While many Stage 2 and 3 subject could defend a choice not consistent wit rights, few could at Stage 5.

### Moral Stages and Political Reasoning

We turn now to the interaction effect moral reasoning and candidate preference o political choice. In comparing political camp we find that the greatest difference involve the most explicitly partisan issue, impeacl ment (Questions 13 and 14, Table 2), fo lowed by the issues of Kalmbach (Question 9 and 10) and Ellsberg (Questions 11 an 12). These situations seem to be distinguishe by their complexity, relative obscurity, an institutional nature. Few people know th procedures involved in either campaign func raising or in national security research. Wher the facts are most ambiguous, individuals ar most influenced by their general political on entations in interaction with their moral rea soning. By comparison, the issue in Question 3, the right to a public defense fund, is com mon and independent of any particular con text. In this case the effect of political prefer ence was nil.

REFERENCE NOTES

1. Jaquette, D. *Helping a sick person: A study* moral thought and action. Unpublished manu script, 1974. (Available from Laboratory of Hu

man Development, Larsen Hall, Harvard University, Cambridge, Massachusetts 02138)

2. Kohlberg, L., & Freundlich, D. Moral reasoning in delinquents. In L. Kohlberg, *Recent research in moral development*. Book in preparation, 1975.

3. Kohlberg, L., Colby, A., Speicher-Dubin, B., & Lieberman, M. *Standard scoring manual for moral judgment interview*. (Available from Center for Moral Education, Larsen Hall, Harvard University, Cambridge, Massachusetts 02138)

## REFERENCES

Candee, D. The moral psychology of Watergate. *Journal of Social Issues*, 1975, *31*(2), 183–192.

Fishkin, J., Keniston, K., & MacKinnon, C. Moral reasoning and political ideology. *Journal of Personality and Social Psychology*, 1973, *27*, 109–119.

Frankena, W. Natural and inalienable rights. *Philosophic Review*, 1955, *64*, 212–232.

Haan, N., Smith, M. B., & Block, J. Moral reasoning of young adults: Political social behavior, family background, and personality correlates. *Journal of Personality and Social Psychology*, 1968, *10*, 183–201.

Hart, H. L. A. Are there any natural rights? *Philosophic Review*, 1955, *64*, 175–191.

Jurich, A., & Jurich, J. The effect of cognitive moral development upon the selection of premarital sexual standards. *Journal of Marriage and the Family*, 1974, *36*, 736–740.

Kelman, H. C., & Lawrence, L. H. Assignment of responsibility in the case of Lt. Calley: Preliminary report on a national survey. *Journal of Social Issues*, 1972, *28*(1), 177–212.

Kohlberg, L. Stage and sequence: The cognitive-developmental approach to socialization. In D. Goslin (Ed.), *Handbook of socialization theory and research*. Chicago: Rand McNally, 1969.

Kohlberg, L. The claim to moral adequacy of a highest stage of moral judgment. *Journal of Philosophy*, 1973, *70*, 630–646.

Krebs, R. *Some relationships between moral judgment, attention and resistance to temptation*. Unpublished doctoral dissertation, University of Chicago, 1967.

Nozick, R. *State, anarchy, and utopia*. New York: Basic Books, 1974.

Piaget, J. *Structuralism*. New York: Harper & Row, 1970.

Rawls, J. *A theory of justice*. Cambridge, Mass.: Harvard University Press, 1971.

Rest, J. New approaches in the assessment of moral judgment. In T. Lickona (Ed.), *Moral development and behavior: Theory, research and social issues*. New York: Holt, Rinehart & Winston, 1976.

Ross, D. *The right and the good*. Oxford, England: Clarendon Press, 1930.

(Received July 28, 1976)

# MORAL REASONING AND MORAL BEHAVIOR IN CONVENTIONAL ADULTS

Dennis Krebs and Alli Rosenwald

*Harvard University*

Traditional approaches to the study of morality have found little relationship between either knowledge of or respect for conventional moral standards and moral behavior. Studies such as those of Havighurst & Taba (1949), Hendry (1960), Lehrer (1967), Mills (1967), and Rau (1964) have supplied consistent support for the conclusions of a classic study on honesty by Hartshorne and May (1928-1930). Hartshorne and May (1928-1930) found that there is little relationship between what people believe is right and wrong and what they do; and that behaviors such as lying, cheating, and stealing are determined mainly by situational demands, not characteristics of individuals. Although a factor analysis of Hartshorne and May's data by Burton (1963) revealed a general factor for cheating, the amount of variance accounted for by the factor was small.

The cognitive-developmental theorist Kohlberg (1964, 1969, 1971) has challenged traditional conceptions of morality, and offered a conceptually different approach to the understanding of the relationship between moral judgment and moral behavior. Kohlberg accepts the two main findings of traditional research: (a) there is not a necessary relationship between the content of moral reasoning (*what* people believe is right or wrong) and moral behavior; and (b) external situational demands determine behavior that is conventionally considered moral. However, he holds that behavior that conforms to conventional standards of right and wrong is not necessarily moral. According to Kohlberg, morality is an aspect of reasoning, not behavior. The only behaviors that can be considered moral are behaviors that spring from the types of moral decisions that are determined by high level moral reasoning. Behaviors such as lying, cheating, and stealing are generally immoral because they generally follow from low-level conceptions of morality. However, such behaviors are not necessarily immoral, or immoral by definition.

The authors gratefully acknowledge the critical reactions of Terence D. Creighton, Phil Zelazo, Roy Hopkins, and Janet Gillmore to early drafts of the study; and they appreciate the time Roger Brown and Larry Kohlberg took to read it over.

Requests for reprints should be sent to Dennis Krebs, Department of Psychology, Simon Fraser University, Burnaby 2, B.C. Canada.

Lying, cheating, and stealing can be moral. For example, a person might lie, cheat, and steal to save a life.

To date, only a small number of published studies have tested the relationship between Kohlberg's measure of moral judgment and moral behavior in adults. Haan, Smith, and Block (1968) found that principled (Stage 5 and 6) subjects were more likely to participate in the original Berkeley free speech sit-in than conventional (Stage 3 and 4) subjects. However, they also found that significantly more preconventional (Stage 2) subjects than conventional subjects sat in. Schwartz, Feldman, Brown, and Heingartner (1969) found that college undergraduates who scored above the median on Kohlberg's test of moral judgment (most of whom were Stage 5 or 6) cheated significantly less than subjects who scored below the median. However, Schwartz et al. (1969) failed to find a significant relationship between level of moral development and helping behavior. Finally, Kohlberg (1969, 1971) made reference to an unpublished study that found that 75% of Stage 6 subjects (vs. 13% of subjects at other stages) refused to obey an experimenter when he demanded that they deliver increasingly dangerous shocks to one another in the classic Milgram (1965) study on obedience.

Although past studies on adults generally have supported Kohlberg's position on the relationship between moral judgment and moral behavior, they have focused almost exclusively on the effect of principled versus conventional moral reasoning. These studies are of theoretical relevance, but their generality is limited because there are relatively few principled adults in the normal population and because the moral decisions they investigated are unusual.

The present study was designed to explore the relationship between moral reasoning and moral behavior in average adults. It focused on the conventional conceptions of morality characteristic of subjects at Kohlberg's Stages 3 and 4. It placed subjects in a situation that demanded a conflict typical of the low-key moral conflicts people face in their everyday lives; it examined subjects' decisions, and analysed the logic of the relationship between the structure of their moral reasoning, as revealed by their verbal responses to Kohlberg's hypothetical dilemmas, and their behavior.

## METHOD

Subjects

Subjects consisted of the first 31 people to respond to a newspaper advertisement reading, "Good pay for little work—Subjects wanted for psychological experiments." Subjects responded by phone and were told that the experiment would involve taking a number of personality tests, for which they would be paid $3.00. Subjects' inquiries were answered with statements designed to reveal that the experimenter was attempting to discover the extent to which certain personality tasks related to one another. The mean age of the subjects was 23, with a range from 17-54. The subjects were from both sexes and came from a wide variety of backgrounds.

Procedure

Subjects met as a group in a large lecture hall. The experimenter, who was a 24-year old female college student, informed them that the purpose of the experiment was to explore redundancy among personality scales in order to examine whether they could be combined into one composite test. She said that the study was both a project for a course and part of the research of a psychologist for whom she worked.

At the beginning of the session, the experimenter explained that she had had considerable difficulty reserving a room for the testing session, and had just been informed that she would only be able to use the lecture hall for one hour, instead of the hour and a half she had requested. Accordingly, she explained, she would begin by administering the tests that were the most difficult to score and put the remainder in a stamped, self-addressed envelope for the subjects to take home. She informed the subjects that she would pay them the full $3.00 after they completed the initial questionnaires, and trust them to complete the remainder. Finally, she informed them that the project for her course was due in a week and a half (which, in fact, was near the end of the school term), and that it was absolutely essential for every subject to complete all remaining questionnaires and send them back to her by the specified date, approximately a week from the testing session. She made it clear that she was trusting them to complete the task for which they would be paid; and that if they let her down they would jeopardize her chances of passing the course.

The subjects were then given two questionnaires, the first soliciting basic demographic information such as age, sex, income, and education; and the second supplying a short form of Kolhberg's test of moral development (Kohlberg, 1964).

After the subjects completed Kohlberg's test of moral development, they were given a stamped, self-addressed envelope which contained the remaining personality questionnaires.[1] As subjects left, they were reminded that by accepting the money, they were contracting to return their questionnaires on time.

## RESULTS

Responses to Kohlberg's moral dilemmas were scored by issue by a professional scorer, who was trained by Kohlberg. A second

---

[1] The tests were a test of Social Responsibility (Berkowitz & Lutterman, 1965), a test of Machiavellianism (Mach IV), (Christie & Geis, 1970), a test of empathy (Hogan, 1969), and a test of values (Rokeach, 1968).

scorer scored all tests. A reliability check revealed 85% agreement on stage assignment. Differences were resolved through discussion between scorers.

None of the subjects was scored as either Stage 1 or 6. Only a small proportion was scored as Stage 2 or 5 (10% [3] and 7% [2] respectively). The majority of the subjects (83%) was scored as Stage 3 or 4, and therefore, fell within the conventional level of moral development.

In all, 39% (12) of the subjects failed to return their questionnaires on time. Sixteen percent (5) returned them late, and 23% (7) failed to return them at all. One set was returned blank. It was classified as unreturned.

Table 1 shows that there was a consistent increase in the proportion of subjects who returned their questionnaires on time at each stage of moral development. With one exception, all subjects at Stage 4 and 5 returned their questionnaires on time. All subjects who submitted their questionnaires late were at Stage 3. Two of the three Stage 2 subjects failed to return their questionnaires.[2] The Pearson $r$ correlation between stage of moral development and the extent to which the contract was honored (fully, somewhat, or not at all) was .49, which was significant at the $p < .01$ level of significance. A $X^2$ test with Yates correction was computed to test the significance of the difference in proportion of subjects at Stage 2 and Stage 3 vs. Stage 4 and Stage 5 who returned their questionnaire on time ($X^2 = 6.90$, df(1), $p < .01$.). Correlations were computed among all demographic variables and the date of questionnaire return. Of the 23 demographic variables assessed, only two correlated significantly with the date of questionnaire return: possession of an intellectually vs. physically oriented job ($r = .506$, n $= 20$, $p < .03$) and years of formal education ($r = .397$, n $= 31$, $p < .05$). Because only 20 of the 31 subjects possessed a job (most of the rest were students), the generality of the association between intellectuality of occupation and moral behavior was limited. Subject's income, subject's father's income, actual job status, and job status desired failed to correlate significantly with the date of questionnaire return. Other demographic variables that failed to correlate significantly with behavior in question were subject's sex, religious background, ethnic background, ordinal position, status as a student, and several aspects of family background. Neither intellectuality of job ($r = .16$) or years of formal education ($r = .29$) correlated significantly with stage of moral development.

----

[2] Kolhberg has revised his scoring system since the data for this study were analyzed. It is possible that the Stage 2 subject who returned his questionnaire on time, and, perhaps the other Stage 2 subjects would now be classified as Stage 4½.

TABLE 1

Questionnaire Return by Subjects at Different Stages of Development

| Questionnaire Return | Stages of moral development | | | | All Stages |
|---|---|---|---|---|---|
| | 2 | 3 | 4 | 5 | |
| On time | 33%(1) | 40%(6) | 91%(10) | 100%(2) | 61%(19) |
| Late | (0) | 33%(5) | (0) | (0) | 16%(5) |
| Not at all | 66%(2) | 27%(4) | 9%(1) | (0) | 23%(7) |

Note.—The n is in parentheses.

## DISCUSSION

The findings of the present study force the conclusion that Kohlberg's test measures *something* that predicts "moral" behavior. In spite of the countless morally neutral forces that could have influenced the subjects' behavior during the time they were given to complete the questionnaires, all but one of the subjects at Kohlberg's highest stages returned their questionnaires on time; and most of those at Kohlberg's lower stages did not.

The traditional way of interpreting results such as those obtained in the present study is in terms of their ability to validate Kohlberg's test of moral development (Kurtines & Greif, 1974). However, common conceptions to the contrary, behavioral measures of morality are in themselves an inadequate basis for either validating Kohlberg's test or testing his theory. Kohlberg does not claim that there is a necessary positive linear relationship between stage of moral development and moral behavior. Isolated acts are inadequate criteria of morality because identical acts often originate from different motives or interpretations of the situation. Not paying income tax to further one's own welfare is not the same as withholding income tax as a public protest. Helping an old lady cross the street becomes an unseemly act when it is a prelude to embezzling her life's savings. In one of the best-known studies in the area, Haan, Smith and Block (1968) found that both principled (Stage 5 and 6) and pre-conventional (Stage 2) subjects sat in to a greater extent than conventional subjects during the Free Speech Movement at Berkeley. The investigators suggested that the principled subjects sat in to support the right to free speech, but the preconventional subjects sat in to better their own lot.

It follows that the frequency of subjects who behaved as predicted at each stage in the present study supplies only a superficial test of Kohlberg's claims. The critical question is why did the subjects behave as they did; and what aspect of Kohlberg's test supplies the predictive power? One answer to this question might be that responses to Kohlberg's test were determined by a third factor such as sex, social class, or education; and the third factor was the primary determinant of the moral behavior. A total of 23 demographic characteristics that could have related to stage of moral development and moral behavior were assessed. Only two correlated significantly with the moral behavior, and neither correlated with stage of moral development. Thus, the present study failed to supply any evidence that responses to Kohlberg's test were determined by more general characteristics that related more closely than it to the behavior that was measured.

What aspect of Kohlberg's test, then, did supply the predictive power? The obvious answer is that the phenomenon that Kohlberg's test purports to measure—moral reasoning—determined the moral behavior.

In order to acquire some insight into the process by which the structure of moral reasoning at the different stages helped determine the responses to the situation that was investigated in this study, a detailed, in-depth analysis of the responses given by subjects to Kohlberg's test was undertaken. This "clinical" method of analysis (cf. Piaget, 1934) does not comprise a rigorous empirical test of Kohlberg's claims. It is essentially interpretive and post hoc. However, it does supply a more adequate way of specifying and elucidating and refining the structural dimensions of Kohlberg's stages, understanding the relationship between moral thought and moral behavior, and generating further tests of Kohlberg's theory than does a frequency count of predicted responses.

Although there were only three subjects who endorsed preconventional points of view; and although only two of them behaved as predicted, the logic of the fit between the structure of Stage 2 moral reasoning and the failure to honor the contract with the experimenter is strong. When one Stage 2 subject was asked whether it would be a citizen's duty to report a reformed escaped convict, he said: "Only if there was a reward." A second gave a similar, but more enterprising suggestion: "The only reason I could see for the tailor reporting Heinz is if there is a reward and if he wanted money, he would get a lot more by blackmailing Heinz." In the eyes of the Stage 2 subjects, the experimenter had made a bad bargain. She had no way of holding them to their contract or catching them and punishing them if they failed to honor it.

The responses of Stage 3 and 4 subjects in the present study help illustrate the difference between the structures that underlie the two types of moral reasoning and show how they could have given rise to the differences in behavior. When asked to advance reasons for stealing the drug, and to explain why stealing it involved a moral problem, Stage 3 subjects were much more prone than Stage 4 subjects to make reference to the role obligations of a good husband— to love, protect, and honor his wife. In all, 73% of the Stage 3 subjects (vs. 36% of Stage 4 subjects) mentioned Heinz's love for or role obligations toward his wife as a reason for stealing the drug.

The question that gave rise to answers that differentiated between the aspect of Stage 3 and Stage 4 reasoning that seemed most relevant to the behavior measured in the present study was "If Heinz [who escaped from jail] was a good friend of the tailor would that make a difference [in reporting him] ? Why?" Sixty-three percent of the Stage 3 subjects (compared to 36% of Stage 4 subjects) argued that the interpersonal status of another would make a difference to the determination of their moral obligation. The responses, especially of those who failed to return their questionnaires on time, revealed that, for a variety of reasons, Stage 3 subjects believed that they have more of a moral obligation toward a friend than a stranger in a situation that involves disobeying the law. Although some Stage

4 subjects realized that they would feel an obligation or desire to favor a friend, most did not identify the obligation as moral. (". . . it [the decision] would become less objective and more personal"; "it would, but shouldn't").

Moral reasoning at Stage 3 is susceptible to inconsistency. Stage 3 subjects hold that the same act is both morally obligatory (when directed toward a friend) and not obligatory (when directed toward a stranger). Similarly, Stage 3 subjects hold that what is right for one person (for example, helping his friend), is not right for someone else (who is not his friend). In the context of the present study, the experimenter was a stranger, and subjects never expected to see her again. Therefore the demands of the situation were less for Stage 3 subjects, who define moral obligation in interpersonal terms, than for Stage 4 subjects, who respond to the more abstract and internal sense of moral obligation implicit in obedience to social rules and norms. It would seem that the external support necessary to engage Stage 3 subjects' principle of ideal reciprocity was insufficient to cause the majority of them to live up to the Golden Rule.

For Stage 4 subjects, the experimenter was a person in authority, and the implicit contract they entered with her was buttressed by a dominant principle of Stage 4 morality, "A good day's work for a good day's pay." Although there was no formal, legal contract between the experimenter and the subjects, Stage 4 subjects were conscious of the ideal that if the existing social order is to prevail, people must honor their commitments to one another. The principles that guided the behavior of Stage 4 subjects were more internal and broad, and, therefore, more dependable than the principles of Stage 3 subjects.

Two studies on children have found a difference between the behavior of subjects who manifest Stage 3 and Stage 4 moral reasoning. Saltzstein, Diamond, and Belenky (1972) found that Stage 3 children were more prone than children at other stages to conform to group consensus in an Asch-type conformity study. The investigators argued that: "It is the tendency to *confuse* one's liking for others and the need for approval with issues of *adherence to truth and fulfilling commitment*" that leads Stage 3 children to conform (p. 335). Turiel and Rothman (1972) found that Stage 4 children were more prone than children at lower stages to behave in a way that was consistent with advice that was one stage above their own. The investigators interpreted their findings as an indication that "in relating behavioral choices to higher-stage reasoning, there is a developmental progression from the segregation of differentiated domains to their integration" (p. 752). The investigators also noted considerable "conflict in inconsistency and indecision" in the reactions of Stage 3 subjects.

The results of the studies on children are consistent with the results of the present study on adults. Group consensus and social approval—the forces that were interpreted as determining the conformity of Stage 3 subjects—were not salient in the present situation; the present Stage 3 subjects were the only subjects to evince the indecision and inconsistency associated with submitting their questionnaires late; and, assuming that most Stage 3 subjects believed it was right to honor their contract with the experimenter, they failed to give evidence that they were able to integrate their moral thought and moral behavior in a consistent manner.

In the context of the behavior measured in the present study Stage 5 subjects would be expected to honor their contract with the experimenter. Subjects who reason in Stage 5 terms look beyond rules, regulations, and laws to the principles on which they were founded. They entered into the contract of their own free will, and, by accepting the money from the experimenter, made a bargain which they were obliged to keep, even if the bargain was a bad one (Stage 2), they felt no affection for the experimenter (Stage 3), or the experimenter's authority was in question (Stage 4). In the words of a Stage 5 subject: "laws are for the benefit and protection of man . . . they cannot be ignored."

In summary, the present study found that Kohlberg's test of moral development predicted an everyday "moral" behavior. It attempted to explain how the structure of moral reasoning at four of Kohlberg's stages could logically have given rise to the behavioral choices that occurred. Because the study was correlational in nature, it could not prove that the differences in the subjects' behavior were caused by the differences in the structure of their reasoning. However, Kohlberg's test is essentially a test of moral judgment; the behavioral decision that was measured was essentially a moral decision; and the subjects' responses to Kohlberg's dilemmas revealed points of view that implied the decisions they made. It is difficult to see how any non-moral dispositions that might have been measured by Kohlberg's test could explain the present subjects' behavior more adequately than the structure of their moral reasoning. The results of the present study must be interpreted as consistent with and as support for Kohlberg's position.

Before concluding, it should be pointed out that as a test of the cognitive dimension of morality, Kohlberg's instrument would be expected to predict behavior best in situations that lend themselves most to moral discussion and moral reasoning. Put another way, Kohlberg's test should be most relevant to behavior that arises from situations that are most similar to the hypothetical dilemmas he employs to measure moral development—situations in which considered moral decisions can be made. The situation created in the present study supplied a low-key, unemotional conflict. It allowed considerable time for subjects to consider its pros and cons in a relatively relaxed atmosphere. Kohlberg's test would not be expected to predict impulsive behaviors that are minimally mediated by cognitive processes as well, including many of the behaviors commonly considered most moral and immoral, like acts of heroism, rape, and murder.

## References

BERKOWITZ, L., & LUTTERMAN, K. The traditionally socially responsible personality. *Public Opinion Quarterly*, 1968, Vol. 32, 169-185.

BURTON, R. V. The generality of honesty reconsidered. *Psychological Review*, 1963, Vol. 70, 481-500.

CHRISTIE, R., & GEIS, F. L. *Studies in Machiavellianism.* New York: Academic Press, 1970.

HAAN, N., SMITH, M. B., & BLOCK, J. Moral reasoning of young adults: Political-social behavior, family background, and personality correlates. *Journal of Personality and Social Psychology*, 1968, Vol. 10, 183-201.

HARTSHORNE, H., & MAY, M. A. *Studies in the nature of character* (Columbia University Teachers College). Vol. 1: *Studies in deceit.* Vol. 2: *Studies in service and self-control.* Vol. 3: *Studies in organization of character.* New York: Macmillan, 1928-1930.

HAVIGHURST, R. J., & TABA, H. *Adolescent character and personality.* New York: Wiley, 1949.

HENDRY, L. S. Cognitive processes in a moral conflict situation. Unpublished doctoral dissertation, Yale University, 1960.

HOGAN, R. Development of an empathy scale. *Journal of Consulting and Clinical Psychology*, 1969, Vol. 33, 307-316.

KOHLBERG, L. Development of moral character and moral ideology. In M. Hoffman & L. Hoffman (Eds.), *Review of child development research.* New York: Russell Sage Foundation, 1964. Pp. 383-432.

KOHLBERG, L. Stage and sequence: The cognitive-developmental approach to socialization. In D. Goslin (Ed.), *Handbook of socialization theory and research.* New York: Rand McNally, 1969. Pp. 347-480.

KOHLBERG, L. From is to ought: How to commit the naturalistic fallacy and get away with it in the study of moral development. In T. Mischel (Ed.), *Cognitive development and epistemology,* New York: Academic, 1971. Pp. 151-235.

KURTINES, W., & GREIF, E. B. The development of moral thought: Review and evaluation of Kohlberg's approach. *Psychological Bulletin*, 1974, Vol. 81, 453-470.

LEHRER, L. Sex differences in moral behavior and attitudes. Unpublished doctoral dissertation, University of Chicago, 1967.

MILGRAM, S. Some conditions of obedience and disobedience to authority. *Human Relations*, 1965, Vol. 18, 57-75.

MILLS, J. Temptation and changes in moral attitudes. Unpublished doctoral dissertation, Stanford University, 1958.

PIAGET, J. *The Moral Judgment of the Child.* Free Press. 1969. (Originally published, 1934.)

ROKEACH, M. *Beliefs, attitudes, and values.* San Francisco: Jossey-Bass. Inc., 1968.

RAU, L. Conscience and identification. In R. R. Sears, L. Rau, & R. Alpert, *Identification and child rearing.* Stanford, Calif.: Stanford Univ. Press, 1965. Pp. 199-240.

SCHWARTZ, S., BROWN, M., FELDMAN, K., & HEINGARTNER, A. Some personality correlates of conduct in two situations of moral conflict. *Journal of Personality,* 1969, Vol. 37, 41-57.

SALTZSTEIN, H. D., DIAMOND, R. M., & BELENKY, M. Moral judgment level and conformity behavior. *Developmental Psychology,* 1972, Vol. 7, 327-336.

TURIEL, E., & ROTHMAN, G. R. The influence of reasoning on behavioral choices at different stages of moral development. *Child Development,* 1972, Vol. 43, 741-756.

VOL. 88, No. 1

JULY 1980

# Psychological Bulletin

# Bridging Moral Cognition and Moral Action: A Critical Review of the Literature

Augusto Blasi
University of Massachusetts—Boston

This essay presents a broad discussion of the conceptual and empirical issues that concern the relations between moral reasoning and moral action. In the first part, two opposite views of the relations between moral cognition and moral action are described, and their contrasting assumptions and implications are clarified. In the second part, the available empirical literature is reviewed; research relating moral reasoning to delinquency, honesty, altruism, conformity, and other real-life moral behaviors is summarized, with special attention given to problems of design, measurement, and interpretation. Although overall these studies seem to support the cognitive-developmental perspective, this support needs to be qualified and interpreted in each of the different areas. At a more general level, the importance of clarifying the meaning of consistency between moral cognition and moral action and the need for a process approach to research in this area are emphasized.

Few would disagree that morality ultimately lies in action and that the study of moral development should use action as the final criterion. But also few would limit the moral phenomenon to objectively observable behavior. Moral action is seen, implicitly or explicitly, as complex, imbedded in a variety of feelings, questions, doubts, judgments, and decisions.

In agreement with cognitive-developmental theory, this article assumes that moral cognition plays a central role in moral functioning, providing unity to the many processes that compose it. From this perspective, the study of the relations between moral cognition and moral action is of primary importance.

Unfortunately, cognitive-developmental theory, as articulate as it is in its specific domain, offers only the vaguest guidelines for approaching the relations of cognition and action, simply hypothesizing a positive correlation between the two. As is pointed out in the present review, this state of affairs is inevitably reflected by the undifferentiated nature of most empirical research in this field. The use of correlational analysis might contribute to our predictive knowledge, but it is incapable of illuminating the articulations among the factors involved.

This is not the appropriate context for providing more precise theoretical formulations. However, one main purpose of this review is

The author would like to thank John Broughton, Ann Colby, Wolfgang Edelstein, John C. Gibbs, Lawrence Kohlberg, Dennis Krebs, Jane Loevinger, James R. Rest, and Abigail J. Stewart for reading and discussing the article.

Requests for reprints should be sent to Augusto Blasi, Department of Psychology, University of Massachusetts, Boston, Massachusetts 02125.

1

to stress, as a general orientation, the necessity of complementing the developmental analysis of cognitive structures with the study of the functional relations among processes from various domains. When it is accepted that the moral phenomenon is, at the same time, complex and unified, it becomes possible to go beyond the search for mathematical correlations and to inquire about the roles that different elements play in an overall scheme in which moral action is the natural end product.

## Two Different Assumptions About Moral Behavior

Morality is ultimately a characteristic of action, and moral development should lead to moral behavior, yet what actions are moral is not easily determined. The history of ethics essentially concerns the criteria by which those actions that are moral can be differentiated from those that are morally neutral.

Social scientists have approached the study of moral action with two very different assumptions. Moral action has been viewed either as the immediate result of action tendencies and of their interplay or as mediated by such cognitive processes as moral definitions, moral beliefs, and moral reasoning.

According to the first view, there are in each person a number of habits, behavioral traits, or generalized action tendencies, leading to a variety of specific behaviors (e.g., sharing, helping, cooperating, sympathizing), that in many cultures are placed in the same generic class of moral action. These tendencies may be simultaneously present or elicited with conflicting tendencies (e.g., aggression, competition, hoarding, self-protection). Which action in a specific situation is performed depends on the relative strength of all simultaneously elicited behavioral tendencies, including inhibiting tendencies, and on their interplay. However complex the set of antecedent factors may be, the outcome is considered to be automatic and objectively determined.

This approach to the understanding of morality is by far the most prevalent among social scientists and is common to theories that are otherwise very different. Thus, the number of moral tendencies and the degree of their generality vary from theory to theory; the processes by which these tendencies originate in a human organism and by which they lead to action are given different accounts. An evolutionary-genetic theory (e.g., contemporary sociobiology, Wilson, 1975) emphasizes adaptation to the physical and social environment, the function of moral tendencies for the survival of the species, and innate mechanisms of an instinctual though not necessarily rigid and fixed nature. Campbell (1975) clearly delineated this viewpoint, suggesting an homeostaticlike model in which the balancing rules between altruistic and egoistic tendencies are determined at each time by the functions of adaptation and survival. A similar explanation is offered in Milgram's (1974) account of obedience to authority. Learning theories characteristically view moral behavior in terms of habits and explain their probability of occurrence and their degree of generality as a function of the reduction of drives, both primary and secondary, of the environmental contingencies under which they were learned, and of schedules of reinforcement (Aronfreed, 1968; Miller & Dollard, 1941; Mowrer, 1960; Skinner, 1953). Although different in many important respects, psychoanalysis, in some accounts, follows a similar general model in explaining moral functioning: Ideas and symbols are endowed with motivational force; a set of such force symbols has a moral meaning and is collectively labeled *superego*. Moral behavior, then, is the result of the relative strength of the superego in conflict with other personality agencies, a conflict complicated by strategies of inhibition, transformation, deception, and disguise.

Recent social psychological research (e.g., on helping behavior, reciprocity, bystander intervention, or obedience) was also guided by a similar model. The action tendencies on which the experimenter focuses change from situation to situation, but in each case the outcome is considered to be the inevitable result of the interplay among the relevant motivational forces. For instance, students' agreement to participate in a boring and perhaps painful experiment could be predicted, in principle with mathematical precision, by knowing the degree by which they fear pain or avoid the unknown, the strength of their need to conform to social norms and particularly to the norm of helping, the intensity of their guilt for having involuntarily jumbled the experimenter's precious notes, the level of embarrassment they may experience in openly refusing the experimenter's request, and so on.

According to the prevalent view, therefore, moral action is essentially irrational and is different from morally neutral action only in terms of specific content categories (helping, obeying, etc.) or in terms of the social function served by morality, for example, of enhancing social cohesion (Hogan, 1973).

Within this model of moral functioning, cognitive processes, including the more complex ones, are frequently assigned an important role, specifically the role of regulating and facilitating the relations between situations and moral tendencies as well as the relations between moral tendencies and behavior. All of the theories mentioned earlier, especially their more contemporary versions, emphasize the advantages and the adaptive nature of a variety of cognitive processes: observation, discrimination, memory and retrieval, labeling, symbol formation, images and rehearsal, abstractions, and hierarchical plans. But perhaps the most important functions of cognition are not recognized in research on moral functioning, namely, the creation of meaning and the determination of truth.[1] The moral meaning, in fact, is considered to be already present in the action tendencies and to be objectively determined either by their function for the individual and for the species or by arbitrary conventions. The question of truth is regarded as irrelevant in this context.

Of course, it is recognized that human individuals engage in behaviors that have been labeled *moral reasoning*, that is, that people wonder about the fundamental criteria for right and wrong, compare different criteria, and inquire about their correctness and truth value. These processes, however, are deprived of any real moral function. These behaviors are frequently interpreted in one of two ways. At times they may be regarded simply as a nonfunctional luxury, some sort of inexplicable vestigial organ. This attitude is implied

by those who tend to emphasize the unrelatedness of moral judgment and moral action (Aronfreed, 1971; W. Mischel, 1969).[2] For example, in a recent article Dreman (1976) stated,

Research has shown that *verbal* moral expressions are influenced mainly by cognitive factors . . . while *manifest* moral behavior is mainly a function of social learning. . . . Thus while a relation may be expected between verbal moral judgment scores and justifications for sharing, there is no empirical basis for predicting that a relation will be obtained between verbal moral judgment and manifest donations. (p. 187; italics in original)

As is concluded later, empirical research, in spite of all its shortcomings, provides a different and more hopeful picture. In fact, the opinion that judgment and action are unrelated seems to renounce the hope of ever finding a unity in human moral functioning.

Others, however, do recognize a function in moral reasoning, but not one serving moral action. Moral reasoning is viewed as rationalization, that is, as a result of rather than as a preparation for one's action and as an expression of the human need for a coherent account of what we are doing. This account may be entirely fictional, but it is useful to the extent that it serves our need for rational coherence. In the words of the Spanish philosopher Unamuno (1921), "Once more I must repeat that our ethical and philosophical doctrines in general are merely the justification *a posteriori* of our conduct, of our actions. . . . What we believe to be the motives of our conduct are usually but the pretext for it" (p. 261; italics added for emphasis).

In contrast with this essentially irrational view that emphasizes needs and action tendencies, a second approach considers moral functioning as essentially rational, namely, as

---

[1] There is ambiguity in the terms *cognition* and *cognitive*, which has become more apparent with their increased popularity. When these labels are applied to theories as diverse as Piaget's and W. Mischel's (1973), the result is utter confusion.

[2] Aronfreed (1976) seems to give cognitive processes an ambiguous role. Whereas, on one hand, he feels that moral categorization is necessary for the definition of actions as moral, on the other, he sees its function as a more flexible and mobile activation of affect, the ultimate determinant of behavior.

a response that is derived from understanding and reasons concerning both the fundamental goals of human beings and the means to pursue them. These goals may not be different in content from those that sociobiologists and social scientists of a functionalist persuasion emphasize. The crucial difference lies, first, in the emphasis given to processes by which these goals are thought to exercise their influence on behavior: categorizing personal and social reality, comparing values and establishing value hierarchies, constructing criteria and rules for evaluations and decisions, and assessing and deliberating. Second, these cognitive processes are considered to be needed not simply to stitch needs and actions together but more fundamentally to construct moral meanings. Morality, then, would not consist in the material achievement of certain goals but in a special meaning that these goals have for the individual and in the special processes by which the goals are achieved. An action beneficial to the welfare of society as a whole or of a fellow human being would not be considered moral if it were performed under hypnosis or under physical constraints but only if it were performed willingly, in response to values that are understood and accepted by the agent. Here lies the reason for the emphasis on judgment that is characteristic of Piaget, Kohlberg, and of cognitive-developmentalism in general. Without judgment, an action, no matter how beneficial, would not be moral.

However, within this view, when moral action is considered to be necessarily mediated by moral judgment, the relations between judgment and action become problematic. How should these relations be conceptualized? How can the connections between the cognitive and the executive functions be explained? Equally important, how can the lack or the breakdown of functional relations be understood? These are the questions that a complete theory of moral functioning should address.

These two views of moral action ultimately reflect two very different conceptions of human actions in general.

According to the first conception, human action, like any other event, is caused by a finite number of elements and their interactions. Examples of elements are genes, stimulus–response associations, attitudes, and traits. In many cases, the situation is a part of the elementary units that produce action. This is clear for habits; but attitudes and traits are also believed to incorporate situational characteristics. A call for taking into account the situation in predicting behavior frequently simply indicates a desire for more specific habits, attitudes, or traits. The interaction among the elements in a specific prediction is mathematically measurable. A failure to predict behavior, then, demands the introduction of new elements in the equation or new interactions among old elements.

Within the second conception of human action, determination is a more appropriate notion than causation. In understanding the type of effect that moral rules have on behavior, useful analogies are the determination of a conclusion from a set of premises or the generation of a new sentence from a set of grammatical and semantic rules. The basic elements, then, are rules and principles, which interact with each other according to superordinate rules and principles. The situation is not literally an intrinsic part of the rules, nor does it interact with the rules as a force with other forces. Rather, a situation is read, interpreted, and assimilated, according to rules, or vice versa, rules are applied to a situation.

As a result, the relative importance of the moral rules by which situations are interpreted and of the situations that are being interpreted by the rules cannot be statistically separated and quantitatively weighted. An action is entirely a response to a situation and entirely a product of rules, in the same way that in a verbal description of an event, both the event and the grammatical rules pervade every single aspect of the description.

Perhaps one of the most important characteristics of the present state of research and theory about moral functioning is the mixture of opposite terminologies and metaphors. This is particularly evident in the tendency among social learning theorists to add the vocabulary of cognition to their traditional conceptual tools. Although convergence is suggested, what is needed is a sharpening of the differences and a fundamental reorganization of the constructs.

## Issues in the Empirical Study of the Relations Between Moral Reasoning and Moral Action

In this section the empirical findings concerning the relations between reasoning and behavior in the area of morality are summarized and discussed. My purpose is less to provide substantive conclusions (although some will be drawn) than to point out certain assumptions that underlie much research activity in this area and to indicate a number of methodological problems.

Before the studies are reviewed, the following general issues should be discussed: (a) Assuming that it makes theoretical sense to study the relations between moral reasoning and moral behavior, how should these relations be conceptualized? (b) How should moral cognition be defined? (c) Which actions will be considered moral? (d) Finally, what specific problems face an investigator starting from a cognitive-developmental understanding of moral functioning, the theoretical focus of the present review?

### Conceptualizing the Relations Between Cognition and Action: The Trait and the Process Approaches to Moral Consistency

Apart from the two basic assumptions about moral behavior that were described earlier, investigators who think that the study of the relations between moral cognition and moral behavior is theoretically sound and empirically viable may still approach the issue with two different questions and objectives. They may be interested in determining the degree of consistency among a number of traits that are all related in terms of morality. For instance, they may ask whether individuals who tend to be interested in moral issues also tend to feel guilty or whether individuals who tend to feel guilty also tend to refrain from cheating in business transactions. This approach can be called the *trait* approach. The traits selected for study may be narrow or broad, but they always represent general tendencies in the individual. Appropriate measures are those that assess the moral characteristics of the individual according to some definition of

morality. The general assumption underlying this approach is that a degree of consistency exists in human beings, not only within the same trait but also across traits that share a common characteristic. This was also the assumption that guided the search for moral character, from the studies by Hartshorne and May (1928), Hartshorne, May, and Maller (1929), and Hartshorne, May, and Shuttleworth (1930) through the efforts of Peck and Havighurst (1960) to the recent studies of Hogan (1973).

Alternatively, investigators may view moral behavior not in terms of personality but rather in terms of processes; they will be interested in studying the components of this process and in discovering the temporal and functional relations that exist among them. For example, they may ask whether a strong attitude against cheating will lead to resisting the temptation to cheat when the need for achievement is aroused and the opportunity to cheat is offered. Whether a child habitually cheats or whether he or she habitually expresses negative attitudes toward cheating is irrelevant. This approach can be called the *functional* or *process* approach. Its focus is on single events and on their temporal relations; the appropriate method is experimental or quasiexperimental. The underlying assumption is not one of consistency among personality traits but rather one of functional unity based on interlocking processes.

Although a point may be found at which these two approaches to the relations between cognition and action merge, in principle the two approaches are different in objective, assumptions, and method. This distinction, however, has largely been ignored, and the theoretical bases for both assumptions of trait consistency and of functional unity have not clearly been delineated. In fact, confusion may result from the legitimate application in both approaches of structural and systemic terminology that has two radically different meanings. Traits may be thought to be parts of the same structure, in a logical Piagetian sense, if among them relations of equivalence and reversibility can be determined. In this sense, the abilities to understand the reciprocal relations in a series of quantities, to systematically classify objects, and to understand that a specific quantity remains the same when it undergoes superficial transformations of shape or appearance, although it is descriptively different, are considered by Piaget to be parts of the same mental structure: concrete operations. The hypothesis is that the same logical principle underlies all three abilities, although it takes different forms for different problems. Processes may be considered to be parts of the same functional system, even though they may come from different logical-psychological domains, if they are related to each other in a temporal and causal sequence that leads to a specific outcome. The specific behavior of classifying objects can be described in terms of perceptual input, conceptual coding, performance, and so on. These components belong to different and logically unrelated mental domains but come together in the effective resolution of a concrete classification problem.

Do moral action and moral reasoning belong to the same logical structure? Or, alternatively, are they related as parts of a functional system? In the first case, logical and correlational analyses are appropriate, and one should expect substantial statistical correlations. In the latter case, the appropriate analyses concern the relations among process components. One may expect statistical correlations among traits, if traits corresponding to the process components should exist, but not as large as in the first case. In fact, correlations may be absent. Although memory and coding strategies are both necessary to resolve a classification task, there is no reason to expect that those who possess highly sophisticated coding strategies are also high in memory strength.

It appears, then, that the term *consistency* has been used with two different meanings; ambiguity has been fostered by extending to one concept what is true and characteristic of the other. The first concept could be called *trait consistency:* the tendency to behave in a similar way at different times and in different situations as well as the tendency of several specific traits to be together in the same individuals and to form a cluster or a superordinate trait. The term *consistency* is appropriate in this context only if a concep-

tual common ground is postulated among traits, over and above their empirical relations.

The second meaning of consistency refers specifically to the agreement between what an individual states about his actions and the actions themselves. Although this relation can be viewed from a trait perspective, the process approach is perhaps a more natural way of viewing it. The latter notion of consistency may be labeled *personal consistency,* since it indicates an important ideal characteristic of the person as person. Although trait consistency has moral meaning only when the traits are moral, consistency between words and actions has a moral significance of its own and corresponds to the notion of integrity. Lack of consistency in the second sense does not simply indicate the situational specificity of traits but suggests expediency and opportunism.

## Meanings of Moral Cognition

The successful investigation of the relations between moral cognition and moral action requires that the two terms be precisely defined. If by moral cognition we mean any verbal statement that has morality as content, three distinguishable kinds of cognitions have traditionally been investigated in their relation to moral action: (a) moral information (i.e., the verbal recognition of moral norms, at least as defined by a specific culture); (b) moral attitudes or values, expressing either a personal belief, an affective inclination, or a tendency to behave in a certain moral manner; and (c) moral judgment or moral reasoning (these two terms are used here interchangeably), characterized by the justification of a moral conclusion and by the general or specific criteria by which moral decisions are supported. Cognitive-developmental theory tends to reserve the label *cognition* to the last of the three types of moral statements.

Hartshorne and May's (1928), Hartshorne et al.'s (1929), and Hartshorne et al.'s (1930) massive and now classical studies on moral character defined cognition in the first sense. One problem with this approach and perhaps a reason for their failure to discover meaningful relations is that after the relatively early age of 7 or 8, there is little progress and small individual differences in the knowledge of the accepted rules.

A recent example of the attitude approach to the relation between verbal statements and moral ideas is provided by Henshel (1971). In this study children (fourth through seventh grades) were asked what they thought about cheating (cognitive component), whether they valued honesty more than intelligence (affective component), and whether they themselves would cheat if they had the opportunity (intentional component). Then they were exposed to one of the traditional cheating tests. Henshel's affective and intentional components correspond to the traditional understanding of attitudes.

The attitude or value approach to behavior is not specific to the moral domain and has a long tradition in psychology. In fact, Henshel's (1971) positive findings are far from typical when viewed in a historical context. As early as 1934, LaPiere had sadly concluded that little consistency existed between people's attitudes, as measured by their statements, and their behavior. Later research seemed to support this conclusion (Deutscher, 1966; Festinger, 1964). Only recently has there been a trend toward a more optimistic outlook about the relevance of attitude research for behavior in general and for moral action in particular. Interestingly, this reversal was mostly affected by the recognition of the complexity of the context in which attitudes operate and by a reorientation toward the individuality of the agent (Ajzen & Fishbein, 1978; Bem & Allen, 1974; D. A. Schwarz, 1976; S. H. Schwartz, 1968, 1977; Warner & DeFleur, 1969; Wicker, 1969).

Regardless of the results, however, some general observations can be made. First, the attitude approach has certain characteristics that provide it with objective advantages in the study of the cognitive antecedents to moral behavior: It seems to elicit the individual's own beliefs rather than a superficial compliance with accepted norms, as the information approach might do, it can be as concrete as the action is, and it may indicate a degree of ego involvement in moral issues. It is thus possible to view attitudes as verbal expressions of action tendencies. Their concreteness and their ego-involving characteristic differentiate attitudes also from moral judgments, as these are usually measured.

Second, the typical strategies by which information and attitudes are described relies on the content of simple statements, frequently formulated by the investigators themselves. Thus it is implicitly assumed (a) that statements about values are understood in the same way by the investigator and by children of different ages, (b) that actions have the same meaning for all those who perform them, and (c) that the meaning of the actions corresponds to the meaning of the verbal expressions for everybody involved in a study. To paraphrase Gertrude Stein, "cheating is cheating is cheating is cheating." The structuralism of Piaget (1932) and Kohlberg (1969, 1971) was meant to be a direct attack precisely on these assumptions. Cheating and other specific contents, whether expressed in words or in action, do not have the same moral meaning for everybody. These ideas, already emphasized by Allport (1937), are now being revived in the context of attitude research and theory (e.g., Bem & Allen, 1974). From a cognitive-developmental perspective, the moral meanings of specific contents depend on the general criteria that constitute the individual's understanding of morality, and these criteria develop with age. Not attitudes or values, therefore, but judgments that express general criteria are crucial.

The review of the empirical literature and the discussion presented here exclusively concern the judgment and the reasoning aspects of moral cognition.

## Definition of Moral Action

The selection of the appropriate actions presents the investigator with problems that are even more serious than those implied in the selection of cognitive behaviors. Which actions can be considered to be moral? Which moral actions can be expected to differentiate the various types of moral thinking?

The usual solution to the first question has been to rely on public moral opinion, on the fact that most people within each culture seem to agree on which behaviors should be considered to be moral and which immoral. Thus, the bulk of available studies focuses on helping, sharing, cheating, and resisting temptations. The relevance to morality of resisting temptations obviously depends on the kind of temptations that moral individuals are expected to resist; however, not much thought has been given to the clarification of this matter. At a more general level, the reliance on an average public morality is unsatisfactory to the extent that individuals can be imagined who, although moral, do not subscribe to it.

In some studies actions were selected that were not clearly moral or immoral (e.g., participation in demonstrations for free speech, Haan, Smith, & Block, 1968, or abortion, Gilligan, 1977). That perhaps the most interesting actions are not clearly moral or immoral should not be surprising when one considers that Lieutenant Calley's behavior at My-Lai, although it left few people indifferent, gathered more approval than disapproval among American adults (Kelman & Lee, 1972). Finally, the action selected for investigation (e.g., the use of marijuana, Haier, 1976), may appear to be not only ambiguous but puzzling. Almost any action can be relevant to morality if it is perceived as relevant by the agent, whereas no action is appropriate if the agent does not see its moral import.

Instead, in the empirical literature, even in those studies that were performed from a cognitive-developmental perspective, the implicit assumption seems to be that there is a developmental dimension of moral action that is conceptually independent of moral judgment. Therefore, the degree of moral maturity in action can be independently and objectively assessed and then correlated to the degree of moral maturity in thinking. Although this may in fact be the case, at present nobody seems to know the parameters by which to evaluate the degree of maturity specifically in moral action, independently of cognition.

It is conceptually and strategically sounder to select behaviors starting from the general moral criteria of the individuals involved in one's study and from the way these criteria are specifically applied. This approach openly acknowledges that moral behavior cannot even be defined independently of moral thinking

and that moral thinking cannot be externall imposed and can only be presumed at th investigator's risk. Perhaps the lack of a empirical relationship between cognition an behavior that is reported in some studies ma simply indicate the impossible task with whic subjects were faced: to be consistent in the behavior with judgments and decisions th they never made and that they may hav found alien to their own mode of thinking. I moral consistency or inconsistency (in th sense of personal consistency, as define earlier) is to be studied, the experiment design should allow the unconfounded man festation of the phenomenon.

### Problems in Implementing the Cognitive-Developmental Approach

The majority of the studies reviewed her used stages of moral thinking as a guidelin to predict moral behavior. This approach, a though theoretically sound, has been marre in practice by a number of conceptual mi understandings and methodological naivet One has been the tendency to treat qualita tively different stages as if they were degree on a quantitative dimension. The strategy dividing subjects into high and low, usin perhaps the median of the sample as a cuto point, and the procedure of calculating corr lations between, for instance, amount c cheating or amount of helping and degree c moral reasoning represent a similar miscor ception.

A second problem with current research that the reasoning structures selected by th investigators have a certain degree of remote ness vis-à-vis the action that they are sup posed to determine. This is particularly ev dent when moral action is related to suc general Piagetian cognitive structures as spa tial perspective taking (Fenyes, 1967) o conservation (Larsen & Kellogg, 1974). Bu there is remoteness from the content of ac tion, even when the moderating variables di rectly concern moral reasoning, in that man of Piaget's (1932) and Kohlberg's (1958 1971, 1976) moral stages frequently do no seem to be related to any specific course o action, but in any one situation they may b compatible with contrasting alternatives

Moral stages concern certain general criteria, such as intention, the importance of punishment, the emphasis on trust and loyalty, and so on. But these same criteria can lead to opposite behaviors, depending on how a situation is appraised.

A convincing demonstration of the loose relations that exist between action and structures of moral judgment is provided by Turiel and Rothman (1972). In this study a group of seventh and eighth graders were faced with an experimental task similar in some respects to Milgram's (1974) well-known "punishing" procedure. However, they also had the opportunity to listen to the arguments that two adults presented for continuing and for terminating the experiment. These arguments were couched in terms of moral criteria either one stage above or one stage below the children's previously measured stage. The plus-one reasoning was used with some children to argue for ending the experiment, whereas with others it was used to support its continuation. The results indicated that at least some children, those who scored at Kohlberg's Stage 4, responded in their actual behavior to the plus-one and not to the minus-one reasoning, regardless of the alternative suggested. A similar independence of the behavioral choice from the level of reasoning was also reported by Haan et al. (1968) in their study of Berkeley free speech demonstrators. Students who participated in the demonstrations belonged, in significantly larger numbers than could be expected by chance, to two different levels of moral reasoning: Kohlberg's preconventional and principled groups. On the other hand, although the majority of conventional students did refrain from demonstrating, some of them did demonstrate for reasons that were consistent with their general moral criteria.

In these and in other instances, the same behavior can be supported by different moral criteria, and the same moral criteria can lead to different moral decisions. Unfortunately, the nature of the relations between specific contents and cognitive moral structures is far from being understood, either in theoretical or in practical terms. Are both solutions of any moral dilemma equally logically consistent with every set of moral criteria? Or, alternatively, are certain specific moral decisions logically incompatible with certain modes of moral reasoning? The first position, which implies that it is impossible to predict moral behavior from moral reasoning, is not only implausible but is not supported, to my knowledge, by any theory or theorist. Candee (1976) explicitly focused his study on the relations between stages of moral reasoning and concrete choices to moral dilemmas. He found that people (mostly college students) at each higher stage of Kohlberg's hierarchy more frequently chose alternatives that were consistent with basic human rights than alternatives that tended to support conventions, institutions, or self-interest. However, too little is known about the specific constraints that cognitive structures exercise on action and about the way these constraints may vary from stage to stage.

It is tempting to conclude from these and similar findings that moral reasoning and moral behavior are unrelated, that Kohlberg's scale is not valid when assessed in terms of behavior (Kurtines & Greif, 1974), or that moral reasoning can be stretched indefinitely to rationalize any kind of action, as W. Mischel and Mischel (1976) skeptically emphasize. But it is also possible to conclude, in closer agreement with common sense and with a rational philosophy of morality (Peters, 1974), that the relations between thinking and action in the moral sphere are less direct and more complex than psychologists expect. If this is the case, it is unreasonable to expect that the knowledge of a person's moral criteria will enable us to predict what specific action he or she will take in a given situation.

It may not be unfair to say that the investigators who have been involved in the study of the present issue have sinned, as a group, by intellectual laziness. Usually too little effort has been expended in deciding what characteristic of the behaviors of cheating or sharing leads individuals of moral stage $x$ to share or cheat more than individuals or moral stage $y$. Or, from the opposite perspective, what characteristic of moral stage $x$ leads to this rather than that specific behavior? An example of a thoughtful approach and of a careful execution is the study by Krebs and Rosenwald (1977). Starting with a conceptual analysis of

Kohlberg's Stages 3 and 4, the investigators selected a situation (the opportunity to honor an informal contractual obligation toward a stranger when social pressures were removed) that was expected to elicit different behaviors from representatives of the two stages. The sample was chosen to guarantee a substantial number of subjects at either one of the two conventional stages, and an attempt was made to statistically control for the possible artifactual effect of irrelevant variables.

A practical way of decreasing the gap between general moral criteria and specific actions is to assess moral reasoning, as Damon (1977) did, using hypothetical situations that resemble the behavior to be studied. In principle, the study of the consistency between moral thinking and moral behavior should include not one but at least two sets of relations: those between specific hypothetical choices and actions and those between hypothetical choices and general structures of moral reasoning. Without information concerning the latter, the moral meaning of the action for the individual remains unknown; without information relevant to the former, moral meanings would not offer an adequate basis for the study of the action–cognition consistency. It is possible that the knowledge of the individual's general attitudes and values —the attitude approach to morality—may eventually play a useful or a necessary role in understanding the relations between cognition and behavior. At present, however, it is not known how general structures of moral reasoning and general attitudes interact in the production of behavior.

Finally, structures of moral reasoning are abstract vis-à-vis moral behavior in yet another respect. They are not only removed from the content of specific actions, but they are also removed from the motivational-affective context of the agent. It is not implied here that general moral criteria have no motivational force. It is implied, rather, that a judgment of morality can be made with different degrees of ego involvement and that this variable is not irrelevant to whether the individual will or will not perform the action in question. It is also implied that there are in the person, next to and perhaps in conflict with cognitive motives (see T. Mischel, 1971),

other motivational sources. How noncognitive motivations interact with moral reasoning as facilitators or inhibitors of moral behavior has been rarely studied (an exception is S. H. Schwartz, Feldman, Brown, & Heingartner, 1969), although the issue is obviously important.

Those who find these considerations sensible and convincing and who are aware of the limitations of the available studies in representing the moral complexities will be surprised by the extent to which the empirical literature supports the hypothesis of a significant relationship between moral thinking and moral behavior. To a large extent, the opposite opinion, that moral reasoning and moral behavior are independent dimensions, is revealed to be a well-advertised myth.

## Review of the Empirical Literature

In the following review certain criteria guided the selection of the studies:

1. Only those studies that included some measure of moral reasoning (i.e., those in which subjects were asked to give reasons for their moral decisions) were examined. The measures, however, differed from study to study. The most frequently used were Piagetian measures, Kohlberg's scale, or other instruments derived from either Piaget or Kohlberg's theory. Moreover, Kohlberg's scale has undergone a number of revisions, and different studies relied on different phases of its developmental vicissitudes. As a result, there is little comparability across investigations.

2. Every study that had some measure of behavior and that related for each subject the behavioral measure to the moral reasoning measure was included. No attempt was made to select the studies on the basis of the moral nature of the behaviors. Those studies in which the behavioral measure consisted of self-reports or of observers' ratings were also included.

3. The review was not limited to published material but included unpublished doctoral theses and mimeographed technical reports. This is admittedly a questionable decision, motivated by the sizable amount of nonpublished material in this area, by the desire to

publicize at least the existence of these research efforts, and, most of all, by the assumption that negative findings more likely would be found in nonpublished reports. The reader should exercise caution and judgment.

## Moral Reasoning and Delinquency

Delinquency offers a natural ground for testing the relations between moral reasoning and moral behavior. And yet, when one looks at the issue closely, some sticky conceptual and theoretical problems appear. First, how should one conceptualize the relation between moral reasoning and delinquent behavior? The 5 studies reviewed here followed a trait approach and implied, at least operationally, that a degree of congruency exists between the reasoning and the behavior of delinquents, as it exists between the reasoning and the behavior of nondelinquents. The delinquent trait would go together with a mode of reasoning about moral issues, characterized by the primacy of one's concrete self-interests, pragmatism, relativism, and opportunism—in sum, what Kohlberg calls preconventional morality. However, there is the possibility that at least some delinquents are characterized not by consistency but by inconsistency. In this case, one should be able to observe the breakdown of those processes that in normal people establish the connections between the level of thinking and the level of execution. Kohlberg and Freundlich (Note 1) think of delinquency in these terms. A trait approach, however, is not suited to trace the differences in processes between delinquents and nondelinquents.

A second problem concerns the definition of delinquency, especially in its conceptual relations to morality. In all of these studies, one of the defining characteristics of delinquency was institutionalization in a delinquent residence or trial and conviction in court or both. These characteristics are too broad and too external to be used as precise indicators of moral functioning. The actual offenses varied considerably from study to study and within the same study, from truancy, vandalism, and car theft to drug dealings, serious arson, and attempted homicide. Only one investigation (Kantner, 1976) exploited these

differences as a possible source of variations in moral reasoning; the investigator grouped the offenses in four categories (violence not related to property, violence related to property, offenses against property without violence, drug-related offenses) but found no significant differences in moral reasoning among them. The delinquent sample, however, was not compared with a nondelinquent group. Kohlberg and Freundlich (Note 1) also argued that inmates convicted for drug-related offenses should show higher moral stages than the other inmates and provided some preliminary supporting evidence.

All in all, as Kantner (1976) himself points out, the single offense seems to be an unsatisfactory solution to the need of introducing some differentiations in the general category of delinquency. Another solution is to resort to a psychological rather than simply to a behavioral classification of delinquency. The three studies following this approach (Campagna & Harter, 1975; Fodor, 1973; Jurkovic, 1976) were successful in finding significant correlates for moral reasoning. The psychological meaning of this procedure, particularly concerning the issue under discussion here, is far from clear. First, the focus shifts from behavior to a variously defined personality trait; second, the precise relations between psychopathy or sociopathy and moral reasoning on one hand and delinquent behavior on the other have not been articulated with any precision.

A methodological difficulty in this type of study, besides the definition of delinquency, concerns the selection of the comparison group. Subjects in this group should not have indulged in delinquent behavior, although they should be matched with the delinquent subjects on all the important factors that may affect moral reasoning scores. All of the investigators were sensitive to this latter requirement: age, race, social class, level of intelligence, and frequently type of social environment or community were either controlled or taken into consideration in the analysis of the data. However, only four studies (Campagna & Harter, 1975; Jurkovic, 1976; Jurkovic & Prentice, 1974; Schmidlin, 1977) described the precautions that were taken to eliminate possible delinquent individuals from their comparison groups (typically, parent reports, school records, and school personnel reports). These precautions are more necessary the more closely delinquents and nondelinquents are matched in terms of social environment and background.

The large majority (11 of 15; see Table 1) of the studies reviewed here resorted to Kohlberg's interview as a measure of moral reasoning. Of the remaining studies, 2 (Kantner, 1976; Schmidlin, 1977) followed Kohlberg's classification but resorted to a format that is objective in administration and scoring, whereas Betke (1944) and Haviland (1977) used procedures of their own construction. Betke followed a classification that was similar to Kohlberg's; Haviland relied on the Piagetian distinction between punitive and restitutive orientation in justice. The important variations in Kohlberg's instruments have already been commented on. In addition, too frequently (at least in 6 studies) the scoring was not done blindly, or no information was given concerning this methodological point.

The findings support the hypothesis that delinquent individuals tend to use developmentally lower modes of moral reasoning than do matched nondelinquents. Of the 15 studies, 10 show statistically significant differences between the two groups. These results are particularly strong because frequently they were obtained with small samples. Perhaps more interesting is the observation that Kohlberg's interview yielded positive findings 9 of 11 times, whereas studies that used other measures gave positive results only 1 of 5 times. Every time objective measures of moral reasoning were used (in 4 studies), no significant difference was found between delinquents and nondelinquents. Whatever the psychological meaning of this observation, it should be taken into consideration in the planning of future research.

It could be asked, beyond within-study differences, whether there are stages that are characteristic of delinquency. Kohlberg believes that the majority of adolescent offenders are preconventional in their moral reasoning, in sharp contrast to noncriminal adolescents who are mostly conventional (Kohlberg & Freundlich, Note 1; Kohlberg, Kauffman, Scharf, & Hickey, Note 2). Of the

12 relevant studies in this group (2 of the studies used measures that are not directly translatable in Kohlberg's terms; 1 used a preadolescent sample), 6 indicated that at least 80% of the delinquent group was at Stages 1 and 2. But other studies reported substantial numbers of delinquents who scored at Kohlberg's conventional level. The varieties of scoring criteria used by different studies makes it impossible at this point to arrive at a more precise conclusion. The most anomalous findings, in this respect, were reported by studies following Kohlberg's classification while using objective tests: Schmidlin (1977) reported the average score of the delinquent group to be between Stages 3 and 4; Kantner (1976) reported that only 10% of his adult delinquent sample was preconventional and that 31% was either principled or in transition to the principled level.

In any event, it is clear that a range of moral reasoning stages can be present among delinquents; the range narrows but does not disappear when psychological classifications such as psychotherapy or sociopathy are introduced. Moral reasoning is an important aspect of delinquency but does not offer alone the explanation of this aberrant behavior.

*Moral Reasoning and Real-Life Behavior*

The 12 studies reviewed in this section have one characteristic in common: They all attempt to relate moral reasoning either to specific behaviors or to habitual actions in real life. In every other respect, specifically in the behaviors investigated and in the methods used, they form a heterogeneous group. Some of the behavioral dimensions (e.g., honesty, social service, or independence from authority) would fit naturally in one or the other of the following sections, all of which focus on behavior in contrived laboratory conditions. The findings about real-life behavior can be compared with those of the corresponding laboratory dimension.

The methods by which behavior was assessed in these studies were teacher ratings (Damon, 1977; Kohlberg, 1958; Santrock, 1975), sociometric nominations (Harris, Mussen, & Rutherford, 1976; Porteus & Johnson, 1965; Harkness, Edwards, & Super, Note 3),

Table 1
Studies That Related Moral Reasoning and Delinquency

| Study | Subjects | Delinquency/ nondelinquency | Basis for matching | Measure of moral judgment | Relation tested[a] | Outcome |
|---|---|---|---|---|---|---|
| Betke (1944) | 50 del, 50 nondel; ages 11–16 | Del: court conviction, institutionalization. Offenses: truancy, larceny, theft. Nondel: NI | Age, IQ, SES, geographic area | Constructed by author, 25 social–moral problems, individual administration; scoring for correct logic and moral criteria (ethical vs. empathic vs. pragmatic) | Delinquency and correctness in logic: $t = 3.48$, $p < .01$. Delinquency and use of ethical criteria: $t = 7.08$, $p < .001$. Delinquency and use of empathic criteria: $ns$. Delinquency and use of pragmatic criteria: $t = 7.13$, $p < .001$. | ? + 0 + |
| Kohlberg (1958) | 12 del, 12 nondel; age about 16 | Del: awaiting trial, institutionalization. Offenses: car theft, burglary, robbery by assault. Nondel: NI | Age, IQ,[b] SES | Kohlberg, interview, 9 dilemmas, global scoring, not blind. Score: MMS. Del stages: approximately 2 as average | Delinquency and MJ: $p < .01$ | + |
| Ruma (1967) | 30 del, 30 nondel; ages 15–17 | Del: court conviction, institutionalization. Offenses: vandalism, theft, assault. Nondel: members of Boys' Clubs | Age, IQ, SES, geographic area | (a) Kohlberg, interview, 6 dilemmas, global scoring. Score: modal stage or stage mixture. Del stages: 1–5 (b) Relevant situation MJ; procedure as in (a) with everyday situations | Delinquency and Kohlberg MJ: $ns$. Delinquency and relevant situation MJ: $ns$ | 0 0 |
| Fodor (1972) | 40 del, 40 nondel; ages 14–17 | Del: court referral. Offenses: from petty larceny to attempted homicide. Nondel: NI (from author's files) | Age, IQ, race, mother's education | Kohlberg, written, 9 dilemmas. issue scoring, blind. Score: MMS. Del stages: approximately 3 as average | Delinquency and MJ: $t = 5.43$, $p < .001$ | + |
| Fodor (1973) | 30 psychopathic del, 30 nonpsychopathic del; ages 14–17 | Institutionalization. Psychopathy: counselors' judgment according to Cleckley's criteria | Age, IQ, race, mother's education | Kohlberg, written, 9 dilemmas. issue scoring, blind. Score: modal stage. Del stages: 1–4 | MJ Stages 1 and 2 vs. 3 and 4 and psychopathy: $\chi^2 = 5.94$, $p < .02$ | + |

(table continued)

135

Table 1 (continued)

| Study | Subjects | Delinquency/ nondelinquency | Basis for matching | Measure of moral judgment | Relation tested[a] | Outcome |
|---|---|---|---|---|---|---|
| Hudgins & Prentice (1973) | 10 del, 10 nondel; ages 14–16 | Del: court conviction. Offenses: car theft, burglary. Nondel: local high school, NI | Age, IQ, race, SES, geographic area | Kohlberg, written, 4 dilemmas, issue scoring. Score: modal stage. MMS. Del stages: 1–3 | Delinquency and MMS: $t = 2.93$, $p < .01$. Delinquency and MJ Stages 1 and 2 vs. 3 and 4: $x^2 = 3.23$, $p < .05$ | + + |
| Jurkovic & Prentice (1974) | 8 del, 8 nondel; mean age approximately 15 | Del: court conviction. probation. Offenses: car theft, burglary. Nondel: school records, counselors, parents', self-reports | Age, IQ, race, SES, geographic area, education, mother's education | Kohlberg, written, 4 dilemmas, issue scoring, blind. Score: MMS. Del stage: approximately 2–3 as average | Delinquency and MMS: ns | 0 |
| Jurkovic (1976) | 36 del (3 groups of 12), 12 nondel; mean age approximately 15 | Del: institutionalization. Offenses: varying according to classification. Psychopathic, neurotic, subcultural: scores on Quay's scales. Nondel: school records, counselors' reports | Age, race, SES, length of institutionalization, social environment | (a) Kohlberg, written, 3 dilemmas, issue scoring, blind. Scores: modal stage. MMS. Del stages: 2–4. (b) Carroll's objective moral reasoning test (after Rest's Defining Issues Test) | Psychopathic vs. neurotic del and MMS (IQ): $p < .10$. Psychopathic vs. subcultural del and MMS (IQ): $p < .005$. Psychopathic del vs. nondel and MMS (IQ): $p < .005$. Differences among other groups: ns. Differences among all groups on Carroll's test: ns. | 0 + ++ 0 0 |
| Campagna & Harter (1975) | 21 sociopaths, 23 normals; ages 10–13 | Sociopaths: institutionalization; selection by Robins's criteria as evident in case history. Normals: school records, counselors' reports, classroom behavior checklist | Age, IQ, SES, geographic area | Kohlberg, interview, 4 dilemmas, global scoring, blind. Score: MMS. Sociopathic stage: 2(1) as average | Sociopathy and MMS: $F = 58.79$, $p < .001$ | + |

Table 1 (*continued*)

| Study | Subjects | Delinquency/ nondelinquency | Basis for matching | Measure of moral judgment | Relation tested[a] | Outcome |
|---|---|---|---|---|---|---|
| Kantner (1976) | 159 adult del | Maximum security prison. 4 categories of offenses: Noneconomic violence, economic violence, economic nonviolence, drugs | Stage groups were matched on age, IQ, race | Rest's Defining Issues Test. Del stages: 2 to principled | Higher vs. lower MJ stages and type of offense (violence vs. drugs) ($\chi^2$): $p < .09$ | 0 |
| Schmidlin (1977) | 30 institutionalized del, 30 community-placed del, 30 nondel; ages 14–17 | Del: institutionalization (past or present). Offenses: runaway, theft, drugs, arson, armed robbery. Nondel: court and school records, self-reports | Age, IQ, race, SES, geographic area, type of offense (for del groups) | Maitland & Goldman's (1974) Moral Judgment Scale, based on Kohlberg's theory; 15 multiple-choice items, each alternative representing a stage. Del stages: 3–4 | Institutionalized del vs. community-placed del vs. nondel and MJ: *ns* | 0 |
| Haviland (1977) | 22 del, 22 nondel; mean age 16 | Del: institutionalization. Nondel: NI | Age, IQ, social environment | Three stories of theft. Score: punitive or restitutive reasoning | Delinquency and punitive vs. restitutive orientation: *ns* | 0 |
| Kohlberg & Freundlich (Note 1) Study 2[c] | 20 del, 14 nondel; mean ages 19.3 and 19.9 | Del: court conviction, institutionalization. Offenses: felonious burglary, assault. Nondel: school records | Age, IQ, SES | Kohlberg, interview, 4 dilemmas, issue scoring, not blind. Score: MMS. Del stages: approximately 2–3 as average | Delinquency and MMS (ANOVA): $p < .05$. | + |
| | | | | | Delinquency and percentage of stage usage: Stages 2 vs. 3 and higher ($p < .05$); Stage 4 vs. lower ($p < .05$) | + |
| Study 3[c] | 13 del, 13 nondel; mean ages 15.5 and 14.9 (Scotland) | Del: probation, institutionalization. Nondel: in institution because home was unfit | Age, race, SES | Kohlberg, interview, 9 dilemmas, global scoring, blind. Score: MMS. Del stages: 2 as average | Delinquency and MMS (ANOVA): $p < .05$. | + |
| | | | | | Delinquency and Stages 1 and 2 vs. 3 and 4: $p < .10$ | 0 |
| Study 4[c] | 8 del, 10 nondel; ages 12–13. 7 del, 10 nondel; age approximately 15 (England) | Del: institutionalization. Offenses: larceny. Nondel: NI | Age, IQ, SES | Kohlberg, interview, 9 dilemmas, sentence scoring, blind. Scores: MMS, percentage of stage usage. Del stages: 2 as average | Delinquency and MMS (ANOVA): $p < .05$. | + |
| | | | | | Delinquency and Stages 1 and 2 vs. 3 and 4: $p < .05$ | + |

*Note.* del = delinquent; nondel = nondelinquent; NI = no information was provided; SES = socioeconomic status; MMS = Moral Maturity Score on Kohlberg's scale; MJ = moral judgment; ANOVA = analysis of variance. All subjects were males. In relation to the hypothesis of a positive relation between moral reasoning and behavior, as interpreted by the investigator: + = support for the hypothesis; 0 = lack of support for the hypothesis; ? = the results are either ambiguous or not directly relevant to the hypothesis.
[a] The variable in parentheses was partialed out.  [b] IQ scores were available only for 5 subjects of the del group.  [c] This study is summarized by Kohlberg & Freundlich (Note 1) without reference to other independent sources.

self-reports (Haan et al., 1968; Haier, 1976; D'Augelli & Cross, 1975; D. A. Schwarz, 1976), and observer ratings (Giraldo, 1972; Krebs & Rosenwald, 1977). It is probably not unfair to say that these are not the most reliable techniques. Although they present, in comparison with laboratory techniques, the advantages of generality and relevance, they may be affected to an unknown degree by the biases of the halo effect, of the temporary context, and of the idiosyncratic interpretations of the variables themselves. Santrock reported a low test–retest reliability, whereas Porteus and Johnson recognized, on the basis of data, that possibly "social visibility, rather than morality, was the major determinant of choice on 'moral' sociometric items" (p. 708). The findings are likely to be more trustworthy, the more objective and specific is the behavior to be reported, as, for instance, being or not being arrested in demonstrations (Haan et al., 1968), using or not using marijuana (Haier, 1976), being or not being virgin (D. A. Schwarz, 1976).

Even more important, in some respects, is the issue of whether and to what extent the behaviors investigated are relevant to mortality and to moral reasoning. This issue is particularly appropriate to the studies in this section. Some of the variables seem to have a prima facie relation to morality. But many others do not, in spite of rationales that connect them to moral reasoning stages. In the latter category should be included organizational participation and political activity (Haan et al., 1968), the ability to be task oriented in group interaction (Forward/Backward dimension from Bales's Adjective Checklist, Bales, 1950), high dominance or sharing of power (Upward/Downward dimension from Bales's Adjective Checklist), the smoking of marijuana (Haier, 1976), the frequency and adventurousness of one's sexual activity (D'Augelli & Cross, 1975; D. A. Schwarz, 1976), and leadership, humor, and gregariousness (Damon, 1977). Of course, all of these behaviors could be relevant to morality, if the agent perceives them as relevant; in none of these studies, however, were subjects' perceptions assessed and reported. One of the problems with these techniques is the relative ease by which they are constructed, administered,

and scored. As a result, it seems, variables are added for purely exploratory purposes or, in any event, without a theoretically solid hypothesis.

With two exceptions (Damon, 1977, who used his own measure; Porteus & Johnson 1965, who used Piagetian-like stories of their construction), all of the researchers resorted to Kohlberg's interview as a measure of moral reasoning. This would offer a welcomed basis for comparing data, if it were not for the well-known lack of standardization of Kohlberg's instrument. In addition, one study reported some problems in scorer reliability (Haier, 1976), and another (D. A. Schwarz 1976) followed the unorthodox procedure of grouping Stage 2 with Stage 5 subjects. Even more seriously, one may wonder at times (e.g. Harris et al., 1976; Porteus & Johnson, 1965; Santrock, 1975) whether the samples offered the minimal range of moral reasoning stages that are required to test the present hypothesis.

The findings, summarized in Table 2, present a confusing picture. Six of the studies (D'Augelli & Cross, 1975; Giraldo, 1972; Haan et al., 1968; Kohlberg, 1958; Krebs & Rosenwald, 1977; Harkness et al., Note 3) reported overall significant relations between moral reasoning and behaviors, three yielded negative data (Haier, 1976; Porteus & Johnson, 1965; Santrock, 1975), and the remaining three mixed results. Moreover, the picture is not clarified by grouping the findings on the basis of the techniques used for behavioral assessment or in terms of the moral face validity of the behaviors. Clearly, apart from the validity of the hypothesis that relates moral reasoning and moral action, the findings have been determined by a number of factors: the far too global and approximate rationale underlying specific hypotheses, the inappropriate selection of the behavioral domain, and the reliance on economical but unreliable techniques.

What can one say of the statistically significant relations found between stages of moral reasoning and behaviors that at least on the surface do not seem moral in nature? In my opinion, they do not help us to determine the psychological relations between reasoning and action but raise instead new questions that concern, specifically, the relations etween moral development and personality evelopment and the respective roles that ioral reasoning and personality traits have i moral behavior. Let us use as an example ne of Bales's dimensions, the Positive/Negaive scale, described as the tendency to be riendly, sociable, interested in group interctions at one pole and, at the other pole, to e unfriendly, disagreeable, self-centered, deached, and negativistic. It is possible that hese behaviors are viewed by an individual s moral and are related to the individual's nderstanding of morality; in this case, one hould expect a noticeable change when the ndividual moves from one stage to a quali- atively different stage. But it is also possible hat these behaviors are a result of person- lity characteristics, noncognitive and perhaps ondevelopmental in nature. In this case, one ould wonder to what extent a natural ten- ency to friendliness affects the development f moral reasoning, and one should not expect ramatic change in group behavior, even when ioral reasoning development has occurred. inally, it is possible that such group inter- ctions are developmental in nature and de- end on massive personality restructuring, oth cognitive and affective, rather than on he narrower cognitive restructuring of moral riteria. Of course, we do not know which is he case, and, moreover, we will not find out f research is not specifically tailored to pre- ise models.

## *Ioral Reasoning and Honesty*

This section examines a group of studies hat attempted to relate some measure of ioral reasoning to honest behavior in labora- ory situations. With the exception of report- ig another person's misbehavior (Arndt, 976; McLaughlin & Stephens, 1974; Rapp, 976), all of the concrete behaviors investi- ated fall under the traditional category of esistance to temptation. As it has been al- eady pointed out, whether resisting tempta- ion is relevant to morality depends on the inds of temptation. In the studies reviewed ere, these were taking candy, not returning he money that was found, touching a for- idden toy, and in each case one form or an- ther of cheating. This research paradigm frequently relies on a presumption that temp- tation has occurred rather than on indepen- dent evidence.

The general hypothesis is that the more mature is one's moral reasoning, the less one will cheat. Although the hypothesis is clear enough, its rationale is much less so. For instance, it is difficult to establish a logical relation between the Piagetian concepts of moral realism or of immanent justice and the inability to resist temptation, except that both characteristics should be outgrown with age. The investigators were apparently assuming a structural consistency among all moral as- pects, such that development in one should be accompanied by development in the others. The problems with this assumption were dis- cussed earlier. Once one shifts the focus from structural consistency to functional articula- tions, the plausibility of each relation must be explicitly argued. The hypothesis is clearer from the viewpoint of Kohlberg's stages, but even then there are difficulties in finding clear rationales. A Stage 2 individual should not want to cheat for fear of being caught; a Stage 3 person should not want to cheat because of social norms and expectations and because of an internalized desire to conform; a more mature person should not want to cheat because of the need for maintaining reciprocal trust, which is the foundation of a viable society. If the experimental manipula- tion is effective in eliminating the fear of being caught, a result that an experienced investi- gator will not readily assume, one ought to be able to obtain different behaviors in Kohl- berg's preconventional individuals and in the others. But questions still remain: Should postconventional people (again, according to Kohlberg's schema) cheat less than the con- ventionals? Is the relation between moral reasoning and resistance to cheating mono- tonic? If so, is it because of the influence of moral reasoning on behavior or because of other developmental processes, also associated with moral reasoning? If gathering clear theo- retical support about this hypothesis is diffi- cult, it is even more difficult when other behaviors (e.g., telling on somebody else's misbehavior or not touching a forbidden toy) are considered. I am fully sympathetic with Arndt's (1976) comment, if not with his

Table 2
*Studies That Related Moral Reasoning and Real-Life Behaviors*

| Study | Subjects | Measure of behavior | Measure of moral judgment | Relation tested[a] | Outcome |
|---|---|---|---|---|---|
| Kohlberg (1958) | 34 M; GR 4, 7, 10; LC to UMC | Teacher ratings; 4 variables: obedience, effort, strength of conscience, fair-mindedness | Kohlberg, interview, 9 dilemmas, global scoring. Score: MMS. Stage range: 2–5 | MMS and strength of conscience: $r = .46$, $p < .01$. MMS and fair-mindedness: $r = .45$, $p < .01$. MMS and other variables: ns | + + 0 0 |
| Porteus & Johnson (1965) | 113 M, 122 F; GR 9 | Sociometric nomination; 4 dimensions: honest, does right even when it harms self, feels bad for doing wrong, takes blame. Score: overall frequency of nominations | 8 Piaget-like stories: immanent justice, moral realism, necessity and efficacy of punishment. Story score: mature/immature. Total score: sum of mature responses | Maturity of MJ and sociometric nominations: ns (for each sex and total sample) ns | 0 |
| Haan, Smith, & Block (1968) | 253 M, 257 F; CS, Peace Corps volunteers | (a) Self-ratings on organizational participation, political activity, social service, protest activity (b) Being arrested in free speech demonstrations | Kohlberg, written, 5 dilemmas, sentence scoring. Score: modal stage ("pure" stages only). Stage range: 2–6 | MJ and organizational participation: curvilinear, conventional level low ($p < .01$). MJ and political activity: curvilinear, conventional level low ($p < .001$). MJ and social service: ns. MJ and political protest: curvilinear, conventional level low ($p < .001$). MJ and political arrest: curvilinear, conventional level low ($p < .001$). | + + 0 + + |
| Giraldo (1972) | 54 M; GR 4–7 | Bales's Interaction Process Analysis; observers' ratings on Upward, Downward, Positive, Negative, Forward, Backward scales | Kohlberg, written, 4 dilemmas, global scoring. Score: MMS. 18 subjects each at preconventional, transitional, conventional levels | MJ and Upward: $r = -.56$, $p < .01$. MJ and Downward: $r = .58$, $p < .01$. MJ and Positive: $r = .32$, $p < .05$. MJ and Negative: ns. MJ and Forward: $r = .69$, $p < .01$. MJ and Backward: $r = -.56$, $p < .01$ | ? ? + 0 + + |
| D'Augelli & Cross (1975) Study 1 | 119 F; CS | Sex Experience Inventory; five behavioral categories forming Guttman scale: neckers, light petters, heavy petters, technical virgins, nonvirgins | Kohlberg, written, 3 standard and 3 sexual dilemmas, global scoring. Score: modal stage. Stage range: 3–5 | MJ and sex experience: curvilinear. Stage 4 low: $F = 6.76$, $p < .01$. Virgins vs. nonvirgins and Stage 4 frequency: $\chi^2 = 11.6$, $p < .005$ | + + |
| Study 2 | 76 nonmarried couples; CS | Revised Sex Experience Inventory, as in Study 1 | Kohlberg, as in Study 1, but based on 4 dilemmas | MJ and sex experience: in M, curvilinear, Stage 4 low: $F = 6.38$, $p < .01$; in F: ns | + 0 |
| D. A. Schwarz (1976) | 140 M, 140 F; CS; MC–UMC | Sex Experience Inventory; 4 levels based on behavioral categories: inexperienced virgins, experienced virgins, traditional nonvirgins, adventurous nonvirgins | (a) Kohlberg, written, 2 dilemmas, issue scoring. Score: modal stage. (b) Sexual Moral Judgment: 2 dilemmas, scored according to Kohlberg's criteria. Stage range: 2–5 | Kohlberg MJ and virgins vs. nonvirgins ($\chi^2$): ns. Sexual MJ and virgins vs. nonvirgins ($\chi^2$): $p < .001$ (major difference between Stages 4 and 5) | 0 + |

Table 2 (*continued*)

| Study | Subjects | Measure of behavior | Measure of moral judgment | Relation tested[a] | Outcome |
|---|---|---|---|---|---|
| Santrock (1975) | 120 M; pre-adolescent; LC, rural/urban | Teacher ratings; 3 factors (10 scales): social conscience, social deviation, sociability | Kohlberg, written, 3 dilemmas, global scoring. Score: for each story major and minor stage; mean of story scores | MJ and teacher ratings on 3 factors (*r*): *ns*. | 0 |
| Haier (1976) | 59 M, 73 F; CS | Use of marijuana. Score: nonuser (never used it) vs. user | Stage range: NI Kohlberg, written, 3 dilemmas, global scoring. Scores: MMS, highest story stage. | MJ and marijuana use: data not reported, "moral reasoning is not related to moral conduct" | 0 |
| Harris, Mussen, & Rutherford (1976) | 33 M; GR 5; LMC–UMC | Sociometric nomination; 2 factors (20 items): honesty, altruism. Score: sum of item scores on each factor | Stage range: 3–5 Kohlberg, interview, 9 dilemmas. sentence scoring. Score: MMS. | MJ and altruism factor (IQ): *r* = .41, *p* < .05. | + |
| Damon (1977) | 15 M + 15 F at each of ages 4, 6, 8, 10; MC | Teacher ratings on leadership, sensitivity, humor, gregariousness, friendliness, generosity | Stage range: NI (a) Hypothetical MJ task: 2 dilemmas, scoring according to age-related levels of distributive justice. (b) Real-life MJ task: reasoning about one actual instance of distribution of rewards; scoring as in (a) | MJ and honesty factor (IQ): *ns* Hypothetical MJ and friendliness: *r* = .24, *p* < .05. Hypothetical MJ and other teacher ratings variables: *ns*. Real-life MJ and all teacher ratings variables: *r* = .21 to .37, *p* < .05 | 0 + <br> 0 <br> + |
| Krebs & Rosenwald (1977) | 31 M and F; ages 17–54 (mean 23); various backgrounds | Return completed tests after having been paid for completing them; trust and need for prompt return were stressed. Score: timely return, late return, or no return | Kohlberg, written, short form, issue scoring. Score: NI. Stage range: 2–5; 83% at 3 and 4 | MJ and degree of honoring the contract: *r* = .49, *p* < .01. Stages 2 and 3 vs. 4 and 5: $x^2$ = 6.90, *p* < .01 | + |
| Harkness, Edwards, & Super (Note 3) | 12 M, adult (Kenya Kipsigis tribe) | (a) 6 elders (moral leaders) and 6 non-elders, matched for age, education, religion, wealth (b) Peer nomination on "the most honest men in village"; all 6 elders, 1 nonelder were nominated | Kohlberg, interview, 3 dilemmas, global scoring. Source MMS. Stage range: 1–3 | MJ and elder status: *t* = 2.83, *p* < .02. MJ and frequency of nominations: *p* = .72, *p* < .01 | + + <br> + |

*Note.* M = male; F = female; GR = grade; LC = lower class; UMC = upper-middle class; MC = middle class; LMC = lower-middle class; MMS = Moral Maturity Score on Kohlberg's scale; *ns* = nonsignificant; MJ = moral judgment; CS = college students; NI = no information was provided. In relation to the hypothesis of a positive relation between moral reasoning and behavior, as interpreted by the investigator: + = support for the hypothesis; 0 = lack of support for the hypothesis; ? = the results are either ambiguous or not directly relevant to the hypothesis.
[a] The variable in parentheses was partialed out.

conclusion, that it is impossible to predict what behavior to expect from each moral reasoning stage.

The findings are briefly reported in Table 3. Simply comparing the number of times the hypothesis of a relation between moral reasoning and moral behavior was supported and the number of times in which it was not would not provide an accurate estimate of the strength of the hypothesis: Among other reasons, the relations tested within each study frequently are not entirely independent of each other. Attempting to determine the gist of the investigations may give us a better estimate. Of the 17 studies, 7 seem to reject the hypothesis (Fenyes, 1967; Grinder, 1964; Linford, 1977; McLaughlin & Stephens, 1974; Medinnus, 1966; Santrock, 1975; Kohlberg, Note 4), 3 give mixed results, supporting the hypothesis for one behavior but not for another, for one measure but not for another of moral reasoning (Arndt, 1976; Nelsen, Grinder, & Biaggio, 1969; Rapp, 1976; Nelsen, Grinder, & Challas, Note 5), and finally, 7 essentially support the hypothesis (Dunivant, 1976; Gallagher, 1975; Harris et al., 1976; La Voie, 1974; S. H. Schwartz et al., 1969; Krebs & Kohlberg, Note 6; Simpson & Graham, Note 7).

This is no more than a rough and even misleading impression. The investigations reported here are not equivalent and frequently not comparable. Different behaviors were assessed and different units of analysis were used. The measures of moral reasoning rely on different theories and different techniques and clearly have different psychometric values. At times, there are also problems of sampling and design. The empirical status of the hypothesis relating moral reasoning and honest behavior can be clarified, to some extent, by a more careful examination of the measures used.

The experimental situations for assessing honesty have some common characteristics: In all of them some incentives to cheat are offered, and the impression is conveyed that it is safe to cheat. Nevertheless, they are far from being equivalent. First, they have a different cheating pull. Krebs and Kohlberg (Note 6), using two individual tasks (Ray-Gun Game and Model-House Game) and

three group tasks (Circles, Squares, a. Blocks Tests), were able to form a Guttm scale of probability to cheat with an accep ble level of reproducibility.

But the behavioral measures are also d ferent in other and more substantive wa Several studies, using more than one cheati task, reported low intercorrelations, thus su porting Hartshorne and May's (1928) cc clusion. Nelsen, Grinder, and Mutterer (196 analyzed six resistance-to-temptation tas (Ray-Gun Game, Magic-Mirror Game, Mu ple-Choice Test, Speed Test, Squares Te and Circles Test) and showed that no mc than 26% of the variance could be account for by either subjects or tasks alone. Nels Grinder, and Biaggio (1969), in an attem to interpret the way the same six behavio measures clustered with each other and wi personality and cognitive measures, differe tiated the type of incentives (e.g., tangib achievement, or competition oriented), t type of skills involved (perceptual–motor academic), the physical characteristics of t situation (e.g., individual vs. group testin These considerations become crucial if t motivational and physical characteristics the tasks relate differently to different se (as seems to be the case in the Nels Grinder, & Biaggio, 1969, study), differe ages, different socioeconomic groups, and d ferent personalities.

One could argue that cheating is cheati regardless of the task and that therefore t very fact that the nature of the task dc make a difference seems to militate agai the major hypothesis examined in this secti But one could also argue that the nature the task may determine whether certain l haviors are defined as cheating by certain pe ple and that, moreover, one's sensitivity the situational context rather than the sup ficial response to each task may have mo meaning and be related to moral reasonir

This is precisely the issue involved in t choice of resistance-to-temptation scor Three types of scores have been used; occ sionally, more than one score was used in t same study. They were (a) complete res tance to cheating versus cheating; (b) degr of cheating, either in one task or summ across tasks; and (c) a consistency scoı

Table 3
*Studies That Related Moral Reasoning and Honesty*

| Study | Subjects | Measure of behavior | Measure of moral judgment | Relation tested[a] | Outcome |
|---|---|---|---|---|---|
| Grinder (1964) | 106 M and F; GR 2, 4, 6 | Ray gun, candy as reward. Scores: complete resistance/yielding; degree of resisting (H, L) | 4 Piaget-like stories about moral realism and immanent justice. Format: written, multiple choice. Score: H, Md, L in moral maturity | Moral realism and complete resistance ($x^2$): ns. Moral realism and degree of resistance: for M, ns; for F, $x^2 = 11.4$, $p < .01$. Immanent justice and complete resistance ($x^2$): ns. Immanent justice and degree of resistance ($x^2$): ns | 0 / 0 + 0 / 0 |
| Kohlberg (Note 4) | 32 M and F; GR 6; WC, MC | Ray gun, badge as reward. Score: never cheated, cheated slightly, cheated frequently | Kohlberg, interview, 6 dilemmas, global scoring. Score: modal stage. Stage range: 1–5 | MJ level and resistance to temptation: $x^2 = 3.48$, ns | 0 |
| Medinnus (1966) | 38 M, 36 F; GR 6; WC | Ray gun, badge as reward. Score: yielding/resisting temptation | One hypothetical dilemma on cheating, written. Score: internalization vs. externalization of control | MJ and resistance to temptation: $x^2 = .01$, ns | 0 |
| Fenyes (1967) | 32 M, 27 F; GR 4; SES heterogeneous | Resistance-to-cheating task, without supervision, prizes as reward[b] | Four MJ measures: (a) intention vs. consequences orientation; (b) external vs. principled orientation, (c) retributive vs. restitutive justice, (d) rule vs. humanistic orientation[b] | From cluster analysis[b]: none of the MJ measures clustered with resistance to temptation. | 0 |
| Nelsen, Grinder, & Challas (Note 5); Nelsen, Grinder, & Biaggio 1969[c] | 45 M, 55 F; GR 6; rural | 6 resistance-to-temptation tasks: ray gun, magic mirror, multiple-choice test, speed test, squares test, circles test. Each task scored on 3-point scale. Total scores: sum across tasks, consistency score | Kohlberg, interview, 4 dilemmas, global scoring. Score: MMS. Stage range: preconventional (50%), conventional[d] | MJ and overall resistance to temptation score: $r = .14$, ns. MJ and consistency score: for M, $r = .37$, $p < .01$; for F, $r = .06$, ns. MJ and consistency score (IQ): for M, $r = .31$, $p < .05$. From factor analysis (14 variables): for M, MJ clustered with consistency and public reward temptation tasks; for M, MJ did not cluster with game-like nor intangible achievement standards temptation tasks; for F, MJ clustered with academic achievement temptation tasks; for F, MJ did not cluster with prolonged temptation and with peeping tasks | 0 / + 0 |
| S. H. Schwartz, Feldman, Brown, & Heingartner (1969) | 35 M; CS | Resistance to temptation: vocabulary test, monetary rewards plus competition with others' scores. Score: cheating/not cheating | Kohlberg, written, 4 dilemmas, global scoring. Score: modal stage. median split. Stage range: 3–6 | MJ and resistance to temptation: $x^2 = 3.64$, $p < .05$ | + |

*(table continued)*

143

Table 3 (*continued*)

| Study | Subjects | Measure of behavior | Measure of moral judgment | Relation tested[a] | Outcome |
|---|---|---|---|---|---|
| La Voie (1974) | 120 M and F; GR 1, 3, 5; MC | Resistance-to-temptation task: play with a forbidden toy. Scores: latency, frequency and duration of forbidden behaviors during 15 min. | (a) 7 Piagetian stories: moral realism (3), expiatory punishment (2), immanent justice (2). Score: 0/1 for each story, sum. (b) Influence on behavior of 4 types of reasons provided by experimenter: intention, consequence, object orientation, person orientation | Total MJ and latency of deviation: $F = 2.82$, $p < .10$. Moral realism and latency: $F = 4.13$, $p < .05$. Moral realism and duration of deviation: $F = 3.27$, $p < .10$.[e] Interaction Total MJ × Object Orientation and Latency: $F = 5.53$, $p < .05$. Interaction Punishment MJ × Focus on Intention × Object Orientation and Duration: $F = 4.39$, $p < .05$ | 0 +  0 + + |
| McLaughlin & Stephens (1974) | 75 retarded, 75 nonretarded; ages 6–10, 10–14, 14–18; stratified SES | 11 honesty tasks: self-control, return found object (2 tasks), return money (2 tasks), tell on other's mishap (4 tasks), cheating by not following rules in speed task, persistence. Score on each task: honest/dishonest | 6 Piagetian measures: lying, retributive justice, punishment, collective responsibility, intentionality, rules of the game. Score: 3- or 4-point scale for each measure | From factor analysis (53 variables): in retarded, MJ and behavior clustered in 1 factor; in nonretarded, MJ and behavior clustered in 2 factors | 0 0 |
| Dunivant (1976) | 122 M, 235 F; CS | Resistance-to-temptation task: vocabulary test, monetary reward, and publicizing of results. Score: degree of cheating | Rest's Defining Issues Test. Score: H, Md, L on principled score | MJ and resistance to temptation: $r = .18$, $p < .05$. | + |
| Gallagher (1975) | 128 M and F; CS; (selected for extreme scores on Hogan's scales) | Resistance-to-temptation task: Quick IQ Test. Score: cheating/not cheating | (a) Kohlberg, written, 4 dilemmas, issue scoring. Score: modal stage. Stage range: 1–6. (b) 4 postexperiment questions about cheating. Score: Kohlberg's criteria | Interaction MJ × Psychosocial Development (Eriksonian) and Resistance to Temptation: in M, *ns*; in F, statistically significant[b] Kohlberg MJ and cheating: $\chi^2 = 14.44$, $p < .01$. Postexperiment MJ and cheating: *ns* | 0 + +  0 |
| Rapp (1976) | 15 M, 15 F; retarded, at each of ages 6–9, 10–14, 14–18 | 5 honesty tasks: (a) do not take candy, (b) do not play with forbidden toy, (c) return lost money, (d) tell on other's mishap, (e) cheating by not following rules in speed task. Score on each task: honest/dishonest | 5 Kohlberg-like stories, similar to experimental tasks. Score on each story: 3-point scale, from irrelevant to mature moral response | MJ and corresponding behavior: on task (a): $r = .19$, $p < .05$; on task (b): $r = .12$, *ns*; on task (c): $r = .01$, *ns*; on task (d): $r = .31$, $p < .002$; on task (e): $r = .17$, $p < .05$ | + 0 0 + + |
| Santrock (1975) | 120 M; preadolescent; LC; rural/urban | 3 resistance-to-temptation tasks: ray gun, word definition test, dynamometer (trophy as reward). Scoring: cheating/not cheating on each task, sum of task scores | Kohlberg, written, 3 dilemmas, global scoring. Score: major and minor stage for each story, mean of story scores. Stage range: NI | MJ and resistance to temptation (r for each task or overall): *ns* | 0 |

Table 3 (continued)

| Study | Subjects | Measure of behavior | Measure of moral judgment | Relation tested[a] | Outcome |
|---|---|---|---|---|---|
| Arndt (1976) | 45 M; ages 13–17 | Opportunity to cheat in test-like situation after witnessing cheating and discussion about it. Scores: (a) cheating/not cheating. (b) reluctance to report cheater (5-point scale), (c) report cheater before or after the experimental manipulation was revealed | (a) Kohlberg, interview, 4 dilemmas, issue scoring. Score: major and minor stage. Stage range: 2–4. (b) Reasoning about cheating, after the experimental task. Score: Kohlberg's criteria | MJ (measures [a] and [b]) and resistance to temptation: ns. / Kohlberg MJ and behavioral measure (b): $r = -.26$, $p < .10$. / Kohlberg MJ and behavioral measure (c) ($t$ test): $p < .01$. / Cheating MJ and behavioral measure (b): $p < .02$ | 0 / 0 / + / + |
| Harris, Mussen, Rutherford (1976) | 33 M; GR 5; LMC–UMC | 2 resistance-to-temptation tasks: word definition test; arithmetic test. Score: cheating/not cheating | Kohlberg, interview, 9 dilemmas. Score: MMS. Stage range: NI | MJ and resistance to temptation: $r = .45$, $p < .05$. / MJ and resistance to temptation (IQ): $r = .27$, $p < .08$. | + / +  0 |
| Linford (1977) | 67 M; GR 12; WC | Resistance-to-temptation task: Mental Measurement Test; two conditions: (a) clear norm, supervision; (b) competitive cues, lack of supervision | Kohlberg, written, 3 dilemmas, scoring NI. Score: major and minor stage. Stage range: mostly 2 and 3 | MJ and resistance to temptation (under both conditions): $r = .15$, ns. | 0 |
| Krebs & Kohlberg (Note 6) | 123 M and F; GR 6; WC, UMC | Resistance-to-temptation task: (a) 2 individual tasks: ray gun, model-house game; (b) 2 group tasks: circles, squares, blocks. | (a) Kohlberg, interview, 5 dilemmas, global scoring. Score: modal stage. Stage range: 1–5 (b) MJ about cheating situation. Score: Kohlberg's criteria | Interaction MJ × Unconscious Cognitive Superego (Holt) and cheating: ns / Principled vs. conventional MJ and complete resistance to cheating: $\chi^2 = 8.65$, $p < .01$. / MJ Stage 4 vs. lower stages and complete resistance to cheating: $\chi^2 = 6.00$, $p < .05$. / MJ Stage 4 vs. lower stages (on Kohlberg) and degree of cheating: $t = 2.00$, $p < .05$. | 0 / + / + / + |
| Simpson & Graham (Note 7) | 302 M and F; ages approximately 11 and 14; WC, MC | 2 resistance-to-temptation tasks: Verbal Test of Intelligence, Test of Creativity. Scores: (a) cheating vs. not cheating. (b) degree of cheating | (a) Modified Kohlberg, 7 dilemmas, global scoring. Score: modal stage. MMS. Stage range: 1–4 (b) Cheating dilemma. Score: Kohlberg's criteria | Interaction Kohlberg MJ × Attention and Cheating (inverse effect of attention): $p < .05$. / Interaction Kohlberg MJ × IQ and Cheating (inverse effect of IQ): $p < .05$ / Kohlberg MJ stage and complete resistance to temptation: $\chi^2 = 11.3$, $p < .02$. / Kohlberg MJ (either score) and degree of cheating: $r = -.14$ to $-.21$, ns. / Cheating MJ and complete resistance to temptation: $r = .05$, ns | + / + / + / 0 / 0 |

Note. M = male; F = female; GR = grade; H = high; L = low; Md = medium; ns = nonsignificant; WC = working class; MC = middle class; LC = lower class; LMC = lower-middle class; UMC = upper-middle class; MJ = moral judgment; SES = socioeconomic status; MMS = Moral Maturity Score on Kohlberg's scale; CS = college students; NI = no information was provided. In relation to the hypothesis of a positive relation between moral reasoning and behavior, as interpreted by the investigator: 0 = lack of support for the hypothesis; + = support for the hypothesis.

[a] The variable in parentheses was partialed out. [b] More detailed information was not reported. [c] This study reanalyzes the same data reported in Nelsen, Grinder, & Challas (Note 5); [d] Kohlberg's interview was administered approximately 1 year later. [e] The investigator accepted $p < .10$ as statistically significant. [f] Clusters varied according to groups and to testing phases.

Table 4
*Outcome of Honesty Studies in Relation
to Moral Reasoning Measures*

| | Moral reasoning measure | | | |
|---------|-----------|----------|--------|-------|
| Outcome | Piagetian | Kohlberg | Ad hoc | Total |
| Positive | 1 | 6 | 1 | 8 |
| Mixed | — | 2 | 1 | 3 |
| Negative | 3 | 3 | 5 | 11 |
| Total | 4 | 11 | 7 | 22 |

*Note.* The sum of the frequencies (22) is higher than the number of studies (17) because some studies used more than one type of measure.

which was expressed by the variance of task scores in Nelsen, Grinder, and Biaggio (1969) and Nelsen, Grinder, and Chalas (Note 5). Krebs and Kohlberg (Note 6) argued that the appropriate analysis should be based on the contrast between complete resistance to temptation and any degree of yielding to it, since "the moral factor . . . implies a qualitative moral decision to cheat or not to cheat" (p. 13). Decisions to cheat a little or to cheat in some of the tasks and not in others are determined by nonmoral considerations. In my opinion, this may be true for various degrees of dishonesty in any simple task but not necessarily for different behaviors in different tasks, unless one assumes that the meaning of each task is objectively determined. There is a noncalculating, nonpragmatic inconsistency that is the norm of moral life, as there is a kind of consistency that is the norm of immoral life. Only four of the studies reviewed here either resorted to a consistency score or contrasted subjects who never cheated across several tasks with those who cheated at least occasionally (Harris et al., 1976; Nelsen, Grinder, & Challas, Note 5; Krebs & Kohlberg, Note 6; Simpson & Graham, Note 7). Of these, three studies used both a qualitative and a quantitative score. (The exception is Harris et al., 1976.) The findings indicate that consistency scores offer indeed a clearer and more discriminative way of investigating the effect of moral reasoning on behavioral honesty.

In accounting for the diversity of the findings, the measures of moral reasoning are even more useful than the methods for assessing resistance to temptation. Moral reasoning measures used in these studies could be grouped in three categories: (a) The first attempted to tap a general structure of moral reasoning according to one or more of the Piagetian constructs (moral realism, immanent justice, etc.), using either the clinical interview or an objective format; (b) the second, also aiming at a general structure of thinking, included Kohlberg's scale and Rest's (1976) objective adaptation of it; and (c) the third category consisted of ad hoc measures (i.e., of measures specifically constructed for one investigation). In these the investigator typically obtained a sample of reasoning about behaviors similar to those required by the practical tasks; the responses were then analyzed according to Piaget's, Kohlberg's, or other categories. By ordering the findings according to this tripartite division, clear differences appear (see Table 4). Of the 11 studies that used Kohlberg's scheme and measure only three (Linford, 1977; Santrock, 1975; Kohlberg, Note 4) did not report a statistically significant relation between moral judgment and honesty in behavior. Of the 11 relations in which moral reasoning was either assessed by ad hoc measures or was analyzed according to Piaget's schema, 8 were not significant, and only 2 supported the hypothesis. Five studies resorted to both a general and an ad hoc measure of moral reasoning. Of these 1 reported negative findings, and another reported positive findings on both measures; the remaining 3 reported positive findings only with the general, Kohlberg-based measure.

In the absence of further evidence, these differences can be explained in terms of the psychometric characteristics of the instruments rather than in terms of the underlying theories. The Piagetian type of measures shared with the ad hoc measures one and frequently several of the following characteristics: They had been constructed by the investigator for the specific study, they frequently consisted of one item, and they relied on an objective multiple-choice format. By contrast, the investigators who chose Kohlberg's scale used between three and seven dilemmas and resorted in each to a series of standard probes. As a result, in spite of important variations f administration and scoring, they were probably able to obtain rich and differentiated information to which the same stage criteria could be applied. Interrater agreement does not seem to be an important difference between the two groups of instruments. Much more important are the single-item characteristic and the fact that an ad hoc constructed measure and coding system may not be able to differentiate relevant from nonrelevant information. Many investigators in this area do not seem to have internalized the basic psychometric principles of the interaction between psychological construct and test medium and thus of the essential variability of subject responses.

When these considerations concerning the measure of moral reasoning and the assessment of honesty are taken into account, it is not unreasonable to conclude that the hypothesis of a significant positive relation between level of moral thinking and resistance to temptation is supported. Frequently, however, even when statistically significant, the relations are low, which suggests that moral reasoning is not the only determinant of moral behavior in the area of honesty. It should be expected that other factors, alone or in interaction with moral judgment, are important. One factor that was consistently found to be related to honest behavior is intelligence. But the results were either negative or inconclusive for many of the variables studied, for example, the exposure to different types of moral reasoning (Arndt, 1976; La Voie, 1974), the degree of temptation, and a measure of "unconscious cognitive superego" (Linford, 1977), an Eriksonian measure of psychosocial development (Dunivant, 1976). As reported earlier, Nelsen, Grinder, and Biaggio (1969) indicated that some temptation tasks cluster with moral reasoning but that others do not and that the tasks interacting with moral stage may be different for different sexes. This finding is interesting for its implications but not clearly understood.

Perhaps more attention should be given to the findings that IQ (Nelsen, Grinder, & Challas, Note 5; Krebs & Kohlberg, Note 6) and the degree of attention (Krebs & Kohlberg, Note 6) interact with moral reasoning

separately and together to produce different behaviors. In the Nelsen, Grinder, and Challas (Note 5) study, an interaction between moral reasoning and IQ was found only for girls: Those high on both measures had the highest consistency scores, whereas those who were high in moral reasoning but low in IQ were the least consistent. Thus a low IQ seems to depress the performance on honesty tasks at higher stages of moral reasoning more than at the lower stages. In Krebs and Kohlberg, the attentional factor and IQ seem to play the same role in interaction with moral reasoning: When attention or IQ are high, there is the highest degree of honesty in Stage 4 children but the lowest in preconventional children. When attention or IQ is low, the honesty of Stage 4 children drops considerably ($p <$ .05), whereas preconventional children have a much higher rate of resistance to temptation. In light of these findings Krebs and Kohlberg consider both IQ and attention to be ego strength factors and suggest that ego strength helps to carry out whatever decisions are derived from one's moral outlook, whether it is high or low. Conscientious children with low ego strength may not be able to behave according to their ideals; on the other hand, pragmatic opportunistic children will use their ego strength to read each situation and to use it for their own advantage. This hypothesis is interesting and deserves careful empirical testing. This hypothesis is functional in nature: Ego strength is undoubtedly a developmental variable but of a different nature than moral reasoning. Finding correlations and interactions, then, is no longer sufficient; the precise articulations should be determined.

## Moral Reasoning and Altruistic Behavior

Kindness, helping one's fellow human beings in their needs, sharing resources with those who lack them, and refraining from hurting others physically and emotionally are behaviors that are most naturally and most universally associated with morality. However, when one analyzes these and similar behaviors more carefully, one realizes that their relation to morality is not always as simple and as direct as it might seem. Although at some abstract level it is always more moral to be kind than to be unkind or cruel, more concretely, it does not follow that it is always better to help than not to help, to share than not to share. These decisions depend on a variety of factors: the genuineness and the urgency of the other's need as well as its relative importance over the agent's needs, the relations of closeness, dependence, or responsibility between the other and the agent, the personal characteristics of the person in need (e.g., his or her pride or arrogance, maliciousness, and, more generally, deservedness of help), and, finally, the possible conflict of altruism with other moral considerations, such as obedience, social expectations, and responsibilities. The important point is that, although each of these considerations can be used to excuse one's selfishness and lack of integrity, they can also be genuinely moral and a part of an overall system of criteria by which a concrete altruistic behavior is evaluated and decided on. In addition to these considerations, the criteria that determine the morality of helping and of sharing may be different at different ages and may follow a developmental understanding of altruistic behavior. The morality of altruism cannot be decided a priori and objectively; the same concrete, physical pattern of action may even be given different labels depending on whether it corresponds to or it conflicts with more general criteria of morality. Thus generosity can become recklessness, helping can become irresponsibility, and compassion cruelty.

The problems in not understanding the ambiguity of "altruism" are clearly manifested in Mussey's (1977) study. One of its aims was to study the degree of congruence between what children say about helping others and what they do. Children's views were gathered by such questions as what people do you help? Which people should you help? Are there people you need not or should not help? Children's behavior consisted of their actual helping or not helping a classmate who had been assigned the task of moving a pile of books from one table to another. To only report on the two extreme age groups, kindergartners said almost exclusively that they help at home and should help their family members, and yet 100% of them did in fact help their classmate.

Eleventh graders said that they mostly help school and should help everyone, and yet only 5% of them helped their classmate to perform his or her task. The investigator concluded that there is a discrepancy between what children say and what they do, that their verbal behavior is grossly in agreement with Piaget or Kohlberg's hypotheses of increasing concern with wider and wider circles of people but that theories based on verbal behavior do not predict actual behavior.

Since Mussey (1977) did not attempt to tap children's reasoning, the parallelism that she establishes between her findings and developmental theories of moral judgment is at best superficial. But even on her own terms one could question the emphasized discrepancy between words and deeds. Kindergartners said almost exclusively that they should help members of their families, but they also said that there is none that they need not help (93%); thus it is not contradictory for them to help their classmates. Eleventh graders said most frequently that they should help everyone, but in 73% of the cases they also said that it is unnecessary or wrong to help people who do not ask, those who are too proud, those who can help themselves, or those who do not help others. The contradiction, then, is not between what they say and do but among their statements. In fact, this contradiction may be simply apparent; older children may be saying that help should not be limited by external categories (such as home, school, etc.) but should be limited by psychological or moral categories. They should help everyone who is morally deserving of help. Whether this was in fact the case and whether from this perspective there still was a contradiction between cognition and behavior cannot be determined. The investigator seems to recognize the possibility of this interpretation: "It may be the case that the absence of helping behavior among 11th graders . . . was in some fashion related to the many qualifying aspects of offering help" (Mussey, 1977, p. 93). She does not recognize, however, that these "qualifying aspects" are precisely those cognitive categories that theories like Piaget's or Kohlberg's emphasize; therefore she does not feel the need to modify her conclusion of the two separate and unrelated bodies of data

It becomes imperative, then, to formulate clear hypotheses concerning the relations between cognitive criteria and altruistic behavior and to select the sample, the cognitive measures, and the behavioral observations that are appropriate to test the hypotheses. Most of the studies reviewed in this section followed this strategy with different degrees of accuracy and success.

The majority of the hypotheses were derived either from Piaget's (1932) or from Kohlberg's (1969, 1976) theory of moral development. For the purpose of bringing out the rationales more clearly, it is useful to break down stage descriptions into their different criterial components. Whether a monotonic relationship between stages and altruistic behavior should be expected will have to be decided subsequently and independently.

The major hypotheses can be summarized as follows:

*Egocentrism.* Children who cannot discriminate their own from others' perspectives will not be able to recognize others' needs when these are in conflict with their own. As a result, one should expect less altruistic behavior in egocentric children but only when there is conflict or competition between needs and desires.

*Moral realism.* This dimension does not seem to be clearly and directly related to altruism. Theoretically, the use of intentions in moral judgments is related to the discrimination on the part of the child of the psychological from the physical, to decentration, and thus to those processes that are themselves directly related to altruism. One should expect children focusing on consequences and not on intentions to be less altruistic, particularly when the consequences are neither physical nor dramatic.

*Authority and rule orientation.* This dimension is more ambiguous than the previous ones. In Piaget's theory, a rigid deference to authority and rules is tied to unilateral respect and thus to egocentrism; it prevents the development of a clear peer orientation, of reciprocity, and therefore of a true sense of fairness and justice. One would expect that authority-oriented children would be less altruistic than those who are less concerned with authority (a) in cases in which altruism conflicts with rules and obedience and (b) in cases in which helping or sharing requires a sense of reciprocity and justice.

Kohlberg's theory distinguishes two different orientations toward authority and rules. The first, which emphasizes punishment, is related to moral realism and in general, to a more egocentric perspective (Stages 0 and 1). The expectations concerning altruism should not be different from those described for Piaget's stage. The second orientation toward rules (Stages 3 and 4) implies a genuine understanding of the moral value of rules and obedience. It is not the contrasting pole of reciprocity and justice, but instead it presupposes the development of role-taking capacities and of idealized reciprocity. Thus, children functioning at this level should be more sensitive to others' needs, even when these conflict with their own, and should be in general more helpful. This sensitivity, however, may be in conflict with other moral considerations that are characteristic of this stage, such as obedience to legitimate authorities and sensible rules, the distribution of roles and tasks, and moral merit. As a result, it becomes difficult to predict the degree and nature of altruistic behavior, especially in noncontrived, real-life situations.

*Equality and equity.* Although Piaget (1932) and Damon (1975) considered these two approaches to justice as having different degrees of maturity along the same developmental sequence, it is impossible to relate them in a general way to different degrees of altruism (e.g., sharing). Whereas children oriented to rigid equality may be expected to follow this orientation in the actual distribution of goods, equity children may appear more or less generous than equality children, depending on the circumstances, such as the age of those involved, their merits, and the psychological consequences. How equality or equity children should behave in situations that do not require distribution of goods or of work (e.g., helping someone in need) is difficult if not impossible to determine.

*Reciprocity.* This is another dimension with a different meaning in Piaget's and in Kohlberg's theories. To Piaget, reciprocity represents the higher of the two moral stages, the contrasting pole of the authority-oriented morality, the necessary basis for fairness and justice.

In Kohlberg's account, reciprocity does not represent any specific stage, but, being synonymous with justice, it is the underlying dimension of all stages, Stage 1 excepted. As a result, there are qualitatively different kinds of reciprocity: Stage 2 is characterized by material reciprocity, by giving to get; Stage 3 and higher stages are characterized by ideal reciprocity and by the golden rule; from Stage 4 reciprocity is seen within a social context and is related to a network of roles. In terms of altruism, one should expect Stage 2 children to be less generous than higher stage children, when the situation offers no prospective of concrete returns. Stage 3 children should be more generous when the situation brings into relief the social norm of helping and promises social approval as reward. It is difficult to think of circumstances in which individuals of more mature stages should necessarily be more generous: An exception may involve help to strangers or under conditions of social disapproval.

It is obvious that whether one follows Piaget's undifferentiated notion of reciprocity or Kohlberg's distinctions may significantly affect the findings. For instance, Dreman and Greenbaum (1973) and Dreman (1976) ordered the reasons for sharing differently from the pattern Kohlberg would have followed: For Kohlberg, emphasis on material reciprocity is developmentally less mature than is emphasis on social norms, whereas for Dreman, as well as for Ugurel-Semin (1952), social norms are assumed to be an earlier concern than reciprocity. From Kohlberg's viewpoint, the negative correlation that Dreman and Greenbaum found between reasons and behavior and the lack of any relation between reasons and age reported in Dreman are not surprising.

*Universal ideals and principles.* Should one expect that people who consider altruism as a universal human value and as having a specieswide application will help more or will be more generous than people who restrict altruism to certain social categories? Will postconventional individuals in Kohlberg's system be more altruistic in action than are conventional individuals? From a logical a priori

viewpoint, the answer may be affirmative on in a general sense, as a lifewide trend. How ever, if one is interested in predicting beha ior in concrete situations, the answer shou depend on whether the situation brings in conflict altruistic beliefs with entrenched co ventions, explicit commands, and restricti and particularistic social expectations.

Probably the most immediate conclusion detailing these expectations concerns the dif culty of formulating, with any degree of pr cision, hypotheses about the relations b tween concrete altruistic behaviors and me sures of moral reasoning. First, the cogniti dimensions listed previously frequently c only offer vague and heavily qualified expe tations. Second, each of these cognitive d mensions is, within a theory, only one aspe of a more general and inclusive stage, perha having various degrees of decalage with o other aspects of the same stage. Finally, stage is part of a sequence in which altruisti related dimensions form a complex networ None of the theories that are presently ava able and that are represented by the mor reasoning scales used in this group of studi has brought the different strands of altruis criteria into a system that is horizontally ( the stage level) coherent and developmenta hierarchical and that allows for precise thou general behavioral predictions in compari stages.

A second conclusion that is derived fro the fragmented and qualified characteristic predicting altruistic behavior from moral re soning is that in this type of research, t heavy burden must be carried by the strat gies for assessing altruism. Usually but n always the investigators have been sensitive this issue. They have tried to circumscribe t meaning of the situations for the subjects t resorting to two methods. Some attempted experimentally characterize the situation bring out certain crucial features, for exampl by contrasting the presence and the absence monetary incentives for helping (Brisse 1977) or by stressing the actual generosity the potential reciprocity of the recipie (Dreman, 1976; Lazarowitz, Stephan, Friedman, 1976). In other studies the mea ing of the situation was clarified by verb instructions and descriptions. Thus, the r ient was a poor child (Rubin & Schneider, 73) or a former mental patient (Brown, 74), competitive interpretations were de-phasized (S. H. Schwartz et al., 1969), or e recipient's generosity was given different tives (Lazarowitz et al., 1976). To what tent these manipulations were successful in oducing the desired perception, which of ese two strategies is more appropriate in neral or for specific cases, are questions at cannot be answered with the data at nd. Probably there is no guarantee that any nipulation will produce precisely the effect at the experimenter has in mind. For in-nce, one could argue that even if S. H. hwartz et al. were successful in eliminating competitive spirit and the social expectation help, their subjects might have been in-ited from helping by the personal chal-ge and the competitive spirit imbedded in e task. Of course, a third strategy would nsist of asking the participants how they rceived the situation. This was never done the studies reviewed here, perhaps because the difficulty of grouping the data in neat tegories.

In terms of the concrete behaviors investi-ted, helping and sharing were the most quent ones; other behaviors were distribu-e justice, reciprocity, and gratuitous ag-ession. Although these behaviors can all be ouped under the category of altruism or osocial action, they are obviously different. eir difference can even be dramatized by at seem to be small experimental manipula-ns. For instance, the traditional candies to shared were at times simply given by the perimenter, like manna from heaven, for no son at all; at other times, they were won in game. Can we assume that this variation is elevant to the child's moral decision? If e views altruism from the standpoint of stice, the two conditions cannot be consid-d to be equivalent. A more appropriate swer is that we do not know, precisely be-se we do not have an articulated psycho-gical theory of altruism within the larger main of morality. The same point will also made in relation to the techniques for sessing moral judgment.

As is demonstrated in Table 5, many of the oral reasoning measures used here are not

different from those resorted to in other areas. Piaget's own stories, Kohlberg's scale, and measures derived from or inspired by Piaget's or Kohlberg's theories (e.g., Damon, 1975; Lee, 1971; Rest's Defining Issues Test) were by far the most frequently used instruments. These measures, in spite of their inadequacies, present a reasonable degree of standardiza-tion and reliability. At times, however, moral reasoning was exclusively assessed by ad hoc measures. In these cases, as it has been al-ready suggested in other contexts, one may question the reliability and the degree of gen-erality of the information. Mussey (1977) is the only research reported here in which children's reasoning was not directly elicited. As explained earlier, it was included because one of the questions uncovered some of the more basic criteria.

Those studies that relied on role-taking measures as the only assessment of reasoning were not included in this review. Although the concept of role-taking is intimately tied to moral reasoning, especially to its prosocial aspect, a recent review of the literature cov-ered those investigations relating role-taking and behavior (Kurdek, 1978) and justifies the decision to focus exclusively on moral judgment. Incidentally, Kurdek concluded his review by pointing out the inconsistency of the findings and his inability to detect a clear pattern, even when the results were organized according to the type of measures used.

The measures of moral reasoning in the present group of studies could be grouped according to their degree of generality. At one extreme there is reasoning about the specific behavior elicited by the experimental task; at the other there are attempts to assess the basic structures of moral cognition (e.g., Kohlberg's scale). In the middle are the at-tempts to assess reasoning about prosocial morality (e.g., Lee's measure) or about posi-tive justice (e.g., Damon's distributive jus-tice tasks). At times the assumption seems to be made that there is no general morality structure and that positive and negative moralities may develop in a partially inde-pendent fashion (see Damon, 1977). Whether one accepts this assumption or not, for the purpose of studying the parallelism between reasoning and action, more specific cognitive

(text continues on page 34)

Table 5
Studies That Related Moral Reasoning and Altruistic Behavior

| Study | Subjects | Measure of altruism | Measure of moral judgment | Relation tested[a] | Outcome |
|---|---|---|---|---|---|
| Wright (1942a) | 31[b] M and F; GR 3; MC | 4 opportunities to give attractive toy to friend or to stranger rather than to self. Score: 5-point frequency scale of generosity | (a) Reasons for preferring friend to stranger or vice versa (after the actual choice).[c] (b) Expectation of peers' generosity (4 questions). Score: 5-point frequency scale of expected generosity | Preferring stranger (associated with higher generosity) is accompanied by less egocentric reasons than preferring friend.[d] <br> Expectation of generosity (in nonconflict situation) and own generosity: $r = .59$ to $.89$, $p < .01$. <br> Expectation of generosity is higher in conflict than in nonconflict situation (l): $p < .02$ | + <br><br> + <br><br> ? |
| Wright (1942b) | 72 M and F; ages 8 and 11 | Sharing 4 attractive and 4 unattractive toys with peer. Score: generous, fair, selfish distribution | Hypothetical situation and reasoning involving distribution of toys[d] | Reasons for sharing and actual sharing: difference in behavior is coordinated with the ideology[d] | + |
| S. H. Schwartz, Feldman, Brown, & Heingartner (1969) | 25 M; CS | Complete a puzzle in noncompetitive group situation, monetary reward; 5 steps of pressure to help peer in this task. Score: median split in frequency of verbal help | Kohlberg, written, 4 dilemmas, global scoring. Score: modal stage, median split. Stage range: 3–6 | H vs. L in MJ and help: $\chi^2 = 40$, $ns$. Principled[e] vs. conventional MJ and help: $p < .02$ | 0 <br> + |
| Rubin & Schneider (1973) | 27 M, 28 F; age approximately 7; LMC | (a) Sharing candy with "poor children." Score: $N$ of candies donated. (b) Helping younger child finish his or her task. Score: amount of help | (a) Lee's measure: 3 authority vs. altruism, 3 peer vs. altruism dilemmas; stories coded according to Lee's 5 levels. Score: sum of story scores. Stage range: NI. (b) Glucksberg, Krauss, & Weisberg's (1966) communicative egocentrism | MJ and sharing: $r = .31$, $p < .05$. (MA) $r = .29$, $p < .05$. MJ and help: $r = .40$, $p < .01$. (MA) $r = .57$, $p < .01$. Egocentrism and sharing: $r = .31$, $p < .05$. (MA) $r = .29$, $p < .05$. Egocentrism and help: $r = .44$, $p < .01$. (MA) $r = .64$, $p < .01$ | + + + + + + + + |
| Dreman & Greenbaum (1973) | 20 M, 20 F; MC Israeli West European; 20 M, 20 F; MC Israeli Middle Eastern; 20 M, 20 F; LMC Israeli; GR K | Sharing odd number of candies. Two conditions: anonymous, reciprocity. Score: $N$ of candies donated | Reasons for sharing (after sharing 4 categories in assumed developmental order: empathy, social norm, in-group, reciprocity | Reasons for sharing[f] and generosity: $r = -.32$, $p < .01$. | – |

## Table 5 (continued)

| Study | Subjects | Measure of altruism | Measure of moral judgment | Relation tested[a] | Outcome |
|---|---|---|---|---|---|
| Anchor & Cross (1974) | 76 M, psychiatric patients; 38 M; CS; ages 18-30 | Modified Prisoner's Dilemma game; competition de-emphasized, monetary reward. Score: $N$ of aggressive moves (damages to other without gain to self) | Kohlberg, interview, global scoring. Score: MJ level. Stage range: Preconventional to principled | From ANOVA (age, IQ, SES, social desirability): MJ and aggression (total group, patients, CS): $p < .001$. Preconventional vs. principled MJ and aggression: $p < .005$ (total), $p < .001$ (patients,) $p < .025$ (CS). Preconventional vs. conventional MJ and aggression: $p < .025$ (total), $ns$ (patients, CS). Conventional vs. principled MJ and aggression: $p < .005$ (total), $p < .001$ (patients), $ns$ (CS) | + + +o ++oo o |
| Brown (1974) | 104 M, 105 F; CS | Commitment to be in team with and help either a former mental patient or a student stranger. Score: $N$ of hours committed | Kohlberg, written, 5 dilemmas, global scoring. Score: MMS, major and minor stage.[a] Stage range: 2-5 | MJ stages and commitment to help: $ns$. Principled vs. conventional MJ and commitment to help: $ns$. Stage 4 and below vs. higher stages and commitment to help: for M, $ns$; for F, $p < .05$ | o + +o ? |
| Emler & Rushton (1974) | 29 M, 31 F; ages 7-13; WC, LMC | Sharing wins with Save the Children Fund. Two conditions: sympathy (emphasis on poverty), nonsympathy. Score: $N$ of tokens donated | (a) Two Piagetian stories of distributive justice coded according to authority orientation vs. equality vs. equity. Score: sum of story scores, median split. (b) Flavell's 2 Role-Taking tasks. Score: 3-point scale | MJ and generosity (ANOVA): $p < .002$. Role taking and generosity: $ns$. MJ × Condition and Generosity: $ns$ | + o ? |
| Staub (1974) Study 8 | 103 F; ages 18-28 | Helping after hearing tape-recorded distress sounds. 5 experimental conditions varying the definition of the situation and modeling. Score: (a) help vs. no help. (b) 4-point scale of helping steps | Kohlberg, written, $N$ of dilemmas and scoring: NI. Score: modal stage. Stage range: up to 5 | MJ Stage 5 vs. lower stages and frequency of help (in situations with sufficient variation): $\chi^2 = 3.97$, $p < .05$. | + |
| Study 9 | 130 M; CS | Interrupt task to help confederate with severe stomachaches; 3 experimental conditions varying permission to help. 7 scores, including (a) distress reaction. 4-point scale; (b) response to expressed need for medicine, 4-point scale; (c) average help across scores | Kohlberg, written, $N$ of dilemmas and scoring: NI. Score: major and minor stage. Stage range: up to 5 | From ANOVA, interaction MJ (major or minor Stage 5 vs. lower stages) × Experimental condition and score (a): $F = 3.66$; $p < .03$; and score (b): $F = 3.22$, $p < .05$; and score (c): $F = 3.37$, $p < .05$. Correlation between MJ and help (permission condition): score (a): $r = .45$, $p < .01$; score (b): $r = .44$, $p < .01$; score (c): $r = .53$, $p < .001$. Correlation between MJ and score (c) for total group: $r = .25$, $p < .05$ | + + + + + + + |

(table continued)

153

Table 5 (continued)

| Study | Subjects | Measure of altruism | Measure of moral judgment | Relation tested[a] | Outcome |
|---|---|---|---|---|---|
| Santrock (1975) | 120 M; pre-adolescent; LC; rural/urban | Two opportunities of sharing candy: with "friend" and with "orphan." Score: sum of candies donated | Kohlberg, written, 3 dilemmas, global scoring. Score: for each story, major and minor stage: mean of story scores. Stage range: NI | From factor analysis (18 measures) MJ and generosity did not cluster[d] | 0 |
| Andreason (1976) | 20 M, 30 F; CS | Helping experimenter to find contact lenses, different degrees of pressure to help via intercom. Score: help (before explicit request)/no help, latency time | Rest's Defining Issues Test. Score: H, Md, L on principled score. Stage range: NI | MJ and helping latency time: $r = -.49$, $p < .01$. MJ and helping before explicit request: $x^2 = 6.10$, $p < .05$ | +<br>+ |
| Dreman (1976) | 180 M and F; GR 1, 4, 7; MC | Sharing candy won at a drawing; 6 conditions varying subject's anonymity and the recipient's generosity. Score: N of candies donated | (a) 3 intentionality stories. Score: H/L (H = 3 mature responses). (b) Reasons for sharing (after sharing), coded as in Dreman & Greenbaum (1973) | Intentionality and sharing: $r = .40$, $p < .001$. Postexperimental reasons for sharing and sharing: ns. Interaction Intentionality × Recipient's Generosity and Sharing: $p < .018$ | +<br>0<br>+ |
| Lazarowitz, Stephan, & Friedman (1976) | 167 F; CS | Matrix game: "partner" gives more points to subject than subject to self and justifies it with one of 3 levels of reasoning; subject has opportunity to give points to partner. Score: difference between points given to partner and to self | Moral Dilemma Inventory based on Kohlberg. Score: H, Md, L on MMS. Stage range: 2–6 | From ANOVA: MJ and altruism (main effects): ns. Interaction MJ × Level of Partner's Justification: $p < .05$. Md MMS: effect of justification on altruism: $p < .001$. L and H MMS: effect of justification on altruism: ns | 0<br>+<br>+<br>0 |
| Brissett (1977) | 223 M; CS | Volunteer to help graduate student in research on learning disability. Two conditions: public vs. private commitment, with or without monetary reward. Score: yes/no; amount of time volunteered | Rest's Defining Issues Test. Score: (a) dominant stage, (b) highest story stage, (c) H, Md, L in principled score. Stage range: 2 to principled | MJ and volunteering (both scores): ns. Interaction MJ × Context of Commitment or × Reward and Volunteering: ns. Three-way interaction and time volunteered: $p < .02$ | 0<br>0<br>+ |
| Eisenberg (1977) | 125M and F; GR 2, 4, 6, 9, 11, 12; UMC | Donation of 1 hour to participate in dull, unpaid task[d] | Prosocial MJ interview: 4 dilemmas. Coding: 9 orientations, from punishment to strongly internalized values. Score: (a) modal altruistic orientation, (b) modal overall orientation, (c) 5-point scale of altruistic decision | MJ and volunteering: for F, ns; for high school M, $p < .005$. Hedonistic vs. other orientations and volunteering: statistically significant[d] | 0<br>+<br>+ |
| Mussey (1977) | 120 M and F; GR K, 4, 8, 11; MC | Helping peer to carry books. Score: help (at least once)/no help | 7 interview questions: What do you help people to do? Which people should you help? Are there people you don't need to help? Codes for each question | Saying that one helps or should help peer and helping peer: K: 24% vs. 100%; GR 11: 79% vs. 5%,[b] Not using limiting criteria for help and helping peer: K: 93% vs. 100%; GR 11: 27% vs. 5%,[b,i] | −<br>+ |

Table 5 (continued)

| Study | Subjects | Measure of altruism | Measure of moral judgment | Relation tested[a] | Outcome |
|---|---|---|---|---|---|
| Rosenn (1977) | 16 M, 20 F; GR 2 | Distribution of wins after 4 games with same-sex and same-age partner. Score: what subject kept for self minus the equity amount, H/L | 5 dilemmas, 2 (from Damon) similar to the behavioral situation. Score: (a) stage score according to Damon's criteria. (b) relative vs. strict equity criteria (0/1). (c) deference to authority (0/1) | MJ stage and fair distribution: $r = -.23$, $p < .10$. | 0 |
| | | | | Use of relativistic criteria and fair distribution: $r = .30$, $p < .05$. | + |
| | | | | Deference to authority and fair distribution: $r = .45$, $p < .01$. | + |
| | | | | Stage score does not add to other two scores in predicting fairness[d] | 0 |
| Damon (1977) | 18 M and 18 F at each of ages 4, 6, 8, 10; MC | Situation patterned after hypothetical dilemma: distribution of rewards among younger, poorer child, child who produced the most, "nice child" (self occupies several roles). Score: percentage of candy bars distributed to each participant | Stage range: 1A–1B (a) Hypothetical MJ task: 2 dilemmas; scoring according to 6 age-related levels of distributive justice. (b) Real-life MJ task: reasoning about the actual distribution task; scoring as in (a) | Hypothetical and real-life reasoning stages: $r = .78$; (age) $r = -.26$, $p < .001$. | ? |
| | | | | MJ stages 0A, 0B vs. others and selfish distribution: $p < .001$. | + |
| | | | | Relations between each of other MJ stages and type of distribution: $ns$. | 0 |
| | | | | Interaction MJ stage (1B and above vs. lower ones) X "producing most" position and tendency to give to self: $p < .001$. | + |
| | | | | Interaction MJ stage (0 vs. others) X "nice child" position and giving more to self: $p < .001$ | + |

Note. M = male; F = female; GR = grade; MA = mental age; MC = middle class; LMC = lower-middle class; WC = working class; H = high; L = low; Md = medium; MJ = moral judgment; NI = no information was provided; MA = mental age; K = kindergarten; CS = college students; ANOVA = analysis of variance; ns = nonsignificant; MMS = Moral Maturity Score on Kohlberg's scale. In relation to the hypothesis of a positive relation between moral reasoning and behavior, as interpreted by the investigator: + = support for the hypothesis; ? = the results are either ambiguous or not directly relevant to the hypothesis; 0 = lack of support for the hypothesis; − = the results show an opposite relation.
[a] The variable in parentheses was partialed out. [b] Not all children were involved in every experiment. [c] Thus, different children were asked different questions. [d] Details were not reported.
[e] These subjects were also high on need for affiliation, which was related to help ($p < .01$). [f] These 4-category reasons for sharing were reported in Dreman (1976) not to be related to age and to be a function of situational factors. [g] Very low agreement was reported between experimenter's scores and the scores obtained in Kohlberg's laboratory. [h] Level of significance was not reported. [i] This relation is explicitly formulated by this reviewer; experimenter suggests its plausibility.

measures should be preferred, provided they offer a satisfactory level of reliability. In this context, Damon's (1975) procedure offered perhaps the best opportunity to study not only the functional relations between moral reasoning and moral action but also their breakdown. In it the laboratory situations are closely patterned after the hypothetical dilemmas. Under both conditions the child is asked to make a decision and to manifest his or her reasons, and the same standardized questions and probes are presented under the two modes. The only difference is that in one condition, what the child says has no practical effects, whereas in the other, the child can determine what he or she actually receives and gives.

In terms of the specific dimensions and hypotheses outlined at the beginning of this section, the moral reasoning measures do not offer a clear picture. Sometimes an instrument fits one dimension closely (e.g., the measures of perspective taking or the Piagetian measures of moral realism), but more frequently a scale includes several dimensions, perhaps a different one for each of the stages represented. (This is the case of Lee's, Damon's, Rest's, and Kohlberg's scales.) Stage scores, then, should be communicated and should be used to organize the results. Unfortunately, the too frequent practice of hiding stage scores behind the high/low dichotomy, as it was pointed out earlier, overlooks the curvilinear relations that stages have with each other and seems to gratuitously assume a monotonically increasing relation between moral reasoning and altruistic behavior.

The results are summarized in Table 5. If a global impression of this body of research were to be given, it could be concluded (with the same qualifications emphasized in previous sections) that of 19 studies, 11 offer a clear and unambiguous confirmation of the hypothesis that relates moral cognition and altruistic behavior, 4 present negative results, whereas the remaining 4 studies (Damon, 1977; Eisenberg, 1977; Mussey, 1977; Rosenn, 1977) report mixed or ambiguous indings.[3] Among the studies with mixed results, Eisenberg found the expected relation only for males and Damon only for one moral

reasoning level. Rosenn, although she did not find a clear influence of stage scores on altruism, was able to read her interview data according to certain dimensions that were cognitive-developmental in nature and that were significantly related to the actual distribution of rewards. Mussey's ambiguity is one of interpretation: The investigator herself, relying on the superficial content of the responses, interpreted the data as indicating a functional separation of reasoning and action. As discussed earlier, I read them in the opposite direction.

The studies reporting negative results present, under attentive scrutiny, some serious methodological shortcomings. Brown (1974) had some rater reliability problems about Kohlberg's scale. Dreman and Greenbaum (1973) based their assessment of moral reasoning on only one question and resorted to a category ordering that was later shown to be inadequate (Dreman, 1976). Rosenn (1977), Santrock (1975), and, again, Dreman and Greenbaum used samples that were homogeneous in age and/or in moral reasoning stage. Similar methodological inadequacies, however, exist also in studies with positive findings. These comments are not intended to explain away nondesirable findings but to point out the importance of following a methodology that is consonant with the questions being asked. For instance, it is essential that the sample include a range of stages, presumably those stages that differ significantly in the structures that underlie altruistic behavior.

In the context of this methodological discussion, an observation, perhaps a simple curiosity, may be worth mentioning: All of the studies that resorted to volunteering for an experiment as the measure of helping behavior (Brissett, 1977; Brown, 1974; Eisenberg, 1977) had negative outcomes. Although it may be premature to derive a general con

---

[3] Two studies, Ugurel-Semin (1952) and De Mersseman (1977), were not included in this review because the investigators did not relate information about moral reasoning to information about behavior for each subject. According to the same investigators, however, their data support the cognitive-developmental hypothesis.

clusion, these findings should make the potential researcher wary of selecting this type of indicator.

## Moral Reasoning and Resistance to Conformity

A central characteristic of Kohlberg's developmental schema is the way various modes of moral thinking are defined in relation to conventional morality. At the conventional level the rules and values of one's group, the laws of one's society, and the commands of the legitimate authority are considered to be the basic moral criteria. At the preconventional level moral expectations are not understood as intrinsically valid and are confused with one's self-interest. At the postconventional level the established morality is recognized as derived from more fundamental and universal concerns and thus as providing legitimate and yet limited criteria. Behavioral conformity to public morality and to authorities can therefore be used to test the relations between moral thinking and moral action, at least within the limits of Kohlberg's theory.

It is important, however, to clarify some common misunderstandings. This theory deals with cognitive criteria and not with need for affiliation or other similar motivational variables; it deals with criteria for morality and not with conformity or independence in other domains. One can legitimately expect that preconventional individuals will not conform to socially accepted moral rules when these contrast with their self-interests, if it is safe to do so; one should also expect that postconventional persons will resist the pressure to modify their individually acquired principles in the direction of established norms or will refuse to change their morally determined course of action for the sake of public expectations, deference to authorities, and social acceptance. But it would be inappropriate to hypothesize, at least on the basis of Kohlberg's theory, that preconventional or postconventional individuals have less intense affiliative needs, generally tend to be less conforming, or, when moral issues are involved, will not conform in cases in which social expectations are not

in conflict either with one's self-interests (for the preconventional) or with one's moral principles (for the postconventional).

A number of studies are available that report data on the relations between Kohlberg's moral stages and behavioral conformity. One of these (Haan et al., 1968) has been discussed previously. The dilemma faced by the Berkeley students in this study was either to obey the legitimate campus authority and refrain from striking or to strike, perhaps in response to one's higher moral principles. It will be recalled that a curvilinear relationship was found between the students' moral thinking and their protesting behavior and that preconventional and postconventional students could be differentiated on the basis of their reasons for striking. These results seemed to support Kohlberg's views of moral development as well as the relations between moral judgment and behavior.

This section reviews 11 studies that addressed the same issue, all using an experimental approach and attempting to study behavioral conformity in a laboratory contrived situation. Three of the studies selected the Asch paradigm: Andreason (1976) used as stimuli true–false statements about altruism; the other two studies (Froming, 1977; Saltzstein, Diamond, & Belenky, 1972) focused on general conformity to group pressure rather than specifically on conformity around moral issues. Even more important, resisting conformity when moral principles are involved may follow radically different parameters than resisting conformity in the judgment of objective physical stimuli. The first type of independence seems to require a high degree of confidence in what is internal, individual, and in some sense subjective. It could be argued that distorting objective reality by yielding to social pressures is in itself a moral issue; however, it is difficult to determine a priori how such behavior should fit this or that moral stage.

Five studies, the largest group, resorted to Milgram's (1974) experimental situation or variations of it. According to the traditional script, the participant, having agreed to cooperate in an experiment, is requested by the experimenter-authority to administer severe punishments whenever the confederate-subject fails in his or her learning task. This situation, therefore, seems to provide an ideal opportunity for investigating moral conformity. In fact, there are some problems: Besides the frequently raised ethical issues, Milgram's paradigm presents crucial interpretive ambiguities. As Mixon (1974) cogently pointed out, the subject of this experiment is faced with a number of contradictory cues such that he or she cannot determine unequivocally the meaning of the situation and the investigator cannot determine the meaning of the subject's behavior, whatever it might be.

Rothman (1971) and Turiel and Rothman (1972) introduced important modifications to Milgram's (1974) script, requiring a special brief description. First, the punishment consisted of taking away previously earned money, in place of the traditional electric shocks. Second, the participating children, before initiating their experimental role, observed two adults perform the same task and then argue opposite viewpoints about the morality of continuing in it. It is hard to tell precisely how these elements affected the children's decision to stop or to continue. One could hypothesize that the need for conforming to the experimenter might have been balanced by the adult example; one could also argue that the adult moral reasoning, aside from its specific content, elicited in the children similar processes and the tendency to view the situation in moral terms. Of course, this or a similar facilitating effect should be desirable if the purpose is to study the influence of moral criteria on behavior.

The remaining studies resorted to less standard procedures. Fodor (1971, 1972) exploited, as an indication of conformity, the challenging of the subject's moral decisions and reasoning that are a standard part of Kohlberg's moral interview. McNamee's (1972) study is probably the most creative because it used a situation that is clearly moral in nature and that requires a certain degree of independence from the authority. As the participant was about to begin the experimental session he or she had signed up for, the experimenter was interrupted by a confederate-subject scheduled for the following session who asked for immediate help: The confederate was feeling very ill as a result of psychedelic drugs and did not know what to do or where to go. The participant was thus given an opportunity to help in spite of his or her own previous commitment to the experimenter and in the face of the experimenter's flat refusal to help.

In sum, these studies are different and not immediately comparable; moreover, their precise meaning in relation to the hypotheses presented previously is frequently unclear.

A similar ambiguity is also present when one looks at the independent variable, the measure of moral judgment. Appropriately enough, all of the investigations reviewed here used Kohlberg's scale; the one exception, Andreason (1976), resorted to Rest's Defining Issues Test, which is related to Kohlberg's instrument both theoretically and empirically. However, there is no uniformity among the hypotheses tested. Several studies (Andreason, 1976; Fodor, 1971, 1972; Froming, 1977) either assumed or simply tested a continuous relation between moral reasoning and conformity; others focused on contrasts that do not correspond to the hypothesis of curvilinearity (e.g., preconventionals vs. postconventionals in Podd, 1972; Stage 3 vs. Stage 4 in Rothman, 1971, and in Turiel & Rothman, 1972). Finally, those studies that contrasted the postconventional with the conventional levels (Epstein, 1974; McNamee, 1972; Saltzstein et al., 1972; Kohlberg, Note 4) frequently offered a weak case because of their samples' ages and stages and resorted, at least in part, to a quantitative rather than to a stage analysis.

The findings are reported in Table 6 and can best be summarized by distinguishing two sets of studies: those dealing with resistance to conformity in judgment (e.g., in the Asch situation) and those dealing with independence in action vis-à-vis an authority figure (e.g., in Milgram's situation). Although different from each other, these two types of behavior have one aspect in common: They are not verbal decisions to hypothetical dilemmas; in either case the consistency with modes of moral reasoning cannot be taken for granted but must be established.

The first group of studies (Andreason

1976; Fodor, 1971, 1972; Froming, 1977; Saltzstein et al., 1972) offers a consistent picture; without exception, they indicate a positive relation between moral stage and resistance to conformity. The independence of judgment associated with higher stages may concern moral content but seems to be a more general characteristic. As to the hypothesis of curvilinearity, Saltzstein et al.'s study is the only one to partially support it. The other investigations could not or did not test it.

The picture provided by the second group of studies is both more ambiguous and more complex. The clearest and strongest support for the relation between moral reasoning and independence in moral action is given by McNamee (1972). Findings obtained with Milgram's situation indicate that no simple direct relation exists between stages of moral reasoning and quitting in the task of administering punishments. Differences in behavior between stages do become more pronounced under certain conditions: when the experimenter is present (Epstein, 1974) or when subjects are exposed to the advice to stop (Rothman, 1971; Turiel & Rothman, 1972). Experiencing a feeling of obligation toward the experimenter seemed also to make a difference in behavior (Epstein, 1974). Otherwise, the differences between stages are mostly in the reasons given or the feelings expressed about the same behavior (McNamee, 1972; Podd, 1972; Kohlberg, Note 4). For instance, in Kohlberg the clear demarcation between moral stages was not given by quitting or not quitting but by the presence or absence of the desire to quit. Explanations and feelings, however, were typically gathered at the end of the experiment: It is therefore difficult to determine to what extent they represent genuine feelings and to what extent they indicate rationalizations.

In sum, moral reasoning stages are clearly related to behavioral independence in judgment but less clearly and only under certain circumstances to independence in moral action. These latter findings could be accounted for by the ambiguity of Milgram's situation but may also suggest that this type of independence requires other factors besides certain modes of moral reasoning. Finally, it is fair to say that the hypothesis of curvilinearity has yet to be tested.

## Discussion and Conclusion

The body of research reviewed here seems to offer considerable support for the hypothesis that moral reasoning and moral action are statistically related. This statement, however, should be qualified as soon as one looks at the findings in more detail. Empirical support, in fact, varies from area to area: It is strongest for the hypotheses that moral reasoning differs between delinquents and nondelinquents and that at higher stages of moral reasoning, there is greater resistance to the pressure of conforming one's judgment to others' views. The support is clear but less strong for the hypothesis that higher moral stage individuals tend to be more honest and more altruistic. Finally, there is little support for the expectation that individuals of the postconventional level resist more than others the social pressure to conform in their moral action.

One may reasonably expect to find higher and more consistently significant statistical correlations, once research is designed and executed with more care. Perhaps the most widespread and consequential shortcoming was the lack of an articulated and theoretically clear rationale for establishing certain specific relations. There frequently seemed to be a lack of fitness between the cognitive-developmental hypotheses and the adopted research strategies. Other methodological problems often seemed to be a result of a muddled or simplistic theoretical basis. They concerned the inadequacies of the measures, particularly of the indicators of moral action, the lack of respect in the empirical procedures for the qualitative nature of stages of moral reasoning, and the selection of samples representing either a too narrow or an inappropriate range of stages to test the specific hypotheses.

These problems, at least in part, are endemic to cognitive-developmental theory at its present stage of articulation. For instance, no serious progress can be made in increasing the predictive power of moral reasoning

AUGUSTO BLASI

Table 6
Studies That Related Moral Reasoning and Resistance to Conformity

| Study | Subjects | Measure of resistance to conformity | Measure of moral judgment | Relation tested[a] | Outcome |
|---|---|---|---|---|---|
| Kohlberg (Note 4)[b] | 32 M; CS | Milgram situation. Score: (a) quitting/not quitting, (b) wanting vs. not wanting to quit (from postexperiment question) | Kohlberg, written, 4 dilemmas, global scoring. Score: modal stage; principled score. Stage range: 3–6[c] | MJ and quitting: ns. MJ and wanting to quit: $p < .01$ (principled scores), $p < .05$ (stage scores). | 0<br>+ |
| Rothman (1971) | 144 M; GR 7, 8, 9 | Milgram-like situation; 4 conditions: (a) exposure to 2 models without reasoning, (b) exposure to 2 models reasoning at Stages +1 or −1, (c) exposure to a quitting model without reasoning, (d) exposure to a quitting model reasoning at Stage +1. Score: quitting/not quitting | (a) Kohlberg, interview, 6 dilemmas, sentence scoring. Score: profile of stage usage, modal stage. Stage range: 3–4. (b) Hypothetical dilemmas replicating experimental conditions (a) and (b). Score: as in (a) | Principled vs. conventional MJ and wanting to quit: 93% vs. 45%[c]. MJ and quitting in conditions (a) and (c) ns. MJ and quitting in condition (b). MJ and quitting in condition (d) | +<br>0<br>++<br>++ |
| Fodor (1971) | 25 M, B; 25 M, W; ages 14–17 | Attempts at changing subject's moral decision during Kohlberg's interview. Score: yielder (changing at least once) vs. resister | Kohlberg, interview, 9 dilemmas, global scoring. Score: MMS. Stage range: 2–4 | MJ and resisting conformity: $t = 3.42$, $p < .01$[d] | + |
| Fodor (1972) | 40 M del; ages 14–17 | As in Fodor (1971) | As in Fodor (1971). Stage range: 2–3 | MJ and resisting conformity: $t = 2.40$, $p < .05$[d] | + |
| McNamee (1972) | 47 M, 55 F; CS; MC; 22 political activists | Opportunity to help a confederate complaining of serious symptoms while experimenter is annoyed and refuses to help. Score: help vs. no help, type of help | Kohlberg, interview, 4 dilemmas, global scoring. Score: modal stage. Stage range: 2–6 | MJ and helping: $F = 19.4$, $p < .01$. Helping increases monotonically by stage. Principled ($N = 6$) vs. other MJ stages and personal help: 100% vs. 0% | +++ |
| Podd (1972) | 112 M; CS; MC | Milgram situation. Score: maximum shock intensity administered | (a) Kohlberg, interview, 4 dilemmas, scoring developed by experimenter. Score: MJ level. Stage range: Preconventional to principled level. (b) Reasons about behavior during the experiment | Preconventional vs. principled MJ and shock intensity: ns. MJ and reasons given for quitting: $\chi^2 = 5.99$, $p < .05$ | 0<br>? |
| Saltzstein, Diamond, & Belenky (1972) | 37 M, 26 F; GR 7; UMC | Modified Asch experiment: groups of 6; judging length of strips; 2 conditions: prize for correctness to individual or to group. Score: conforming (at least once)/not conforming | (a) Kohlberg, interview, 4 dilemmas, global scoring. Score: modal stage. Subjects grouped in Stages 1–2, 3, 4–5. (b) Postexperimental questions about the group's right to individual conformity | MJ and conformity: curvilinear, Stage 3 high: $p < .02$. Belief in group's right to conformity and conformity: for M, Stages 1–2 is least consistent, $p < .01$; for F, Stage 3 is most consistent, $p < .10$ | +<br>?<br>? |

Table 6 (continued)

| Study | Subjects | Measure of resistance to conformity | Measure of moral judgment | Relation tested[a] | Outcome |
|---|---|---|---|---|---|
| Turiel & Rothman (1972) | 43 M; GR 7, 8; UMC | Approximately as in Rothman (1971), condition (b) | (a) As in Rothman (1971). Stage range: 2–4. (b) Postexperimental questions concerning subject's decisions and the model's advice | Stage 4 vs. lower MJ stages and following advice to quit: $p < .001$. Stage 4 vs. lower MJ stages and following +1 advice: $p < .01$. MJ Stage 4 vs. Stage 3 and consistency between evaluation of advice and behavior: $p < .08$ | +<br>?<br>0 |
| Epstein (1974) | 78 M; CS | Role-played Milgram situation; 2 conditions: Experimenter present vs. experimenter absent. Score: maximum shock intensity administered (H, Md, L). | (a) Kohlberg, written, 5 dilemmas. Score: conventional vs. principled (b) Postexperimental questions about victim's rights and subject's obligation to experimenter | MJ and intensity of shock: $ns$. MJ and intensity of shock: experimenter present: $p < .10$. Concern for victim's rights and intensity of shock: $ns$. Obligation to experimenter and intensity of shock: $p < .001$. MJ and conformity: $r = -.36$, $p < .01$ | 0<br>0<br><br>0<br><br>+<br><br>+ |
| Andreason (1976) | 20 M, 20 F; CS | Asch-like experiment: groups of 5, answering 50-item questionnaire (25 about altruism). Score: median split | Rest's Defining Issues Test. Score: principled score. Stage range: NI | | |
| Froming (1977) | 120 M and F; CS | Asch-like experiment: groups of 3, judgment metronome ticks; 2 conditions: self-aware (in front of mirror) vs. non-self-aware. Score: (a) one-step compliance in one-step discrepancy, (b) one-step compliance in two-step discrepancy, (c) two-step compliance in two-step discrepancy, (d) sum | Kohlberg, written, 5 dilemmas, global scoring. Score: MMS. Stage range: 3–5. | MJ and total compliance (IQ): $p < .08$. MJ and compliance (score [a]): $p < .05$. MJ and compliance (scores [b], [c]): $ns$. Interaction MJ × Self-Awareness × Type of Compliance: some relations were significant | 0<br>+<br>0<br>? |

*Note.* M = male; F = female; CS = college students; MJ = moral judgment; $ns$ = nonsignificant; GR = grade; B = black; W = white; MMS = Moral Maturity Score on Kohlberg's scale; del = delinquent; MC = middle class; UMC = upper-middle class; H = high; Md = medium; L = low; NI = no information was provided. In relation to the hypothesis of a positive relation between moral reasoning and behavior, as interpreted by the investigator: + = support for the hypothesis; ? = the results are either ambiguous or not directly relevant to the hypothesis; 0 = lack of support for the hypothesis.

[a] Accounts of this unpublished study are also given in Milgram (1974). [b] When moral reasoning protocols are scored according to the most recent scoring manual, there are no clear-cut principled scores, and the differences, though still significant, tend to decrease. [c] Yielders and resisters were approximately equal in age, race, IQ, and mother's education.

[d] The variable in parentheses was partialled out.

vis-à-vis action until the relations between general moral criteria and the choice of specific alternatives are better understood. It is plausible that prediction can only be improved by including in the equation personality characteristics that are unrelated or only partially related to moral cognitive structures.

Implicit in the last comment is that methodological improvements alone will not resolve the problems. At times, what seemed to be a well-thought-out design yielded inconclusive findings. The fact that different hypotheses gathered various degrees of support does not have any immediately obvious explanation. At other times, positive correlations were found with imperfect measures, with the treatment of moral reasoning measures as continuous, with less than adequate samples, and, most puzzling, with behaviors that do not appear to be specifically moral. The last finding raises the question of how even positive correlations should be interpreted: Could they be an artifact of variables that, although related to the development of moral reasoning, are not themselves moral in nature? From a methodological perspective, it is imperative that investigators control, more systematically than they have been doing, such variables as age, IQ, and cognitive development.

What was not learned in reviewing these studies, the successful as well as the unsuccessful ones, is the psychological meaning of significant statistical correlations between moral reasoning and action. This meaning would not be revealed even if, after improving experimental designs and methods, one were able to predict with a high degree of probability which actions can be expected in diverse situations from individuals of various stages.

A different focus and different questions are needed than those that have been guiding research in this area. The processes that fill the space between a concrete moral judgment and its corresponding action should be determined. One could ask, for instance, in what way a general structure of moral reasoning is applied to a concrete situation to invest it with moral meaning. Do people differ in their readiness to interpret the world in moral terms? What types of motivational forces lead individuals from judgment to action? What kinds of defensive or coping strategies are used to avoid an unpleasant decision that follows from one's moral judgment, or what kinds of strategies are used to keep the consistency between judgment and action, in spite of external or internal interfering factors? Only rarely and indirectly have the studies reported here touched on some of these questions. Probably the closest example is provided by Krebs and Kohlberg (Note 6), who considered IQ and attention as an ego strength factor moderating the relations between moral reasoning and cheating.

The process approach is more congenial with the social learning tradition and has been mostly used by psychologists that persuasion (e.g., Aronfreed and W. Mischel). These efforts, however, in keeping with their theoretical sources, did not take seriously the problem of judgment–action consistency. Parallel observations should be made about those studies that investigated variables such as defensive and coping mechanisms (Haan, 1977; S. H. Schwartz, 1968, 1973, 1977; Sykes & Matza, 1957),[4] the control and management of fantasy (W. Mischel, 1974), the ability to tolerate anxiety and ambiguity (Frenkel-Brunswik, 1949; Harrington, Block, & Block, 1978). Even though these variables are potentially useful for understanding the processes that bridge moral reasoning and moral action, they were not studied for the purpose of clarifying this question.

What appears to be needed is an explicit and direct focus on the psychological nature of integrity or of personal consistency, that is, on the processes and skills involved in the capacity to invest one's life with the meanings that are personally understood and accepted and to act in ways that are consistent

---

[4] Haan's (1978) study addresses more directly than any other investigation known to this author the issues presented here. Her study appeared in print after the present article had been submitted for publication; it was therefore impossible to comment on it in a way that would do justice to it complexity. Haan's approach and findings, however seem to agree with the overall thrust of this discussion.

with one's normal insights. These issues not only seem important, at least from a commonsense viewpoint, but should be a natural part of a theory that emphasizes cognitive structures. And yet, as the series of studies reported here testify, cognitive-developmental theory has completely neglected them. Perhaps avoidance rather than neglect or even deeper incompatibilities are operating here.

A reasonable explanation for this neglect is the overwhelming influence that Piaget's rationalistic views of human nature and of human functioning have had on cognitive-developmental theory as a whole. The term *rationalistic*, having a different meaning here than *cognitive* or even *rational*, refers specifically to two central characteristics of Piaget's overall philosophy. The first is the tendency to study cognitive, including moral reasoning, structures, and cognitive processes as disengaged from their psychological context, as if they were not parts of a more complex organism, the psychological subject, to which in some way they would be subordinated. The second characteristic, related to the first, is the view that other processes are organically and not simply functionally dependent on cognitive processes. Accordingly, affect and cognition are seen as indivisible harmonious aspects of the same reality, whereas action structures are viewed as closely related to cognitive structures. As a result, the lack of consistency between action and cognition simply becomes another instance of logical disequilibrium, to be resolved through the normal reciprocal influence of assimilation and accommodation. From this perspective, the relations between cognition and action are not problematic, and moral personal inconsistency is either a matter of error or an incomprehensible mystery.

Integrity and its failure cannot be studied without taking seriously into account the self and related constructs, such as self-definition, self-organization, self-awareness, and sensitivity to internal inconsistency. There is no reason why processes related to the self could not be integrated with the general principles of cognitive-developmental theory; this integration, however, as necessary as it

appears, cannot be obtained by simply applying or extending familiar ideas and principles but requires a substantial shift in emphasis and a careful rethinking of concepts and relations.

## Reference Notes

1. Kohlberg, L., & Freundlich, D. *Moral judgment in youthful offenders*. Unpublished manuscript, Harvard University, 1977.
2. Kohlberg, L., Kauffman, K., Scharf, P., & Hickey, J. *The just community approach to corrections: A manual*. Unpublished manuscript, Harvard University, Moral Education Research Fund, 1974.
3. Harkness, S., Edwards, C. P., & Super, C. M. *Kohlberg in the bush: A study of moral reasoning among the elders of a rural Kipsigis community*. Paper presented at the meeting of the Society for Cross-Cultural Research, East Lansing, Mich., 1977.
4. Kohlberg, L. *Relationships between the development of moral judgment and moral conduct*. Paper presented at the biannual meeting of the Society for Research in Child Development, Minneapolis, Minn., 1965.
5. Nelsen, E. A., Grinder, R. E., & Challas, J. H. *Resistance to temptation and moral judgment: Behavioral correlates of Kohlberg's measure of moral development*. Unpublished manuscript, University of Wisconsin—Madison, 1968.
6. Krebs, R., & Kohlberg, L. *Moral judgment and ego controls as determinants of resistance to cheating*. Unpublished manuscript, 1977. (Available from L. Kohlberg, Laboratory of Human Development, Harvard University, Cambridge, Mass. 02138.)
7. Simpson, A. L., & Graham, D. *The development of moral judgment, emotion and behavior in British adolescents*. Unpublished manuscript, 1975. (Available from L. Kohlberg, Laboratory of Human Development, Harvard University, Cambridge, Mass. 02138.)

## References

Ajzen, I., & Fishbein, M. Attitude-behavior relations: A theoretical analysis and review of empirical research. *Psychological Bulletin*, 1978, *84*, 888–918.

Allport, G. W. *Personality: A psychological interpretation*. New York: Holt, Rinehart & Winston, 1937.

Anchor, K. N., & Cross, H. J. Maladaptive aggression, moral perspective, and the socialization process. *Journal of Personality and Social Psychology*, 1974, *30*, 163–168.

Andreason, A. W. The effects of social responsibility, moral judgment, and conformity on helping behavior (Doctoral dissertation, Brigham Young University, 1975). *Dissertation Abstracts Inter-*

*national*, 1976, *36*, 5856B. (University Microfilms No. 76-9,829)

Arndt, A. W. Maturity of moral reasoning about hypothetical dilemmas and behavior in an actual situation (Doctoral dissertation, University of California, Berkeley, 1975). *Dissertation Abstracts International*, 1976, *37*, 435B. (University Microfilms No. 76-15,099)

Aronfreed, J. *Conduct and conscience*. New York: Academic Press, 1968.

Aronfreed, J. Some problems for a theory of the acquisition of conscience. In C. M. Beck, B. S. Crittenden, & E. V. Sullivan (Eds.), *Moral education: Interdisciplinary approaches*. Toronto, Ontario, Canada: University of Toronto Press, 1971.

Aronfreed, J. Moral development from the standpoint of a general psychological theory. In T. Lickona (Ed.), *Moral development and behavior*. New York: Holt, Rinehart & Winston, 1976.

Bales, R. F. *Interaction process analysis: A method for the study of small groups*. Reading, Mass.: Addison-Wesley, 1950.

Bem, D. J., & Allen, A. On predicting some of the people some of the time: The search for cross-situational consistencies in behavior. *Psychological Review*, 1974, *81*, 506–520.

Betke, M. A. Defective moral reasoning and delinquency: A psychological study. *Catholic University of America Studies in Psychology and Psychiatry*, 1944, *6*(No. 4).

Brissett, M. J., Jr. Moral judgment level, social context of commitment, monetary incentive, and altruistic behavior in college students (Doctoral dissertation, Purdue University, 1976). *Dissertation Abstracts International*, 1977, *37*, 5317B. (University Microfilms No. 77-7,422)

Brown, P. I. M. Moral judgment and helpfulness toward a former mental patient (Doctoral dissertation, University of Texas at Austin, 1974). *Dissertation Abstracts International*, 1974, *35*, 2399B–2400B. (University Microfilms No. 74-24,835)

Campagna, A. F., & Harter, S. Moral judgment in sociopathic and normal children. *Journal of Personality and Social Psychology*, 1975, *31*, 199–205.

Campbell, D. T. On the conflicts between biological and social evaluation and between psychology and moral tradition. *American Psychologist*, 1975, *30*, 1103–1126.

Candee, D. Structure and choice in moral reasoning. *Journal of Personality and Social Psychology*, 1976, *34*, 1293–1301.

Damon, W. Early conceptions of positive justice as related to the development of logical operations. *Child Development*, 1975, *46*, 301–312.

Damon, W. *The social world of the child*. San Francisco: Jossey-Bass, 1977.

D'Augelli, J. F., & Cross, H. J. Relationship of sex guilt and moral reasoning to premarital sex in college women and couples. *Journal of Consulting and Clinical Psychology*, 1975, *43*, 40–47.

De Mersseman, S. L. A developmental investigation of children's moral reasoning and behavior in

hypothetical and practical situations (Doctoral dissertation, University of California, Berkeley 1976). *Dissertation Abstracts International*, 197 *37*, 4643B. (University Microfilms No. 77-4,435

Deutscher, I. Words and deeds: Social science an social policy. *Social Problems*, 1966, *13*, 235–26.

Dreman, S. B. Sharing behavior in Israeli schoo children: Cognitive and social learning factor *Child Development*, 1976, *47*, 186–194.

Dreman, S. B., & Greenbaum, C. W. Altruism reciprocity: Sharing behavior in Israeli kinde garten children. *Child Development*, 1973, *4* 61–68.

Dunivant, N., Jr. Moral judgment, psychologic development, situational characteristics, and mor behavior: A mediational interactionist mod (Doctoral dissertation, University of Texas Austin, 1975). *Dissertation Abstracts Internationa* 1976, *36*, 5342B–5343B. (University Microfilm No. 76-8,021)

Eisenberg, N. H. The development of prosoci moral judgment (Doctoral dissertation, Unive sity of California, Berkeley, 1976). *Dissertatio Abstracts International*, 1977, *37*, 4753B. (Un versity Microfilms No. 77-4,444)

Emler, P. N., & Rushton, J. P. Cognitive-develop mental factors in children's generosity. *Britis Journal of Social and Clinical Psychology*, 197 *13*, 277–281.

Epstein, J. A. The effects of moral orientation an external pressure on the violation of internalize norms (Doctoral dissertation, University of Mich igan (Ann Arbor), 1974). *Dissertation Abstrac International*, 1974, *35*, 2426B. (University Micro films No. 74-25,196)

Fenyes, C. M. Moral judgment and appropriateness f self-blame and resistance to temptation (Doctor dissertation, University of California, Berkeley 1967). *Dissertation Abstracts International*, 196 *28*, 1682B–1683B. (University Microfilms No. 6 11,619)

Festinger, L. Behavioral support for opinion chang *Public Opinion Quarterly*, 1964, *28*, 404–417.

Fodor, E. M. Resistance to social influence amon adolescents as a function of level of moral de velopment. *Journal of Social Psychology*, 197 *85*, 121–126.

Fodor, E. M. Delinquency and susceptibility of so cial influence among adolescents as a function c moral development. *Journal of Social Psycholog* 1972, *86*, 257–260.

Fodor, E. M. Moral development and parent be havior antecedents in adolescent psychopath. *Journal of Genetic Psychology*, 1973, *122*, 37–4:

Frenkel-Brunswik, E. Intolerance of ambiguity a an emotional and perceptual personality variabl *Journal of Personality*, 1949, *18*, 108–143.

Froming, W. J. The relationship of moral judgmen self-awareness, and sex to compliance behavic (Doctoral dissertation, University of Texas a Austin, 1977). *Dissertation Abstracts Internationa* 1977, *38*, 2397B. (University Microfilms No. 7 22,955)

Gallagher, M. J. A comparison of Hogan's and Kohlberg's theories of moral development (Doctoral dissertation, Columbia University, 1975). *Dissertation Abstracts International*, 1975, *36*, 2446B–2447B. (University Microfilms No. 75-25,680)

Gilligan, C. In a different voice: Women's conception of the self and morality. *Harvard Educational Review*, 1977, *47*, 481–517.

Giraldo, M. Moral development and its relation to role-taking ability and interpersonal behavior (Doctoral dissertation, Catholic University of America, 1972). *Dissertation Abstracts International*, 1972, *33*, 1285B. (University Microfilms No. 72-23,545)

Glucksberg, S., Krauss, R. M., & Weisberg, R. Referential communication in nursery school children: Method and some preliminary findings. *Journal of Experimental Child Psychology*, 1966, *3*, 333–342.

Grinder, R. E. Relations between behavioral and cognitive dimensions of conscience in middle childhood. *Child Development*, 1964, *35*, 881–891.

Haan, N. *Coping and defending: Processes of self-environment organization*. New York: Academic Press, 1977.

Haan, N. Two moralities in action contexts: Relationships to thought, ego regulation, and development. *Journal of Personality and Social Psychology*, 1978, *36*, 286–305.

Haan, N., Smith, M. B., & Block, J. Moral reasoning of young adults: Political-social behavior, family background, and personality correlates. *Journal of Personality and Social Psychology*, 1968, *10*, 183–201.

Haier, R. J. Moral reasoning and moral character: A comparison of the Kohlberg and the Hogan models (Doctoral dissertation, Johns Hopkins University, 1975). *Dissertation Abstracts International*, 1976, *36*, 3672B. (University Microfilms No. 76-1514)

Harrington, D. M., Block, J. H., & Block, J. Intolerance of ambiguity in preschool children: Psychometric considerations, behavioral manifestations, and parental correlates. *Developmental Psychology*, 1978, *14*, 242–256.

Harris, S., Mussen, P., & Rutherford, E. Some cognitive, behavioral, and personality correlates of maturity of moral judgment. *Journal of Genetic Psychology*, 1976, *128*, 123–135.

Hartshorne, H., & May, M. A. *Studies in the nature of character: Vol. I. Studies in deceit*. New York: Macmillan, 1928.

Hartshorne, H., May, M. A., & Maller, J. B. *Studies in the nature of character: Vol. II. Studies in self-control*. New York: Macmillan, 1929.

Hartshorne, H., May, M. A., & Shuttleworth, F. K. *Studies in the nature of character: Vol. III. Studies in the organization of character*. New York: Macmillan, 1930.

Haviland, J. M. The punitive beliefs and behaviors of adolescent delinquent boys. *Developmental Psychology*, 1977, *13*, 677–678.

Henshel, A. M. The relationship between values and behavior: A developmental hypothesis. *Child Development*, 1971, *42*, 1997–2007.

Hogan, R. Moral conduct and moral character: A psychological perspective. *Psychological Bulletin*, 1973, *79*, 217–232.

Hudgins, W., & Prentice, N. M. Moral judgment in delinquent and nondelinquent adolescents and their mothers. *Journal of Abnormal Psychology*, 1973, *82*, 145–152.

Jurkovic, G. J. The relationship of moral and cognitive development to dimensions of juvenile delinquency (Doctoral dissertation, University of Texas at Austin, 1975). *Dissertation Abstracts International*, 1976, *36*, 5262B. (University Microfilms No. 76-8,054)

Jurkovic, G. J., & Prentice, N. M. Dimensions of moral interaction and moral judgment in delinquent and nondelinquent families. *Journal of Consulting and Clinical Psychology*, 1974, *42*, 256–262.

Kantner, J. E. The relationship between moral judgment and personality variables in adult offenders (Doctoral dissertation, Purdue University, 1975). *Dissertation Abstracts International*, 1976, *36*, 5262B–5263B. (University Microfilms No. 76-7,088)

Kelman, H., & Lee, H. L. Assignment of responsibility in the case of Lt. Calley: Preliminary report on a national survey. *Journal of Social Issues*, 1972, *28*, 177–212.

Kohlberg, L. *The development of modes of moral thinking and choice in the years ten to sixteen*. Unpublished doctoral dissertation, University of Chicago, 1958.

Kohlberg, L. Stage and sequence: The cognitive-developmental approach to socialization. In D. A. Goslin (Ed.), *Handbook of socialization theory and research*. Chicago: Rand McNally, 1969.

Kohlberg, L. From is to ought: How to commit the naturalistic fallacy and get away with it. In T. Mischel (Ed.), *Cognitive development and epistemology*. New York: Academic Press, 1971.

Kohlberg, L. Moral stages and moralization. In T. Lickona (Ed.), *Moral development and behavior: Theory, research and social issues*. New York: Holt, Rinehart & Winston, 1976.

Krebs, D., & Rosenwald, A. Moral reasoning and moral behavior in conventional adults. *Merrill-Palmer Quarterly*, 1977, *23*, 77–87.

Kurdek, L. A. Perspective taking as the cognitive basis of children's moral development: A review of the literature. *Merrill-Palmer Quarterly*, 1978, *24*, 3–28.

Kurtines, W., & Greif, E. B. The development of moral thought: Review and evaluation of Kohlberg's approach. *Psychological Bulletin*, 1974, *81*, 453–470.

LaPiere, R. T. Attitudes vs. actions. *Social Forces*, 1934, *13*, 230–237.

Larsen, G. Y., & Kellogg, J. A developmental study of the relation between conservation and sharing behavior. *Child Development*, 1974, *45*, 849–851.

La Voie, J. C. Cognitive determinants of resistance to deviation in seven-, nine-, and eleven-year-old children of low and high maturity of moral judgment. *Developmental Psychology*, 1974, *10*, 393–403.

Lazarowitz, R., Stephan, W. G., & Friedman, S. T. Effects of moral justifications and moral reasoning on altruism. *Developmental Psychology*, 1976, *12*, 353–354.

Lee, L. C. The concomitant development of cognitive and moral modes of thought: A test of selected deductions from Piaget's theory. *Genetic Psychology Monographs*, 1971, *83*, 93–146.

Linford, J. L. Conscious and unconscious moral judgment, moral character and conventional conduct in adolescence (Doctoral dissertation, California School of Professional Psychology, 1977). *Dissertation Abstracts International*, 1977, *38*, 2834B. (University Microfilms No. 77-27,601)

Maitland, K. A., & Goldman, J. R. Moral judgment as a function of peer group interaction. *Journal of Personality and Social Psychology*, 1974, *30*, 699–704.

McLaughlin, J. A., & Stephens, B. Interrelationships among reasoning, moral judgment, and moral conduct. *American Journal of Mental Deficiency*, 1974, *79*, 156–161.

McNamee, S. M. Moral behavior, moral development, and needs in students and political activists (Doctoral dissertation, Case Western Reserve University, 1972). *Dissertation Abstracts International*, 1972, *33*, 1800B–1801B. (University Microfilms No. 76-26,187)

Medinnus, G. R. Behavioral and cognitive measures of conscience development. *Journal of Genetic Psychology*, 1966, *109*, 147–150.

Milgram, S. *Obedience to authority: An experimental view*. New York: Harper & Row, 1974.

Miller, N. E., & Dollard, J. *Social learning and imitation*. New Haven, Conn.: Yale University Press, 1941.

Mischel, T. Piaget: Cognitive conflict and the motivation of thought. In T. Mischel (Ed.), *Cognitive development and epistemology*. New York: Academic Press, 1971.

Mischel, W. Continuity and change in personality. *American Psychologist*, 1969, *24*, 1012–1018.

Mischel, W. Toward a cognitive social learning reconceptualization of personality. *Psychological Review*, 1973, *80*, 252–283.

Mischel, W. Processes in delay of gratification. In L. Berkowitz (Ed.), *Advances in experimental social psychology* (Vol. 7). New York: Academic Press, 1974.

Mischel, W., & Mischel, H. N. A cognitive social-learning approach to morality and self-regulation. In T. Lickona (Ed.), *Moral development and behavior*. New York: Holt, Rinehart & Winston, 1976.

Mixon, D. If you won't deceive, what can you do? In N. Armistead (Ed.), *Reconstructing social psychology*. Baltimore, Md.: Penguin Books, 1974.

Mowrer, O. H. *Learning theory and behavior*. New York: Wiley, 1960.

Mussey, P. M. An analysis of children's helping behaviors as related to moral development (Doctoral dissertation, University of Tennessee, Knoxville, 1976). *Dissertation Abstracts International*, 1977, *37*, 4223B. (University Microfilms No. 77-3,668)

Nelsen, E. A., Grinder, R. E., & Biaggio, A. M. Relationships among behavioral, cognitive-developmental, and self-report measures of morality and personality. *Multivariate Behavioral Research*, 1969, *4*, 483–500.

Nelsen, E. A., Grinder, R. E., & Mutterer, M. L. Sources of variance in behavioral measures of honesty in temptation situations: Methodological analysis. *Developmental Psychology*, 1969, *1*, 265–279.

Peck, R. F., & Havighurst, R. J. *The psychology of character development*. New York: Wiley, 1960.

Peters, R. S. *Psychology and ethical development*. London: Allen & Unwin, 1974.

Piaget, J. *The moral judgment of the child*. London: Routledge & Kegan Paul, 1932.

Podd, M. H. Ego identity status and morality: The relationship between two developmental constructs. *Developmental Psychology*, 1972, *6*, 497–507.

Porteus, B. D., & Johnson, R. C. Children's responses to two measures of conscience development and their relation to socio-metric nomination. *Child Development*, 1965, *36*, 703–711.

Rapp, L. R. An investigation of the development of moral conduct and moral judgment among trainable mentally retarded children (Doctoral dissertation, Ohio State University, 1975). *Dissertation Abstracts International*, 1976, *36*, 5870B. (University Microfilms No. 76-10,033)

Rest, J. R. New approaches in the assessment of moral judgment. In T. Lickona (Ed.) *Moral development and behavior*. New York: Holt, Rinehart & Winston, 1976.

Rosenn, M. M. The relation of moral reasoning to prosocial behavior: A developmental perspective (Doctoral dissertation, University of California, Berkeley, 1976). *Dissertation Abstracts International*, 1977, *38*, 967B–968B. (University Microfilms No. 77-15,838)

Rothman, G. R. An experimental analysis of the relationship between moral judgment and behavioral choice (Doctoral dissertation, Columbia University, 1971). *Dissertation Abstracts International*, 1971, *32*, 3624B. (University Microfilms No. 72-1,381)

Rubin, K. H., & Schneider, F. W. The relationship between moral judgment, egocentrism, and altruistic behavior. *Child Development*, 1973, *44*, 661–665.

Ruma, E. H. Conscience development in delinquents and non-delinquents: The relationship between moral judgment, guilt, and behavior (Doctoral dissertation, Ohio State University, 1967). *Dis-*

*sertation Abstracts International,* 1967, *28,* 2631B. (University Microfilms No. 67-16,331)

Saltzstein, H. D., Diamond, R. M., & Belenky, M. Moral judgment level and conformity behavior. *Developmental Psychology,* 1972, *7,* 327–336.

Santrock, J. W. Moral structure: The interrelations of moral behavior, moral judgment, and moral affect. *Journal of Genetic Psychology,* 1975, *127,* 201–213.

Schmidlin, S. S. Moral judgment and delinquency: The effect of institutionalization and peer pressure (Doctoral dissertation, University of Florida, 1975). *Dissertation Abstracts International,* 1977, *37,* 3630B. (University Microfilms No. 77-124)

Schwartz, S. H. Words, deeds, and the perception of consequences and responsibility in action situations. *Journal of Personality and Social Psychology,* 1968, *10,* 232–242.

Schwartz, S. H. Normative explanations of helping behavior: A critique, proposal, and empirical test. *Journal of Experimental and Social Psychology,* 1973, *9,* 349–364.

Schwartz, S. H. Normative influences on altruism. In L. Berkowitz (Ed.), *Advances in experimental social psychology* (Vol. 10). New York: Academic Press, 1977.

Schwartz, S. H., Feldman, K. A., Brown, M. E., & Heingartner, A. Some personality correlates of conduct in two situations of moral conflict. *Journal of Personality,* 1969, *37,* 41–57.

Schwarz, D. A. The relationships among sexual behavior, moral reasoning, and sex guilt in late adolescence (Doctoral dissertation, Columbia University, 1975). *Dissertation Abstracts International,* 1976, *36,* 6400B. (University Microfilms No. 76-12,782)

Skinner, B. F. *Science and human behavior.* New York: Macmillan, 1953.

Staub, E. Helping a distressed person: Social, personality, and stimulus determinants. In L. Berkowitz (Ed.), *Advances in experimental social psychology* (Vol. 7). New York: Academic Press, 1974.

Sykes, G. M., & Matza, D. Techniques of neutralization: A theory of delinquency. *American Sociological Review,* 1957, *22,* 664–670.

Turiel, E., & Rothman, G. R. The influence of reasoning on behavioral choices at different stages of moral development. *Child Development,* 1972, *43,* 741–756.

Ugurel-Semin, R. Moral behavior and moral judgment of children. *Journal of Abnormal and Social Psychology,* 1952, *47,* 463–474.

Unamuno, M. *The tragic sense of life.* London: Macmillan, 1921.

Warner, L. G., & DeFleur, M. L. Attitudes as an interactional concept: Social constraint and social distance as intervening variables between attitudes and action. *American Sociological Review,* 1969, *34,* 153–169.

Wicker, A. W. Attitudes versus actions: The relationship of verbal and overt behavioral responses to attitude objects. *Journal of Social Issues,* 1969, *25,* 41–78.

Wilson, E. *Sociobiology.* Cambridge, Mass.: Harvard University Press, 1975.

Wright, B. Altruism in children and the perceived conduct of others. *Journal of Abnormal and Social Psychology,* 1942, *37,* 218–233. (a)

Wright, B. The development of ideology of altruism and fairness in children. *Psychological Bulletin,* 1942, *39,* 485. (Abstract) (b)

Received February 2, 1979 ∎

CHAPTER 7

# Moral Identity:
# Its Role in Moral Functioning

AUGUSTO BLASI

*The general issues of this chapter concern moral action and the relations between moral cognition and moral action. Specifically, the chapter will focus on the role of identity in mediating moral knowledge and practical moral decisions. From this perspective, the problem of moral action becomes a question of self-consistency.*

*Three central psychological concepts and their functional articulations will be discussed. The first is the concept of self-identity and the importance that morality plays in it (self-as-moral). The role of morality in one's identity is viewed as a dimension of developmental and individual differences. The second, the concept of responsibility, is understood here specifically as an extension of one's identity into the domain of action. The third is the concept of self-consistency, which becomes integrity in the area of morality.*

*Both the theoretical and the practical implications of the identity approach to moral development and moral functioning will be analyzed.*

The relations between moral knowledge and moral action represent a central issue for a philosophical as well as for a psychological understanding of moral functioning and moral development. This question, however, has received relatively little theoretical attention, even among cognitive-developmental psychologists. This is particularly clear when one considers the amount of energy and the degree of conceptual sophistication that has been devoted to the understanding of moral reasoning and of the development of cognitive moral structures. Chapter 4, by Kohlberg and Candee, is an important but rare attempt to address the issue from a cognitive-developmental perspective. This state of affairs is also surprising because there is a widespread skepticism, among psychologists and philosophers alike, concerning the motivational power of cognition. A cognitive-developmental solution to the problem of moral functioning remains not only incomplete but also theoretically unconvincing, unless it is shown how moral understanding is indeed a motive for action.

Recently I (Blasi, 1980, 1983) presented a model, labeled "self model," which attempted to deal, in a tentative and sketchy way, with both consistency and inconsistency between moral judgment and moral action. In it I hypothesized (1) that the outcome of moral judgments becomes, at least in some cases, the content of judgments of responsibility; in other words, that the agent, having decided the morally good action, also determines whether that action is strictly obligatory for him or her; (2) that the criteria for responsibility (in the sense of strict obligation) are related to the structure of one's self, or to the essential definition of oneself; (3) that the motivational basis for moral action lies in the internal demand for psychological self-consistency; and (4) that moral action will be more likely to follow moral judgment if the individual has the ability to stop defensive strategies from interfering with the subjective discomfort of self-inconsistency.

In this chapter I will focus on the self, the core element of the self model, and will further explore its nature and its role in moral action. In Chapter 6 Damon presents a research project aimed at describing the development of the self in children and adolescents. His findings seem to be perfectly compatible with my understanding of the role of the self in moral functioning. My chapter, however, does not present empirical data; it focuses, instead, on certain conceptual features of the moral self, which will be globally designated by the term *identity*. The advantage of the term *moral identity* may not necessarily lie in its conceptual clarity. Within the Eriksonian tradition, however, this concept is more or less consistently used to refer to certain psychological processes and has acquired certain properties that, when properly understood, seem to be necessary in a complete theory of moral functioning.

This chapter will raise two questions, one in each of the two main sections. First, what is meant by moral identity and what are the advantages of introducing this concept in the scheme of moral action? Second, what are the relations between moral cognition and moral identity? In this second section, as a way of introducing the problems that identity raises for a cognitive-developmentalist, two noncognitive approaches to the moral self will first be discussed: the ideal self of psychoanalysis and the self-regarding sentiment of McDougall. With the help of these two contrasting views, a cognitive solution to the issue of moral identity will be very briefly outlined.

The general framework of this chapter, therefore, is frankly cognitive. In other words, I assume that it is impossible to understand the moral quality—positive or negative—of an action without resorting to the agent's judgment, that moral judgments reflect the individual's general understanding of himself or herself, other people, social relations, and situations, and that this understanding can and does change as a result of the development of one's intelligence and of richer and more complex experience with the social world. Admittedly, a great deal is being assumed, considering the importance that these ideas have in the development of my argument. Because these assumptions are mostly philosophical in nature and are aimed at defining the moral phenomenon, however, their discussion seems to be unnecessary and out of place in the present context.

## MORAL IDENTITY

There are three characteristics of identity that not only seem to be central in Erikson's account (particularly in *Insight and Responsibility, 1964*) but also are useful for my purposes: First, identity is experienced as rooted in the very core of one's being; second, identity is described as involving being true to oneself in action; third, it is associated with truthfulness, namely, with respect for one's own understanding of reality. The latter two meanings are part of the cluster of characteristics by which Erikson defines fidelity, the human virtue that is intimately associated with the development of identity. My use of this concept of identity is somewhat opportunistic: Erikson's descriptions of these characteristics are useful for my purpose, independently of the overall theoretical context in which they are embedded and from which they derive their specific Eriksonian meaning.

One of the most frequently heard criticisms of the contemporary emphasis on moral reasoning is that moral understanding and moral knowledge give a rather abstract and lifeless perspective on the moral reality. The doubts that moral reasoning may be reliably tied to moral action seem frequently to reflect the same kind of bias with which life and soul are associated only with emotions and desires. Erikson (1964) himself appeared to imply a similar view, when he distinguished between ethical or moral ideas ("nobility and rectitude as cultivated by moralities," p. 211), on one hand, and what he calls "virtues" or "strengths," on the other. The first, by themselves, are "nonvital," "despirited" superstructures and need the latter in order to acquire not only psychological roots but also validity and actuality. "Virtues," instead, are vital, "essential," "animated," and "spirited" qualities, originating from the convergence of "unfolding capacities with existing institutions" (p. 142); they exercise the function of giving human beings the same sense of rootedness that animals possess as a privilege of nature (p. 117). Ethical ideals will provide strength and trustworthy guidelines for adapting to the real world only to the extent that they are built on, and integrated with, the substructure and the rock bottom of these inherent natural strengths.

McDougall (1936), as we shall see, starting from very different assumptions, arrived at a similar conclusion: Moral ideals are powerless if they are not rooted in a moral self. Thus, despite different theoretical frameworks, a common belief is stressed, a belief that also seems to be shared by common sense: Morality is more a characteristic of the agent than of either action or thinking; the ultimate source of goodness lies in good will, and good will is at the core of what a person is.

In this chapter, then, identity is considered equivalent to the essential self.

Each individual, beginning relatively early in development, has an image, a perception, a scheme, or a theory of himself or herself (all these terms are awkward; none captures precisely the type of reality to be conveyed), being at the same time a principle of cognitive organization and the source of a special class of motives, the self motives.

The self is not simply a collection of characteristics, traits, or percepts; it is an organization of self-related information in which the various elements are brought together according to certain principles of psychological consistency. The organizing principle, varying from person to person, determines the order and the hierarchy among the characteristics that are included in the self, along such metaphorical dimensions as central peripheral, deep superficial, important unimportant, and so on. It also defines what could be called the essential or the core self, namely, the set of those aspects without which the individual would see himself or herself to be radically different; those so central that one could not even imagine being deprived of them; those whose loss would be considered and felt as irreparable.

Defined in this manner, identity includes at least some elements of the ideal self and functions as the ideal principle of action. Understanding that a specific ideal is a goal for one's becoming already involves a restructuring of the very core of the actual self, introducing in it a new principle of tension between what one understands and what one does. The seemingly curious psychoanalytic expression "identification with one's self" (Sandler, Holder, & Meers, 1963) begins to make sense when it is understood to indicate that parts of the actual representation of oneself have acquired the function of self ideal.

Although already implicit in what has been said, it may be useful to point out explicitly that the psychological construct of self-perception and similar constructs, which have been guiding empirical work in this area, are a feeble if not distorted version of the reality that is suggested by the term *identity*. This is so even when attempts are made to capture the organizing aspects of self-perceptions. The essential self or identity cannot be found simply, or mainly, in what one says about oneself, particularly through the framework of checklists, rating scales, and questionnaires. One would have to uncover the unverbalized, and to some extent unverbalizable, assumptions that underlie what one says about oneself and about others, the decisions one makes, the emotions one experiences.

Much of this material may be unconscious (though not necessarily in the Freudian sense of the term), may appear in fantasy, in day and night dreams, and may elicit the whole range of defenses. One can think of experiences such as the sense of futility and waste in one's life, of uselessness of one's work, of incompetence in one's chosen field, of inadequacy in one's love. People's essential selves may vary; however, one should get to this level of analysis to even hope to find it. Anything less would be "lifeless" and "despirited," in the sense that Erikson gave these words.

Identity, as has been described here, is relevant to moral functioning in two ways. First, being moral, being a good person, being fair and just in a general sense, may be, but need not be, a part of an individual's essential self. From a psychological perspective, it seems plausible (or at least not impossible) that some people's identity does not include morality (see Chap. 6). In fact, one can hypothesize for morality different degrees of centrality in people's identities. The individual who lacks a moral identity will still understand and use moral speech, will be able to make moral judgments and to engage in discussions about the appropriateness of certain moral decisions and the validity of certain moral criteria. However, a moral perspective will play no significant role in his or her life, in the decisions that really matter, in the fundamental outlook on the world and on history, or in eliciting strong emotions and deep anxieties. Second, one can hypothesize that different moral aspects characterize the moral identity of the individual who does have one; where one person sees compassion as being essential to his or her identity, another emphasizes instead fairness and justice; where one considers obedience as a central ideal, another stresses moral freedom.

Moral identity, in sum, both in its general and in its specific aspects, can be looked at as a dimension of individual differences. Quite possibly, some of these variations are developmental in nature. It should not be surprising if moral identity cannot be found before a certain age, even when moral reasoning and cognitive moral criteria are already present. Similarly, it is not improbable that one's moral identity undergoes changes, for instance, from focusing on obedience as a central virtue to emphasizing loyalty and, finally, moral autonomy. There are, at present, no data directly relevant to the preceding hypotheses, with the possible exceptions of anecdotal, biographical, and clinical materials. In fact, there are no readily available methods by which these hypotheses could be empirically addressed. But the questions are clearly empirical, and adequate methods are not beyond our empirical imagination.

From my present perspective, moral identity is directly related to moral action, providing one of its truly moral motives. As already mentioned, one aspect of fidelity, the basic virtue that Erikson considers as inherently tied to the development of identity, consists of a concern with being authentic and true to one's self in action. In my self model (Blasi, 1980, 1983), the connection between moral identity and action is expressed through the concepts of responsibility (in the sense of strict obligation to act according to one's judgment) and integrity. These two concepts are closely related and derive their meaning from a view of moral action as an extension of the essential self into the domain of the possible, of what is not but needs to be, if the agent has to remain true to himself or herself. Responsibility, in this sense, stresses the self as the source of "moral compulsion." Integrity, instead, emphasizes the idea of moral self-consistency, of intactness and wholeness—all essential connotations of the self as a psychological organization. Neither of these ideas is new. Over a century ago, the French philosopher J.-M. Guyau wrote: "Thought, action—they are at bottom identical. And what is called moral obligation is, in the sphere of the intellect, the sense of this radical identity; obligation is an internal expansion, a need for completing our ideas by making them pass into action. Morality is the unity of the being" (quoted in Baldwin, 1899, p. 56). It should be added that moral cognition and moral action are not the same; their relation is not a matter of fact but is a matter of obligation and depends on the unity of the self.

## MORAL IDENTITY AND MORAL COGNITION

The second section of this chapter is much more controversial and is more on the side of philosophy than on the side of psychology. It raises questions concerning the cognitive nature of the moral self and the functional relations between moral judgment and moral identity. The issue is important for a cognitive approach to moral functioning and development; it also has some practical implications, particularly with regard to the origin and the transformations of moral identity.

The problem can be stated as follows: If, at least in some instances, moral judgment, derived from cognitive criteria and other cognitive considerations, is not sufficient to motivate moral action, but requires motives originating from within one's identity, what becomes of the cognitive basis of moral action? To use a concrete example, two hypothetical individuals may share the same structure of moral reasoning but are characterized by a different identity with respect to morality (e.g., the first has but the second lacks a moral identity). In a specific situation, the first man behaves consistently with both his moral judgment and his moral identity, whereas the second behaves in a way that is inconsistent with his moral judgment but not inconsistent with his identity. In this and similar cases, can we still maintain a cognitive approach to the understanding of morality? Can we say that moral understanding is functionally related to moral action? Or should not we say, in contradiction with the premises of this chapter, that structures of moral reasoning are ultimately sterile and play no real significant role in moral functioning? In sum, is it possible to make one's moral understanding alive, full-blooded, animated, and rooted in one's deeper psychological nature without losing in the process its cognitive characteristics?[1]

Anticipating a later discussion, a cognitive solution will be possible to the extent that the essential self is sensitive to, and indeed biased toward, cognitive considerations, not only in moral decisions but also in setting up goals and ideals for itself, namely, in constructing its very self. First, however, I will illustrate the risks presented by a psychological approach to morality that is based on the self and on identity. Of course, the assessment of risk depends

---

[1] The conflict between moral judgment and identity is problematic for a cognitive theory of moral functioning in a way that other conflicts—for example, between moral judgment and hedonistic desires, or between moral reasoning and career ambitions—are not. The reason is that moral consistency can be understood only as a part and within the broader domain of self-consistency, and not in opposition to it; one type of consistency cannot be pursued at the expense of the other.

on the assumption adopted in this chapter that reason is of the essence of morality and cannot be eliminated without destroying the moral phenomenon itself. I will do so by commenting on the psychoanalytic theory of the ideal self, or one version of it, and McDougall's (1936) concept of the self-regarding sentiment.

Freud's (again, in some interpretations of his thinking) and McDougall's views share two characteristics: Both attempted to anchor morality in the total personality of the individual and looked skeptically at a morality that relies on abstract ideals; they both constructed the moral personality around a core of instinct-like impulses and their transformations. The differences, however, are as important as the similarities: Freud's basic motive (in the version discussed here) concerned hedonistic desire; McDougall relied instead on social needs, particularly on the need for social acceptance and approval, while rejecting egocentric and hedonistic needs as inadequate to account for the truly moral experience. Echoes of McDougall can be found in Chapters 13 and 16 in this book.

From the perspective of the present chapter, the aim and the interest in comparing psychoanalysis and McDougall's theory are to show that the risks involved in a self-based approach to the psychology of morality lie not in the type of needs or instincts that one places at the core of the self, but in the noncognitive, nonrational nature of needs and instincts. Social impulses are frequently considered higher, and more obviously moral, than hedonistic needs; this was certainly McDougall's (1936) opinion (see particularly pp. 162–164). To the extent that the social self is not a response to understanding and reason, however, to this extent a moral functioning based on the self seems incompatible with a cognitive-developmental account.

### The Psychoanalytic Ideal Self

It is well known that Freud did not leave a coherent account of the moral agencies, that is, an account in which ego, conscience, superego, and ego ideal are clearly defined and clearly distinguished from one another. My comments follow the reconstruction that Sandler et al. (1963) gave of one such agency, the ideal self, on the basis of Freud's own writings and of later psychoanalytic discussion. The purpose here is not to offer a reliable account of what Freud really thought or said, but to discuss one way of approaching moral functioning from the perspective of the self.

According to the Sandler et al. (1963) account, the ideal self is one element of the representation of oneself that is constructed on the basis of three contents: a very early identification with the "admired object" (frequently the father); identification with the "ideal child," namely, with the "parents' ideal of a desirable and loved child, as perceived by the child" (p. 154); and identification with the self, namely, with those earlier shapes of the self that were associated with a high degree of narcissistic gratification.

These authors also point out the special "economic gains" (measured, namely, on the basis of libidinal gratification) that derive from constructing the ideal self on the identifications just described: By internalizing compliance to the authority, the child "gains a feeling of being loved"; by identifying with the admired object, "he can love and admire himself as he does the object" (p. 153); the third identification, finally, is a direct attempt "to restore . . . the primary narcissistic state of the earliest weeks of life" (p. 156). In sum, the construction of the ideal self is guided by the wish to obtain as much libidinal gratification as possible, either by way of primary narcissism or by way of secondary narcissism.

Thus, instinctual self-love is the motivational spring guiding the construction of the ideal self. Moreover, the specific shape that the ideal self acquires in any situation, including situations in which a moral decision is called for, is "a compromise between the desired state of instinctual gratification and the need to win the love of, or to avoid punishment from, authority figures, internal or external. The ultimate criterion at any given time is an economic one" (p. 153).

Other later influences will affect the ideal self, but its stable core will be mostly unconscious and will be based "upon the ideals created in childhood" (p. 155). Knowledge and reality are indeed given a role, but only a prudential one: Their function is not to shape ideals, but simply to make the individual aware of his or her own limitations and potentialities as well as of the possibilities for gratification offered by the environment.

When this psychoanalytic account is stripped of its metapsychological terminology, it appears quite similar in its essential message to other, more familiar, views of morality: Moral standards in the best of cases (namely, by comparison with the aggressive and limiting superego morality) are based on the self and on the ideal for the self; the latter is rooted in the most natural and vital of needs, the need to obtain love and the most intensive pleasure that is possible; at its best, morality cannot be but a form of self-interest. Therefore, so-called higher virtues, disinterested ideals (and these would include several stages suggested by cognitive theories of moral reasoning), have no grounding in real human substance and should be suspiciously regarded as hypocritical and devious maneuvers to serve one's self-interest.

It should perhaps be added, parenthetically, that ego-psychoanalytic theorists, when they attempt to balance the previous account of morality by adding certain cognitive-developmental principles such as those of Jean Piaget or Lawrence Kohlberg, frequently do not seriously consider the constraints that are presented by an instinctual view of the self and of the ideal self. Rationality and truth are not brought back in by relying on the "economic principle," that is, on the best possible compromise between truth and instinctual self-interest.

## McDougall's Self-regarding Sentiment

In McDougall's (1936) system, the concept of self-regarding sentiment plays, with regard to moral action, the same roles that the ideal self plays in the preceding psychoanalytic account. The self-regarding sentiment is said to integrate within it the moral sentiments, namely, those emotional orientations that lead to moral judgments, and, most important, to provide the motivational force for moral action. On one hand, it motivates the acceptance of rules and of the moral tradition; on the other, it informs volition and sustains the determination to pursue moral ideals despite strong contrary desires. In contrast, moral inconsistency and backsliding are explained on the basis of a weak self-regarding sentiment.

Therefore, the self is, in its emotional substance, the center of moral functioning. Moral victories are achieved because "the personality as a whole, or the central feature or nucleus of the personality, the man himself, or all that which is regarded by himself and others as the most essential part of himself, is thrown upon the side of the weaker (but moral) motive" (McDougall, 1936, pp. 206–207).

But what is the self-regarding sentiment? It is a sentiment, first of all, namely, an organized system of emotions and tendencies, a cluster of affects and impulses, centered around a specific object. In this case, the object is the idea of self. As the self originates in social interaction and maintains throughout life a structure that reflects its origin, the emotions and motives that constitute the self-regarding sentiment are mostly social in nature: admiration, awe and reverence, altruistic feelings and sympathy, and particularly shame and pride, self-respect and self-satisfaction. From these originate the two central motives: search for social approval and avoidance of social disapproval. In turn, the roots of the self-regarding sentiment lie in primitive, essentially inborn, instincts: passive sympathy, the gregarious instinct, and the instincts of self-display and self-subjection.

McDougall rejected very strongly any attempt to reduce the self-regarding sentiment and morality to a concern with punishments and rewards and to material interests. On the other hand, he thought that people's desire for social approval has such a degree of intensity as to be unexplainable on rational grounds. Here lies the living source of that type of morality that is specifically human.

Of course, cognition is also important; emotions and motives require an idea, the idea of self, in order to be clustered together and are modified with the changes that this idea undergoes. However, as McDougall (1936) writes, "The relation between the cognitive disposition and the emotional dispositions comprised within a sentiment is that the latter remain the conative-affective root of the whole system . . . furnishing to it the energy, 'drive,' conative force or interest by which all thinking of the object is sustained" (p. 438). His views on this matter are particularly clear when he discusses the role and the nature of moral judgments.

McDougall (1936) realized the limitations of a moral system based on social approval and was aware that a higher type of moral functioning can occasionally be observed, namely, a moral functioning in which "man . . . is capable also of standing up against public opinion and of doing what he judges to be right in defiance of it" (p. 183). A central factor that characterizes this level and makes it possible is moral judgment. But moral judgments are also said to originate from emotions and sentiments.

There are, in fact, two kinds of judgments: The first is purely classificatory and consists in applying to concrete instances emotionally charged labels that are provided by one's society (lie, theft, etc.); this judgment does not proceed from emotions. By contrast, the second kind of moral judgment, called original moral judgment by McDougall and corresponding approximately to moral reasoning in contemporary cognitive-developmental theory, is a result of sentiments, particularly of abstract moral sentiments (e.g., love of justice, love of truth, hatred of deception). It seems that emotions of this type depend on, and originate from, certain kinds of understanding. According to McDougall, however, they are acquired from absorbing the finer aspects of one's moral tradition, through the admiration (another sentiment) of those exceptional individuals who embody them. Much, of course, is left unexplained in this account: How does one recognize the more refined aspects of a tradition? According to which criteria are certain people judged to be exceptional and worthy of admiration? How is it possible to make original judgments that go beyond the tradition of one's society?

In sum, McDougall's central explanation of moral strivings lies in the self-regarding sentiment, which he considers to be structured around the search for approval and the emotions that are associated with it. He saw the need for a postconventional morality, to use Kohlberg's term, and for personal autonomy. He was able to describe these characteristics, but he was unable to account for them and to transcend the level of moral praise and blame. From my understanding, the central reason for McDougall's failure lies in the assumptions that moral judgment is noncognitive and that reasoning is powerless to affect the emotive core of the self.

## CONCLUDING REMARKS

It was argued, first, that it is important for a psychological theory of morality to study the relations between moral action and personality and to recognize that a morality that actually works, not only in this or that action but also in one's life in general, must be rooted in some form of identity. Erikson's approach through the idea of a naturally unfolding set of "virtues," the psychoanalytic approach, based, in the version presented here, on the ideal self, and McDougall's self-regarding sentiment are all attempts to ground morality in the nature of the psychological being. The notion of moral identity was aimed at the same purpose.

It was pointed out, then, that an attempt to establish morality on personality runs the risk of eliminating from morality what seems one of its essential characteristics, namely, its being based on judgment and reason. Neither Freud nor McDougall avoided this risk. Erikson's position is more ambiguous in this respect, mostly because it is not clear to what extent his virtues depend on a genuine understanding of and not simply on adaptation to our social world.

All these views share the idea of a naturally occurring morality, namely, of a morality spontaneously evolving from natural impulses, basic instincts, and the like. One could blame, then, the "naturalistic" approach of these theories for eliminating from morality the foundation of reason. But it is not clear what "natural" and "naturalistic" mean, or what would be contrasted to these terms. I certainly do not suggest an unnatural or a supernatural morality.

As already mentioned, moral functioning inevitably becomes divorced from reason and truth when morality derives from the self, personality, identity, or similar constructs, *and* when personality, identity, or the self are impervious, in their basic structure, to the influence of reason. The dilemma is this: If moral identity is based on natural impulses, egoistic or social, one loses the cognitive basis of morality; if cognition and reason are stressed as establishing moral motives, one risks losing the person as the center of morality. It would appear, then, that the only hope of grounding morality on the essential self without losing morality's reason is to hypothesize that the self's very identity is constructed, at least in part, under the influence of moral reasons.

The steps could be the following:

1.  General moral structures would be constructed through social interactions and would reflect a genuine understanding of the social reality, namely, an understanding that is, in principle, independent of one's personality biases, objective, and open to revision as a result of better and more complete evidence and experience.

2.  General moral structures would influence the construction of more concrete ideals of actions and ideals of agents.

3.  This would lead, in turn, to the construction of an ideal moral self and, eventually, to the moralization of the self and personality.

4.  At this point, the self, partially constructed under the influence and the guide of moral reason, could become, itself, the source of concrete moral judgments. These judgments would be grounded on one's identity but would also be cognitive and genuinely moral. Fundamentally, however, the direction of influence would be from moral understanding to moral identity, rather than the other way around, as Freud, McDougall, and possibly Erikson seemed to think.

Of course, the crucial question is, Can the self and identity be influenced in their shape by knowledge and truth? This question is as yet unanswered, at least through research data. Leaving this issue aside for the time being, I am suggesting that the self and identity *should* be influenced by knowledge and truth; that one should not be indifferent as to whether one has a moral identity or not, or as to the type of moral identity that one has; that the construction of such an identity is indeed a genuine moral issue, more important than altruism, honesty, or truthfulness; and, finally, that morality and the good life, to use a Kantian distinction, cannot be separated.

## REFERENCES

Baldwin, J. M. *Social and ethical interpretations in mental development*. New York: Macmillan, 1899.

Blasi, A. Bridging moral cognition and moral action: A critical review of the literature. *Psychological Bulletin*, 1980, *88*, 1–45.

Blasi, A. Moral cognition and moral action: A theoretical perspective. *Developmental Review*, 1983, *3*, 178–210.

Erikson, E. H. *Insight and responsibility*. New York: Norton, 1964.

McDougall, W. *An introduction to social psychology*. London: Methuen, 1936.

Sandler, J., Holder, A., & Meers, D. The ego ideal and the ideal self. *The Psychoanalytic Study of the Child*, 1963, *18*, 139–158.

*The Journal of Genetic Psychology*, 1974, **125**, 277-283.

# POSSIBLE ENVIRONMENTAL CAUSES OF STAGES IN MORAL REASONING*[1]

*State University of New York College at Buffalo*

NANCY WADSWORTH DENNEY[2] AND DIANE M. DUFFY

## SUMMARY

Both children (6-, 10-, and 14-year-olds) and their mothers were interviewed. The children's responses to moral dilemmas were classified into Kohlberg's three main categories—preconventional, conventional, and postconventional. The mothers were presented with a variety of hypothetical situations—e.g., they had just found out that their child had stolen something, and were asked to tell what they would say or do to their child in each situation. The mothers' hypothetical responses to such situations were divided into either the preconventional, conventional, or postconventional category depending on the level or moral reasoning such responses would imply to their children. The results indicated that as the age of the children increased, both the level of moral reasoning used by the children and the level of moral reasoning implied by the mothers' treatment of the children increased. Even with age partialed out, there was a significant positive relationship between the mothers' implied level of moral reasoning and the children's level of moral reasoning. Thus, although causality cannot be established, the results indicate that there is at least the possibility that environmental changes—i.e., changes in the way the mother treats the child—may be responsible for the appearance of stages in the child's development of moral reasoning.

## A. INTRODUCTION

Kohlberg has described three distinct stages in the development of moral reasoning (1). In the first or preconventional stage, there is an orientation toward the physical consequences of an act (e.g., rewarded acts are good

* Received in the Editorial Office, Provincetown, Massachusetts, on August 31, 1973. Copyright, 1974, by The Journal Press.
[1] This research was partially supported by funds from the National Science Foundation Institutional Grant Awards Program in conjunction with the State University of New York College at Buffalo.
[2] Now at the University of Kansas.

and punished acts are bad) and toward deference to superior power. In the second or conventional stage, there is an orientation toward pleasing others and maintaining social order (e.g., obeying the rules set forth by the family or school). In the third or postconventional stage, the orientation is toward autonomous moral principles which are independent of other people or groups.

Kohlberg has suggested that the developmental changes which take place in moral reasoning occur as a result of internal changes in the child's cognitive structure. He contends that cognitive stages, such as those observed in moral reasoning, do not result from environmental influences alone. The following exemplifies his reasoning:

> In contrast, if structural stages do define general ontogenetic sequences, then an interactional type of theory of developmental process must be used to explain ontogeny. If the child goes through qualitatively different stages of thought, his basic modes of organizing experience cannot be the direct result of adult teaching, or they would be copies of adult thought from the start. If the child's cognitive responses differed from the adult's only in revealing less information and less complication of structure, it would be possible to view them as incomplete learning of the external structure of the world, whether that structure is defined in terms of the adult culture or in terms of the laws of the physical world. If the child's responses indicate a different structure or organization than the adult's, rather than a less complete one, and if the structure is similar in all children, it is extremely difficult to view the child's mental structure as a direct learning of the external structure (1, p.354).

Kohlberg seems to be assuming that the "external structure" remains the same for children of all ages. He implies that adults try to teach children of all ages the same things and in the same ways. However, at least with respect to moral reasoning, parents probably do not teach children of different ages the same things. It seems unlikely, for example, that parents would expound upon their own moral reasoning to a four-year-old child. It seems more likely, that with respect to moral situations, parents treat children of different ages very differently and, thereby, imply different types of moral reasoning to children of different ages. For example, it is not too surprising that one of the first stages in the development of moral reasoning that is of an orientation to the physical consequences of an act and deference to superior power. How often does one hear a parent saying something like the following to a very young child: "If you hit your sister one more time, you'll come into the house!" The parent in this example is implying that the child should not hit his sister *because* of the consequences of the act. It is not surprising that children who are frequently given "explanations," such as the above, would be oriented toward punishment and authority. The parent in this case is teaching the child a preconventional type of reasoning. Surely not all parents who make such statements are, themselves, in the preconventional stage. Rather, for some reason they are not exposing their children to their own moral reasoning. From this example, it is clear that parents are capable of implying types of moral reasoning to their children that may be very different from their own type of moral reasoning.

It seems likely that the level of moral reasoning that is implied by parents would increase with the age of their child. If this is indeed the case, then the stages that occur in the child's thinking may simply occur because the child is learning these types of thinking from his parents. Thus, it is possible that the observed stages may really originate in the external environment rather than in internal changes in the child's cognitive structure. The purpose of the present study was, first, to determine whether parents actually do imply different moral principles to children of different ages and, second, to determine whether there is a relationship between the type of moral reasoning that the parents imply and the level of moral reasoning used by the child.

## B. Method

### 1. Subjects

The subjects were 17 six-year-olds, 17 ten-year-olds, and 17 fourteen-year-old students at the campus school of the State University of New York College at Buffalo and their mothers. The age ranges of the three groups of children were from 6 years and 2 months to 6 years and 11 months, from 10 years and 3 months to 10 years and 10 months, and from 14 years and 1 month to 14 years and 11 months. Due to the lottery student selection employed by the campus school, the students came from a variety of racial and social class backgrounds. Approximately half of the subjects were male and half, female.

### 2. Procedure

The children and their mothers were interviewed separately. Neither was told that the other was being interviewed.

a. *Child interview.* The children were brought individually from the classroom to the experimental room. The experimenter spent a few minutes talking with the children in order to establish rapport before beginning the interview. The children were then asked 11 questions, each of which demanded a moral judgment. Examples of such questions are as follows: (a) "Kathy's parents told her that if she didn't do well in school she would be punished. On the next big test Kathy didn't know many of the answers. When the teacher wasn't looking Kathy copied someone else's answers. Kathy got a good grade on the test. Kathy's mother was so happy that Kathy got a good grade on the test that she took her out for an ice cream sundae. Was Kathy right to copy the answers? Why?"; and (b) "A woman had an accident on the highway. One man saw the accident and just kept on driving. Another man saw the accident and stopped to help the lady. He lifted the injured lady into his car and drove her to the hospital. There the doctor told the man that by moving the lady he had made her injuries worse. Which man did the best thing—the man who drove by or the man who stopped to help? Why?" After the child's response to each question, a number of probing questions were asked to determine why he answered the way he did.

The answers to all of the questions were tape-recorded so they could be scored at a later time. The responses were divided into Kohlberg's three main stages—preconventional, conventional, and postconventional.

b. *Mother interview.* The mothers were interviewed individually during school hours. They were presented with 15 questions that were intended to get at the moral principles that the mothers convey to their children by the way they respond to their children's behavior. Examples of such questions are as follows: (a) "If you found out that (child's name) had stolen something from a department store but did not get caught, what would you say or do to (child's name)?"; (b) "If you asked (child's name) to clean up the dishes because you had to go to a meeting right after dinner and he (she) said "no", what would you say or do?"; and (c) "let's say that (child's name) came home from school and said that someone at school had told him that if a person was in great pain and dying of cancer, the doctor should just kill him. What would you say to him (her)?"

The mothers' responses were also tape-recorded so they could be scored at a later time. The mothers' responses were scored according to which of Kohlberg's stages of moral reasoning their actions would imply to the child. For example, if, in response to the first question cited above, the mother said that she would spank her child and tell him that if he ever stole something again he would get another spanking, she would be given a preconventional score. In this case the mother is implying to the child that the reason for not stealing is so that he will not get spanked. Thus, she is stressing to the child that the consequences of the act are what make it either good or bad. Likewise, the mother who says that she would tell her child that he should not steal because, if he got caught, the owner of the store might call the police would get a preconventional score.

Examples of responses that would be categorized into conventional stages are: "What would Mr. Jones think if he found out that you were stealing from his store? Do you want people to think that you are a thief?" and "It's against the law to take something that doesn't belong to you so we are going to have to return it to the store."

Examples of responses that would be classified as postconventional are "I know I wouldn't feel right if I stole something. I wouldn't want other people to take things that belong to me, so I wouldn't take things that belong to other people." or "Do you think it's right for people to just go take whatever they want? What would happen if everyone just went around taking whatever they wanted no matter who it belonged to?"

## C.  RESULTS

All of the mothers' responses and all of the children's responses were categorized into either the preconventional, conventional, or postconventional category of moral reasoning. Then the most frequent category used by each mother and each child was taken as that mother's or that child's overall score. All of the analyses were performed on these overall scores.

Interrater reliability was established on both the children's and the mothers' overall scores by the first author and another rater who was unfamiliar with the project. The two raters independently categorized the protocols of 25 randomly selected mothers and the protocols of 25 randomly selected children. The interrater reliability obtained on the mothers' protocols was .89 and the interrater reliability obtained on the children's protocols was .85.

All of the data analyses were performed on the first author's categorizations of the data.

### 1.  *Mothers' Responses*

The frequencies of the mothers' implied levels of moral reasoning for the 6-, 10-, and 14-year-old children are presented in Table 1. There was a significant relationship between the age of the child and the level of moral reasoning implied by the mother in her treatment of the child, $X^2(4) = 14.43$, $p < .01$. The older the child, the higher the level of moral reasoning, the mother implied in her treatment of the child.

TABLE 1
LEVELS OF MORAL REASONING IMPLIED BY MOTHERS AND
DISPLAYED BY CHILDREN

| Children's age | Preconventional | Conventional | Postconventional |
|---|---|---|---|
| | | *Implied by mothers* | |
| 6 | 12 | 1 | 4 |
| 10 | 5 | 4 | 8 |
| 14 | 2 | 7 | 8 |
| | | *Displayed by children* | |
| 6 | 15 | 2 | 0 |
| 10 | 7 | 9 | 1 |
| 14 | 5 | 8 | 4 |

## 2. Children's Responses

The frequencies of the 6-, 10-, and 14-year-old children's levels of moral reasoning are also presented in Table 1. There was a significant relationship between the age of the child and his level of moral development, $X^2(4) = 16.06$, $p < .01$. The older the child, the higher the level of moral reasoning he used.

## 3. Relationship Between the Mother's and the Children's Responses

The correlation between the mothers' and their children's responses was $+.59$ which was significant at the .01 level. This is not too surprising in light of the fact that both the mothers' implied level of moral reasoning and the children's level of moral reasoning increased with the age of the child. However, even with age partialed out, the relationship between the mother's implied level of moral reasoning was significant, $r = .51$.

## D. DISCUSSION

The results of the present study indicate that (a) the older the child the higher the level of moral reasoning he employs; (b) the older the child, the higher the level of moral reasoning his mother implies; and (c) even with age partialed out, there is a significant positive relationship between the level of moral reasoning implied by the mother and the level of moral reasoning employed by her child.

If one can assume that the mothers' responses to the hypothetical situations presented reflect the way in which they ordinarily treat their children, then the results indicate that the mothers do, indeed, treat children of different ages in ways that imply different types of moral reasoning.

Thus, it appears that there is at least one environmental factor—how the parent treats the child—which could be responsible for the stages that have been observed in the development of moral reasoning. Consequently, environmental factors should no longer be quickly dismissed as possible causes of the stages observed in young children. The environment is simply not the same for children of different ages, and thus, environmental factors should be considered as possible causes of developmental changes in the child's thinking.

Of course, the results of the present study do not prove that the stages observed in the development of moral reasoning are a result of external, adult teaching rather than a result of internal changes in cognitive structure. Because the present study was correlational, causality cannot be established. One could always argue that the mothers simply tailor their explanations to what they have found, through experience, to be understandable for the children. Thus, the children might be causing the stages in the mothers. In order to establish the direction of causality, noncorrelational research will have to be done. Until that time, one can at least conclude that environmental factors should not be discounted as possible causes of the stages in the development of moral reasoning.

## REFERENCE

1.  KOHLBERG, L. Stage and sequence: The cognitive-developmental approach to socialization. In D. A. Goslin (Ed.), *Handbook of Socialization Theory and Research*. Chicago: Rand McNally, 1969.

*Department of Psychology*
*The University of Kansas*
*Lawrence, Kansas 66044*

# 𝒳 *3* 𝒳

# Fair Distribution and Sharing: The Development of Positive Justice

*F*or a young child, sharing is probably the largest part of friendship. Playing with friends in early childhood means spending time together, using each other's playthings, trading toys, and taking turns. What is the significance of such activity to the child, or to the child's social development? How does a child represent his own sharing to himself? Do children share resources because they think that it is "right" to do so in some sense; and, if so, what is the basis of this moral value? Or are there a variety of reasons for sharing, and a variety of modes of sharing, representative of different children at different developmental levels? These questions are the focus of the present chapter.

Let us begin, in a sense, at the top, by examining how

some sophisticated adults have analyzed the rationale and significance of resource sharing. The crux of sharing is the logic of distribution; that is, the range of ways in which goods may be awarded in a society (whether the society consists of a nation or of three-year-old children at play). When attempts are made to award the resources fairly, we have a problem in what Aristotle first called "distributive justice." Of course, one may attempt *not* to make fair awards but, rather, to distribute resources in a pragmatic or selfish manner. Mimicking Aristotle, we might call this a problem in "distributive pragmatism." Nevertheless, justice is commonly invoked as a means of resolving social conflicts between competing parties (see Rawls, 1971). Even when the self is one of the parties, and even when the chosen distribution of resources seems blatantly to favor the self, it is normal for all but the very youngest children to justify the distribution with some reference to fairness.

Distributions of resources may be constructed and justified in various ways. Frankena (1963), a contemporary philosopher, has suggested three categories of distribution modes. The following analysis is adapted rather loosely from Frankena's original distinctions. Each of the three main modes represents a different means of dividing resources among competing persons; and each mode tends to favor and reward different qualities in persons. For example, a *meritarian* mode of distributing goods favors persons who possess certain valued characteristics (such as age, sex, intelligence, goodness, race, physical beauty, diligence, or friendliness) and thus allegedly deserve a greater share of the resources than others. Probably the truest claims to merit, however, are based on notions of payback or reciprocity; that is, someone deserves more than someone else because he has contributed more, worked harder, or invested greater talent. Often, the underlying assumption in this kind of merit argument is that it is in the interest of all persons in society to encourage such achievement (Rawls, 1971); but this assumption is by no means necessary for the belief that people should be paid back materially for meritorious deeds or service.

Another mode of distributing resources is the *egalitarian* mode. The assumption here is that all persons—simply because they are human beings—are entitled to equal shares of resources, or at least to equal opportunities for acquiring the resources. Therefore, the egalitarian mode may assure all parties of equal shares or may distribute resources according to luck (as long as everyone has an equal chance). A combination of egalitarian and meritarian modes might ensure everyone an equal chance to compete and then allow the best competitor to win the largest share of the reward.

A more active means of obtaining egalitarian distributions, beyond simply giving everyone equal chances, is the *benevolent* mode. Benevolence attempts to establish equality between persons not merely through equal distributions or equal opportunity but, rather, by giving extra to persons with special need or prior deprivation. In this manner, benevolence attempts to compensate for inequalities that may have existed prior to the distribution of resources in any given situation. Rather than doling out equal shares all along, regardless of individual circumstance, this mode of distributing goods tries to achieve an end state of equality.

These three basic modes of distributing resources are not, of course, mutually exclusive. Each may be combined with another in any distribution decision. In addition, each may be used differently in different circumstances, or when different types of resources are to be shared. For example, one might choose one mode for distributing food, another for distributing luxuries, and still another for distributing intangible resources, such as power or praise. Nevertheless, the above analysis of basic modes of resource sharing enables us to proceed with a description of children's knowledge of sharing and affiliated activities and to distinguish between developmental levels of this knowledge. The following three studies in positive justice (the aspect of justice that is concerned with who in society should get what proportion of the available resources, praise, and other rewards) explore how children at different ages conceive of and deal with distribution-of-reward conflicts common to the social world of childhood. The first study examines children's positive justice solutions to such conflicts as they are presented hypothetically to the children; the second reports longitudinal evidence of the development of positive justice reasoning in early and middle childhood; and the third study examines children's positive justice reasoning and conduct in a real-life distribution-of-reward situation.

## Study 1: Hypothetical Dilemmas

The subjects of Study 1 were fifty boys and girls—five boys and five girls at each age from four through eight—from middle- and upper-middle-class families in Berkeley, California. All children were given the hypothetical positive justice interview described in Chapter Two. In addition, there was an initial attempt to give these children two of Kohlberg's moral judgment dilemmas, in order to establish the relation between children's positive justice reasoning and their more general moral judgment. This attempt, however, was unsuccessful; the youngest children (six and under) failed to respond intelligibly to the Kohlberg dilemmas, and the oldest children showed no variation in their reasoning beyond Kohlberg's stage 1. In contrast, the positive justice interview revealed great variation in children's reasoning throughout this entire age span. The fifty children in Study 1 were also given five of Piaget's logical-operational tasks: two classification tasks, one seriation task, one spatial perspectives task, and one numerical proportionality task. (This aspect of the study is discussed in Chapter Seven.)

A distinct sequence of age-related levels of justice emerged from children's reasoning in Study 1, as well as from a previous pilot study (Damon, 1973). (The extent to which these levels may be called formal developmental "stages"—and the implications of this term—is discussed in relation to Study 2, where the longitudinal evidence directly bears on this issue. For now, we shall simply refer to *levels* of positive justice reasoning.) Six primary levels of positive justice reasoning were discerned in the subjects of Study 1; these are labeled 0-A, 0-B, 1-A, 1-B, 2-A, and 2-B. Table 1 offers brief, somewhat cryptic, descriptions of each of the positive justice levels. Perhaps the best way to conceptualize these levels is as a sequence of unfolding confusions in the mind of the child. Each mental confu-

Table 1
Brief Descriptions of Early Positive Justice Levels

---

*Level 0-A:*  Positive justice choices derive from *S*'s wish that an act occur. Reasons simply assert the choices rather than attempting to justify them (that is, I should get it because I want to have it).

*Level 0-B:*  Choices still reflect *S*'s desires but are now justified on the basis of external, observable realities such as size, sex, or other physical characteristics of persons (that is, We should get the most because we're girls). Such justifications, however, are invoked in a fluctuating, *a posteriori* manner, and are self-serving in the end.

*Level 1-A:*  Positive justice choices derive from notions of strict equality in actions (that is, that everyone should get the same). Justifications are consistent with this principle but are unilateral and inflexible.

*Level 1-B:*  Positive justice choices derive from a notion of reciprocity in actions: that persons should be paid back in kind for doing good or bad things. Notions of merit and deserving emerge. Justifications are unilateral and inflexible.

*Level 2-A:*  A moral relativity develops out of the understanding that different persons can have different, yet equally valid, justifications for their claims to justice. The claims of persons with special needs (that is, the poor) are weighed heavily. Choices attempt quantitative compromises between competing claims (e.g., He should get the most, but she should get some too).

*Level 2-B:*  *S* coordinates considerations of equality and reciprocity, so that *S*'s positive justice choices take into account the claims of various persons and the demands of the specific situation. Choices are firm and clearcut, yet justifications reflect the recognition that all persons should be given their due (though, in many situations, this does not mean equal treatment).

---

sion is less sophisticated than the following one. At the most primitive level, 0-A, fairness is confused with the child's own desires. This is certainly the most basic confusion of all, since— as the Canadian philosopher Beck (1970) has said—the essence of fairness and morality is the eventual subordination of purely selfish desire. For example, a child at 0-A might say that it is fair for him to get more ice cream than his sister because he likes ice cream and wants more. At level 0-B egocentric desires are justified by references to some quasi-objective criterion; for example, a child might say that he should get what he wants because he's the fastest runner in his house, or because he's a boy, and so on, even if such criteria are illogical, untrue, or irrelevant to the reward under consideration. At the next level, 1-A, fairness is confused with strict equality in actions: It is fair for everyone to get the same treatment, regardless of special considerations like merit or need. We may recognize an egalitarian mode of distribution here. Next, at 1-B, comes a confusion of fairness with deserving: Those who worked hardest, were smartest, acted best, and so on, should be rewarded because they deserve it. This is certainly one form of a meritarian argument, relying on the notion of reciprocity or payback for good deeds. We are at this point normally into middle childhood, in the early elementary school years. Among children a bit older, at 2-A, fairness is confused with compromise, special attention being paid to those with special needs. The child might say that everyone with a claim should get some justly determined proportion of the resources in question, but perhaps the poor people, who have less to begin with, should receive more to make up the difference. We see here a benevolent mode. Finally, the oldest children (at 2-B) confuse fairness with a situational kind of ethic. All potential justice claims—equality, need, deserving, compromise—are considered, but the one that is selected is chosen with a view to the specific function of the reward in the specific situation under question. Often these children sound like utilitarians. For example, a child might argue that people who work the hardest and do the best jobs should be rewarded most, because that way everyone will be encouraged to do better next time, and then all of the class will earn more money. Or another child at this same level might argue that all should be rewarded equally, because this is by nature a cooperative situation and all other considerations would violate the implicit agreement of all present. At all levels, however—as will be noted in the quantitative results section following this discussion—it is rare to see a child employ any one type of reasoning exclusively; rather, children tend to use the more advanced levels in greater frequency as they get older, just as they tend to use the lower levels less.

The ordering of these early levels bears no implication about the relative worth of meritarian, egalitarian, or benevolent philosophies of distribution as employed by adults. The positive justice levels demonstrated by young children in their reasoning represent primitive uses of such philosophies as they may be applied to distribution problems commonly found in childhood. A distribution-of-rewards problem in adulthood is usually considered in the context of major political traditions and prevailing economic realities. In such a case, positive justice reasoning takes on an entirely different form, with different sorts of organizing principles at work. For this reason, the primitive (and, of course, naive) uses that the young children in the present study make of egalitarian, meritarian, and benevolent philosophies have no direct relation to similar-sounding ideas when applied by adults to the complex distribution problems of their social world. There may, of course, be a *developmental* relation between the two, in the sense that children's early construction of justice principles in their own social world prepares them for the later reorganization and amplification of the justice principles necessary for functioning in the adult social world. But it would be a mistake to expect, for example, an eight-year-old child, demonstrating 2-A benevolence, to construct a benevolent solution to a problem in adult social welfare.

*Levels of positive justice reasoning.* In the ensuing discussion, examples of children's reasoning at each of the six levels are quoted and analyzed. As in all of our analyses of children's social knowledge, the discussion focuses on the organizing principles underlying each mode or level of reasoning. In the case of positive justice, organizing principles at each level function in four related ways: (1) to determine the type of justice conflict that the child recognizes and considers; (2) to determine by what means the child resolves the justice conflict; (3) to determine the collection of persons whom the child considers signifi-

cant in his/her construction of a "fair" resolution to the justice
conflict; and (4) to determine the nature of the justification
that the child invokes in support of his/her resolutions to the
justice conflict.

At the most primitive level, 0-A, the child's conception of
positive justice is confused with his conception of his own desire. Judgments like "I should get more candy than Jimmy" are
not distinguished from statements like "I want more than
Jimmy." The child's distribution choices derive from his wish
for a given act to occur and from his attempt to ensure pleasant
consequences for himself or his close associates.

James (4 yrs. 8 mos.): Suppose you and Sammy are playing together and you have these [five] toys? Would you give
him any? *I would give him these two.* Why those two? *Because I
got to keep three. These are the ones I like.* Suppose Sammy
said, "I want to have more"? *If he took one then I would take
one back from him.* Why is that? *Because I want three.* What
will Sammy do then? *He will say that's OK, because he likes
these* [the two toys originally given].

Mary (4 yrs.): Who should Miss Townsend [the teacher]
give the ice cream to? *Clara.* Why Clara? *Because she likes ice
cream.* Well, Ed likes ice cream too. Should Ed get some ice
cream? *Yes.* Suppose there is not enough, and all the kids like
ice cream. Who should she give it to? *Rebecca.* Why Rebecca?
*She likes Rebecca.* Is it fair to the boys just to give the girls ice
cream? *Yes.* Why is that fair? *Because they don't like the boys.*
So is it OK not to be fair to the boys? *If they don't like the ice
cream, they won't want to eat the ice cream.*

At 0-A the types of conflict recognized by the child are
simply conflicts between the self's desire and any obstacles to
the fulfillment of these desires. Where there is potential conflict
between the desires of the self and those of another, the child at
0-A generally reconciles the two by assimilating one to the
other. In each of the protocols cited above, for example, the
child assumes that all parties will be in accord with his wishes,
even when certain parties are receiving less, or even none, of the
desired reward.

The means of resolving conflicts at 0-A is to assure pleasant consequences to the self or to those associated with the self. Significant persons are the self and those associated with the self through bonds of affection (as in "liking"), familial relation, sex type, or other kinds of identification (youth, size, race, and so on). The nature of justification at 0-A is egocentric and subjective. There is no awareness of a need to support a justice choice with external, objective reasons; rather, justifications are limited to a reassertion of one's own wishes. Reasoning at this primitive level does not go beyond statements of what the child, or the figure associated with the child, wants or likes.

0-B justice choices, like those at 0-A, primarily serve the purpose of gratifying the self. But, in his reasoning, the child at 0-B considers certain external, observable characteristics of persons: "The biggest should get the most" or "She should have it because she's pretty." This initial citing of personal attributes constitutes a rudimentary (nonreciprocal) use of merit, lacking the more advanced notion of deserving or payback for good deeds. In addition, rudimentary usage of equality appears in the form of one-to-one correspondences: "Give them all some" (though not necessarily the same). Also, rudimentary notions of reciprocity appear in the form of action-reaction sequences: "If I don't share with her, she'll get mad at me." In none of these rudimentary forms is true reciprocity or equality employed accurately or consistently, but we do see the germinal roots of these later organizing principles. The distinguishing characteristic of 0-B reasoning is not this rudimentary usage of later principles but the child's tendency to invoke "objective" considerations solely in support of his own egocentric wishes. Typical of 0-B is that these new considerations are invoked in a fluctuating, *a posteriori* manner and are consistent more with the principle of self-gratification than with any constant, objective standard of fairness. In a sense, at 0-B we have an 0-A mode of judgment justified on grounds that sound, on the surface, like objective standards.

Miriam (4 yrs. 5 mos.): [Keeps four blue chips and gives Jenny two white chips.] You would keep all the blues for your-

self? *Yes, because I like blue. And then I'd play with them.*
Let's pretend Jenny said, "I like blue." Would you give her any
blue? *Never, because I have a blue dress at home.* So you
wouldn't give her any blue at all. Is it fair to do it this way? *Ah,
ha, I've got it. I'd give her two of the white—I'd give her those
[two] because she's younger than me, and I get four because
I'm four.*

Jack (5 yrs. 2 mos.): Suppose your friend Johnny is sitting here. Would you give him any of your toys [five poker
chips]? *Yes, I'd give him this one.* You would keep these four
for yourself? *Yes.* Why would you keep more for yourself and
only give him one? *Because I'm bigger than him.* What if I
wanted some of these. Would you give me any? *Yes, you can
have this one.* Why do you get to have more than me? *Because
I'm bigger than you.* You're bigger than me? *Yes.* But I say I'm
bigger than you and I should get more than you. *No, I want to
keep [all] these.*

The types of conflict recognized at 0-B include conflicts
between the self's desires and those of others; hence, the child
realizes that there is a need to justify his decisions on grounds
more universally acceptable than a reference to his own wishes.
Related to this is a realization that others may react negatively
to a decision that affects the self positively, a realization that
enables the subject to describe realistically the reciprocal nature
of some social exchanges (for example, "She'll get mad if I
don't share with her").

As at 0-A, the 0-B means of resolving conflicts is the awarding of preferential treatment to the self or to those associated with
the self. The definition of significant persons also remains unchanged. But in 0-B justifications, as noted above, there is a significant advance: The subject for the first time supports his decisions by referring to external, observable events or to physical
characteristics of persons. The fluctuating, after-the-fact nature
of 0-B reasoning is demonstrated by Miriam, and the self-serving
aspect of 0-B reasoning is demonstrated by Jack. Despite these
limitations, however, 0-B represents an increasing differentiation
of the subject's conception of justice from his naked desire.

At level 1-A the operating justice principle is one of equal action; that is, everyone should get the same treatment under any circumstances. This principle permeates both the subject's choices and his justifications at 1-A, so that there is an inevitable logical consistency between the two. In fact, the subject's unilateral use of the equal-action principle is so overridingly consistent that 1-A reasoning often takes on a quality of inflexibility and absolutism.

Anita (7 yrs. 4 mos.): How would you give it out? *You can give them each a quarter, or you can give them each a dime, a penny, a nickel, and all kinds of things you would like to give them.* Do you think anyone should get any more than anyone else? *No, because it's not fair. Somebody has 35 cents and somebody has one penny. That's not fair.* Clara said she made more things than everybody else and she should get more money. *No. She shouldn't because it's not fair for her to get more money, like a dollar, and they get only about one cent.* Why isn't that fair? *Well, she couldn't make all those things, 'cause if she did she would've got tired. She didn't make all the money.* She didn't make them all, but she did make more than anybody else. Should she get a little more? *No. People should get the same amount of money because it's not fair.* Here's another thing. George said that he thought the one who made the best stuff should get the most money. *The best person who makes the best stuff is not polite, because you should make them have the same alike—give everything the same. The same, because it's not polite when you give people the most and they [the rest] don't have one. It's fair to the other children that they have to get it too.*

Mike (6 yrs. 11 mos.): Would you give Kevin any of these to play with? *Yeah.* You would? *I'd give these, so it'd be equal, so we can each have five.* Well, where would you put that [extra] one? *Put it back.* You wouldn't use it then? *Yeah.* Why is that a good thing? *'Cause like if I have six, that wouldn't be equal, like see—and if he has six, it wouldn't be equal.* Why wouldn't that be a good thing? *Because then we would start fussin'. Like, say I have four and you have seven, then we start fighting.*

Iris (6 yrs. 8 mos.): What do you think "fair" means? *If somebody gets, like after lunch—one of my friends, I asked him if I could have some of their lunch and they said OK, and then they gave somebody else two pieces and they only gave me one, and I said that wasn't fair.*

The type of conflict recognized at 1-A is that of persons against persons, each person now being considered a distinct, objective, yet essentially similar individual. Each party in a conflict situation is seen as having an identical goal, that of self-interest. In other words, the child at 1-A knows that persons may compete with one another for goods and favors, but he understands this competition as an inevitable conflict of separate individuals, each with similar selfish desires; he does not recognize the psychological uniqueness, the subjectivity, the disparate intentions and motivations of the competing individuals. Therefore, he does not see the problem as one of weighing one type of consideration against another qualitatively different one.

The child's means of resolving conflicts at 1-A is to treat all persons equally, through the administration of equal acts. No mitigating circumstances or reasons are allowed or recognized. Anita, for example, considers behavior that would lead to a claim to differential treatment "impolite." Since no claim beyond another's simple assertion of self-interest is recognized, all other types of justice claims are understood to be further, and thus overassertive, statements of this self-interest. Equality—or absolute similarity of treatment—is derivable at 1-A from the subject's belief in the similarity of persons' wants, needs, and claims to justice.

Significant persons at 1-A are all those present in a conflict situation. Justifications assert the principle of equal treatment and further support this principle with reference to the self-interest of each party concerned. Mike, for example, wants to prevent "fussing" and fighting, a common 1-A rationale for equal treatment. Since equality in treatment is seen at 1-A as the only sensible way to deal with conflicting persons (con-

ceived as quarreling, selfish individuals), reasoning appears unilateral and inflexible.

At 1-B justice judgments operate on the principle of a
reciprocity of acts, employing notions of merit and fair exchange. The child at 1-B regards positive justice as a payback for
being or doing good (for example, being smart or working
hard). Similarly, there is now a sense of obligation in the exchange or reward—so that, for example, a friend *should* be paid
back for a favor or a gift. What was merely descriptive at 0-B in
the subject's recognition of action-reaction sequences becomes
prescriptive at 1-B.

Alison (6 yrs. 8 mos.): What if your mother told you,
"No, you can't play with Colin anymore"? *I would say to my
mother, "But he's my friend."* And what difference would that
make? *Because he shares his things with me, so I've got to share
my toys with him.* Suppose you don't like this person? *Then if
he won't play with me, I won't play with him, and I won't share
anything with him.*

Steven (6 yrs. 6 mos.): But Rebecca thought that she
should get the most because she made the most things. Do you
think that's fair? *Well, if she made more things, then she'd get
more money.* What if she didn't make . . . *If she didn't want to
make anything, then she wouldn't get as much as all of these
kids.* Well, what about the poor kid here, who doesn't have any
money to begin with? *Well, the poor kid should make some
stuff, then he'd get more.* What about the lazy kid? *Well, he
shouldn't get as much if he didn't work as much, if he didn't do
his work.* What's the very best way of giving the money out? *I
think Rebecca should get the most because she made the most,
and if she didn't make the most, then she wouldn't get as much
money. But I'll bet she made pretty much.*

The type of conflict recognized at 1-B is that of some
persons with "deserving" claims versus other persons with
"deserving" claims; but only one type of claim is understood to
be "deserving": that of merit. The 1-B means of resolving conflicts, therefore, is to treat people differentially according to

their possession of merit criteria. As Steven illustrates, reward at
1-B is seen as a direct payback for work, achievement, or any
investment of talent or effort. Related to this is the 1-B notion
that friends should be paid back for their favors and that sharing is an instrumental means toward this end. For Alison,
sharing seems mainly to serve the purpose of establishing a fair
exchange.

Significant persons at 1-B are those who have made a contribution, and the significance of the person varies with the
degree of his contribution. At 1-B justification incorporates
notions of reciprocal obligation; but, since the valuing of reciprocity is as unilateral as was the valuing of equality at 1-A,
reasoning still maintains its absolutistic, inflexible quality.

At 2-A the child extends his justice reasoning beyond the
unilateral modes of judgment that prevail at 1-A and 1-B. The
child at 2-A, realizing that there may be a plurality of acceptable justice claims, which may lead to a number of morally
acceptable decisions, demonstrates a moral relativity in his
reasoning. Associated with this relativity is a new respect for the
equality of persons; that is, since all persons should be considered as equals, all persons' claims must be considered equally
(though not necessarily judged to be of absolutely equal worth).

Because there is at 2-A an emphasis on the equality of
persons (rather than on an equality of acts, as at 1-A), the condition of need, understood as a special form of personal inequal-
ity, is given a special preference in positive justice judgments. A
child at 2-A considers that rewarding need may be necessary to
maintain the equality of persons; for example, giving extra food
to a hungry person helps to maintain him as an equal person,
even though the act itself is an unequal act.

The new notion of need, alongside the previously realized
notion of merit, makes the child aware of a number of conflicting claims. At 2-A choices generally attempt compromises between the conflicting claims, rather than direct resolutions of
them.

Andy (7 yrs. 9 mos.): What if Rebecca made more stuff?
Should she get more money? *Oh, about seven more pennies. It*

*depends on what she made—if she made something easy or hard.* What if she made something hard? *About ten cents more.* What about Peter, who made the best stuff? Should he get more? *Well, maybe he should. But since she made more, she may have some good ones, so then maybe he can get around five cents more.* What about Billy, who doesn't get any allowance? *He should only get about three cents more because—if he got a lot more, he might even have more than anybody adding up their allowance.* What about these others? *No, because they don't have such a big reason.*

Dan (8 yrs. 11 mos.): So, would you give Rebecca, who made more things, more of the money? *Well, she would get a little more. She would be getting about three dollars more.* Billy says that he should get more, too, because he doesn't get any money at home. *I'd give him a little more. Because everybody deserves an allowance.* What about Melissa, the best-behaved kid? Would you give her more? *Probably.* You would? *Yeah, but not too much more, because being a real nice kid isn't much, you know. I'd probably give her same as Billy, but not as much as Rebecca.* Well, Peter said, "No, the kids who made the best stuff should get the most." Now what do you think? *Well, if we keep doing it this way, there'll probably be one kid left with nothing. And so, I think what we do is, first we'd have everybody say all their reasons, then we'll pick the three best reasons. Because everybody in the class could come up with one.* Well, if you had to decide, which ones were the best reasons? *These kids—he [Billy] really needs it because he doesn't get money too often, and she [Rebecca] earned it and so did he [Peter]. And she [Melissa] did very good—So we take these four and we give them each about ten cents more.*

The type of conflict recognized at 2-A is that of a plurality of disparate claims to justice. The means of resolving such conflicts is to mediate between them through mechanisms of compromise. Such compromise in a positive justice situation often takes a quantitative form, awarding the most to the party with the "best" claim and awarding shares to each of the other parties in proportion to "how right" each is considered to be (see Dan above). In this manner, quantitative compromises serve the purpose of respecting all parties' perspectives equally, while

at the same time weighing each of them and arriving at a concrete judgment regarding this weighing. Often, the stress on
equal weighing at 2-A leads the child to favor the claim of special need or deprivation, since this is seen as the best way to
establish ultimate equality between persons. Significant persons
at 2-A are all persons present. Justifications reflect a moral relativity associated with the 2-A attempt to respect all parties
equally; there is frequently the assertion that, when two or
more parties conflict, each of them is right "in a way."

The child at 2-B, like the child at 2-A, weighs the relative
value of all competing justice claims; but at 2-B a further-order
judgment is made as to which of the competing claims is most
justifiable in the current context. Most significantly, the child at
2-B is able to exclude certain justice claims as irrelevant to the
particular conflict under consideration. In positive justice problems, the child makes such exclusions considering the function
of the reward. The subject sees that a decision concerning just
reward can be a means toward various ends, and he doles out
the reward according to which end he deems most appropriate.

Sally (7 yrs. 6 mos.): Should anyone get any more than
anyone else? *That depends on how nice their things were—If
Peter sold like a belt he'd made, for about nine dollars, then
Peter should get nine dollars.* Do you think that's the fairest
way to do it? *Yes—so everybody would get what their things
sold for.* Is that the best way, or should all the kids get equal
shares of the class's profits? *Well, it seems that would be fair if
everybody got an equal share, but probably some kids didn't
sell as much as others. I would give the most to the kids that
sold the most.* Why is that? *That way they'll all do better next
time.* Should the kids who were most cooperative get bigger
shares? *No! Because that really doesn't make much sense. They
are not in a contest about attitude and how you share with
other people. They don't care about that. They just want to
have people do good stuff, they don't care about that.* How
about giving bigger shares to the poor kids? *No. They [the
class] don't care if they [the poor kids] are poor or not. Well,
we might feel a little sorry for them. But they don't care about
that. They just want the ones who did the best to get the most*

*money.* And why is that? *I just said, that way they'll all try to do better next time.*

Louise (8 yrs. 5 mos.): Should Melissa [the well-behaved girl] get a little more of the fair money? *No. Because behavior doesn't help make the things. It doesn't make the fair get more money just because she acted better.* What about the people who made the best things? *No. 'Cause, look, they can't help it if their things aren't as good as someone else's.* What is the fairest way? *Take it and split it all up evenly.* And what about Billy, because he didn't get any allowance at home? *He would have to go along with it, probably—a few extra dollars isn't going to help much, because he doesn't have that much money. It isn't going to buy his father some job or something.*

As at 2-A, the type of conflict recognized at 2-B is that of a plurality of disparate justice claims. But the means of resolving conflicts at 2-B is to systematically exclude all but the "best claim." In this way a clearcut, definitive judgment is made, while at the same time all persons' claims have been recognized and respected. The judgment as to which is the best claim may vary from subject to subject, as in the two examples cited. But the distinguishing feature of a 2-B judgment is the way in which this determination is made—most notably, with particular concern for the special demands of the current situation. Sally, for example, excludes all claims other than those that will lead to having people "do good stuff," because she judges this as the purpose of this situation. On a similar basis, Louise opts for an equality solution.

Significant persons at 2-B are all persons present in a conflict situation. Justifications coordinate the various claims to justice, including those of equality (need, equal acts) and those of reciprocity (merit, fair exchange). At 2-B the claims are integrated in such a fashion that they can be differentially employed in different contexts.

In Chapter One we noted that the development of social knowledge consists, in part, of an increasing differentiation between practical and moral orientations to social problems. A practical orientation focuses on realistic consequences of

actions to the self, whereas a moral orientation focuses on justice and how to obtain it. As a child develops, we hypothesized,
his ability to distinguish between practical and moral ideas
should increase. In the development of children's positive justice reasoning, we have seen just such a trend. Children at the
0-A level show almost total confusion between what is best for
themselves and what is fair. At the 0-B level there is a recognition of this dichotomy only in the sense that children begin to
see the need to justify their choices on some quasi-objective
ground. But their choices still tend to confuse practical and
moral ends, just as their justifications shift uneasily back and
forth between practical and moral claims. At 1-A there seems to
be a greater respect for fairness, defined as strict equality; and
children at this level do consistently maintain this newfound objective standard of distribution. But when probed for their
reasons for this respect for fairness, the children reveal a vestigial confusion between practical and moral goals; the rationale
behind equality at 1-A is inevitably the child's desire to avoid
troublesome consequences, such as everyone's getting mad,
fighting, and hurting each other. Only at 1-B and above does
fairness seem valued in its own right, regardless of practical consequences. At 1-B fairness is considered a right of those who
deserve it through meritorious achievement, and at 2-A fairness
is considered a general right of all persons, especially those who
are in intrinsically unequal circumstances to begin with. Children have come so far by 2-B that they actually begin to make
consciously reasoned distinctions between practical and moral
considerations. Both 2-B subjects quoted above seem to be carefully weighing practical against moral concerns. The first child
favors the practical; the second, the moral. But both decisions
are based on judgments about the nature of the specific distribution situation—and especially about which concern, practical
or moral, is more appropriately served in this particular situation. Even among eight-year-olds, we already can see a relatively
sophisticated distinction between the two major orientations to
social problems.

It is certainly true that a child at 2-B positive justice reasoning has come a long way from the moral egocentrism of level

0-A. But a child's positive justice development is far from complete at level 2-B. For example, still missing at 2-B is the ability to remove oneself from the immediate distribution situation, to view it from a perspective wider than that of the parties actually involved. A child at 2-B might say that any distribution agreed on by all persons competing for rewards would be fair, even if the agreement seems to violate objective standards of fairness. As one example, if an adult could get a child voluntarily to trade five dollars for a candy bar, this might be seen as "fair" at 2-B, as long as the two parties attest to the fairness of the arrangement. There is no sense yet that the adult has "taken advantage" of the child, because in this early form of reasoning there is no way to establish a moral perspective outside of the immediate, concrete situation. Objective "third-party" social perspectives are established by organizing principles more advanced than anything found at 2-B and earlier. Since the province of this book is children up to the age of ten or so, we shall conclude here only that a formidable amount of social development continues beyond the age range described in this book.

*Quantitative empirical findings.* A scoring manual, containing lengthy descriptions of the six justice levels as well as examples of children's reasoning at each level, was prepared for Study 1. The descriptions and examples in the manual were drawn from a small sample of children in a pilot study completed prior to the present study (Damon, 1973). All fifty protocols from Study 1 were scored on the basis of this manual. The unit of scoring in a protocol was called a "chunk" of reasoning, a chunk being any statement or group of statements by the child that conveyed a coherent idea or meaning. After all of the reasoning chunks in a given protocol were scored, a composite justice score for the protocol was obtained by taking the highest level of reasoning consistently used by the subject. The final consideration of only the subject's highest reasoning is consistent with the "testing-the-limits" philosophy of the clinical interview method employed in this study (see Chapter Two). In a sense, the interview and scoring techniques when combined may be seen as a means of obtaining the best performance, or the reasoning competence, of children in the course of their hypothetical positive justice reasoning. This "best-performance" approach is necessary to control for incidental differences between children that may affect some scores on a child's protocol but that should not be considered in assessing the child's ability to reason about justice. For example, some children may misunderstand the questions at first or may take longer than others to formulate clear expressions of their beliefs. Others may answer impulsively at first but then work through the justice problem in a more careful, reasoned manner. The intention both of testing-the-limits interviewing and of best-performance scoring is to allow the child every chance to demonstrate his fullest reasoning ability in the positive justice area, without assigning scores based on parts of the subject's performance that do not represent the subject's true ability. On the average, approximately 42 percent of children's reasoning chunks in Study 1 were at the level of their best performance. Most (75 percent) of the remaining 58 percent of the chunks were at one or two levels below this, with occasional inconsistent chunks at one or two levels higher or at more than two levels lower. There was, of course, considerable variation between subjects on this matter, with one subject demonstrating as little as 24 percent of reasoning at his best level, while two others showed an extremely consistent 94 percent of reasoning at their best levels. The standard deviation of subjects' mean percentage of reasoning chunks from their best performance levels was 15.6 percent.

Interjudge reliability of scoring for Study 1 was determined for a randomly chosen subset of approximately one fourth (twelve) of the subjects' protocols. Two judges, or "raters," were given copies of the twelve protocols, as well as copies of the scoring guide. Reliability was determined by calculating the percentage of perfect agreement between the two raters on each subject's score, in addition to the percentage of disagreement by one level, two levels, and so on. For composite positive justice scores, there was 83 percent perfect agreement between the two raters and 17 percent disagreement by one level. The two judges' ratings were never more than one level apart.

There was a strong association between age of subject and

positive justice reasoning level. A rank-order correlation between age of subject and justice reasoning level yielded a coefficient of $r$ (48) = .85, $p < .001$. Justice level 0-A was found predominantly at age four; 0-B, at ages four and five; 1-A, at age
five (with some subjects scattered at higher ages); 1-B, at ages
six and seven; 2-A, at age eight; and 2-B, at age eight.

The close association between age and positive justice
level found in Study 1 suggests that children's justice reasoning
develops in a regular and predictable age-related manner during
early and middle childhood. The closeness of the association
found in this study was probably amplified by the homogeneity
of the sample. Children from a more economically or culturally
mixed community would probably have produced weaker age
trends, since major variance in justice scores might have arisen
from factors other than the age-related development of the children. Still, it was possible to conclude from Study 1 that sex-
related socialization patterns do not play a major role in the
development of children's justice reasoning; no sex differences
overall or at any of the five age levels were found in justice
scores.

## Study 2: Longitudinal Data

In the previous study we described six positive justice
levels and found evidence that these six levels were age-related
in children aged four to eight. That is, the younger children in
our sample tended to use the lower levels, whereas the older
children tended to use the higher levels. This kind of "cross-
sectional" evidence suggests that a child's knowledge of justice
develops according to the sequence defined by the six levels.
But, in itself, cross-sectional evidence is not strong enough to
support such a statement with any great confidence. It is possible, for example, that the older children in our sample used a
different form of justice reasoning than the younger children
simply because their age group had been exposed to different
kinds of instruction or other information from their social
world. Perhaps older children had teachers who had different
values than younger ones' teachers. Or perhaps eight-year-olds

in our society have lived through a different chain of social events than have six-year-olds, and these different events were reflected in the reasoning differences found in Study 1. In such cases, the age trends reported would say nothing about how children in general develop a sense of justice. Rather, the age trends would attest only to "cohort" differences between the age groups studied, such differences being due merely to incidental environmental factors.

Study 2 was an attempt to collect more direct data on the development of positive justice reasoning in young children. It was longitudinal as well as cross-sectional in design. Not only did we study children from different age levels, but we studied them over the course of a year, in order to witness developmental changes as they actually occur in individual children. In this manner, we could ascertain whether age differences in children's reasoning were due only to environmental-cohort factors that may apply differently to different groups or whether they were due to developmental changes that occur generally as children grow older.

Also at issue in Study 2 was the "stagelike" nature of the six positive justice levels. Developmental psychologists (for example, Piaget, 1967; Langer, 1969) have generally reserved the term *stages* for developmental sequences that have the following characteristics: (1) *universality,* in the sense that the sequence does not characterize development in merely one culture or subgroup but, rather, is general to all human development; (2) *invariance of sequence,* in the sense that the order of the stages must be constant, stage 1 always preceding stage 2 in development, and so on; and (3) *wholeness,* in the sense that a stage must characterize an organization or pattern of behaviors, rather than the acquisition or development of only a single trait or ability. Study 2 was designed to provide some information relevant to the first two properties of stages noted above. Though this information was not intended to be conclusive, we nevertheless hoped that it would suggest the extent to which the six positive justice levels could be regarded as "stages." More specifically, because Study 2 was conducted with a different type of subject population than was Study 1, we believed that the "universality" property of the levels would be tested (though not as thoroughly, of course, as if the new study had been conducted among, say, Communist Chinese); and, because Study 2 was longitudinal in design, we expected that the nature and relative invariance of the six-level justice sequence could be observed. In other words, we should be able to confirm, from reasoning changes in subjects as they grow a year older, whether the six justice levels develop in order or whether, on the contrary, subjects skip levels, reverse levels, or otherwise vary the justice sequence in the course of their development. Study 2 was not designed to test the "wholeness" property of the justice levels, although this issue will be discussed in Chapter Seven, where the notion of related structures is considered.

The subjects of Study 2 were forty boys and girls from Worcester, Massachusetts. The children were from a range of middle-, lower-middle-, and upper-middle-class backgrounds. The sample was, therefore, less homogeneous than that of Study 1. At the beginning of Study 2, the children ranged in age from four through nine: There were 6 four-year-olds, 6 five-year-olds, 7 six-year-olds, 9 seven-year-olds, 7 eight-year-olds, and 5 nine-year-olds. At the end of the study, all children were one year older.

The procedure of Study 2 was first to give all children an original positive justice interview (in year 1 of the study) and then to give the same children a second interview one year after the first (year 2 of the study). The first interview, given in year 1, was the same as that quoted in Chapter Two and used in Study 1. The second interview, one year later, consisted of two parts. The first part of the second interview was a repeat of the original interview that was given a year earlier to all subjects (referred to here as the "year-2 original interview"). But it was also necessary to give the subjects something new in the second interview, to control for test-retest effects; therefore, the second part of the year-2 interview differed in detail from the original positive justice interview, although it probed for the same general issues. This second part of the year-2 interview is quoted below, complete with the basic set of probe questions.

*211*

These four kids—Michelle, George, Norman, and Ellen
Scott—are brothers and sisters. They came from a family that
doesn't have too much money, so they don't get much of an
allowance. [Make sure that child at this point knows what an
allowance is; and, if not, explain or rephrase.] But they all want
to have some spending money for candy or for going to the
movies and stuff like that.

One day, Ellen has a real good idea. She says that they
should all go out and deliver papers. They could all share a
paper route together and split up the money. The kids decided
to do this, and the paper route earned them ten dollars every
week. [Make sure that child knows what paper route is, and
how it could earn money for the kids.] The kids work the paper
route together and do a real good job. They all carry papers,
although George and Norman carry the most because they're
boys and they can lift more. Ellen and Michelle carry some
papers too, even though Michelle is a very young girl and can't
work as hard as the other kids. But, together, the kids make ten
dollars every week.

Now after the first week, the kids found out right away
that they have a problem. How do they split up the ten dollars
they have made?

1. What do you think? What is the best way for them to
   split the money up? [Use ten poker chips if it helps the
   child think about the ten dollars.] Why is that a good
   way?

2. Ellen says that it was her idea in the first place, so she
   should get some extra money. Is she right? How much
   extra [if appropriate]?

3. George and Norman said they do the most work, so
   they should get the most money. What do you think?

4. Is it fair to give more to Michelle and Ellen because
   they're girls? Is it fair to give more to George and Norman because they're boys?

5. What about Michelle, who doesn't work as hard as the
   other kids? Should she get less? The reason that she
   doesn't do as much is because she's younger and she's a
   girl. Does that matter? What if the reason were because
   Michelle was just plain lazy? Should she get less then?

6. Ellen and Norman are the two oldest kids. They say that they should get more of the money because it's in place of an allowance, and older kids should get more allowance than younger kids. Are they right? How much more [if appropriate]?

7. George, here, is a real sweet kid and everyone likes him a lot. Should he get some extra money?

8. What's the fairest way to split up the money? Why?

The order of the two parts of the year-2 interview varied from subject to subject, so that in half of the cases the new part was given first, and in the other half the original interview was given first. This was necessary to control for fatigue effects that might have influenced subjects' scores on whichever part was given last. For the older children it was possible to give both parts in one forty-minute session, whereas for the younger children the second interview was divided into two twenty-minute sessions. Both interviews in Study 2 were scored on the basis of the same scoring manual used in Study 1. A test of interjudge reliability of scoring in Study 2 yielded almost identical results to those obtained in Study 1.

The results of Study 2 were as follows. First, as in Study 1, children's positive justice scores were strongly associated with age. Though in Study 2 the magnitude of the correlation coefficient between age and justice scores was a bit lower than in Study 1, the associations found in Study 2 were still highly significant. For age and the year-1 original justice interview, $r$ (38) = .64, $p <$ .001; for age and the year-2 original interview, $r$ (38) = .64, $p <$ .001; and for age and the new part of the year-2 interview, $r$ (38) = .56, $p <$ .001. In addition, scores on all justice interviews were correlated significantly with one another. This indicates that children who scored high on one interview tended to score high on the others, and likewise for low scorers. The association between scores on the year-1 original interview and on the year-2 original interview was $r$ (38) = .61, $p <$ .001; the association between year-1 original interview scores and scores on the new part of the year-2 interview was $r$ (38) = .48, $p <$ .01; and the association between scores on the original and new parts of the year-2 interview was $r$ (38) = .73, $p < .001$. Thus, as we might predict, the closest association was between subjects' performances on the two dilemmas administered during the same year (year 2). Next in closeness was the relation between subjects' performances on the same dilemma (the original interview) given a year apart. Weakest, though still significant, was the relation between subjects' performances on different dilemmas a year apart.

For many subjects there was no change in justice scores from one year to the next. Out of the forty subjects, fourteen (or 35 percent) scored at the same justice level on the original interview in year 1 as they did on the original interview in year 2. Twelve (or 30 percent) scored at the same level on the original interview in year 1 as they did on the new part of the year-2 interview.

It could be argued that the percentage of subjects who remained at the same level from year 1 to year 2 was artificially high because of "floor" and "ceiling" effects. That is, 0-As from year 1 could never be scored lower, nor could 2-Bs ever be scored higher, since there was no possible score lower than 0-A or higher than 2-B. Thus, children moving down from 0-A or up from 2-B would still be scored 0-A and 2-B, respectively, thereby inflating the percentage of children remaining at the same level from one year to the next. This is a valid objection, though of little import in the present case, since no 0-As and only two 2-Bs were given the same score from one year to the next. Thus, the "floor" and "ceiling" effects, if any, on the percentage of subjects remaining the same were minimal.

Of the subjects whose scores did change from one year to the next, there was generally a small amount of change. Only five subjects (13 percent) changed by more than one level from year 1 to year 2 on the original interview. Only four (10 percent) changed by more than one level from the year-1 original to the year-2 new interview. There was change in both directions (up and down) from the year-1 to the year-2 interviews, though there was a significant tendency for subjects to advance in the course of the year. Eighteen subjects (45 percent) had higher justice scores on the year-2 original interview than on the year-1 original interview, whereas eight (20 percent) had lower scores in year 2. Nineteen subjects (48 percent) had higher scores on the new interview in year 2 than on the original interview in year 1, whereas nine subjects (23 percent) had lower scores. A nonparametric sign test indicated that the tendency of subjects to change their scores positively from one year to the next was significant at $p < .05$, regardless of which year-2 interview score was used (original or new part). Finally, out of the subjects who showed some change, those who changed by more than one level invariably changed in an upward direction, with only one exception.

Although the results from this small study are hardly conclusive, nevertheless some of the findings do shed light on the nature of the positive justice levels. First of all, the age relatedness of the levels was once again confirmed, this time with children from a different geographical and cultural environment. That the magnitude of the age-justice correlations was somewhat smaller in Study 2 than in Study 1 probably attests to the greater socioeconomic homogeneity in the Study 1 sample. Regardless of this difference, the results from the Worcester, Massachusetts, children were close enough to those from the Berkeley, California, sample to add one bit of evidence in favor of the universality of the positive justice levels. Needless to say, the world extends a long way beyond Worcester and Berkeley, so we have barely opened the door on the universality problem.

Not only were the relations between age and positive justice level confirmed with a new sample of children, but they were replicated in a longitudinal as well as in a cross-sectional design. Over three fourths of the subjects in the present study either stayed at the same level of justice reasoning from one year to the next or progressed upward (regardless of which year-2 interview score was considered). Further, of the children who changed, there was a significant tendency for these changes to be in a positive direction. These findings argue against an environmental-cohort explanation for the positive justice age trends. The pattern and direction of changes from one year to the next suggest rather that positive justice reasoning is a developmental phenomenon, improving as subjects grow older. In addition, the maintenance of the rank-order correlations from one year to the next argues against the importance of incidental environmental influences on subjects' reasoning levels.

As for the sequence of levels, the evidence from Study 2 was not strong enough to confirm the notion that the levels develop in an invariant order. We saw some change in a negative as well as a positive direction, though there was a significant tendency for these changes to be mostly positive. Probably if there had been more time between interviews, we would have seen a clearer tendency for children to advance rather than to move both upward and downward (or, in many cases, to stay the same). In any case, the findings from the present study suggest that children generally do move forward with age along the sequence of justice levels but that one year is too short a time to notice much of this movement. Not only do many children not change at all in the course of a year, but a certain number of children seem to move downward as well. Whether this downward movement should be considered a measurement error, or whether it is evidence against the invariant, forward "steplike" development of positive justice knowledge, cannot be resolved by the present study. For the present, rather than claiming that our positive justice sequence has the formal properties of stages (in particular, the property of invariance of sequence), we shall retain the more conservative term *levels* to describe this sequence.

More striking than the pattern of change in the present study was the considerable stability of the justice levels over time. A sizable group of subjects showed no change at all in the course of a year, and those that did change showed only the smallest degree (usually no more than one level) of change. In one sense, this might be taken as confirmation of the "test-retest" reliability of the justice instrument, since it is clearly possible to obtain from the original justice interview a fairly stable score, even over the course of a year. (In addition, the rank-order correlations between year-1 and year-2 justice scores offer another such confirmation.) But, in a more profound sense, the stability of the justice levels over a year's time suggests that the development of positive justice knowledge in young children is a long, slow process. It simply seems to take a sizable amount of time for a child to reorganize his thinking about justice in a progressive manner. Progress, when it does occur, normally takes place slowly and in small steps. Constructing new justice principles is clearly a complex and difficult task, requiring more than a year for many young children. We shall be interested to note, later in this book, whether the development of new organizing principles for other aspects of social knowledge takes a similar length of time.

### Study 3: Hypothetical Context and "Real-Life" Setting*

The hypothetical interview technique, as used in Studies 1 and 2, has become an increasingly common instrument for the assessment of children's social and moral development (see Lickona, 1976). With the increasing reliance of psychologists and educators on hypothetical-verbal measures, we are naturally interested in the relation between children's performance on such tasks and their behavior in real-life social settings. We may phrase the question of interest in the following manner: Will a child's theoretical reflections on hypothetical stories or dilemmas predict the child's actual judgment and conduct in a real-life social situation? As noted in Chapter One, psychological data on this question are so sketchy that "the connection between 'story problem morality' and conduct is still . . . mostly unknown" (Brown and Herrnstein, 1975, p. 326). Study 3 was an experimental attempt to investigate this problem in the area of children's positive justice knowledge.

Most previous laboratory studies have dichotomized social thought and social action and have attempted to demonstrate correlations between the two. The most common of these attempts have looked for relations between children's moral judgment and children's ability to resist the temptation to engage in "immoral" deeds. These experimental attempts by and large have been unsuccessful. The classic Hartshorne and May failure to establish a relation between children's moral

*Study 3 was done with the collaboration of Randy P. Gerson.

knowledge and their refusal to cheat or lie was noted in Chapter One. Similarly, Grinder and his associates (Grinder, 1964; Nelson, Grinder, and Biaggio, 1969) found low, insignificant, or nonexistent correlations between the maturity of children's moral judgments and their tendencies to resist cheating. In fact, only in rare instances has a relation between social judgment and social action been reported; and in such cases the relation seems to be an indeterminate one. Haan, Smith, and Block (1968), for example, found that college students assessed at Kohlberg's moral judgment stages 2, 5, and 6 were more likely to join a campus sit-in than were students at other stages. But the stage-2 students sat in for different reasons than did the stage-5 and stage-6 students, and a large number of students at stages 2 and 5 chose the opposite action of not sitting in.

The Haan study points to the difficulty inherent in any attempt to specify a relation between judgment and action. As Kohlberg (1969b) has written, any mode of judgment conceivably may lead to a number of disparate (and even contradictory) actions, just as almost any action may theoretically be justified at any judgment level. When social judgment fails to predict social action, therefore, it may be a result of either (or both) of two possibilities: (1) there is sometimes inconsistency between what a person says and what he does in the social realm or (2) judgment cannot predict action because there is never a one-to-one relation between a mode of judgment and a particular act. It is this twin-based, generic uncertainty that has confounded attempts to construct scientific models describing the judgment-conduct relation. As noted in Chapter One, such uncertainty arises from the conceptual problem of attempting to distinguish between two inseparable aspects of human knowledge: thought and action.

With a reformulation of the original problem, however, it becomes possible to investigate the relation between "story-problem" social judgment and real-life social behavior in a less ambiguous fashion. In Chapter One a distinction was drawn between two types of social knowledge: (1) theoretical, reflective social knowledge of the kind tapped by a hypothetical interview and (2) real-life knowledge that is expressed in everyday social interaction. This real-life (or practical) knowledge is an active kind of judgment that is manifested both in a person's real-life reasoning and in his real-life conduct. Both theoretical and real-life knowledge include observable as well as nonobservable components of action (or, in other words, "thought" as well as action). If we therefore redefine our original problem as the connection between theoretical social knowledge and real-life social knowledge, several interesting questions may be investigated directly. First, there is the question of whether children's real-life social knowledge develops in an age-related manner, similar to that found, for example, in children's theoretical positive justice knowledge (as manifested in the hypothetical-verbal interviews of Studies 1 and 2). If so, the relation between the two may be further explored and further questions asked. For example, we may ask how closely the level of a child's real-life social knowledge can be predicted from the level of his hypothetical social knowledge. Does one type of knowledge tend to be more advanced than the other, or do they tend to be at the same level, or is there no consistent developmental direction one way or the other? Piaget (1932) has asserted that active knowledge should precede theoretical knowledge developmentally, regardless of the specific domain of knowledge (logical, physical, social, and so on). On the other hand, our intuitions tell us that a child's real-life social judgment may not always "live up to" his hypothetical reasoning. It is possible, with the present formulation of the problem, empirically to test this commonsense position against the opposing position suggested by Piaget.

The relations between hypothetical and real-life social knowledge still tell us nothing about what a child actually will do in a real-life situation. In fact, we can never predict a specific social act from a mode of judgment, for reasons of intrinsic uncertainty noted above. But we may be able to predict from a child's social knowledge the child's general *tendencies,* or *patterns* of observable acts. For instance, in a distribution-of-rewards problem we can never predict from a child's positive justice level exactly how he will apportion a reward in a given situation, but we may be able to predict his tendency to reward one type of justice claim over another—his tendency to favor or not to favor himself, and so on. For such patterns of observable acts we shall use the term *conduct*.

Study 3 is an attempt experimentally to unravel and investigate both of the above problems of interest: (1) the relation between a child's hypothetical and real-life social knowledge and (2) the relation between children's modes of social knowledge and their patterns of social conduct. As in Studies 1 and 2, the study focuses on children's responses to distribution-of-rewards problems. Our first research question concerns the relations between hypothetical and real-life positive justice knowledge, as manifested by children's reasoning in the two types of contexts. Here we may test the predictions noted in the last two paragraphs. Second, with reference to the six positive justice levels described in Study 1, we may make and test the following predictions concerning relations between children's levels of positive justice reasoning and their patterns of distribution conduct: (1) Children at 0-A and 0-B should be the ones most likely to prefer themselves in a distributive justice problem; (2) children at 1-A should be most likely to prefer equal distributions; (3) children at 1-B should be most likely to prefer distributions weighed in favor of those who have demonstrated "deserving," or merit; (4) children at 2-A and 2-B should be most likely to consider need or special circumstances in their distributions. These predictions arise from direct inferences about the action implications of the different positive justice levels. The assumption here is that certain organizing principles of positive justice are more compatible than others with certain patterns of distribution. Therefore, these principles should set limits to what a child will or will not do in a real-life situation. The justice principles are too abstract to determine specific acts but do lead to certain general tendencies or patterns of conduct.

The choice of the distributive justice area also enables us to compare the present investigation with some recent studies of children's sharing and distribution behavior. In some of these studies the findings seem consistent with the predictions made above. For example, Lane and Coon (1972) found that four-year-olds tend to distribute rewards selfishly, taking significantly more than their share. Most five-year-olds, on the other hand, tend to construct equal distributions. Neither the four- nor the five-year-olds in the Lane and Coon study chose "equity" (or meritarian) distributions. This reported behavior seems to parallel children's positive justice as described in Study 1, in that four-year-olds normally are at levels 0-A or 0-B (self-interest), five-year-olds are at 1-A (equality), and neither is normally found at 1-B (merit).

Other studies, however, suggest that factors beyond the justice reasoning level of a child may influence the child's mode of distributing rewards. Leventhal and his associates (Leventhal and Anderson, 1970; Leventhal and Whiteside, 1973) conclude that interactions between sex-related socialization patterns and self-interest may be important determinants of children's reward-distribution behavior. In the Leventhal studies girls tended to prefer equal distributions more than did boys; boys tended to construct unequal distributions, particularly when it was in their self-interest to do so. Other investigators (Lerner, 1974; Peterson, Peterson, and McDonald, 1975) suggest that conditions of the specific reward-allocation task largely determine how a child distributes rewards. Lerner found that equal distributions were more likely when children thought of themselves as members of a team than when they thought of themselves as working independently of one another. The Peterson study also pointed to the cognitive complexity of the reward-allocation task as an additional factor in determining equal or unequal distributions.

In none of the above reward-allocation experiments were factors such as sex, self-interest, and differing task variables studied in relation to children's developing ability to reason about justice. Yet it seems that a child's real-life justice decisions must derive from some interaction of situational (and/or socialization) factors with the child's moral judgment. One purpose of the present study was to witness such external and internal factors operating in combination with one another, as children at various ages and developmental levels reach decisions about distributive justice.

The subjects of Study 3 were 144 middle-class children:

18 boys and 18 girls at each of the ages four, six, eight, and ten. Subjects were drawn from preschools and elementary schools in Worcester, Massachusetts.

The procedure was as follows: One third of the boys and girls, evenly distributed across the age groups, were administered the hypothetical positive justice interview used in Study 1 and, one to two months later, were placed in a "real-life" distributive situation with peers. The second third of the subjects were given the same tasks, only in opposite sequence. The remaining third of the subjects were treated the same as the first group, except that they were administered a second hypothetical justice interview immediately after the first hypothetical interview.

The "real-life" distributive justice situation presented to all subjects was the experimental technique described in Chapter Two, where three same-aged subjects and a younger child who is not a subject are asked to make some bracelets for the experimenter. The actual distributive justice task arises when the three subjects, in the absence of the younger child, are asked to apportion among the group a reward of ten candy bars. As noted in Chapter Two, there were three experimental conditions in this "real-life" situation, though in a sense the conditions were self-assumed by the children. The three conditions were those of "prettiest and most," "biggest boy or girl," and "nice," each of these criteria representing a different kind of claim to merit. The truest claim to merit, of course, is "prettiest and most," because this claim represents reciprocal payback for a good deed. We believed that this merit claim would carry the most weight with children at 1-B justice reasoning or above and that "biggest" and "nice" would be 0-level types of claims, irrelevant to higher-level children. In addition, the fourth party in the situation (the younger child who was not a subject) occupied a role which, we believed, would carry weight mostly with children at 2-A or above, because only at 2-A does there develop an appreciation for special needs or circumstances (in this case, incompetence due to age).

Each subject's distribution decisions were recorded at three choice points: at the beginning of the child's individual interview following the bracelet-making session, at the end of the interview (after the child had expressed his justice reasoning), and at the end of the group decision session. These three choice points will be referred to as the subject's initial choice, his final choice, and his group choice. (In group discussions where the three subjects failed to reach a consensus, each subject's final expressed preference in the group was taken as his or her group choice.) These three distribution choices were considered the subject's actual conduct and were scored according to percentage of candy bars—out of those actually given out— that the subject distributed to each of the four original participants: the child who made "prettiest and most," the "biggest" boy or girl, the "nice" child, and the nonpresent younger child. Percentage of candy bars out of those given out was used as a measure rather than raw number of candy bars, since several subjects refused to distribute all ten bars. Since the subject himself was always one of the participants, the percentage of candy bars given to self was automatically coded by simply recording the experimental condition assumed by the subject.

In addition, each child's justice reasoning during both the individual and group sessions was recorded on tape. Though it was not possible to obtain reliable scores for children's reasoning in the group sessions, a "real-life" reasoning score was obtained for each child from the individual interviews. This score was derived from the child's reasoning in the same manner as in the hypothetical justice interview described in Study 1. Interjudge reliability of scoring for children's real-life justice reasoning was performed on twenty protocols and yielded 85 percent perfect agreement among judges and 15 percent disagreement by no more than one level, results almost identical to interjudge reliability on hypothetical positive justice reasoning reported in Studies 1 and 2.

Because the hypothetical positive justice story and the experimental justice situation were not identical in all details, the possibility existed that variance in children's moral judgment between the two contexts might be due to factors extrinsic to the relations of interest. For example, there were simply more persons to distribute rewards to in the hypothetical situation than in the real-life one, and the quantitative nature of the rewards differed. Thus, it is possible that the cognitive complexity of the two tasks may have differed. Also, the hypothetical interview was presented in the third person, whereas the real-life interviews, of course, were conducted in the first person. As a control for such incidental differences between the hypothetical and real-life tasks, one third of the subjects were given a second hypothetical story prior to their engagement in the experimental situation. This second "control" story paralleled more closely the actual events in the experimental situation and ended with hypothetical first-person queries addressed to the subject. The second story is quoted at the end of Chapter Two. Since it was possible that responding to a story so similar to the experimental situation might affect the subject's performance in the real-life context, only one third of the subjects were given this second hypothetical interview. It was always given one or two months prior to the child's engagement in the practical situation, rather than afterward, since it did not make sense to ask a child hypothetically about a situation that he or she had already been in.

For the subjects who were administered both hypothetical interviews, a rank-order correlation of $r$ (46) = .81, $p < .001$ was found between level of justice reasoning on the two interviews. Among the subjects who demonstrated some variance in their response to the two stories, there was no trend for one or the other story to yield higher justice scores. From these results it was inferred that the basic positive justice interview from Study 1 was an appropriate instrument for assessing children's justice reasoning about hypothetical stories similar to the experimental "real-life" situation. In other words, it did not seem that differences between subjects' performances in the hypothetical and real-life situations could be due to incidental differences between the two tasks used in the present study. Rather, any such differences could now be attributed to differences between children's hypothetical and real-life social judgment and conduct.

As a measure of subjects' real-life social behavior outside of the experimental situation, each subject's teacher was asked to complete a teacher-rating scale of social competence designed by Rothenberg (1970). The scale consists of rating systems for seven social competence dimensions: leadership, sensitivity, humor, gregariousness, friendliness, cruelty, and mood. In the present study teachers were asked to rate children on all of these dimensions except cruelty and mood, which were not believed relevant to the present study. In addition, a new scale for generosity was constructed, following the Rothenberg model, since this dimension seemed to be particularly related to positive justice. Thus, a total of six social competence dimensions were measured in the present study. Of the 144 subjects in Study 3, teacher ratings were obtained for 120 subjects (all but 24). The 24, evenly divided between ages and sexes, were pupils at a school that declined to provide such ratings.

The results of Study 3 are reported in two parts. The first part pertains to relations between hypothetical and real-life positive justice knowledge. The second part pertains to the actual distribution conduct of the subjects during the experimental "real-life" situation.

*Reasoning in hypothetical and real-life contexts.* Subjects' justice reasoning scores on both the hypothetical interview and in the "real-life" experimental situation were closely associated with age. The association of real-life reasoning scores (R) with age was $r$ (142) = .85, $p < .001$; and the association of hypothetical reasoning scores (H) with age was $r$ (142) = .83, $p < .001$. Both of these rank-order correlations were of approximately the same magnitude as the relation found between hypothetical justice reasoning and age in Study 1. The association between R and H was $r = .78, p < .001$. With age partialed out, this association became $r = 26, p < .001$.

For 50 percent of the subjects ($N = 72$), justice reasoning scores on R were at the same level as justice reasoning scores on H. For the remaining seventy-two subjects the deviation of R scores from H scores conformed to the following pattern: for nineteen subjects R scores were more advanced than H scores; and for fifty-three subjects, H scores were more advanced than R scores. In the seventy-two cases of deviation between R and H, only fourteen represented deviations of more than one level;

and in each of these fourteen instances the deviation was in the direction of H being higher than R. A chi-square analysis of the distinct tendency for subjects to reason at more advanced levels on H than on R was significant at $p < .001$. When the "deviating" subjects were broken down into age groups, however, this tendency was found to disappear at age ten. In other words, of the eighteen ten-year-olds who showed deviations between H and R scores, nine scored higher on H and nine scored higher on R. In a chi-square analysis, this was a significant variation from the usual trend for subjects to score higher on H ($p < .05$).

There were no significant sex differences in either R or H reasoning scores. Neither were there significant sex differences on R or H reasoning scores at any of the four age levels, taken separately. In addition, no significant differences in patterns of deviation between R and H could be attributed to sex, to experimental condition (whether subject was "prettiest and most," "biggest," or "nice"), or to task order (whether subject was given H before R, or R before H, or whether the subject was given the second "control" hypothetical interview in addition to H and R). Relations between teacher ratings of subjects' social competence and subjects' H and R justice scores were tested through rank-order correlations. No significant associations were found between H justice scores and any of the six social competence dimensions, with the exception of one relation between H scores and the social competence dimension of friendliness, $r (118) = .24$, $p < .05$. But subjects' R justice scores correlated significantly with all six social competence dimensions, yielding correlations at the $p < .05$ level of significance, which ranged from $r (118) = .21$ (on leadership) to $r (118) = .37$ (on friendliness).

From the present set of findings, certain conclusions can be reached about children's social reasoning in real-life contexts, as well as about the relation between real-life and hypothetical social reasoning. At least in the area of positive justice, children's real-life social reasoning seems to go through the same kind of closely age-related progression that characterizes children's hypothetical social reasoning. In large part because both real-life and hypothetical reasoning are so closely age-related, there is also a strong association between the two during the age span studied. Even aside from the age factor—that is, with age partialed out—a significant association can be found between real-life and hypothetical reasoning. But with age controlled in this manner, this association seems to be of too small a magnitude to predict a child's real-life reasoning from his or her hypothetical reasoning with any confidence. In addition, the relation between children's real-life and hypothetical reasoning may have been inflated by "practice effects"—that is, by a possible tendency for children's performances on either H or R (whichever was given first) to have influenced their performances on whichever of the two tasks was given second. This consideration casts doubt on even the small relation remaining between H and R after age had been partialed out. Thus, the relation between hypothetical and real-life social reasoning in children seems to be determined chiefly by the developmental factor, which is responsible for the strong age bonds shared by both types of reasoning. Beyond this powerful age and development factor, there seems to be only a moderate connection between children's reasoning in the two contexts.

The clear trend for children's hypothetical reasoning to be at the same level as, or higher than, their real-life reasoning conforms to our commonsense intuitions but directly contradicts predictions made by Piaget concerning the developmental priority of active to reflective knowledge. This contradiction may be due to the differences between the moral issues investigated by Piaget and by the present study.* When Piaget (1932)

---

*Or the contradiction may be due to a combination of theoretical and methodical differences between Piaget's approach and our own. Piaget's "active" knowledge does not exactly parallel the "real-life" knowledge investigated in the present study. For Piaget (1932, 1976), a child's knowledge is no longer active once the child is asked to explain it (at which point the child's "reflective" knowledge is being tapped). Thus, according to Piaget, our present technique of interrogating a child for the meaning behind his or her actions in the real-life situation would elicit reflective rather than active knowledge. We, on the other hand, have used children's responses to this technique as one index of their real-life knowledge, since verbal reasoning is very much a part of real-life contexts. Thus, in this sense, Piaget's distinction between active and reflective knowledge is operationally somewhat different from our distinction between theoreti-

made his prediction that reflective reasoning would lag behind real-life judgment in the social realm, he was discussing the issue of moral intentionality. His own children, he said, showed a real-life understanding that good intentions should excuse a harmful act well before they demonstrated similar understanding in a hypothetical context. But a young child may well be severe with impersonal characters in an imaginary story and, at the same time, show sympathetic understanding of extenuating intentions and circumstances when discussing the real-life moral problems of himself or friends. It is clearly easier, and more in a child's self-interest, for him to consider intentions that excuse his own misdeeds than to consider the extenuating intentions of hypothetical others. In distributive justice problems, on the other hand, the child's self-interest plays a different role. Here it is often in a child's interest to use a lower rather than a higher mode of judgment, since the lower modes tend to be more ego-centric and self-serving. Therefore, it is not surprising that children demonstrate higher levels of positive justice reasoning when considering an imaginary moral story than while engaged in a real-life situation. In the present study, only at the most advanced age level studied (age ten) did children consistently resist the tendency to employ a lower mode of judgment in the real-life context. (This last finding may reflect a certain objective quality associated predominantly with the more mature positive justice levels.)

If the above analysis is correct, it is the interaction of the child's self-interest with his social judgment, rather than developmental relations between theoretical and active thought, that often accounts for lags between hypothetical and real-life social reasoning. Such an interaction would account for instances

---

cal and real-life knowledge. Still, it is our own belief that a real-life situation taps "active" knowledge—even in Piaget's sense—far more directly than does a hypothetical-verbal interview. In fact, it is hard to imagine how children's real-life social knowledge could be studied without eliciting from them some verbal explanations of their actions. For this reason, we have maintained that Piaget's assertions concerning the relations between active and reflective social knowledge are relevant to the issues investigated in the present study and should be examined in light of the present set of findings.

where real-life reasoning precedes hypothetical reasoning and also for instances where hypothetical reasoning precedes real-life (as found in the present study). The direction of the lag between the two types of reasoning is determined by the way in which self-interest is best served in the particular social area considered. Self-interest can therefore act as either an instigator or a retardant for advanced social judgment, depending upon the type of social problem that the child encounters. But there do seem to be limits on how much reasoning can be advanced or retarded, since even a two-level discrepancy between hypothetical and real-life reasoning was rare in the present study.

The finding that children's reasoning in the experimental situation correlated significantly with all six social competence measures, whereas the hypothetical measures correlated only once with one of the six dimensions, was taken as a validation of the "real-life" quality of the experimental situation. The children's teachers, in rating each child's social competence, apparently were responding to something about the child's usual behavior that was also evoked in the practical context but not in the course of the child's hypothetical reasoning. This finding suggests both the validity of our real-life measure and the distinctness of hypothetical and practical social knowledge.

*Conduct in the practical situation.* A series of analyses of variance were conducted to test predicted relations of subjects' H and R reasoning scores to their actual distributions at the initial individual choice point (IC), the final individual choice point (FC), and the group choice point (GC). The analyses also considered subjects' sex and experimental condition ("prettiest and most," "biggest," and "nice"). In reporting these results, we shall focus on relations between subjects' H scores and their conduct at IC, since our central research question is the extent to which a child's actual moral conduct (prior to unusual verbal probing) can be predicted from the child's hypothetical moral reasoning. However, for cases in which there were important differences in children's conduct at FC or GC, or in cases where children's R reasoning scores bore a significantly different relation to their conduct than did their H scores, these additional results will be included. Table 2 presents the basic findings regarding relations between subjects' reasoning levels on H and their conduct at IC. In Table 2, subjects' conduct is reported in terms of the mean percentage of candy bars distributed to the child who made "prettiest and most" (M), the "biggest" (B), the child who made "nice" ones (N), the younger child (Y), and the self, by subjects at each of the six H levels. The following results report the main and interaction effects found in the analyses of variance described above.

Table 2

Mean Percentage of Candy Bars Distributed at Initial Choice Point (IC)
by Subjects at Six Hypothetical Reasoning Levels

| Hypothetical justice scores | Child receiving reward[a] | | | | |
|---|---|---|---|---|---|
| | M | B | N | Y | Self |
| 0-A | 22.1 | 24.4 | 40.0 | 21.0 | 39.0 |
| 0-B | 26.2 | 24.5 | 30.0 | 22.2 | 30.6 |
| 1-A | 26.4 | 26.8 | 25.3 | 23.2 | 28.3 |
| 1-B | 28.0 | 24.2 | 25.2 | 22.8 | 25.9 |
| 2-A | 27.9 | 25.4 | 23.8 | 23.3 | 26.9 |
| 2-B | 26.6 | 26.0 | 24.2 | 24.0 | 26.0 |

[a]M = "prettiest and most"; B = "biggest boy or girl"; N = "nice"; Y = "younger child."

We had predicted that 0-A and 0-B subjects would show the greatest propensity for self-reward. The planned comparison for distributions to self showed a significant tendency for subjects at 0-A and 0-B justice reasoning to distribute more to themselves than did subjects at other reasoning levels: $p < .001$. Table 2 shows this tendency clearly. In addition, there were indications that subjects at all levels tended to favor themselves, though not as strongly as did the 0-A and 0-B subjects.

In all three experimental conditions (M, B, and N), subjects tended to give more to their own position than did other subjects. Specifically, subjects in the position of M gave an average of 28.6 percent of the candy bars to M, whereas subjects who were not M gave only an average of 23.8 percent to M.

Subjects in the position of B gave B an average of 26.7 percent, whereas subjects who were not B gave B an average of 23.7 percent. Subjects in the position of N gave N 31.8 percent, whereas subjects who were not N gave N only 24.4 percent. In all three instances, the tendency to favor the self's position more than did others was significant at $p < .001$. There were also specific predictable interaction effects between subjects' reasoning levels and the three experimental conditions. Subjects at 1-B and above, unlike lower-level subjects, gave significantly more to themselves when they were in the condition of M than when they were in the conditions of B or N: $p < .001$. Likewise, subjects at 0-A and 0-B reasoning, unlike other subjects, gave significantly more to themselves when they were in the condition of N than when they were in conditions of M or B: $p < .001$. Therefore, being in the position of M instigated self-favoring for the older subjects, whereas being in the position of N encouraged this same tendency for the younger subjects.

But there was also a universal tendency for all subjects to give at least something to each of the other parties in the experimental situation. Never did a subject deny any participant some percentage of the candy. Even at the youngest ages, where the tendency toward self-reward was greatest, subjects normally gave a minimum of 20 percent of the candy (two candy bars) to each of the other three participants. At the most self-oriented extreme, two 0-A subjects gave themselves 70 percent of the candy and each of the remaining three parties 10 percent. But the normal pattern was for subjects to vary their distributions between 20 percent and 40 percent for any given person, as the mean percentages in Table 2 show. Thus, even in the most extreme cases, children's self-preference had its limits, succumbing to the general tendency toward awarding everyone some share of the reward. Though the exact share of the reward given each participant varied according to a number of factors, the decision to make some award to all parties was universal in this study.

We also predicted that subjects at 2-A and 2-B would show more consideration for the younger child than would subjects at other levels. The planned comparison showed a nonsignificant tendency at IC for 2-A and 2-B subjects to give more to

Y than did other subjects. This tendency is shown in Table 2. A further analysis revealed that this tendency was significant at choice points FC and GC: $p < .001$ for both choice points. Accordingly, there was a significant interaction effect, $p < .001$, between subjects' reasoning levels and the three choice points on distributions to Y. Nevertheless, there were no *overall* differences, when all reasoning levels were combined, between subjects' distributions to Y at IC, FC, and GC. Thus, the extra time or probing represented by FC and GC did have a positive influence on children's sharing with the younger child, although this influence registered only on subjects at justice levels 2-A and 2-B.

The prediction that subjects at 1-A would be more likely than other subjects to construct equal distributions was tested through a series of Fisher Exact analyses. Subjects constructing equal distributions (25 percent of candy bars to each of the four participants) were compared with those not doing so, across subjects scoring at 1-A compared with those scoring at all other levels. Contrary to predictions, there were no significant differences between 1-A and other subjects at any of the three choice points. Neither was there a significant tendency at any of the three choice points for girls to be more likely than boys to construct equal distributions, contrary to the findings reported by Leventhal and Anderson (1970) and Leventhal and Whiteside (1973). Combining all subjects, there were significantly more equal distributions at GC than at either IC or FC on a chi-square analysis: $p < .01$. Thus, children at the end of the group session were more likely to opt for equal solutions than were children during their individual interviews.

There were no main or interaction effects of sex on distributions to M, B, N, Y, or self, or on equal versus unequal distributions (as noted above).

We had made two predictions concerning relations between social competence measures and the subjects' conduct in the practical situation. First, we predicted that children ranking high on the social competence dimension of generosity would give fewer candy bars to themselves than would subjects low on social competence. This prediction was borne out weakly at all three choice points: *combining* IC, FC, and GC, $p < .05$. The second prediction, that children high on the social competence dimension of sensitivity would tend to give more to Y, was borne out only marginally: with the three choice points combined, $p < .1$. An assortment of post hoc analyses revealed no other noteworthy social competence relations.

The prediction that children at hypothetical justice level 1-A would be the ones most likely to construct equal distributions was not borne out significantly; nor was the prediction that 1-Bs more than others would favor the meritorious child (the one who made the "prettiest and most" bracelets). The prediction that 2-As and 2-Bs would reward the younger, less competent child more than would other subjects was established significantly only at the final choice point in the distribution situation, after the children had had a chance to reason and reflect on their decisions. At the initial choice point, when children's spontaneous conduct was tapped, this tendency at 2-A and 2-B was nonsignificant. The only strong, predictable relation found between reasoning and conduct was the tendency of the 0-As and 0-Bs to favor themselves more than the others favored themselves. However, the 0-A and 0-B children were not the only ones who acted in their own self-interest, even though these younger children did so in a more exaggerated way than did the more advanced ones. The tendency of all children to favor themselves is evident in the finding that subjects tended to give more to whichever of the three roles ("prettiest and most," "biggest" boy or girl, "nice") they themselves assumed.

If self-interest generally had a major influence on children's conduct, this influence was manifested differently at different levels of justice reasoning. Two interactions between self-interest and reasoning level are particularly noteworthy. The first is the finding that children at 1-B and above, unlike other subjects, were particularly likely to favor themselves when in the merit condition (M). The second is the finding that 0-As and 0-Bs, unlike others, showed a particularly strong propensity to favor themselves when in the "nice" condition (N). Taken together, these two findings indicate that, although self-interest does not disappear with development, its nature changes. The claim of merit (payback for having made the prettiest and most) was more accessible to children at 1-B and above than to younger children and therefore was used disproportionately at the highest levels in constructing self-serving distributions. This is not surprising, since it is at level 1-B that notions of merit, earning, and reciprocal payback are first truly understood. The 0-A and 0-B children, on the other hand, seemed to be particularly influenced by the claim of "nice," a more general and diffuse form of praise. Probably because "nice" did not represent real merit or investment, the older children did not take it seriously, even when it was in their self-interest to do so. For the younger children, however, it represented the one comprehensible and believable criterion by which they could distinguish themselves favorably from others.

We must conclude from the present set of findings that predicting a child's social conduct from his or her reasoning remains a complex and risky task. However, it is sometimes possible to predict, from a child's hypothetical positive justice judgment, both the child's level of reasoning and the child's general pattern of distribution conduct in a real-life situation. Both such predictions, however, must take into account the manner in which the child's self-interest interacts with the child's reasoning level. First of all, self-interest frequently seems to retard children's real-life reasoning, though not more than one level and not among children at the highest age level. On the other hand, in other social situations (for example, situations involving moral intentionality as reported by Piaget), self-interest may provoke more advanced real-life judgment. Similarly, predictions concerning children's conduct must also consider the different ways in which self-interest may influence different modes of reasoning in different contexts. In the present study, differences in self-interested choices were found not only between reasoning levels but also between the three choice points in the experimental situation. Finally, factors other than self-interest may color or distort the relations between children's moral reasoning and their patterns of moral conduct. Though the present study did not yield any significant effects of variables such as sex or task order, there may still be factors other than self-interest that explain the uneven and complex results bearing on our original judgment-conduct predictions. For example, some children may have understood the meaning of the four experimental roles (M, B, N, and Y) differently than intended; or the adult presence may have affected the children's behavior in some way; or, finally, the influence of the children upon each other in the group decision context undoubtedly had some effect on the children's group choices, as evidenced by the greater number of equal distributions at this choice point. A further investigation into developmental group dynamics is warranted here for a richer understanding of how young children construct group decisions and the conditions under which they will or will not reach a consensus with a peer group.

Concerning this last point, it is possible to get some initial sense of children's peer-group behavior from the present study, even though this study was not really designed to explore social-psychological process or group dynamics. The one striking finding from Study 3 about the development of group process in young children was the increasing ability, with age, of children to reach agreement with their peers. In the oldest groups (the eight- and ten-year-olds), all children reached a consensus by the final *group* choice point. On the other hand, 8 percent of the six-year-old groups and 22 percent of the four-year-old groups failed to reach a consensus—even though all groups were given as much time as they needed to come to an agreement, and the experimenter encouraged agreements by refusing to distribute candy bars until all members of the group concurred in the decision. Only after it was clear that there would be no progress toward a consensus did the experimenter arrange a compromise and finally distribute the candy. In spite of this encouragement, a sizable number of younger children failed to arrive at a group agreement.

We shall now quote some typical group discussions, ranging from a session of four-year-olds to a session of ten-year-olds. As will be seen, there is quite a different flavor to the social interactions of children at different age levels. The differences, of course, can be partly attributed to differences between primitive and advanced justice reasoning. Justice to a four-year-old bears little resemblance to justice in a ten-year-old's eyes, as demonstrated by each study in this section. But there are other group process variables at work here, including different modes of communication and varying levels of attention. These variables shall remain untapped in the present analysis, though intuitively we can witness their operation in the dialogues quoted below.

*Three four-year-olds: Jason, Sean, and Bonnie*

**Experimenter:** OK, here are the ten candy bars, and we want to ask you as a group how to split them up. Any ideas?

**Sean:** I want seven. Then one for you, one for you and one for her [Tina, not present].

**Experimenter:** And you are going to take seven and put them in your bag.

**Sean:** Yeah, 'cause I have seven friends at home.

**E:** What do you guys think?

**Sean:** And some of the kids want some of these.

**Jason:** That wouldn't be fair.

**E:** How should it be different?

**Jason:** It should be different like that [gives himself four, Sean three, Bonnie two, and Tina one]. I'm gonna' get four.

**Bonnie:** [Picks up candy and gives everyone two, with two left over.]

**Jason:** No! I get four. [Takes two extra bars for himself.] Look how they cheat.

**Bonnie:** Put them back.

**Jason:** I get four because I'm four and you're only two.

**Bonnie:** I'm four too.

**Jason:** She's [Tina] only one.

**Bonnie:** No she's not, she's three.

Jason: One.

Bonnie: Three.

Jason: One.

Sean: I want to get seven for my seven bosses at home.

E: Do you think you should?

Sean: Yeah, 'cause my bosses want some of these.

E: What do you mean, bosses?

Sean: 'Cause I like them.

Bonnie: I want three.

Sean: But I want seven.

Bonnie: Well, I'm going to take three. [Takes three, gives Sean three, Jason two, and Tina two.]

Sean: [Grabs one of Tina's.]

Bonnie: No! That one's for Tina.

E: Why are those two for Tina, Bonnie?

Bonnie: 'Cause she's the littlest.

Sean: She just wants one.

E: How do you know she just wants one?

Sean: 'Cause I know she says she wants one. She needs one. She says she wants one.

Bonnie: She wants two.

Sean: No! If you do that, I'm going to punch you out of the room.

Jason: Well, then we'll all agree on this.

E: What do you mean, Jason?

Jason: We'll just talk about the candy bars.

Sean: Yeah, 'cause I want seven.

**Jason:** Well, I'll just take two. [Takes two.]

**Bonnie:** Well, I'll just take one more. [Takes three in all.]

**Sean:** But that one's Tina's. [Takes all of the remaining five and holds them in front of himself.]

**Bonnie:** No, you've got Tina's.

**Sean:** [Goes to other end of room with his five.] No, I need five 'cause my mother needs five. And I need five for all my bosses.

[The discussion continues in this manner until the experimenter is forced to arrange a compromise.]

### Three four-year-olds: Jonathan, Ben, and Kerri

**E:** How do you think we should give them out?

**Jonathan:** [Gives two to everyone, has two left over. Then takes the extra two for himself.] I'm going to take these and eat them for supper.

**E:** What do you think, Ben? Do you think they [the extra two] should go to you and Jonathan?

**Ben:** [Nods yes.]

**E:** What do you think, Kerri?

**Kerri:** No.

**E:** What way do you think would be best?

**Kerri:** I don't know.

**E:** What do you think, though? Put them out again and let Kerri give them out.

**Kerri:** [Gives two to Jennifer, not present; two to Ben; two to Jonathan; and two to herself.]

**E:** What about these two?

**Jonathan:** These two go for me and Ben.

**E:** Is that what you wanted to do?

Kerri: [Nods no.]

E: What do you think, Jonathan? You think two and two, three and three? Do you think that way would be fair?

Jonathan: Yes.

E: Why would it be fair?

Jonathan: 'Cause I hate girls.

E: Would that make it fair?

Jonathan: Yes.

E: What do you think about that, Kerri?

Kerri: I don't know.

Jonathan: Girls never fuss.

E: Why do you think it would be fair?

Jonathan: Girls never fuss.

E: Do you ever fuss, Kerri? Does anyone think Ben ought to get more because he made more bracelets?

Jonathan: No.

Ben: No.

E: Does anyone think Kerri should get more because she's the tallest girl?

Jonathan: No, because she's dumb. She doesn't get more. She's a girl.

E: Should boys get more? Why should they get more?

Ben: Because they always need more.

E: Why do they need more?

Ben: Because that's how I want it.

E: What do you think about that [to Kerri]? Think that's fair?

Kerri: No.

Jonathan: Yes.

Ben: It's fair.

E: Kerri doesn't think it's fair.

Ben: I do. I hope Jenny would.

Jonathan: Yeah, Jenny would, 'cause she always thinks.

E: OK. So the two boys want to give the boys more, and Kerri wants to give everybody the same? Does anyone think they might change their mind?

All the children: No.

*Three six-year-olds: Jay, Juan, and Susan*

E: So what Jay said is he put them out, three for him and three for Juan, two for Susan and two for Jennifer [not present]. And Susan said that's OK too. That's the way she did it.

Jay: [To Juan] You should think that's fair too. You have three, and I have three, and they have two.

Juan: I don't think that's fair.

Jay: Why?

Juan: We shouldn't give the boys more than the girls. We should break them in half and give the girls two, the boys two, then . . .

Jay: No, No, No. I said ours were the prettiest, that's why we get more.

Juan: Wait a second. Whose is this?

Jay: Yours.

Juan: No, it isn't.

Jay: See, we made the prettiest. I say we made the prettiest. Do you think that's a nice one? And you made nice ones, and we made the prettiest. I think that's fair because we made the prettiest.

**Juan:** We should break them in half, and then that would be really fair.

**Susan:** That's what I said, but then he said what if we can't break them in half.

**Jay:** But I think that we can.

**Jay:** She thinks this is fair like this [three, three, two, two]. Susan doesn't care, do you? She thinks if she has two that's OK. She doesn't care, and we can have the most.

**Juan:** If I was you, I would cut them in half and give everyone the same.

**E:** What do you think, Susan? Didn't you at one point say you thought we should split them in half?

**Susan:** That's what I said. Now I say . . . [Susan gives them out —three, three, two, two, as Jay wishes.]

**E:** What? This way?

**Jay:** Yeah. Because she thinks that we made the prettiest.

**Juan:** She got some in her lunch box. Do you have candy?

**Jay:** Do you have a Hershey bar? She's got some Nestlés or a Hershey bar.

**E:** Susan says it's OK. How about Jennifer?

**Jay:** I think she would say it's OK.

**Juan:** If she didn't leave, I think it wouldn't be OK.

**E:** So what are you going to do?

**Jay:** I think that this is the way to do it, because me and Juan made the prettiest.

**Juan:** She [Jennifer] made pretty, and she made the same.

**Jay:** No, No, No. What I mean, Juan—see how yours is pretty, and see how pretty this is too. I think these two are pretty, right. And all of these are pretty. And I think hers too and these are nice too. But I think these are pretty.

Juan: They're all the same, they're all pretty.

Jay: I know, but I think these are the prettiest.

Juan: They all are.

Jay: No, No.

E: So what about now? What do you guys want to do?

Jay: Juan, that's fair!

Juan: She has one in her lunch, but I don't know about Jennifer.

Jay: Think that would be fair! She would have three, and we would all have three.

E: We don't have eleven, we have ten.

Jay: But she only made one, and it's not pretty.

Juan: It's good. She's only in kindergarten. She would think it's fair, I think. Yeah, she would.

E: What are you guys going to do?

Jay: If you think it's fair, and Susan thinks it's fair, and I think it's fair, she [Jennifer] might think it's fair.

E: Well, let's see what Juan thinks. What do you suggest, Juan? What's the best way? What's the best thing to do with the candy bars?

Juan: I think that's [three, three, two, two] the best way, if she's only in kindergarten.

Jay: She has two, and we have three.

Juan: You made the most.

Jay: You see I had four bracelets.

Juan: I had the second most. Give these two candy bars to her.

Jay: You see, what I was thinking was, Juan and I get three 'cause we, ours are pretty and I made the most. Susan already has one in her lunch box.

Juan: And Jennifer's only in kindergarten.

Jay: She doesn't get more, 'cause she just made one and it's not pretty.

E: Do you agree, Susan?

Susan: OK.

[Children agree on three, three, two, two distribution.]

E: Juan, do you want to do this, or not?

Jay: How about keeping it this way, and the next time, if we only have . . . if just us came and we had ten candy . . . then we would all have three. No, that would equal nine, and we would have one left. We could put that one in the box.

E: OK. Can anyone think of a better thing to do than this?

Juan: [Shakes his head.]

E: Can you think of something else that might be better, Juan?

Juan: The only thing I know is cut them in half.

Susan: Yeah, I want to do that now.

E: What do you think of that?

Jay: See, if she has a candy in her lunch box, I think it wouldn't be fair to us, because see if we cut two in half, she would have four.

Juan: 'Cause she has some in her lunch box, I think it would be fair to cut one in the middle, it would.

Susan: Since he made three, and you made two, and I made two, then since . . .

Juan: Well, you got one in your lunch bucket. You would have four.

E: What were you thinking, Susan?

Jay: I would think that this is the best way. If she has one in her lunch box, and if we split that in half, it wouldn't be fair. She would have four, and we would have three.

E: What were you thinking, Susan?

Susan: I was thinking that since he made two, and I had one . . .

Jay: Hold it, I had an idea. You have a Hershey bar in your lunch box?

E: Wait a second, OK?

Susan: Since he made three, he should have three. Since he made two, he should have two. Since I have one in my lunch box, I'll have three.

Jay: Hold it! Know what I had in mind? You had . . . Do you have one of these in your lunch box?

Susan: [Head shake "no."]

Jay: Do you have a different kind of candy?

Susan: Yeah. The same size, but a different flavor. Nuts, the nut kind.

E: Well, I don't know if we want to get into that. I never heard the end of Susan's idea. What was that . . . you said he should have three?

Susan: He should have two. Since I have one in my lunch I should have two . . .

E: Then what? Do you know?

Jay: I have a great idea. Since I made three. See, if she had one, right? I would think me and Juan had three, right?

Juan: No, she would have the same. She's a . . .

Jay: I think this way is best.

Juan: I don't think so.

E: So you still think we should split them?

Juan: I think we should.

E: Susan, what do you think?

Susan: I think we should split them too now.

E: But you still think we should give them out this way, Jay? Well, how are we going to decide this? Can anyone think of any better way? Are there some ways that are better than either of these?

Jay: Hold it! I think . . . see, she has two. We could have two too. So she would have to go to him . . . or you could have one for one of your friends, and I could have one for one of my friends.

Juan: No, if she would want one, she would have one. And he would have one. It would be fair.

E: Is that what you guys want to do? I wonder, if you guys were all going to have two, wouldn't it be just the same if you all had two and a half?

Jay: No, hold it! She has three. She made the littlest and pretty, she should have two. Now I think that's the best way, huh, Juan?

Juan: ["No," head shake.]

Jay: Hold it, see, three for me; three for Susan, right? And with her, she only made the littlest one, and she also had . . . a little pretty one. I think she should have two.

E: We are almost to recess time. So we simply have to decide.

Jay: I think this is the best way, Juan.

E: Well, I think we can't go much further, Jay. The vote is two to one; so unless one of those guys changes his mind, I think we're going to have to split them, OK? Want to still cut them in half? OK. I would have liked to get you guys to decide, but we are out of time, so I'll cut them in half, OK?

Jay: I've got an idea. She has three, right? Hold it. The best way we should do it is take two away.

*Three ten-year-olds: Craig, Norman, and Bonnie*

E: We talked with you all and couldn't decide, so we thought you should decide together. What do you think is the best way to give it out?

Craig: Would Dennis [the younger child] get some?

E: If you think so.

Norman: He has to be here too.

E: Well, you all decide among you.

Bonnie: I was thinking, we could give it out one a bracelet, because Dennis did one and we all did three. Or give two and a half to everybody. That way everybody gets the same thing.

Craig: Maybe he [Dennis] should get one and we get three.

Norman: No. It ain't fair.

Bonnie: Also, Dennis is younger and he left earlier.

E: Well, what do you think? Is that the best way?

Norman: No.

E: Why not, Norman?

Norman: Because if he were here too, and he's a child too, so he should get even.

Bonnie: Yeah, well lookit. His was bigger so it would have taken longer. And he used more black, but that made it shorter. But he left earlier, he's younger and, you know, didn't do it neat.

Norman: I know. That's beside the point. That means we don't expect as much from him.

Bonnie: A kindergartner could do better work than me though, probably.

Norman: Yeah, probably. Probably my sister could too. Probably my brother Scott could too. He's only two years old.

Bonnie: Who said that?

E: So far you've got one for Dennis, three for you, Craig, three for you, Norman, and three for you, Bonnie.

Bonnie: [Mumbles something.] That's what he [Dennis] should get.

Norman: No. He's not. That's what I'm getting at. That's what I'm putting in your mind, in your mind, in his mind [pointing to each member in group. Stated rather belligerently].

Bonnie: Well, let's split these in half. Everybody gets two and a half.

Norman: Right.

E: What do you think? Do you agree, Craig?

Craig: [Does not reply.]

Norman: It's the best way. Everybody gets the same amount.

Bonnie: Craig's is the prettiest, Norman's is the neatest, and I did the most.

Norman: I was the most well behaved.

E: So, does everyone agree? What's the best way to do it?

Craig: I was thinking. Two and a half, or somebody flip up a coin, or . . .

Norman: That was my idea. Don't you steal my idea.

Craig: Or give three to her [Bonnie], three for Norman, and three for me, and one for Dennis.

E: And why do you think that is the best way, Craig?

Craig: [No reply.]

Norman: You're not putting his [Dennis's] mind into your little mind.

Craig: Yes, I am.

Norman: I know—how would he feel—

Craig: Yes, I am.

Norman: Well, you're not reasoning about him. If we did that he would say [mimics child's whining voice] "Come, come, you guys got this and I only got this." And he'd start bawling his brains out.

Bonnie: Well, his isn't that neat or anything.

Norman: I know, but he is younger.

Bonnie: Well, wouldn't you say, supposing that you had a younger dog and an older dog, right? You could teach them both the same tricks. And if you had a box of dog bones, you'd give them a dog bone for every trick. Supposing the little one or even the big one just wanted the dog bones and he wouldn't do any tricks. You wouldn't give him one for that.

Norman: I know, but he did something. It's not like he didn't do anything. Least he did one. You're getting on the point like he didn't do anything.

Bonnie: No, I know he did something. He did the best he could.

Norman: Yeah, so he should get as much as we do. [Pause for a few moments.]

E: What do you think, Bonnie?

Bonnie: Yeah, well you know, Dennis only did one.

Craig: I know, but he had his birthday.

Bonnie: What do you mean, "his birthday"?

Craig: He had his birthday a couple of days ago.

Norman: Yeah, you get lazy after your birthday.

Craig: But I don't mean it that way. He had some, he might have had some sweet or—

**Norman**: Remember when he dropped some beads on the floor. That would have taken more time for him to pick them all up.

**Craig**: He didn't drop them. He just dropped them on the table.

**Norman**: Yeah, and then they fell all over the floor.

**Bonnie**: Yeah, well, Norman, you remember the other time you did it and the whole bottom fell off and you had to string it again? That took a little bit of time too.

**E**: Wait, I still don't understand. What do you think—first, Norman?

**Norman**: I think we should all get the same amount. Because his got dumped on the floor, plus you didn't start him until we got here and he had to leave before we did. So he had less time to do it than us.

**E**: What do you think, Bonnie?

**Bonnie**: I think we should give one for each bracelet. Because Dennis only made one and everybody else made three.

**E**: What do you think about Norman's argument?

**Bonnie**: Well, Norman's was the neatest, and Craig's was the prettiest, and mine had the most yellow. Dennis's was not—

**Norman**: He had the most black.

**Bonnie**: Yeah, I don't know what I would do.

**Norman**: [Counts how many black beads are on each of the bracelets of each of the members of the group.]

**E**: What difference does it make how many black beads you have?

**Bonnie**: None.

**Norman**: What difference does it make on how many yellows she has?

**Bonnie**: What difference does it make that yours are the neatest?

Norman: Right, and what difference does it make if his is the prettiest?

Bonnie: None. Because I have the most yellow and Norman was the neatest.

Bonnie: Everybody has something special about their bracelet. And he [Dennis] does.

Craig: And Dennis has . . . a lot of pink.

E: What do you think, Bonnie?

Bonnie: I think we should cut this in half.

E: What do you think, Norman?

Norman: We should cut it in half.

E: Craig, what do you think?

Craig: I don't know.

Norman: C'mon, buddy, do what I do. Last year you were always following me around. Why can't you this year? You're cheating Dennis out. You wouldn't like it if you got short-changed at a store. When you deserved five bucks and you only got one buck. And so it's like shortchanging him.

E: She changed her mind. Did you change your mind?

Craig: That's what I thought at first.

Bonnie: Cut these in half.

E: And what do you think, Craig?

Craig: I think the same thing. I thought of that at first, when I came here.

E: So what's the best way? [Everybody agrees to split evenly among the four.] Anybody that doesn't think it's fair, tell me before it's too late?

Bonnie: I don't know what to do. Because Dennis only made one.

Craig: Yeah.

E: So, Craig and Bonnie, you're still undecided, huh?

Bonnie: I think it's better the other way. Dennis only made one.

Norman: But he won't like to get shortchanged.

Craig: But he might not mind. Is Dennis here?

E: He can't come.

Craig: I wish Dennis was here.

Norman: Yeah, then we could get a better idea.

E: What do you think Dennis would say if he was here?

Norman: He would say: "I want just as much as you guys get. Because I did my best."

Bonnie: So listen to this: he didn't make as much. He didn't make them that neat, he didn't make them that pretty—

Craig: He might not even mind.

Bonnie: Supposing you got four kids in a family and one of them got in a rock fight. So he could only have one candy bar for dessert.

Norman: I know. But this isn't symbolizing a rock fight. I busted bottles down at the park and I still got as much as the others. But in my allowance instead of getting twenty-five cents I got fifteen.

Bonnie: Well, with him it's the same thing. He got less than somebody else because he did something bad.

E: What do you think, Craig?

Craig: I think we should get Dennis and let him figure it out.

Bonnie: No, because he'll say "I should get the same amount" but he didn't do as much.

Norman: He does, even though he didn't do as much.

**Craig:** Can't we take Dennis for a minute?

**E:** No, it's all up to you three.

**Bonnie:** I think we should get more because we did more. We spent more time doing it.

**Craig:** Norman, if you don't want to have three why don't you give two to him and then he'll have three, and you'll have one?

**Bonnie:** Yeah.

**Norman:** No, it isn't fair. It goes the same way—if we give three to Dennis it goes the same way. Just split them in half. Would you let someone make a big deal about it if you were younger and this big kid could do something and you couldn't?  .

**Bonnie:** If he was older he could have the privilege of doing everything else. He could go to certain movies like young kids can't.

**Norman:** I know. [Almost shouting.] We know it. They know it. But does Dennis know it?

**Craig:** Don't yell!

**Norman:** I can do what I want. It's a free country.

**E:** So what do you think? What's the best way?

**Norman:** Split them in half is the best way—we get them even.

**Bonnie:** What do you think [to Craig]? It's up to Craig. You want to split them in half, I want them the other way.

**E:** It's up to you, Craig.

**Craig:** No.

**E:** No what?

**Craig:** I don't want to split them in half.

**Bonnie:** All right.

**E:** Is there anything else you want to say to convince him [to Norman]?

**Norman:** [No reply.]

**E:** Craig, is there anything you would want to say to convince Norman?

**Craig:** [No reply.]

[Group begins to put candy into bags according to Bonnie and Craig's criterion.]

**Norman:** Hold it. You know he wasn't here so we can't get his point of view. So that's why it's spoiling us—we can't get his point of view.

**Craig:** Why can't we get him now?

**E:** What do you think he would say if he was here?

**Norman:** I think he would say he deserves as much, because he was younger.

**Bonnie:** I could prove it to him because he could have done just as much as we did but you know, he did it slower, he was talking more for one thing and—

**Craig:** Maybe he just wanted to make one. Maybe he doesn't like beads.

**Bonnie:** Maybe he didn't really enjoy doing them.

**E:** So you think you could talk him into it, thinking that's fair?

**Craig:** I could talk him into it.

**Bonnie:** I think so. We should get a bigger reward because we made more. Just supposing I could go back just as early as him.

**Norman:** He is little, for one. Besides, we're not thinking about him. You're not thinking about him. You're leaving him out and just thinking about us three. Just because he's not here doesn't mean you shouldn't think about him.

**Craig:** I didn't say that.

**Norman:** I know. But—you didn't say anything. We're the ones bickering and arguing about it and you're sitting there not saying a single word.

**Bonnie**: Craig, which do you want to do? One for Dennis and three for the rest of us?

**Craig**: I want to give Dennis the same as us.

**Bonnie**: It's the only fair way—I think we should.

**E**: How come?

**Bonnie**: I just thought it over.

**E**: What made you change your mind?

**Craig**: Besides, I was waiting for the answer.

**E**: Wait. Listen to Bonnie.

**Bonnie**: Dennis wouldn't think it's fair. Maybe he didn't want to do it as much, though. If he doesn't like it and I was doing a lot and he was talking a lot with Norman and that's why I got more done. And we used not as big a string as he had. So it probably would take him a little longer.

**Craig**: His [Dennis's] is bigger than mine.

**Norman**: This is my biggest—it's bigger [Dennis's is bigger].

**E**: So, do you agree with Bonnie, Craig? What do you think?

**Craig**: It's a good idea.

[They all begin to give out the candy spontaneously at this point, according to Norman's criterion.]

**E**: So before you do it, make sure everybody thinks it's fair.

**Norman**: Do you [to Craig]?

**Craig**: Sure! Do you [to Bonnie]?

**Bonnie**: Yes, I guess so.

**Craig**: You sure?

[No reply. They continue giving out candy bars. They give out two and a half to each of the four members.]

# 3

# The Development
# of Social-Conventional
# and Moral Concepts

## ELLIOT TURIEL

The topic of this chapter is somewhat different from those of the other chapters in this volume. While all the others deal mainly with moral development, the primary emphasis here is on the development of concepts of social convention and on the basis for distinguishing social convention from morality. Concepts of social convention stem from the child's efforts at understanding social systems. From a relatively young age, children partake in social groups and social organizations. In the process of such interactions, children develop a sociological orientation through which they form concepts of culture and social organization. A central aspect of interaction in social systems is the normative regulation reflected in *conventionally* shared behaviors; as part of their understanding of social organization, children develop concepts of social conventions. Through their social interactions children also develop moral judgments, which are prescriptions about behavior.

Therefore, two separate questions require investigation: (1) How does the individual think about culture and social organization? (2) How does the individual make moral judgments? In turn, these two questions require separate developmental analyses. This chapter deals with theory and research pertaining to these two issues, from the perspective of a structural-developmental approach. The structural-developmental approach is also represented in this book by Damon (*see* Chapter 2) and Rothman (*see* Chapter 4) in their discussions of moral judgment and behavior. Basic to this framework are the following propositions, which apply not only to social development but also to other aspects of cognitive development (cf. Kaplan, 1966; Langer, 1969a; Piaget, 1947/1950, 1970; Piaget & Inhelder, 1969; Strauss, 1972; Werner, 1948): (1) The individual's development progresses through a series of organized structures of thought and action, which (2) are transformed in an ordered way through (3) interaction with the social and physical environments. This approach is termed *structural-developmental* because it rests on analyses of the organization of thought and action and of the transformations that structures undergo in development. Mental structures define the ways the child actively organizes experiences, and out of efforts at active organization of experience, structural changes occur (Inhelder, Sinclair, & Bovet, 1974; Langer, 1969b; Snyder & Feldman, 1977; Strauss, 1972; Turiel, 1973, 1974, 1977).

Approaching the development of social concepts from a structural viewpoint implies that children construct social concepts that form organized patterns. Social judgments are not determined by environmental content, but are constructions stemming from the individual's *interactions* with the environment. Development involves progress through a series of organized structures, not derived directly from the environment, but generated out of interaction with the environment. This interactional thesis was formulated by Piaget: "Knowledge, at its origin, neither arises from objects nor from the subject, but from interactions—at first inextricable—between the subject and those objects" (Piaget, 1970, p. 704). Piaget's proposition is that the development of knowledge is not a function of direct instruction: "Each time one prematurely teaches a child something he could have discovered himself, that child is kept from inventing it and consequently from understanding it completely" (Piaget, 1970, p. 715).

As both Damon and Rothman maintain in their chapters, within the structural approach, moral development is not seen as a process of internalizing socially acceptable behaviors or cultural values. Rather, it is seen as a construction of concepts of right or wrong or of justice. Moreover, I take the position that if morality is to be viewed as involving judgmental processes, then it is necessary that moral judgments be distinguished from other forms of social judgments, particularly from judgments about the conventions of social systems.

The role of convention in social organization has been differentiated from that of morality by the sociologist, Max Weber (1922/1947). Weber actually identified three categories of social action: custom, convention, and ethics. He used the term *custom* to refer to actions that are performed with some regularity, but that do not serve a social-organizational function and are, thus, readily alterable. Consequently, customs are not regulated by external sanctions: "Today it is customary every morning to eat a breakfast which, within limits, conforms to a certain pattern. But there is no obligation to do so" (Weber, 1922/1947, p. 122). In contrast, conventions are a significant aspect of the "legitimate order" of social organization and are regulated by sanctions:

The term *convention* will be employed to designate that part of the custom followed within a given social group which is recognized as "binding" and protected against violation by sanctions of disapproval . . . . Conformity with convention in such matters of the usual forms of greeting, the mode of dress recognized as appropriate or respectable, and various of the rules governing the restrictions on social intercourse, both in form and in content, is very definitely expected of the individual and regarded as binding on him. (pp. 127-128).

In turn, the conventional is distinct from the ethical:

Every system of ethics which has in a sociological sense become validly established is likely to be upheld to a large extent by the probability that disapproval will result in its violation, that is, by convention. On the other hand, it is by no means necessary that all conventionally or legally guaranteed forms of order should claim the authority of ethical norms. (p. 130).

## SOCIAL CONVENTION AS DISTINCT FROM MORALITY

At this point brief definitions of the terms *social convention* and *morality* are in order. By social convention I am referring to behavioral uniformities that coordinate interactions of individuals within social systems. Thus, social conventions constitute shared knowledge of uniformities in social interactions and are determined by the social system in which they are formed. Some illustrative examples of social-conventional acts include uniformities in modes of dress, usages of forms of address (e.g., first name or titles plus last name), and modes of greeting. Research has shown that these types of conventional uniformities are based on accepted usage and are regulated by social organization. For instance, it has been found (Brown & Gilman, 1960; Slobin, Miller, & Porter, 1968) that usage of forms of address reflects the relative social status of individuals within a social organization. Forms of address are regulated by the social relations between the speaker and addressee, which in turn are partially regulated by the social structure. These conclusions are based on analyses of pronouns of address (e.g., *tu* or *vous* in French) in a number of languages in different historical contexts (Brown & Gilman, 1960), as well as on uses of first names or titles (Brown & Ford, 1961) in a variety of contexts (e.g., usage in modern American plays and in business firms). Furthermore, it has been shown that modes of greeting in Mexican (Foster, 1964) and African (Goody, 1972) societies serve to affirm social status and maintain different levels of social distance between individuals.

Social conventional acts in themselves are arbitrary, in that they do not have an intrinsically prescriptive basis—in other words, alternative courses of action can serve similar functions. A conventional uniformity within one social unit may serve the same function as a different conventional uniformity in another social system. Consider, for example, conventional uniformities regarding modes of dress. Typically, formal attire (e.g., suit and tie) is worn in certain social contexts (e.g., a business firm or place of religious worship) and the content of this conventional uniformity is arbitrarily designated. Uniform modes of dress other than a suit and tie could just as well be designated as appropriate for the business office or church.

In the case of conventions, therefore, the content of the regularity can be varied without altering the functions served; conventional uniformities are defined relative to the social-situational context. Accordingly, within the conventional domain, only violations of implicit or explicit regulations would be regarded as transgressions. For an individual to regard a particular act as a transgression, he or she would have to possess culture-specific information about the act's status as a socially determined regularity. This is not the case in the moral domain. Within the moral domain, actions are not arbitrary, and the existence of a social regulation is not necessary for an individual to view an event as a transgression. For example, when one person hits another, thereby causing physical harm, perception of that event as a transgression stems from features intrinsic to the event (e.g., from a perception of the consequences to the victim). Thus, moral issues are not relative to the social context, nor are they determined by social regulations.

The distinction between convention and morality implies a narrow definition of morality as justice. The proposition is that children develop concepts of justice, which apply to a relatively limited range of issues, including the value of life, physical and psychological harm to others, trust, and responsibility. In contrast to convention, moral considerations stem from factors intrinsic to actions, such as their consequences (e.g., physical and psychological harm to others, violation of rights, effects on the general welfare, etc.). On this basis we can distinguish between (1) convention, which is part of social systems, as structured by an underlying conceptualization of social organization: and (2) morality, which is structured by an underlying conceptualization of justice (cf. Damon, this book; Piaget, 1932/1948; Kohlberg, 1969; Turiel, 1974).

### Theories of Moral Development

Research into the development of concepts of social convention is important in its own right as a means of explaining a central aspect of the child's understanding of the social world. In addition, such study has a bearing upon our understanding of moral development. As Richard Brandt stated in his philosophical overview of *Ethical Theory:*

Some branches of the more experimental social sciences also do, or should, draw on the concepts and distinctions that metaethics aims to criticize and clarify, particularly those parts of anthropology, sociology and psychology that are concerned with values and attitudes and conscience . . . . Some scientists have no criterion for distinguishing between ethical beliefs or judgments and nonethical ones. Hence, in their descriptive work they mix the two together indiscriminately, missing many opportunities for observations of theoretical importance . . . . Some social scientists ignore the difference between beliefs about the good or desirable and beliefs about duty and obligation, and thereby overlook the possibility that quite different accounts of the genesis of the two may be in order. (1959, p. 12).

Carrying Brandt's position even further, it is my contention that students of moral development have traditionally failed to distinguish social convention from morality, and that this failure has been a major obstacle in social scientific explanations of morality. There have been two main trends in social scientific analyses of moral development from at least the 1920s until the present time. One trend is represented by internalization theories and the other by structural-developmental theories. In the 1920s and 1930s, some of the prominent social scientists maintaining internalization positions were Durkheim (1924/1974, 1925/1961), Freud (1923/1960, 1930/1961), and Hartshorne and May (1928-1930). The structural view, at the time, was represented by Piaget (1932/1948). More recently, the neo-behaviorists (Sears, Maccoby, & Levin, 1957; Whiting, 1960) and the social-learning theorists (Aronfreed, 1968, 1976; Grinder, 1962; Mischel & Mischel, 1976) have maintained the internalization position, while followers of Piaget have extended his explanations of moral development (Kohlberg, 1969, 1976; Lickona, 1976; Rest, 1976). Although doing so in rather different ways, both approaches have assumed that convention and morality are part of one domain and that they do not develop independently of each other. Internalization theorists, for instance, have maintained that moral development is the learning of socially acceptable behavior and the incorporation of transmitted values. By viewing social behaviors and values as the incorporation of externally determined and imposed content, theorists taking this view make no conceptual distinction between different social behaviors.

While structural theorists have maintained that moral development is *not* an internalization of values, the specific stage formulations proposed by Piaget (1932/1948) and, more recently, by Kohlberg (1969) have been based on the presumption that moral judgments apply to *all* forms of social behavior. Thus, those explanations have also fused the moral and social-conventional domains: convention is treated as a subclass of the moral domain. Piaget originally proposed that moral development proceeds through two stages (following a nonmoral or premoral phase). The first is labeled *heteronomous* (generally corresponding to ages three to eight), and the second is labeled *autonomous*. According to Piaget, the child's moral orientation develops from an attitude of unilateral respect for adult authority to relationships of mutual respect among equals. At the heteronomous level, morality is based on a nonmutual, but unilateral, respect the child feels toward adults (regarded as authority). Rules are viewed as fixed and unalterable. In turn, the social order and its adult authorities are regarded as sacred. Developmentally, the young child's morality of unilateral respect becomes transformed into a morality of cooperation and mutual respect (the autonomous level). The basis for this stage is the emergence of the concepts of reciprocity and equality. Rules are no longer regarded as fixed or sacred; rather, they are viewed as products of mutual agreement, serving the aims of cooperation, and are, thus, regarded as changeable.

Piaget's two-stage system was modified and extended by Kohlberg (1958, 1969) into a six-stage system. Summary definitions of those six stages are presented elsewhere in this book (*see* Chapter 8), and need not be repeated here. It should be noted, however, that the major modifications of Piaget's moral stage scheme made in the stages formulated by Kohlberg are: (1) at the earliest levels (Stages 1 and 2), moral judgments are based not on respect for authority and rules, but on an orientation to punishment; and (2) those early stages are followed in adolescence by levels (Stages 3 and 4) in which there is an orientation toward maintaining the rules of social groups and society. At the next levels (Stages 5 and 6), moral judgments are autonomous and based on principles that are "universal principles of justice: the equality of human rights and respect for the dignity of human beings as individual persons" (Kohlberg, 1976, p. 35).

In spite of their differences, both Piaget's and Kohlberg's formulations are based on the assumption that moral development progresses from (1) judgments in which morality and convention are undifferentiated, to (2) judgments in which the two are differentiated, with convention subordinate to morality. In both stage sequences, the most advanced forms of morality are defined as ones in which concepts of justice are differentiated from and *displace* concepts of convention. Correspondingly, in both stage sequences, lower levels of judgment are ones in which justice is undifferentiated from convention. This was stated explicitly by Piaget in the way he contrasted the heteronomous and autonomous stages:

> Law now [autonomous stage] emanates from the sovereign people and no longer from the tradition laid down by the Elders. And correlatively with this change, the respective values attaching to custom and the rights of reason come to be practically reversed. In the past [heteronomous stage] custom had always prevailed over rights. (Piaget, 1932/1948, p. 64).

> For very young children, a rule is a sacred reality because it is traditional; for the older ones it depends upon mutual agreement. (Piaget, 1932/1948, pp. 96-97).

There are two points to be noted here. One is that morality and convention are treated by Piaget as closely intertwined within one domain.

The second is that Piaget attributes a great deal to the young child; the six year old is seen as having a sense of culture, custom, and tradition.

### Classification of Stimulus Events
### Used in Research

If social convention is to be distinguished from morality, then it is necessary that stimulus events used in research be appropriate to the domain being investigated. That is, the use of events in the social-conventional domain would be inappropriate in research on moral judgment or behavior. This point can be illustrated through an example from a domain clearly different from the moral. Suppose that in order to investigate moral reasoning a researcher posed a series of mathematical problems to subjects of different ages. Of course, such a procedure would be questionable; we could not be at all confident that subjects in the study had engaged in moral reasoning. The inadequacy of using mathematical problems to study moral development is quite apparent, and as far as I know no one has done so. Similarly, the adequacy of many types of social situations used by moral development researchers is open to question. As one example, in an experiment (Stein, 1967) on the role of imitation in moral development, children were assigned to do a boring task while a very attractive film was being shown in the same room. Children who left their assigned task to look at the film were considered to have violated a moral standard. The researcher classified "duty and responsibility in performing a job" as a moral standard on the grounds that such behavior reflects a moral value of the society. It is not self-evident, however, that the performance of an assigned task is a valid measure of moral behavior. Does it reflect a moral standard or a non-moral standard which relates to social and economic organization?

Another example comes from an often-used experimental paradigm for studying children's acquisition of moral behavior. Children's behaviors in response to a prohibition against playing with designated toys are measured. This paradigm has been labeled the *forbidden toy paradigm*. The basic experimental event is one in which the child is prohibited by an experimenter from touching or playing with certain toys that are available in the experimental room. (Generally, the subject is prohibited from playing with the more attractive of pairs of toys.) The effects of a number of variables on the internalization of the (presumed) moral prohibition have been studied. These have included nurturance (Parke, 1967; Parke & Walters, 1967), modeling (Parke & Walters, 1967; Slaby & Parke, 1971; Walters, Parke & Cane, 1965), intensity and timing of punishment (Aronfreed, 1966; Aronfreed & Reber, 1965; Parke & Walters, 1967; Walters, Parke, & Cane, 1965), and verbal instructions (Aronfreed, 1966; Cheyne, 1971; Cheyne, Goyeche, & Walters, 1969; Cheyne & Walters, 1969; Stouwie, 1971). In the usual procedure, the child is left alone with the toys used in the experimental treatments; thereby, a measure is obtained of the degree of internalization of the response (i.e., resistance to the temptation to play with the prohibited toys). From the viewpoint of the convention/morality distinction, the forbidden toy paradigm would not be classified as a moral situation. The prohibition against playing with a designated toy is an arbitrary restriction established by the experimenter for the experimental situation. An experimenter could just as well, without altering the moral value of the act, establish the opposite prohibition and restrict the child from playing with the less attractive toys. The restrictions placed upon the child are related solely to the scientific aims of the experiment: how the child responds to a prohibition when there is presumably some temptation to violate it. Given the arbitrary (nonmoral) nature of the restriction imposed, it is likely that children would view the restriction as a rule or convention specific to the social interactions of the experimental situation.

Several other events of questionable status have been used ostensibly to study moral judgment and behavior. In one case, children's concepts of game rules were used as a means of assessing moral judgments (Piaget, 1932/1948). In other cases, events involving material damage to objects were used to study moral judgments (Piaget, 1932/1948), as well as the moral emotion of guilt (Aronfreed, 1963; Aronfreed, Cutick, & Fagen, 1963).

In sum, an adequate understanding of the individual's social development requires both delineation of domains of social concepts and specification of the domain of social stimulus events. When faced with a social stimulus, the subject's response is, in part, determined by the nature of the event. Generally, the individual applies social-conventional concepts to certain types of events and moral concepts to other types of events. The use of stimuli that do not correspond to the conceptual domain being studied (as has often been the case) is likely to produce inaccurate results. Consequently, the choice of stimulus events in research should be based on criteria (Turiel, 1978a) for their appropriateness to the domain of the social concept or behavior under investigation.

## SOCIAL DOMAINS AND CONCEPTS OF
## SOCIAL RULES

As stated earlier, previous structural-developmental explanations of moral development (i.e., those of Piaget and Kohlberg) have not distinguished between morality and social convention. It is my contention that those explanations have defined the moral domain in too broad a fashion. An adequate application of the principles of structural-developmental theory requires that distinctions be made between different aspects of social concepts. It will be recalled that one of the premises of the structural approach is that concepts are constructions stemming from the individual's interactions with the environment. This is to say that the child's concepts are formed out of his or her actions upon the environment; to form concepts about objects and events, the child must act upon them. In turn, interactions with fundamentally different types of objects and events would result in the production of different conceptual frameworks (Turiel, 1975). More specifically, social-conventional concepts originate from experiences that are distinguishable from experiences that produce moral concepts. For instance, experiences with distribution of goods and infliction of harm or theft would relate to moral development, while experiences with social order, rules, or being different from the group would relate to developing concepts of social convention.

A recently completed study (Nucci & Turiel, 1978) demonstrates how young children's social interactions revolving around social-conventional events may differ from their interactions around moral events. In this study, observations of social behaviors were made in ten different preschools. In these schools the social class backgrounds of the children and the teachers' instructional and socialization practices varied. At each school an observer tape-recorded narrative descriptions of a series of naturally occurring events that entailed social-conventional and moral transgressions. (The described events were reliably classified as social-conventional or moral.) For each of these events, the observer rated the responses made by children and adults to the transgressions. These ratings were done on a checklist that contained a listing of categories of potential responses (statements pertaining to injury or loss, emotional reactions, rationales; statements about feelings of others, physical reactions; statements about disorder, rules and sanctions, and commands). The observer tallied the number of responses displayed in each observed event.

The frequencies of responses on the category checklist showed that the types of social interactions associated with moral transgressions differed from those associated with social-conventional transgressions. In the first place, children were much more likely to respond to moral transgressions than to social-conventional transgressions; children and adults responded at about equal frequencies to moral transgressions. Moral transgressions frequently produced direct communications (regarding injury or loss and emotional reactions) by the victim to the transgressor. The children's responses revolved around the intrinsic consequences of actions and often resulted in direct feedback regarding the effects of the acts upon the victim. Adult responses to moral transgressions complemented the responses initiated by children. Adults often responded either by pointing out to the transgressor the effects of his actions upon the victim or by encouraging the victim to do so.

Adults responded to children's social-conventional transgressions differently from the way they responded to children's moral transgressions. Adult responses to social-conventional events consisted mainly of communications focusing on aspects of the social order of the school. In large part, such communication entailed commands to refrain from violating norms and statements specifying school rules. Adult responses to social-conventional transgressions also focused on the maintenance of classroom order.

These findings suggest that the social context for learning social-conventional concepts may differ from that related to the learning of moral concepts. In other words, the types of social interactions experienced by the children differed according to the domain of the transgression. However, these findings do not demonstrate that the two domains constitute different conceptual systems in children's development. In that regard, it is necessary to show that children of different ages indeed do make the distinction. In explaining conceptual development, it is not sufficient (although it is necessary) to draw distinctions on definitional or philosophical grounds. As the concern here is with structure and development in ontogenesis, the issue in question requires empirical investigation.

A recent series of studies on individuals' concepts of rules pertaining to moral and social-conventional acts provide support for the proposition that the distinction between the two domains is made across developmental levels. The findings of these studies speak to a second issue as well: namely, how do children understand social rules. Social rules and regulations constitute a pervasive and important aspect of the child's social environment. From an early age the child deals with rules—in the home, in the school, among peers, and in the broader societal context. Undoubtedly, social rules influence the child's behavior and contribute to development. To understand the influence of rules on development, it is necessary to keep in mind that a rule always pertains to an action (or class of actions) and, as I have maintained, actions can be classified according to domain. It follows, therefore, that the meanings and functions attributed by individuals to rules would vary on the basis of the act to which the rule pertains; the meaning attributed to moral acts would be different from the meaning attributed to rules pertaining to social-conventional acts.

This point can be illustrated by considering an example of a child's responses to questions about rights to possessions. It will be recalled that social-conventional acts, in themselves, are defined as arbitrary and as having no intrinsically prescriptive basis independent of social organization. Rules related to moral acts, however, are not defined by their social context, but by factors intrinsic to actions. Consider the following responses made by a ten-year-old boy who was questioned about a story in which an adolescent had cheated an old man out of money (taken from Turiel, 1979). The subject was asked whether or not taking the man's money would be wrong if no rule prohibited such cheating and if everyone agreed it was acceptable.

I still think that would be wrong.
*Why?*

Because you're still cheating the old man. It doesn't matter whether he's stupid enough or not, and it's not really fair to take the money.

*What do you mean, it's not fair to steal?*

It's not nice to do it, because maybe he needs it too.

*What if the rule were changed about calling people by their first names so that everybody could call their teachers by their first names? Do you think it would be right or wrong in that case to do it?*

I think it would be all right then because the rule is changed. Right? And everybody else would probably be doing it too.

*How come the two things are different?*

Because it's sort of a different story. Cheating an old man, you should never do that, even if everybody says you can. You should still never cheat off an old man.

These responses illustrate that the relation between a moral act and a rule is conceptualized differently from the relationship between a conventional act and rule. In the moral domain, the regulations are explicit formulations of prescriptions, and thus the rule stems from the act to which it pertains. Consider as an example, a rule prohibiting theft. Such a rule stems from the judgment that it is wrong to take someone else's possessions. The rule, therefore, is an explicit formulation of a prescription regarding the justice or injustice of an action. If an act is intrinsically valued, then a rule pertaining to the act will be viewed as unchangeable and universally desirable. Furthermore, the aims served by the rule will not be regarded as specific to a given social context.

In the social-conventional domain, in contrast, the rule does not stem from the act to which it pertains. A rule is an explicit formulation of the convention. Thus, the uniformity leads to the rule, which guides the action. Since this aim can be served by a variety of actions, such rules will be viewed as changeable and relative to their social context.

Studies have been done with subjects of various ages on the ways they view the relation between acts and rules. One finding comes from the Nucci and Turiel study (1978). Preschool children were questioned about the spontaneously occurring moral and social-conventional events that they had witnessed. The children were asked whether or not the act would be wrong if there were no rule in the school pertaining to the act. When questioned about social-conventional events, in 81 percent of the cases the children stated that the act would be all right if no school rule existed. When questioned about moral events, in 86 percent of the cases the children stated that the act would not be right even if no rule existed.

In a study by Nucci (1977) the subjects were of a wider age range—from 7 to 19 years. They were presented with a series of statements describing transgressions of rules pertaining to moral and social-conventional acts. Subjects were then requested to select those statements which described acts that they considered "wrong regardless of the absence of a rule." At all ages, subjects selected almost all the statements depicting moral transgressions and only a very few of the statements depicting social-conventional transgressions.

One additional study (Turiel, 1978b) dealt with conceptions of the relativity of rules. Subjects ranging from 6 to 17 years of age were interviewed about a variety of moral and social—conventional rules, some of which they themselves had generated (e.g., rules in their homes and schools) and some of which the experimenter had presented (e.g., a rule prohibiting theft). They were questioned about their view of the relativity of those rules (e.g., suppose there is another country in which the rules do not exist?). As expected, it was found that subjects discriminated between the two types of rules. Most subjects, at all ages, regarded the conventional rules as legitimately changeable from one setting to another. But they did not regard the moral rules as legitimately changeable from setting to setting. The most striking finding was that the large majority of subjects at every age stated: (1) that it would *not* be right for a social system to have no rule regarding theft, and (2) that it would be wrong to steal even if there were no rule prohibiting stealing. *

Taken together, the findings from these studies on social rules demonstrate that the distinction between morality and convention is made across developmental levels. It appears, therefore, that concepts of social convention and moral concepts develop in parallel fashion. Having thus presented some evidence regarding the ways in which the two domains are distinguished, I can now turn to other research which has focused directly on the form and development of concepts of social convention.

## CONCEPTS OF SOCIAL CONVENTION

The development of concepts of social convention has been studied through interviews with children, adolescents, and young adults. In that research, the method termed the *clinical method* by Piaget (1928) was used. In the clinical method the subject is administered a semi-structured interview designed to obtain information about the form of reasoning, rather than just the conclusions or attitudes held (content). The interview

---

*In the Turiel (1978b) study, subjects were also questioned about rules in games. Regardless of age, subjects stated that game rules were changeable and specific to the functions of the game. Therefore, the meaning and function attributed to game rules by children is different from the meaning and function attributed to moral rules. As was stated in the previous section, assessments of children's concepts of game rules have been used as a means of assessing moral judgments (Piaget, 1932/1948). However, these findings show that the use of game rules is not an appropriate way to study moral development. See Turiel, 1978a for further discussion.

contains questions aimed at stimulating the subject to explain the basis for his or her conclusions as fully as possible. Accordingly, the interviewer probes in such a way as to obtain the type of information adequate to an analysis of the organization of thought.* (For more extensive discussions of the rationale behind the clinical method, *see* Damon, 1977; Piaget, 1928/1960; Turiel, 1969; and Chapter 2 in this book.)

In the study of social convention (Turiel, 1978a), 110 subjects aged 6 to 25 years were administered an interview that revolved around a series of hypothetical stories. Each of these stories dealt with a form of conventional usage, about which subjects were extensively probed. The stories dealt with: (1) forms of address (a boy who wants to call teachers in school by their first names), (2) modes of dress (dressing casually in a business office), (3) sex-associated occupations (a boy who wants to become a nurse caring for infants when he grows up), (4) patterns of family living arrangements in different cultures (fathers living apart from the rest of the family), and (5) modes of eating (with hands or with knife and fork). I can provide a concrete example of the type of story used in the interview by referring to the situation dealing with forms of address. The story concerns a boy, brought up by his parents to call people by their first names, who is expected to address teachers in his new school by their formal titles. He comes into conflict with the teachers and the principal who insist that he use titles and last names rather than first names.

---

*It is essential to understand that the clinical interview method is based on different methodological criteria from those of the method of standardized testing (i.e., the method used in IQ tests and most personality tests). Unlike the clinical method, standardized tests are designed to elicit answers from the subject (such as an answer to a mathematical problem), without analysis of the form of reasoning that produced the answer. Again unlike the clinical method, standardized tests yield a score reflecting some quantitative assessment of the testee's capacity or trait (such as an IQ score). The clinical method, and the theory from which it stems, is based on contrasting assumptions. For instance, early in his career Piaget concluded that standardized tests did not yield sufficient information regarding the reasoning used by the individual to arrive at his or her answers. Piaget concluded that investigation of the nature or form of thinking required an alternative method to standardized testing and, thus, he formulated the "clinical method."

Clearly, the differences in theoretical assumptions and methodological criteria between the clinical method and standardized tests are fundamental ones. Unfortunately, these differences are not always understood. I have in mind an article by Kurtines and Greif (1974) in which they purport to critically evaluate Kohlberg's methods for assessing moral judgments. However, Kurtines and Greif evaluated Kohlberg's structural theory, which is based on data obtained through the clinical method, using criteria derived from standardized testing. They committed a major fallacy by evaluating one methodology with criteria from an alternative methodology. Moreover, they evaluated a structural theory with some criteria explicitly rejected by structural theorists in their alternative methodology. I do not mean to say that is is not legitimate to debate the relative merits of the criteria of one approach over those of another. But Kurtines and Greif did not do this. Instead, they accepted the tenets of one approach as if they were absolute, and then mechanically applied them to another (contrasting) approach. This procedure is scientifically untenable since the methodology evaluated was designed to meet empirical objectives different from most of the criteria used in the evaluation. It can be safely assumed that conclusions derived from scientifically illegitimate procedures hold no scientific weight.

The analyses of responses to the interview showed that there is a progression in social-conventional concepts from childhood through early adulthood. This progression is characterized through the seven ordered levels that are summarized in Table 3-1. It should be noted that the progression, represented by the levels summarized in Table 3-1, is not one of straightforward linear development. Rather, the pattern of development is one in which there is a series of oscillations between *affirmation* and *negation* of convention and social structure. Each affirmation entails a construction of concepts of conventions and social structure. Each phase of affirmation is followed by negation of the validity of that construction. In turn, each phase of negation leads to a new construction of concepts of convention and social structure.

The forms of affirmation and negation vary from level to level. At all of the levels, however, conventions are understood to be social constructions. Throughout the levels, two factors are salient: one is the conceived arbitrariness of social-conventional acts, and the other is the conceptual connections made between such acts and the social context. At each of the levels, conventional acts are (1) viewed, in some sense, as arbitrary, and (2) related to a conception of social structure. The phases of affirmation of convention entail the formation of concepts of social structure. The phases of negation of convention entail reevaluation of the social structure conception of the previous level. Development within this domain progresses toward viewing conventions as shared knowledge of uniformities in interactions within the social systems and toward viewing such uniformities as functional to the coordination of social interactions.

In what follows, each of the levels is described and corresponding illustrative responses are provided. I will keep the descriptions brief and limit the number of subject responses (all of which are taken from Turiel, 1978a) used to illustrate the levels. A fuller description can be found in Turiel (1978a).

### First Level: Convention as Descriptive of Social Uniformity

It is necessary to begin the description of the first level with a cautionary statement. The data supporting an explanation of the social-conventional concepts of six or seven year olds are still quite limited. The younger children in this sample were administered a short interview containing only two of the hypothetical stories. (This caution applies to the description of the second level, as well.) Those subjects were given a less extensive interview than the rest because a highly verbal procedure could only be used in limited ways with children of those ages. (Young children's thinking is currently being studied by using methods less dependent upon verbal explanations.)

**Table 3-1.** Major changes in social-conventional concepts.

| Level | Description | Approximate Ages |
|-------|-------------|------------------|
| 1 | *Convention as descriptive of social uniformity.* Convention is viewed as being descriptive of uniformities in behavior. Convention is not conceived as part of the structure or function of social interaction. Conventional uniformities are descriptive of what is assumed to exist. Convention is maintained to avoid violation of empirical uniformities. | 6-7 |
| 2 | *Negation of convention as descriptive of social uniformity.* Empirical uniformity is not seen as a sufficient basis for maintaining conventions. Conventional acts are regarded as arbitrary. Convention is not conceived as part of the structure or function of social interaction. | 8-9 |
| 3 | *Convention as affirmation of the rule system; early concrete conception of the social system.* Convention is seen as arbitrary and changeable. Adherence to convention is based on concrete rules and authoritative expectations. One's conception of conventional acts is not coordinated with the conception of rules. | 10-11 |
| 4 | *Negation of convention as part of the rule system.* Convention is now seen as arbitrary and changeable regardless of the rules. Evaluation of rules pertaining to conventional acts is coordinated with evaluation of the act. Conventions are "nothing but" social expectations. | 12-13 |
| 5 | *Convention as mediated by the social system.* Systematic concepts of social structure emerge. Convention is regarded as normative regulation in a social system built on uniformity, fixed roles, and static hierarchical organization. | 14-16 |
| 6 | *Negation of convention as societal standards.* Convention is regarded as codified societal standards. Uniformity in convention is not considered to serve the function of maintaining the social system. Conventions are "nothing but" societal standards that exist through habitual use. | 17-18 |
| 7 | *Convention as coordination of social interactions.* Conventions are regarded as uniformities that are functional in coordinating social interactions. Shared knowledge, in the form of conventions, among members of social groups facilitates interaction and operation of the social system. | 18-25 |

One of the stories used with these young subjects dealt with forms of address (described earlier in this section). The other story dealt with a young boy who claims that he wants to become a nurse and care for infants when he grows up; his father thinks that he should not do so.

Let's begin the description of this level with presentation of some responses made by a six year old. The basis of conventional thinking at this level is in the assumption, and interpretation, of the existence of descriptive social uniformities.

First the responses to the story dealing with forms of address:

### Joan (6 years:10 months)

*Should Peter call his teachers by their first names?*

He is wrong because if like if everyone called her Mrs. Loomis, and he called her by her first name, she expects to be called Mrs. Loomis instead.

*Why is that better than by her first name?*

Because it sounds a little bit better and everyone else calls her Mrs. Loomis.

*What if he wants to do something different than everyone else does, do you think he would be right or wrong in calling her Carol instead of Mrs. Loomis?*

No, wrong. Because if everyone else calls her Loomis, she would want him to call her Loomis and like when he says hey Carol, and not Mrs. Loomis, it would sound different.

*Do you think it matters if you call people by first names or Mr. or Mrs. or doctor, do you think it makes a difference?*

Yes. If you were Mrs. and they called you Miss, it would be wrong because you would be married.

*What if they called me Helen instead of Mrs., what would you think of that? Does it make a difference?*

Yes. Helen is a girl's name.

The following responses were made to the story dealing with the boy who wants to become a nurse.

### Joan

*Should he become a nurse?*

Well, no because he could easily be a doctor and he could take care of babies in the hospital.

*Why shouldn't he be a nurse?*

Well, because a nurse is a lady and the boys, the other men would just laugh at them.

*Why shouldn't a man be a nurse?*

Well, because it would be sort of silly because ladies wear those kind of dresses and those kind of shoes and hats.

*What is the difference between doctors and nurses?*

Doctors take care of them most and nurses just hand them things.

*Do you think his father was right?*

Yes. Because well, a nurse, she typewrites and stuff and all that.

*The man should not do that?*

No. Because he would look silly in a dress.

Insofar as social convention has relevance to the thinking of subjects at this level, it is related to the meaning attributed to what they perceive to be uniformities in behavior. Uniformities in social behavior are not understood to be regulations or coordinations of social interactions or part of a social system. Uniformities in behavior are descriptive of what is assumed to exist. In turn, what is assumed to exist uniformly is interpreted as necessary and requiring conservation. For instance, these subjects stated that titles are necessarily associated with certain classes of people and that occupations (nurse, doctor) are necessarily associated with the class of male or female. Thus, for these subjects, titles are not signs of role or status, nor do they serve communicative functions. Rather, titles are descriptive of the person. Titles may describe the marital status or age of an individual.

Similarly, observed behaviors or physical traits of classes of persons are interpreted as fixed and necessary for individuals within the classification. This notion was most clearly apparent in the subjects' consideration of whether or not a male could become a nurse. It was maintained that two types of (nondesirable) violations of empirical uniformity would result if a male became a nurse: type of activity and type of dress. Activities and physical characteristics (e.g., dress) serve to classify roles and persons for these subjects. The role of a nurse is defined by: (1) activities like taking care of babies, giving injections, typewriting, etc., and (2) wearing a particular kind of dress. In turn, females are defined by similar activities and types of dress. According to subjects at this level, if a male were to become a nurse, the necessary associations of activities or dress to the classes male and female would be violated because a male would be engaging in female activities and wearing female dress.

We shall see that at the next level—one of negation of social convention—it is asserted that empirical uniformity is not sufficient for judging behaviors as necessary, fixed, or requiring conservation.

## Second Level: Negation of Convention as
## Descriptive of Social Uniformity

By about the age of eight or nine, there is a shift in children's thinking about uniformity and convention. While at the first level perceived empirical regularities are regarded as requiring specified behavior by individual actors, at the second level children cease to see empirical uniformities as implying fixed or necessary behaviors. Furthermore, children at the second level have yet to construct notions of social structure or of the functions of convention as a means for coordinating social interactions. Consequently, at this level there is a negation of the necessity for adherence to convention.

### Susan (8:6)

Right, because it doesn't matter. There are men nurses in the hospitals.

*What if there were not any in Joe's time, do you still think he should have done it?*

Yes. It doesn't matter if it is a man or woman it is just your job taking care of little children.

*How come it doesn't matter if you are a man or woman?*

Like we talked about before, a man is the same as a woman.

*Why do you think his parents think he should not take care of little kids?*

Because his father might be old fashioned and he would think that men could not take care of babies.

*Why do you think he thinks that?*

Because it is a lady's job, because ladies know what babies are because they have them.

*You don't think that is true?*

No. Because ladies are the same and men might know a lot about babies too.

*What about the fact that women have them and know more about them, do you think that is true?*

No. Men might take care of babies when the mother is not home.

It can be seen from these responses that empirical uniformities in behavior no longer have the force that they did at the previous level. Subjects at the second level understand that there may exist (or at one time there may have existed) uniformities in these behaviors. Uniformity does not imply necessity. The empirical associations of activities, roles, or labels

(e.g., titles) with classes of person are no longer seen as necessary associations. Viewing uniformities as implying social necessity is attributed to
others; but it is not accepted by these subjects. One eight-year-old boy
stated the following:

> *Why do you think his parents see that job as for women only?*
>
> Because most women do it. But on my baseball team there is a girl.
> So you can't say he can't. She is a good player in fact.

The most salient feature of social-conventional thinking at this level is
that the acts are regarded as arbitrary. It is assumed that there is no intrinsic
basis for acting one way or the other. It is on the basis of the assertion of
the arbitrariness of these actions that subjects at the second level negate the
necessity for convention. However, there is no awareness of the coordinative functions of convention, except at the level of the need to determine
others' specific preferences.

### Third Level: Convention as Affirmation of the Rule System

For the first time, social convention is related to elements of the social system at the third level. Subjects at this level still regard social-conventional
acts as arbitrary—in the sense that it is assumed there is no intrinsic basis
for the action. The basic change at this level is that concrete conceptions of
social structure begin to emerge. Subjects evaluate social-conventional acts
in relation to the rules and authoritative expectations which are part of a
social system or institution.

The responses that follow illustrate these changing conceptions. The
first set of responses were in reply to questions pertaining to the story dealing with forms of address. The second set of responses were to questions
dealing with formal and informal dress. In the latter story, one lawyer
(Ken) decides to dress informally in the law office despite objection from
his partner (Bob).

#### Bruce (11:5)

> *Do you think Peter was right or wrong to continue calling his teachers
> by their first names?*
>
> Wrong, because the principal told him not to. Because it was a rule.
> It was one of the rules of the school.
>
> *And why does that make it wrong to call a teacher by his first name?*
>
> Because you should follow the rules.
>
> *Do you think if there weren't a rule, that it would be wrong—or
> would it be right to call teachers by their first names?*

Right. Because if there wasn't a rule, it wouldn't matter.

*What do you mean, it wouldn't matter?*

It wouldn't matter what they called her if there wasn't a rule.

*What about the rule makes it wrong?*

They made the rule because if there wasn't any rules, everybody would just be doing things they wanted to do. If they didn't have any rules everybody would, like, be running in the corridor and knocking over people!

## Bruce

I guess it was all right to wear sports clothes.

*How come?*

Because—he shouldn't wear rags or anything, but I think it's all right to wear sports clothes.

*What about Bob's concern for it not looking professional? Do you think that doesn't matter?*

Well, I guess he should look some professional. But you don't judge by his clothes, you judge by what he does.

*Could you explain what you mean by that?*

Well, you don't go judging a person by what he wears, you should see whether he's good at it.

*Do you think it's right or wrong for Bob to expect Ken to dress in a particular way?*

Wrong. Because he should be able to wear what he wants to the office.

*What if it's an office rule to wear a suit and tie to the office? Is Ken right or wrong in breaking the rule?*

If it's a rule to wear a tie, I guess you should.

*Why is that?*

Because that's one of the rules.

It is clear that in one sense these subjects regard social-conventional acts as arbitrary and changeable. Apart from concrete rules or specific demands for compliance from authorities, conventional acts are not seen as necessary. In the absence of rules or authoritative expectations, conventions, like forms of address, modes of dress, or manner of eating, "do not matter."

The third level represents the beginning of conceptions of social structure. Three notions of social structure are related to convention at this level: (1) authority, (2) adherence to rules, and (3) maintenance of social order. Social relationships are now seen as governed by a system in which individuals hold positions of authority, such as principals or teachers in a school or employers in a business firm. The authority is seen to come primarily from the power of individuals in such positions. Rules pertaining to conventions (i.e., acts otherwise regarded as arbitrary) are viewed as requiring adherence. Additionally, rudimentary notions of social order emerge at this level. It is assumed that maintenance of an existing social order is based on conformity to rules and authoritative expectations. At this level, therefore, conventions are contingent upon the social context: rules and authoritative expectations require adherence to the conventions. The demands of authority or existing rules may vary from one context to the next—as from one school to another.

For subjects at this level, therefore, the evaluation of what are regarded as arbitrary conventional acts is dependent upon whether or not a rule exists. This means that the subject's conception of convention is not coordinated with his or her conception of rules or social context. That is, the rule is treated as obligatory and invariable even though it pertains to an act which is otherwise treated as variable. At the next level, which takes the form of negation of convention, there is a coordination of rules and action.

### Fourth Level: Negation of Convention as Part of the Rule System

At the fourth level, the basic conception of conventional acts as arbitrary is maintained, as was the case with subjects at the previous two levels. Unlike subjects at the third level, however, subjects at the fourth level coordinate their evaluation of an act with the evaluation of the rule or expectation to which the act pertains. Viewing conventional acts as arbitrary, subjects at the fourth level maintain that rules or expectations about such acts are not valid. This level, therefore, represents another form of negation of convention.

#### <u>Bill</u> (12:11)

*Do you think Peter was right or wrong to continue calling his teachers by their first names?*

I think it is up to him what he calls them because a name is just like a symbol or something and it doesn't really matter, just as long as the teacher knows or everybody else knows who you are talking about.

*What about the rule, do you think it would be wrong to disobey it in the school?*

No.

*In some schools it is generally accepted to address teachers by their first names. Do you consider it wrong to call a teacher by his name even in a school where it is allowed?*

No.

*Is there a difference in doing it in a school where it is allowed and in a school where it is not allowed?*

I don't think so.

*How come?*

I don't really think it makes that much difference. I think that kids should call teachers by their first names, so I don't see any difference in it.

*Why do you think kids should call teachers by their first names?*

They call everybody else by their first names, and it seems more friendly, too.

*Some people might argue that it shows a lack of consideration and respect to call a teacher by his first name. What would you say to that?*

I think that is stupid. There is nothing wrong with a name no matter which you say. It doesn't really matter.

The distinguishing features of thinking at the fourth level are: (1) social-conventional acts are regarded as arbitrary; (2) rules and authoritative expectations are evaluated on the basis of the acts involved; and therefore, (3) those rules pertaining to social-conventional acts are unnecessary and unduly constraining. The use of titles or modes of dress, for instance, are regarded as arbitrary. It is the ability to communicate with others that these subjects regard as important. Names are seen as ways of identifying people and it is thought that communication can be achieved via the use of first names or titles. Similarly, modes of dress have little meaning to these subjects. It is believed that these kinds of decisions are up to individual choice. Therefore, each individual has the right to make his or her own choice of how to address teachers or how to dress.

The changes from the third to the fourth level in the conception of rules pertaining to conventional acts result in the view that conventions are *nothing but the expectations of others.* This nothing-but-the-expectations-of-others orientation stems from an awareness that, indeed, expectations do exist regarding what appear to these subjects as arbitrary acts. Consequently, social expectations are rejected as an insufficient basis for prescriptions of behavior.

At this level, therefore, expectations of authorities regarding conventional acts are not regarded as sufficient justification for adherence to convention. At the previous level, such expectations or rules were regarded as sufficient justification. The fourth level is different because such rules or ex-

pectations are regarded as arbitrary labels of expected and unexpected behavior. In addition, the necessity for adherence to a rule is evaluated prag-
matically. But, the role and function of convention in social organization is
neither negated nor affirmed at this level.

### Fifth Level: Convention as Mediated by the Social System

The previous two levels can be viewed as forming the foundations for concepts of convention as mediated by social structure. At the third level, conventions formed part of the individual's uncoordinated concepts about
concrete rules and authoritative expectations. The fourth level constitutes
a negation of convention through the coordination of conventional acts
and prescriptions (rules and expectations). This phase of negation of convention leaves the adolescent without a systematic understanding of the
organization of social interactions. It is at the fifth level that we see the formation of systematic concepts of social organization.

The basic change at this level, therefore, is the formulation of conceptions of society as a system. Notions about individuals as part of more
general social units or of a collective system have been formed. Social units
are defined as systems of individuals interconnected in an organization
with a hierarchical order.

At this level, convention is defined as shared behavior mediated by
common concepts of society. Normative characteristics are viewed as central to social units. Therefore, one of the defining characteristics of a social
system is uniformity. Conventionally shared behavior is necessary because
of the function served by uniformity in the social system. At this fifth level,
therefore, convention is normative regulation in a system with uniformity,
fixed roles, and static hierarchical organization.

There are two phases to the fifth level. During the first phase uniformity is a defining characteristic of a collectivity, and adherence to conventional uniformities is necessary for participation. In the second phase
uniformity represents a general consensus that is codified and that functions to maintain the social order. First, let's consider examples of the first
phase.

#### Richard (17:1)

*Do you think Peter was right or wrong to continue calling his teachers by their first names?*

I think he was wrong, because you have to realize that you should
have respect for your elders and that respect is shown by addressing
them by their last names.

*Why do you think that shows respect?*

Informally, you just call any of your friends by their first names, but you really don't have that relation with a teacher. Whereas with parents too, you call them Mom and Dad and it's a different relation than the other two.

*What if Peter thought it didn't make any difference what you called people, that you could still respect them no matter what you called them?*

I think he'd have to realize that you have to go along with the ways of other people in your society.

*Why do you have to go along with the societal part of it in this case?*

I think in society when you talk to an elder or teacher you have a more formal—you do it more formally, whereas a first-name basis would be informal and it would be just ordinary, really. As if it was just anybody.

### Richard

*Do you think Ken was right or wrong in his decision to continue wearing sports clothes to the office?*

I think he was wrong, because you have to sacrifice some things if it would be better for the company. But if he really felt that strongly about it, I guess it's his prerogative to do it.

*Do you think he'd be right in doing it, sticking to his beliefs?*

I don't know, I think he should go along with what is set up, really, by the office to begin with, because when he first worked there he did dress up. So he's working on the understanding that you should dress up because it's a professional service.

*Why do you think you should dress up in a professional service?*

Your appearance sometimes makes them either for you or against you, and if you saw someone dressed up in dungarees you'd think less of him than if you saw someone in a tie and suit.

*Why is that?*

Because people feel that if he has that much pride in the way he dresses, he'd be apt to have pride in the other things he does.

In a general sense, these responses illustrate the changes at the fifth level. Social acts are now judged in relation to a group or social system in which the individual is subordinate. Social systems are viewed as providing a context for rules and expectations. More specifically, Richard made clear distinctions between different social units and defined social units by the specified uniform behavior. For subjects at the first phase of the fifth level, the individual's adherence to uniformities is a necessary accommodation to the group in order to be a participant. Participation in group or collective life is not considered an obligation for the individual. However, if an individual is part of the group, then adherence to its uniformities is necessary. Deviance from the prescribed behavior is a violation of the legitimate expectations of others who are part of the group.

That these subjects view conventions as social constructions of group life is demonstrated by the fact that they maintain that sanctions for deviations should take the form of exclusion from the group. The following response illustrates this point:

### Mike (14:6)

I don't think he should be punished just because it's an accepted custom. If there's some reason that this custom is terribly bad there's a law against it, so that you won't be doing it. But if there's no law, I think that the punishment itself comes from society, and that's why you don't find a lot of people eating with their hands, because society has taught them not to. And those that have learned to, which are very few, you know, from their families or something, learn not to because society itself punished you by regarding you as an outcast.

In the second phase of the fifth level, there is an extension of the subject's conception of social systems. While in the first phase uniformity is related to group participation, in the second phase it is also assumed that conventional uniformities in social groups, particularly at the societal level, are also necessary for the maintenance of the society. During the first phase, variance in an individual's behavior results in group exclusion for that person; at the second phase variance or diversity can additionally imply a breakdown of the social unit.

### James (15:11)

I think he's wrong, because in his family he can call his mother and father by their first names. But when he's in public he's got to respect the rules of the school.

*Why does he have to respect the rules of the school?*

How can you be one individual? If everyone else—he's one individual and his family is brought up with first names. In school, it's a rule to call people by their last names, and if it's a rule he can't be the only one who's not going to do it. He's just going to have to live with it. Even if his family taught him like that, he doesn't have to tell them . . . he cannot do it. It's just the principle of the thing. Because it's different if a lot of families did it, but I think he probably is just one exception. And he should obey the rules of the school.

*How would it be different if a lot of families brought their children up that way?*

It depends. Usually in schools they allow the parents to have some opinion on how the school is run. And so if there's umpteen million families that are brought up like this, like I know, most of the time (maybe this is an exception, but it's a good example), most families I think will teach kids to call adults and older people by their last names. But if it's the other way around—say, it was more polite to call them by their first names now, and there was a lot of people and say the principal said, "if you don't call me by my last name," I guarantee you if they—they'd finally take a vote through the town, and it would probably be passed that they would call them by first names. So it really depends on what the customs are. Like I know right now that usually it's appropriate to call them by their last names. If he's only one in twenty maybe, even more than that, then he should call them by their last names.

We can see from these responses that at this level conventions are codified. They represent common shared knowledge of the part of the members of a social system. Conventions are determined by general acceptance and are thereby binding on all members. Furthermore, the nature of relations between members of a social group are determined by social organization. For instance, the relation between student and teacher is determined by the social context of the school. Within the school context, the use of titles represents a uniform means for signifying the student-teacher relation.

Having formed systematic concepts of social organization, subjects at the fifth level now define society as hierarchically ordered. Individuals are thereby classified on the basis of their role and status within the system. Conventions symbolize both roles and status. An example of the way in which conventions symbolize roles can be seen in the following response:

Actually my answer would depend on what kind of firm it was, and actually I am not sure, but if it was an old established law firm and he had several law partners who dressed like lawyers do and then he came in wearing very casual clothes, I think he would be jeopardizing the people he worked with, compromising their willingness to wear clothes as part of their occupation. It would be unfair to them in the sense that since they are lawyers and dealing with people this guy would have certain responsibilities towards the company he worked for and by wearing casual clothes, he would create a bad impression that others would want to avoid; if he were a clerk and nobody ever saw him, then it wouldn't really matter.

*Do you think it makes a difference if people dress appropriately or not for their job?*

For your job, your dress, unfortunately, I guess people's first impression of you is on how you look, which I guess is only right because they have no other way of judging you. I guess most of how you look is what clothes you wear, so if you want to create a favorable impression you should wear clothes that create a favorable impression.

At this level, hierarchical distinctions are made between people of differing roles and status. Status distinctions are based on the roles and functions within the social system. Status distinctions place constraints upon relationships, and interactions between individuals of unequal status require conventional forms of address. In this sense, conventions regulate those relations between individuals which are determined by the social context and the relative status of the actors.

### Sixth Level: Negation of Convention as Societal Standards

The sixth level represents another swing to the negation of convention. The previous form of negation (fourth level) entailed the assertion that conventions are "nothing but" social expectations. This was followed (fifth level) by the formation of social-system concepts where conventions were interpreted as societal standards providing necessary uniformity. The sixth level is, once again, a phase of negation—in this case conventions are regarded as "nothing but" societal expectations. Conventions are interpreted as codified standards. However, uniformity in convention is no longer considered to serve the function of maintaining the social system. The following responses provide examples of this sixth level:

#### Kevin (17:10)

*Do you think Peter was right or wrong to continue calling his teachers by their first names?*

Well, obviously he was right. Just the fact that teachers in schools have to be called Mr. and Mrs. is no valid reason for that. And also they simply refuse to acknowledge the fact that he's used to calling people by their first names, which is a natural thing to do.

*Why is there no valid reason for calling teachers by . . .*

Well, there is no good reason for it, the reason is to give the teacher in the classroom respect and give him a feeling of power and authority over the kids in the class.

*And why don't you think that's a good reason?*

Well because classroom situations don't turn into learning situations, they turn into situations where there is one person in the class who has all the knowledge and has all the controlling force over the class. And you have a bunch of students who are supposed to play a role which is subservient to him. And it's a different situation when one person obviously has more knowledge than the other people but he doesn't require them to be subservient to him.

*What about calling people like doctors or professors by their first names, would that be wrong?*

Well, I don't know whether it's right or wrong. I usually call people by their first names. I don't think it's very important, the fact that teachers want to be called Mr. or Mrs. People want to be called Doctor or Professor . . . . It's not a very urgent problem.

### Jerry (17:9)

*Do you think Ken was right or wrong in his decision to continue wearing sports clothes to the office?*

I don't know whether that is a place where you have to get dressed up—in the sense of a coat and tie. Maybe he should wear whatever is comfortable. Like in schools most dress codes are abolished and there's a move to have faculty dress codes abolished. So in that sense the strict coat and tie code is going out. So he's just a little bit ahead of the time in that office.

*What if the style wasn't changing and people still had to dress pretty traditionally. Do you think he'd be right or wrong in wearing casual clothes?*

I think it's up to him to decide whether he should wear them. He will probably in that case be a minority of one; he would be in the position where he would be forced to either conform to the rest of the business or society or leave the business.

*Why do you think it's up to him?*

I don't see that it makes any difference for society to set the code. I think a personal code is the ultimate that you should have for dress that is possible.

The negation of convention at this level represents a rejection of the reasoning of the previous level. Conventions are still regarded as part of collective opinion or of the social system. Conventions are defined as codified societal standards that serve the purpose of providing uniformity of behavior within the group. At the sixth level, however, uniformity per se is no longer regarded as a necessary condition for the adequate functioning of social systems. Diversity or variation in the behavior of individuals is not seen as incompatible with the organization of a social system. Changes in conventions are interpreted to mean that uniformity within a social system is not necessary. Without the uniformity requirement, conventions are regarded as arbitrary. Conventions are not yet understood to serve integrating or coordinative functions, and they are considered to be arbitrary dictates.

### Bob (17:8)

Calling someone Professor or something isn't wrong because you are not doing physical harm. It is just a social rule, the way you have been brought up. Society says you call people Mr. and Mrs. That is not going to do anything to actual relationships, it is just something someone says—now you call him Mr. or Mrs.

For subjects at this level, conventions are societal standards for uniform behavior. Conventions are arbitrary, but habitual, forms of behavior that in some instances serve nonsocietal functions. Perceived changes in conventions over time are taken to support the idea that conventions are arbitrary and maintained through habitual use.

### *Seventh Level: Convention as a Coordination of Social Interactions*

We have seen that by the fifth level, conceptual connections are made between convention and uniformities in social organization. At that level, it is assumed that uniformities are societal standards necessary of all members of the group. The negation of convention at the sixth level is based on the premise that conventional uniformities are not necessary for maintenance of a social system. Conventional concepts at the seventh level maintain conceptual connections between convention and the social system. The social system mediates convention, which is defined as uniformity that is functional in coordinating social interactions.

At this seventh level, conventions are conceptualized as integral elements of the interactions of groups of people in a more or less stable relationship (e.g., school, business firm, society) forming an organizational system. The basic function of convention is to coordinate interactions between individuals and to integrate different parts of the system. Conventional acts are regarded as arbitrary in that there is no principle intrinsic to acting in a particular way. Alternative (and perhaps opposing) courses of action may be equally valid. However, uniform or specified courses of action on the part of members of the social system are necessary. These are generally agreed-upon and known modes of behavior. The purpose of these uniformities is to coordinate interactions and thereby facilitate the operation of the social system. For subjects at the seventh level, such uniformities constitute social conventions.

It is also assumed that a system of conventions is based on general knowledge (shared norms) within the social system. The need for uniformity is based on the mutual expectations held by members of the social system that each individual will act in specified ways in order to achieve coordination. Achieving coordination entails recognizing that members interact in a way that makes conventional uniformities in behavior necessary. It is assumed that individuals adhere to convention on the basis of: (1) the expectation that others do so, and (2) the view that conventional acts are arbitrary (no intrinsic consequences to the act). Conventions are, therefore, based on the premise that there is common knowledge (by all likely participants) that individuals will adhere to the specified behaviors. In part, shared knowledge is based on the past behavior (the traditional and customary) of members of the social system.

Consider examples of this seventh level:

### Joseph (26:8)

Well to the extent that conformity to these social norms is necessary probably even from the standpoint of his best interests, he has to get used to using the modes of address. They are social customs that are acceptable.

*You said to the extent that social conformity is necessary, to what extent is it necessary?*

Looking at it strictly from his point of view, he is going to be measurably better off if he learns to accept these things.

*Better off in what way?*

Well, from the standpoint of being able to get a job, just getting along with people. If he has some strong feeling about this in this matter, that would weigh in the balance on the other side. But it would probably be a mistake in our society today to allow a child to continue to deviate from the norms that he is going to be expected to follow, that are necessary in his success in anything that he would want to do.

*Why do you think these norms are necessary?*

I didn't say they were necessary. I said his conforming to them is necessary.

*Why do you think his conforming is necessary?*

Well, it doesn't matter to me, but probably every society has had some sorts of distinctions about what to call people under titles that are given, possibly meaningless or possibly they have some meaning. It goes back to the old sociology that people have to have some method of determining how they are expected to act, and they have to have some way of knowing how other people are going to act to them in order to carry on day to day interpersonal relations. They can't be carried on completely in the dark as to what other people are going to do.

### Tom (19:0)

*Do you think Peter was right or wrong to continue calling his teachers by their first names?*

He was wrong.

*Why?*

Because the teacher didn't like to be called by his first name, and I think this was right, if that was how he wanted to be addressed. . . .

*Why shouldn't the teacher just change for him, why should he change for the teacher?*

Well, I'd say the teacher has to make a general—rules have to be accepted between teacher and student. If it was tutorial then the student would probably be able to convince the teacher that it would be all right to do that, as long as the student is not showing any lack of respect by addressing the teacher by his first name. The thing is, in a class that has several kids, assuming the rest of the kids have been brought up the same way we have, and they address the teacher formally, it would be breaking the generality of all the students addressing the teacher in the same manner if she lets this one student address her by her first name.

*What do you mean showing respect for the teacher calling him by his first name?*

I can see she would only be offended by the student calling her by her first name if she connected that with the students possibly thinking of her as a peer instead of someone with authority and a higher status.

*Would that be wrong?*

Would it be wrong for the student to think of the teacher as a peer? It wouldn't be wrong. It would only be inconvenient if the student thought he was just as authoritative on anything that comes up between the teacher and the student. Because in that case he would argue with the teacher who in the vast majority of the cases is bound to be right or would show better judgment because she is experienced a lot more. So it would be all right for the student to consider the teacher a peer as long as—the thing is it entails a definition of considering a peer, if you feel you have just as much authority when you say something as the other person. You can't, it isn't true. It would be wrong if the student considered himself just as authoritative as the teacher.

For subjects at the seventh level, convention is based on common or shared knowledge that facilitates social interactions. Violations of conventions produce the "inconveniences" stemming from the failure to coordinate interactions or to maintain a social organization. It is thought that to facilitate interactions the individual within social organizations needs to have ways of knowing how others will act in a given situation. This is accomplished through convention.

That convention is based on the shared knowledge and expectations is made more explicit in the following responses:

### Tom

*What would you prefer to be called or to call a teacher?*

I don't really care, it is not what you call them, but what you think calling them a certain thing means. I would just address the teacher by what I thought was conventional and be thinking all the time or have established in my mind what my relationship with the teacher is. The name doesn't really matter.

*Why would you do what was conventional?*

Because it is the easiest thing to do. If I did something unconventional then I would have to stop and explain to the teacher why I am doing things that are unconventional and it is really trivial, the reason for it.

*What are the reasons for conventions?*

Well, conventions make things move along smoothly and also—are most consistently understandable communication. If something involved in the communication of two people involves a certain way, if you communicate with somebody about something, you probably have some conventional way of talking about the thing you want to communicate and the person you are trying to communicate to is also familiar with the general way of communicating this convention. Therefore he is able to follow you more quickly because he automatically is familiar with the way you start to do something, if it is the conventional way of doing something. So he doesn't have to stop and think how is that working, how is this thing said, because he has already been familiar with it. It shortens the process in many cases.

At this seventh level, therefore, the primary function of convention is to facilitate interactions. By utilizing conventions, shared forms of knowledge allow for smoother interactions. Each participant assumes a common understanding based on past experiences in similar situations.

## CONCLUSIONS AND APPLICATION

The levels of social-conventional concepts just described demonstrate that social convention is structured by underlying concepts of social organization. At each level, conventions are seen in relation to social structure. The levels reflect changes in conceptions of the social system and changes in the understanding of the connections between convention and the social system. In other words, the individual, in taking a sociological perspective, develops a conception of society in which convention is an integral part. From this viewpoint, the individual's adherence to convention would not be regarded as the result of the acquisition of specific attitudes or habitual behavior. Rather, adherence to convention stems from the individual's conceptualizations of systems of social interaction. Conventions may vary in their specifics, but they are structured by the underlying concepts of social organization. As Dewey put it: "The particular form a convention takes has nothing fixed and absolute about it. But the existence of some form of convention is not itself a convention. It is a uniform attendant of all social relationships" (1938/1963, p. 59).

The findings on the development of concepts of social convention have direct bearing upon explanations of moral development. As discussed earlier, most explanations of moral development have failed to adequately distinguish between convention and morality. As a consequence, the development of moral concepts has not been described in a sufficiently precise way. For instance, in the moral development theories reviewed earlier (e.g., Kohlberg, 1969; Piaget, 1932/1948) a dichotomy is made between what is assumed to be the nonreasoning or conformist states of individuals at earlier developmental levels and the reasoning of individuals at advanced developmental levels. Within those formulations it is assumed that convention is equivalent to conformity, which constitutes a less advanced developmental level.

The proposition of a dichotomy between the "less developed" conformists and the "more developed" reasoners has its parallel in some anthropological explanations of "primitive" and "advanced" societies. That type of anthropological explanation has been characterized by Malinowski:

> Underlying all these ideas was the assumption that in primitive societies the individual is completely dominated by the group—the horde, the clan or the tribe—that he obeys the commands of his community, its traditions, its public opinion, its decrees, with a slaved, fascinated, passive obedience. (1926/1962, pp. 3-4).

Criticizing the assumption that individuals in primitive societies merely conform to the social system, Malinowski (1926/1962) argued that individuals from primitive societies reason about custom and law in ways that are not dissimilar from the reasoning of individuals in other types of societies. Similarly, I am proposing that the dichotomy of the nonreasoning, conforming child and the reasoning, principled adult is a false dichotomy. Children possess both distinctively moral and distinctively social-conventional concepts that each follow a developmental course.

The failure of moral development theories to distinguish social convention from morality has an important implication for educational applications. Namely, since our knowledge is still tentative, there is need for much caution in any application of theories in practical educational settings. It appears, however, that there has been a recent proliferation of moral education programs that are primarily aimed at moving students through stages of moral judgment. As it was stated a few years ago in an issue of *Newsweek*, the efforts in the 1950s to upgrade the teaching of science and math stemming from Sputnik are paralleled in the 1970s by increased efforts at teaching morality in the schools as an aftermath to Watergate and revelations of illegal corporate payoffs.

> Most parents seem willing to allow the schools to pick up the moral slack. According to the Gallup poll's latest annual report on American education, 79 per cent of the people surveyed favor "instruction in the schools that would deal with morals and moral behavior."

> In their search for such a curriculum, many educators are turning to the theories of Dr. Lawrence Kohlberg . . . who claims that moral development—like intellectual development—is a natural process that teachers can nurture in children. . . . Kohlberg's theories are now being introduced into a variety of U.S. classrooms . . . . Last month, the public school district of Tacoma inaugurated a program that over the next three years will expose every student from kindergarten through grade 12 to Kohlberg's method of moral education . . . . In addition, more than 6,000 public-school districts are now using sophisticated audio-visual aids that are based on Kohlberg's six stages. *

In my view, moral education should proceed with an awareness of the limitations of our understanding of the sequence of moral development and of the processes of developmental change. Furthermore, as much as possible, moral education should be coupled with educational research. The research on social convention discussed here, I believe, shows that much still needs to be done before moral development is fully understood.

## REFERENCES

Aronfreed, J. The effects of experimental socialization paradigms upon two moral responses to transgression. *Journal of Abnormal and Social Psychology,* 1963, *66,* 437-448.

Aronfreed, J. *The internalization of social control through punishment: Experimental studies of the role of conditioning and the second signal system in the development of conscience.* Proceedings of the XVIIIth International Congress of Psychology, Moscow, USSR, August, 1966.

* Reprinted with permission from *Newsweek*, March 1, 1976, pp. 74-75.

**Aronfreed, J.** *Conduct and conscience: The socialization of internalized control over behavior.* New York: Academic Press, Inc., 1968.

**Aronfreed, J.** Moral development from the standpoint of a general psychological theory. In T. Lickona (Ed.), *Moral development and behavior: Theory, research and social issues.* New York: Holt, Rinehart and Winston, 1976.

**Aronfreed, J., Cutick, R. & Fagen, S.** Cognitive structure, punishment, and nurturance in the experimental induction of self-criticism. *Child Development,* 1963, *34,* 281-294.

**Aronfreed, J., & Reber, A.** Internalized behavioral suppression and the timing of social punishment. *Journal of Personality and Social Psychology,* 1965, *1,* 3-16.

**Brandt, R. B.** *Ethical theory.* Englewood Cliffs, N. J.: Prentice-Hall, Inc., 1959.

**Broughton, J.** *The cognitive-developmental approach to morality: A reply to Kurtines and Greif.* Unpublished manuscript, Wayne State University, 1975.

**Brown, R., & Ford, M.** Address in American English. *Journal of Abnormal and Social Psychology,* 1961, *62,* 375-385.

**Brown, R. & Gilman, A.** The pronouns of power and solidarity. In T. A. Sebeok (Ed.), *Style in Language.* New York: John Wiley & Sons, Inc., 1960.

**Cheyne, J. A.** Some parameters of punishment affecting resistance to deviation and generalization of a prohibition. *Child Development,* 1971, *42,* 1249-1261.

**Cheyne, J. A., Goyeche, J. R. M., & Walters, R. H.** Attention, anxiety and rules in resistance to deviation in children. *Journal of Experimental Child Psychology,* 1969, *8,* 127-139.

**Cheyne, J. A. & Walters, R. H.** Intensity of punishment, timing of punishment and cognitive structure as determinants of response inhibition. *Journal of Experimental Child Psychology,* 1969, *7,* 231-244.

**Damon, W.** *The social world of the child.* San Francisco: Jossey-Bass, Inc., Publishers, 1977.

**Dewey, J.** *Experience and education.* New York: The Macmillan Company, 1963. (Originally published, 1938.)

**Durkheim, E.** *Sociology and philosophy.* New York: The Free Press, 1974. (Originally published, 1924.)

**Durkheim, E.** *Moral education.* Glencoe, Ill.: The Free Press, 1961. (Originally published, 1925.)

**Foster, G. M.** Speech forms and perceptions of social distance in a Spanish-speaking Mexican village. *Southwestern Journal of Anthropology,* 1964, *20,* 107-122.

**Freud, S.** Some psychological consequences of the anatomical distinction between the sexes. In S. Freud, *Collected Papers* (Vol. 5). New York: Basic Books, 1959. (Originally published, 1925.)

**Freud, S.** *The ego and the id.* New York: W. W. Norton & Company, Inc., 1960. (Originally published, 1923.)

**Freud, S.** *Civilization and its discontents.* New York: W. W. Norton & Company, Inc., 1961. (Originally published, 1930.)

**Goody, E.** "Greeting," "begging," and the presentation of respect. In J. S. LaFontaine (Ed.), *The interpretation of ritual.* London: Tavistock Publications, 1972.

Grinder, R. Parental child-rearing practices, conscience, and resistance to temptation of sixth-grade children. *Child Development*, 1962, *33*, 803-820.

Hartshorne, H., & May, M. S. *Studies in the nature of character* (Vol. I, *Studies in deceit;* Vol. II, *Studies in self-control;* Vol. III, *Studies in the organization of character).* New York: Macmillan, Inc., 1928-1930.

Inhelder, B., Sinclair, H., & Bovet, M. *Learning and the development of cognition.* Cambridge, Mass.: Harvard University Press, 1974.

Jones, V. *Character and citizenship training in the public schools.* Chicago: University of Chicago Press, 1936.

Kaplan, B. The study of language in psychiatry. In S. Ariete (Ed.), *American handbook of psychiatry* (Vol. 3). New York: Basic Books, 1966.

Kohlberg, L. *The development of modes of moral thinking and choice in the years 10 to 16.* Unpublished doctoral dissertation, University of Chicago, 1958.

Kohlberg, L. Stage and sequence: The cognitive-developmental approach to socialization. In D. A. Goslin (Ed.), *Handbook of socialization theory and research.* Chicago: Rand McNally & Company, 1969.

Kohlberg, L. Moral stages and moralization: The cognitive-developmental approach. In T. Lickona (Ed.), *Moral development and behavior: Theory, research and social issues.* New York: Holt, Rinehart and Winston, 1976.

Kurtines, W., & Greif, E. B. The development of moral thought: Review and evaluation of Kohlberg's approach. *Psychological Bulletin,* 1974, *81*, 453-470.

Langer, J. *Theories of development.* New York: Holt, Rinehart and Winston, 1969. (a)

Langer, J. Disequilibrium as a source of development. In P. H. Mussen, J. Langer, & M. Covington (Eds.), *Trends and issues in developmental psychology.* New York: Holt, Rinehart and Winston, 1969. (b)

Lickona, T. (Ed.). *Moral development and behavior: Theory, research and social issues.* New York: Holt, Rinehart and Winston, 1976.

Malinowski, B. *Crime and custom in savage society.* Totowa, N. J.: Littlefield, Adams and Co., 1962. (Originally published, 1926.)

Mischel, W., & Mischel, H. N. A cognitive social learning approach to morality and self-regulation. In T. Lickona (Ed.), *Moral development and behavior: Theory, research and social issues.* New York: Holt, Rinehart and Winston, 1976.

Nucci, L. P. *Social development: Personal, conventional and moral concepts.* Unpublished doctoral dissertation, University of California, Santa Cruz, 1977.

Nucci, L. P., & Turiel, E. Social interactions and the development of social concepts in preschool children. *Child Development*, 1978, *49*, 400-407.

Parke, R. Nurturance, nurturance withdrawal and resistance to deviation. *Child Development*, 1967, *38*, 1101-1110.

Parke, R., & Walters, R. Some factors influencing the efficacy of punishment training for inducing response inhibition. *Monographs of the Society for Research in Child Development*, 1967, *32*, 1.

Piaget, J. *The moral judgment of the child.* Glencoe, Ill.: The Free Press, 1948. (Originally published, 1932.)

Piaget, J. *The psychology of intelligence.* New York: Harcourt, Brace, 1950. (Originally published, 1947.)

**Piaget, J.** First discussion. In J. M. Tanner & B. Inhelder (Eds.), *Discussions on child development IV.* New York: Basic Books, 1958. (Originally published, 1954.)

**Piaget, J.** *The child's conception of the world.* Patterson, N. J.: Littlefield, Adams and Co., 1960. (Originally published, 1928.)

**Piaget, J.** Piaget's theory. In P. H. Mussen (Ed.), *Carmichael's manual of child psychology.* New York: John Wiley & Sons, Inc., 1970.

**Piaget, J., & Inhelder, B.** *The psychology of the child.* New York: Basic Books, 1969.

**Rest, J. R.** New approaches in the assessment of moral judgment. In T. Lickona (Ed.), *Moral development and behavior: Theory, research and social issues.* New York: Holt, Rinehart and Winston, 1976.

**Sears, R. R., Maccoby, E. E., & Levin, H.** *Patterns of child rearing.* Evanston, Ill.: Row, Peterson, 1957.

**Slaby, R. E., & Parke, R. D.** Effect on resistance to deviation of observing a model's affective reactions to response consequences. *Developmental Psychology,* 1971, *5,* 40-47.

**Slobin, D., Miller, S., & Porter, L.** Forms of address and social organization in a business organization. *Journal of Personality and Social Psychology,* 1968, *8,* 289-293.

**Snyder, S. S., & Feldman, D.** Internal and external influences on cognitive developmental change. *Child Development,* 1977, *48,* 937-943.

**Stein, A.** Imitation of resistance to temptation. *Child Development,* 1967, *38,* 157-169.

**Stouwie, R. J.** Inconsistent verbal instructions and children's resistance to temptation. *Child Development,* 1971, *42,* 1517-1531.

**Strauss, S.** Inducing cognitive development and learning: A review of short-term training experiments. I. The organismic-developmental approach. *Cognition,* 1972, *1,* 329-357.

**Turiel, E.** Developmental processes in the child's moral thinking. In P. H. Mussen, J. Langer, & M. Covington (Eds.), *Trends and issues in developmental psychology.* New York: Holt, Rinehart and Winston, 1969.

**Turiel, E.** Stage transition in moral development. In R. M. Travers (Ed.), *Second handbook of research on teaching.* Chicago: Rand McNally & Company, 1973.

**Turiel, E.** Conflict and transition in adolescent moral development. *Child Development,* 1974, *45,* 14-29.

**Turiel, E.** The development of social concepts: Mores, customs and conventions. In D. J. De Palma & J. M. Foley (Eds.), *Moral development: Current theory and research.* Hillsdale, N.J.: Lawrence Erlbaum Associates, 1975.

**Turiel, E.** Conflict and transition in adolescent moral development: II. The resolution of disequilibrium through structural reorganization. *Child Development,* 1977, *48,* 634-637.

**Turiel, E.** The development of concepts of social structure. In J. Glick & A. Clarke-Stewart (Eds.), *The development of social understanding.* New York: Gardner Press, 1978. (a)

**Turiel, E.** Social regulation and domains of social concepts. In W. Damon (Ed.), *New directions for child development* (Vol. 1). San Francisco: Jossey-Bass, Inc., Publishers, 1978. (b)

**Turiel, E.** Distinct conceptual and developmental domains: Social convention and morality. In C. B. Keasey (Ed.), *Nebraska symposium on motivation, 1977.* Lincoln, Nebraska: University of Nebraska Press, 1979.

**Walters, R., Parke, R. & Cane, V.** Timing of punishment and the observation of consequences to others as determinants of response inhibition. *Journal of Experimental Child Psychology,* 1965, *2,* 10-30.

**Weber, M.** *The theory of social and economic organization.* Glencoe, Ill.: The Free Press, 1947. (Originally published, 1922.)

**Werner, H.** *Comparative psychology of mental development.* New York: International Universities Press, Inc. 1948.

**Whiting, J. W. M.** Resource mediation and learning by identification. In I. Iscoe & H. W. Stevenson (Eds.), *Personality development in children.* Austin, Texas: University of Texas Press, 1960.

# Conceptions of Personal Issues: A Domain Distinct from Moral or Societal Concepts

**Larry Nucci**

*University of Illinois at Chicago Circle*

NUCCI, LARRY. *Conceptions of Personal Issues: A Domain Distinct from Moral or Societal Concepts*. CHILD DEVELOPMENT, 1981, **52**, 114–121. The study employed a series of sorting tasks with 80 subjects (age 7–20) to determine whether children and adolescents make a conceptual distinction between events defined as personal matters and issues of morality or social convention. It was found that subjects at all ages ranked moral violations as more wrong than violations of convention. Social conventional violations, in turn, were ranked as more wrong than the commission of acts in the personal domain. Reasons given for event rankings were consistent with the moral, conventional, or personal nature of acts. In other sorting tasks, subjects ranked moral transgressions as wrong even in the absence of governing rules. In the final task, subjects sorted acts in the personal domain as their own business and, as such, acts which should not be rule governed.

This article presents research examining one aspect of the thinking of children and adolescents about the set of social actions which are within what is identified as the personal domain. The study investigated whether children and adolescents make a conceptual discrimination between personal issues and those which are either moral or social conventional. The distinction between personal issues and matters of convention or morality can be made with reference to Turiel's (1978a) proposal that the development of reasoning about social events is structured within distinct conceptual domains stemming from qualitatively different aspects of the individual's social interactions. From this premise Turiel has proposed that individuals construct moral judgments out of their experiences with the range of social actions having an intrinsic effect upon the rights or well-being of others. Conceptions of social convention, on the other hand, are hypothesized to be constructed out of the individual's experiences with actions whose propriety is defined by the societal context (i.e., implicit or explicit societal norms). For a more complete discussion see Turiel (1978a). Research investigating Turiel's proposal has provided evidence that children and adolescents distinguish between moral and social conventional issues (Nucci & Turiel 1978; Turiel 1978b); that

both children and adolescents experience different social interactions in the context of social conventional and moral events (Nucci & Turiel 1978; Nucci & Nucci, Note 1); and that social conventional concepts follow a developmental sequence (Turiel 1978a), differing from the sequence of changing conceptions of justice (e.g., Damon 1975).

The present research extends Turiel's domain analysis to take into account the individual's conceptions of personal issues. While the previous two domains are concerned with matters of justice and societal organization (Turiel 1978a), the personal domain is defined by actions considered to be outside the realm of societal regulation and moral concern. Personal issues comprise the set of social actions whose import and effects are perceived to be primarily upon the actor rather than other individuals or the societal structure. As such, the personal represents the circumscribed set of actions that define the private aspects of one's life; the set of social actions for which the issue of "right or wrong" is one of preference rather than obligation or custom. Examples of actions viewed as personal matters include: one's choice of friends or associates, the content of one's correspondence or creative works, one's recreational activities, and actions which focus on the state of one's own body

This paper is based on a dissertation submitted by the author to the University of California, Santa Cruz, in partial fulfillment of the requirements for the degree of Doctor of Philosophy. Thanks are due to Elliot Turiel and Neal Gordon for their helpful comments on the manuscript. Thanks are also due to Ernest Pascarella for his suggestions regarding data analysis. Reprints may be obtained from the author, College of Education, University of Illinois at Chicago Circle, Box 4348, Chicago, Illinois 60680.

(e.g., masturbation, smoking, or aspects of physical appearance).

As a first step toward investigating children's and adolescents' concepts about personal issues, the present study employed a series of sorting tasks to examine the hypothesis that individuals distinguish among moral, social conventional, and personal matters. It was expected (a) that subjects would classify actions in the personal domain on the basis that the acts did not affect others, were the person's own business, and should not be governed by rules; (b) that their judgments of social conventional events would be based on their perception of the acts as affecting the social order established by rules emanating from authority or social consensus; and (c) that their judgments of moral events would be based on the intrinsic consequences of actions upon others rather than on the presence of a rule. It was also hypothesized that on the basis of those criteria subjects would distinguish among actions violating rules governing moral, social conventional, or personal behaviors in terms of their degree of "wrongness." It was expected that moral transgressions would be rated "most wrong," while rule violations stemming from actions in the personal domain would be viewed as "least wrong" or "not wrong."

*Subjects.*—The study employed eight male and eight female subjects in each of five grade levels (second, $\bar{X}$ age 7-4; fifth, $\bar{X}$ age 10-8; eighth, $\bar{X}$ age 13-4; eleventh, $\bar{X}$ age 16-7; and college sophomore, $\bar{X}$ age 19-6). All of the school-age children came from schools within the same district, situated in a middle-income area of Santa Cruz, California. The college-age subjects were from the University of California at Santa Cruz.

*Materials.*[1]—For the children in the second and fifth grades the materials consisted of 12 cartoon strips, each composed of a three-frame sequence with accompanying captions. Each sequence depicted an action contained in one of the three domains such that each domain was the focus of four of the 12 cartoons. Cartoons were used with the younger children to maximize their attention to the social actions being examined and to make the task concrete and comprehensible. The cartoons were drawn by an artist on thick posterboard $45 \times 15$ cm. Settings depicted in the cartoons varied from the classroom and playground to the home. Though adults appeared in some of the se-

quences, the main character in each cartoon segment was a child. Each sequence depicted the main character engaged in an act which violated either an explicitly stated rule or generally held cultural expectation.

Scenes were defined by the experimenter as content for the moral or social conventional domains on the basis of Turiel's (1978a) distinction between moral and social conventional issues. Sequences depicting the main character engaged in an unjust act such as injuring another person, stealing, etc., were classified in the moral domain. For example, one scene showed the main character taking a doll from another girl. Scenes depicting violations of rules or norms which serve to maintain the social order were classified as social conventional. An example of such an act is included in the segment in which a boy addresses his teacher by her first name when the rules of the school state that the students call their teachers by their proper names.

Scenes depicting personal issues were constructed within the framework of the definition of the personal provided here (introduction). Personal issues were the subject of scenes depicting the main character engaging in actions, which, though counter to a stated norm, resulted in consequences primarily affecting the actor. Cartoon sequences showing a school-age boy wearing long hair in violation of the school's rules, or a girl playing with a friend her parents have forbade her to interact with are examples of scenes defined by the experimenter as content for the personal domain. Personal acts were presented in conflict with social rules or social authority in order to: (a) match the format of the moral and conventional stimuli (both of which included information that the acts portrayed ran counter to social norms); and (b) to provide a context in which to test the general hypothesis that subjects would view personal acts as within the discretion of the characters engaging in the action and, hence, beyond the realm of normative regulation.

Experiences with these stimulus materials during the pilot study indicated that, though the cartoon sequences worked well with the younger children, they were not optimally suited for investigating adolescents' and young adults' classification of social acts. Though older subjects in the pilot study sorted these materials in essentially the same fashion as the second- and fifth-grade children ($\chi^2$ analyses

[1] A complete description and/or copies of the materials may be obtained from the author.

revealed no significant differences among the sortings provided by older and younger subjects), it quickly became apparent that the older subjects found it quite uninteresting to be dealing with cartoon segments showing elementary school-age children engaging in actions (e.g., doll stealing) not common to the day-to-day events encountered by most adolescents or college-age subjects. Thus, subjects in the eighth, eleventh, and college sophomore levels participating in the present study were not given the above mentioned cartoon sequences. The sorting-task materials used with these age groups consisted of 15 descriptions of actions typed on separate 3 × 5 inch cards. The content of these descriptions was similar to that of the cartoon sequences shown to the younger children. However, the characters in these descriptions were portrayed as adolescents or young adults. In addition, the content of some of the sequences depicted in the cartoons was altered to be more age appropriate. For example, the doll-stealing episode was replaced by a description of a student who steals a library book which other students need to pass an exam. Experience with a second pilot group of adolescent and college-age subjects indicated that this latter set of materials sustained the interest and involvement of older subjects.

A listing, by domain, of the actions presented to subjects at each grade level is presented in tables 3 and 4.

*Procedure.*—There were three classification tasks which together made up the sorting-task portion of the study. The first of these tasks required the subject to sort the various social acts according to their degree of wrongness following a standard set of instructions (see Nucci, Note 2). Following the reading of the instructions, the cards were presented in a standard order to the subject. The cards were ordered in sets of three, with each set containing one card from each domain. Within sets the cards were arranged in random order. In the case of the second- and fifth-grade children, the experimenter read aloud the accompanying caption as each cartoon segment was presented. They were asked to restate the story depicted by each of the three cartoons before ordering them. The older students, on the other hand, were asked to read each of the typed event descriptions aloud themselves. Once all of the cards had been ordered, subjects were asked to explain why they had ordered them as they did. The interview was designed to

elicit a central reason for the ranking of each card.

At the completion of the initial sorting task, subjects were presented all of the cards in their standard order and were asked to indicate which of the cards depicted actions the subject considered wrong, regardless of the presence or absence of a governing rule. This procedure, based on an interview developed by Turiel (1978b), has been used to indicate which actions subjects consider to be in the moral domain.

Finally, the subjects were presented the cards a third time in their standard order and were asked to indicate which of the actions should be considered the person's own business, or should not have a rule governing them. This final task was used to see if subjects would employ these criteria as a basis for identifying sequences defined as content for the personal domain.

**Results**

*Ranking of events.*—The average ranks for moral, social conventional, or personal events as a function of grade level are presented in table 1. Separate one-way analyses of variance for ranked data (Winer 1971) performed on scores at each grade level yielded significant effects for domain ($p < .001$). However, similar analyses performed on scores within each domain yielded no significant effects for grade level (subject age). Pair-wise comparisons ($t$ test for correlated samples) revealed that, at each grade level, moral transgressions were ranked as more wrong than transgressions of convention; and that social conventional transgressions were ranked as more wrong than transgressions of rules governing personal matters ($p < .001$).

Supplemental analyses examining the numbers of subjects providing modal rankings for transgressions of a given type as most, less, or least wrong demonstrated that the observed differences in mean scores resulted from consistent event rankings by the bulk of subjects at each grade level. It was found that, at each grade level, significant (binomial one-tailed test: $p < .01$) numbers of subjects (81% grades 2 and 5; 94% grade 8; 100% grades 11 and college) provided modal ranking 1 (most wrong) for moral items. Only one subject (grade 8) in the study provided a modal rank of 2 (less wrong) for moral items; no subject ranked a predominant number of moral items as least wrong. Analyses of subjects' modal

TABLE 1

MEAN RANKINGS OF WRONGNESS OF TRANSGRESSIONS IN EACH OF
THREE DOMAINS AS A FUNCTION OF GRADE LEVEL[a]

| | DOMAIN | | | |
| Grade Level | Moral | Social Conventional | Personal | $\chi^{2}$[*] |
|---|---|---|---|---|
| 2 ($\bar{X}$ age 7-4) | 1.19 | 2.02 | 2.79 | 28.22 |
| 5 ($\bar{X}$ age 10-8) | 1.19 | 1.97 | 2.84 | 30.55 |
| 8 ($\bar{X}$ age 13-4) | 1.12 | 2.07 | 2.79 | 29.15 |
| 11 ($\bar{X}$ age 16-7) | 1.06 | 2.14 | 2.80 | 29.37 |
| College ($\bar{X}$ age 19-6) | 1.05 | 2.16 | 2.79 | 29.94 |
| $\chi^{2}$ | 5.25 | 4.67 | 2.66 | ... |

[a] Rank of 1 = most wrong; 2 = less wrong; 3 = least wrong.
[*] $p < .001$.

rankings of personal items showed that significant (binomial one-tailed test: $p < .05$) numbers of subjects at each grade level (81% grade 2; 75% grade 5; 87% grade 8; 94% grades 11 and college) provided modal rankings of 3 (least wrong) for such items. Three subjects (one each at grades 8, 11, and college) provided modal rankings of 2 (less wrong) for personal items; no subject ranked a predominant number of personal items as most wrong.

*Reasons given for event ranking.*—On the basis of subject responses, a set of 12 categories was devised for classifying the reasons given for ranking actions as most wrong, less wrong, or least wrong. These categories were defined as follows: (1) Act should never be committed—the act is always wrong and/or should always be prohibited. (2) Unjust act—the act violates rights, causes harm, or deprives another of what is rightfully theirs. (3) Act affects many others—the act adversely affects a number of other people. (4) Act shows lack of character—committing the act shows lack of character, judgment, or responsibility. (5) Transgressor impolite—acting in the prescribed manner shows common courtesy, while not following the rule is impolite or unmannerly. (6) Transgressor creates disorder—by violating norms the transgressor is disruptive, creates disorder, makes a mess. (7) Law, rule, or authority prohibits act—the act is wrong because it is counter to an existing standard or the wishes of authority; commission of the act will get the person in trouble. (8) Minor offense—the act is only a little bit wrong; the actor will probably not get in trouble. (9) Consequences only affect actor—the consequences of the act only affect the actor; there are no significant consequences for others. (10) Personal matter—decisions regarding commission of the act should reside entirely with the actor; it is the

person's own business; (11) Rule rejected—the rule is rejected as uncommon, absurd, or serves no useful purpose; (12) Rule unjust—the rule is unjust, and the act should not be prohibited. The interjudge reliability for classifying reasons within the set of categories was estimated by a second judge's classification of reasons for the 10 subjects (69 reasons). The two judges were in agreement on 94% of their classifications.

Table 2 summarizes the frequencies (in percentages) of the reasons which subjects at each of the grade levels gave for ranking a stimuli as most wrong, less wrong, or least wrong. Only 6% of the 1,104 reasons scored were categorized as unscorable. The statistical significance of relationships between event rankings and reasons was determined using sign tests. For each reason category, the number of subjects providing reasons with greater frequency in one direction or the other for each of the following comparison pairs was measured against chance expectation: (a) most wrong versus less wrong and least wrong; (b) less wrong versus most wrong and least wrong; (c) least wrong versus most wrong and less wrong. The contingencies for these comparisons are summarized in table 3.

At all ages there was a greater tendency to rank an action as most wrong rather than less wrong or least wrong because the transgression was perceived as an unjust act which resulted in harm or negative consequence to another person ($p < .001$). Only at the youngest ages (grades 2 and 5) was there a significant tendency to classify an act as most wrong simply because the act should never be committed ($p < .05$). On the other hand, there was a significant tendency for subjects at the two oldest ages (grade 11 and college) to judge an action as most wrong because they perceived that the adverse consequences of the act affects many others ($p < .001$) and because commission of the act shows lack of character or sense of responsibility ($p < .05$).

At each age there was a significant tendency to classify an act as less wrong rather than most or least wrong because a law, rule, or authority prohibits the act ($p < .01$) and because the transgression creates disorder ($p$

TABLE 2

FREQUENCIES OF REASONS GIVEN FOR EVENT RANKINGS (%)

| | | | | | | | | | | | | | | | |
|---|---|---|---|---|---|---|---|---|---|---|---|---|---|---|---|
| | RANK | | | | | | | | | | | | | | |
| | Most Wrong (Grade) | | | | | Less Wrong (Grade) | | | | | Least Wrong (Grade) | | | | |
| REASON | 2 | 5 | 8 | 11 | Col-lege | 2 | 5 | 8 | 11 | Col-lege | 2 | 5 | 8 | 11 | Col-lege |
| Act should never be committed | 20 | 19 | 4 | 5 | 4 | 3 | 2 | 0 | 0 | 0 | 0 | 0 | 0 | 0 | 0 |
| Unjust act | 39 | 56 | 65 | 51 | 56 | 6 | 3 | 2 | 3 | 1 | 0 | 0 | 0 | 0 | 0 |
| Act affects many others | 3 | 2 | 5 | 23 | 21 | 0 | 2 | 0 | 3 | 2 | 0 | 0 | 0 | 0 | 0 |
| Act shows lack of character | 0 | 0 | 2 | 9 | 8 | 0 | 0 | 0 | 0 | 0 | 0 | 0 | 0 | 0 | 0 |
| Transgressor impolite | 6 | 2 | 4 | 0 | 0 | 6 | 11 | 18 | 31 | 36 | 0 | 0 | 0 | 0 | 0 |
| Transgressor creates disorder | 2 | 0 | 3 | 0 | 0 | 11 | 19 | 23 | 11 | 13 | 0 | 0 | 0 | 0 | 0 |
| Law, rule, or authority prohibits act | 21 | 14 | 10 | 6 | 4 | 58 | 48 | 30 | 31 | 28 | 0 | 2 | 1 | 0 | 0 |
| Minor offense | 0 | 0 | 0 | 0 | 0 | 5 | 5 | 13 | 11 | 13 | 9 | 9 | 15 | 13 | 9 |
| Consequences only affect actor | 0 | 0 | 0 | 0 | 0 | 0 | 0 | 0 | 0 | 0 | 13 | 13 | 43 | 21 | 23 |
| Personal matter | 0 | 0 | 0 | 0 | 0 | 0 | 1 | 4 | 2 | 0 | 44 | 47 | 24 | 43 | 49 |
| Rule rejected | 0 | 0 | 0 | 0 | 0 | 6 | 7 | 6 | 2 | 0 | 28 | 19 | 5 | 8 | 8 |
| Rule unjust | 0 | 0 | 0 | 0 | 0 | 0 | 0 | 0 | 0 | 0 | 0 | 2 | 4 | 9 | 8 |
| Unscorable | 8 | 6 | 7 | 5 | 7 | 5 | 2 | 4 | 6 | 6 | 6 | 8 | 8 | 6 | 3 |

TABLE 3

N OF SUBJECTS PROVIDING REASONS OF A GIVEN TYPE AS A FUNCTION OF EVENT RANKING[a]

| | | | | | |
|---|---|---|---|---|---|
| | GRADE | | | | |
| REASON | 2 | 5 | 8 | 11 | College |
| | Most Wrong vs. Less or Least Wrong | | | | |
| Act should never be committed | 9/1* | 9/0** | 3/0 | 3/0 | 4/1 |
| Unjust act | 12/0*** | 15/0*** | 16/0*** | 16/0*** | 15/0*** |
| Act affects many others | 2/0 | 1/1 | 4/0 | 10/1** | 9/0** |
| Act shows lack of character | 0/0 | 0/0 | 1/0 | 7/0** | 6/0* |
| | Less Wrong vs. Most or Least Wrong | | | | |
| Transgressor impolite | 2/3 | 6/1 | 10/1** | 11/0*** | 12/0*** |
| Transgression creates disorder | 8/1* | 8/0** | 11/0*** | 7/0** | 6/0* |
| Law, rule, or authority prohibits act | 14/1*** | 13/2** | 12/2** | 12/2** | 15/0*** |
| | Least Wrong vs. Most or Less Wrong | | | | |
| Consequences only affect actor | 6/0* | 6/0* | 12/0*** | 10/0** | 10/0** |
| Personal matter | 16/0*** | 15/0*** | 10/1** | 14/0*** | 15/0*** |
| Rule rejected | 10/1** | 8/1* | 3/4 | 6/0* | 6/0*· |
| Rule unjust | 0/0 | 1/0 | 3/0 | 7/0** | 6/0* |

ᵃ For sign tests, $N$ of subjects include only those providing reasons of a given type with greater frequency in one direction or another. Subjects not providing reasons or those providing reasons with equal frequency in each direction are not included in the analysis.

\* $p < .05$.

\*\* $p < .01$.

\*\*\* $p < .001$.

< .05). Only at the older ages (grades 8, 11, and college) was there a significant tendency to rank an item as less wrong rather than least or most wrong because the rule prescribes common courtesy, or the transgressor is impolite (p < .01). At none of the grade levels did reasons stating that the act was a minor offense significantly differentiate between acts rated less wrong or least wrong. However, there was a significant tendency for subjects at grades 8, 11, and college to rate an item as less wrong, rather than most wrong, because the act was perceived to be a minor offense (p < .05). It should be noted, however, that no subject used minor offense as a justification for ranking a majority of items as either less or least wrong. Thus, the resulting event rankings cannot be attributed simply to a circular set of criteria focusing upon the relative importance of the misdeeds (i.e., ranking an item as less or least wrong because it is a minor offense).

At all ages there was a significant tendency to rank an action as least wrong because the resulting consequences only affect the actor (grades 2 and 5, p < .05; grades 8, 11, and college, p < .01), and because the act is a personal matter and should be person's own business (p < .01). At all levels except the eighth grade, there was a significant tendency to reject the rule governing acts rated least wrong because subjects perceived the rule as absurd or inordinate (p < .05). In addition, subjects in the two oldest age groups (grade 11 and college) tended more often to view as unjust those rules governing acts ranked least wrong than those governing acts ranked as most or less wrong (p < .05). Though reasons regarding the act as a minor offense did not distinguish between acts rated least wrong from less wrong, there was a significant tendency for this reason to appear more frequently at grades 8, 11, and college for acts rated least wrong than those rated most wrong (p < .05).

*Sorting of actions as wrong even in absence of rule.*—Table 4 shows the number of subjects sorting acts as wrong, regardless of the absence of a rule. As can be seen, at each age group all of the acts defined by the experimenter as moral were sorted in the positive direction at significant frequencies (p < .01). In addition, all of the items considered to be social conventional or personal were sorted in the negative direction at significant frequencies (p < .01). There were no significant age differences on this task.

*Sorting of actions as should be the person's business.*—The numbers of subjects sorting

items as depicting actions which should be the person's own affair and should not be governed by a rule or law are also presented in table 4. At each grade level all of the actions defined by the experimenter as personal issues were sorted in the positive direction at significant frequencies (p < .05). One item, "Eating lunch with fingers," was sorted on a chance basis. All other social conventional and moral issues were sorted in the negative direction at significant frequencies (p < .02). As measured by this procedure, there were no significant age differences in subjects' perceptions of actions as personal issues.

## Discussion

The results of the varied sorting tasks employed in this research support the proposal that individuals make a conceptual distinction between personal issues and matters of morality or social convention.

It was found that events the experimenter classified as entailing moral transgressions were ranked by subjects at all ages as most wrong when contrasted with events involving personal issues or transgressions of social convention. This result is consistent with findings from previous research (Turiel 1978b) demonstrating that most subjects 6–17 years of age rank rules pertaining to moral issues as more important than rules regulating social convention. In the present study, moral transgressions were ranked most wrong because they were considered to be unjust acts (i.e., behaviors which harm others or deprive people of what is rightfully theirs). The youngest subjects categorically condemned such acts, while older subjects labeled such acts as indicative of a lack of character or sound judgment. At all ages these actions were considered wrong even in the absence of a governing rule or law. This last result confirms earlier findings (Nucci & Turiel 1978; Turiel 1978a) that children consider moral transgressions to be wrong in the absence of a governing rule and is consistent with research (Turiel 1978b; Weston & Turiel, 1980) showing that most subjects 6–17 years of age view rules pertaining to moral events as not legitimately changeable from one social setting to another, since the regulated acts are seen as having an intrinsic effect upon the rights or well-being of others.

Events classified as entailing transgressions of social conventions were rated at all ages as intermediate in degree of wrongness between moral transgressions and actions the subject defined as personal. Subjects considered the wrongness of violating social convention to be that of creating a disturbance or causing disorder, and violating social standards or the wishes of authority. Older subjects looked upon acts of this kind as violating the norms of polite conduct or respectful behavior. Consistent with findings from previous research (Nucci & Turiel 1978; Turiel 1978b; Weston & Turiel, 1980), such acts were viewed at all ages to be wrong only if the governing rule was in effect.

As was expected, events the experimenter classified as depicting personal matters were considered by subjects at all ages to be either not wrong, or less wrong than either moral or social conventional transgressions, even though the action entailed the violation of a social norm. The behaviors portrayed were considered one's own business: personal matters having results which primarily affect the actor. Subjects at all ages indicated that these acts should not be governed by a societal rule or law. Subjects rejected rules governing these actions as inordinate or absurd. In addition, the oldest subjects labeled the rules unjust.

The high degree of correspondence among subjects' classifications of social events and the lack of variability in such judgments as a function of age provide strong support for the proposition that personal issues are organized within a conceptual framework distinct from matters of convention or morality. Such data misinterpreted can lead to the false assumption that particular events are universally regarded as content for respective domains (e.g., personal). That is not the claim being made here. On the contrary, the data are interpreted to mean that individuals employ a common set of criteria for classifying social events but may vary in their interpretation of which events meet which criteria.

The classification of specific acts as social conventional or personal may be variable, in part, since what constitutes a matter of convention is established by each culture or social group. Within a given social group, the norms relevant to the maintenance of the societal order are generally understood. Thus, acts not pertaining to such societal functions may be considered by individual members of the group to be personal matters with a high degree of

TABLE 4

$N$ OF SUBJECTS OUT OF 16 AT EACH GRADE LEVEL SORTING ACTIONS AS "WRONG EVEN IN ABSENCE OF RULE" (W) AND "SHOULD BE PERSON'S BUSINESS" (PB)[a]

| | GRADE | | | | | | | | | |
|---|---|---|---|---|---|---|---|---|---|---|
| | 2 | | 5 | | 8 | | 11 | | College | |
| ACTION | W | PB | W | PB | W | PB | W | PB | W | PB |
| Moral:[b] | | | | | | | | | | |
| Lying[b] | 16 | 0 | 16 | 0 | ... | ... | ... | ... | ... | ... |
| Stealing | 16 | 0 | 15 | 0 | 15 | 0 | 16 | 0 | 16 | 0 |
| Hitting | 16 | 0 | 16 | 0 | 16 | 0 | 15 | 0 | 16 | 0 |
| Selfishness | 16 | 0 | 15 | 0 | 15 | 0 | 14 | 0 | 16 | 0 |
| Athlete throwing game[e] | ... | ... | ... | ... | 16 | 0 | 15 | 0 | 16 | 0 |
| Damaging borrowed property[e] | ... | ... | ... | ... | 16 | 0 | 16 | 0 | 16 | 0 |
| Social convention: | | | | | | | | | | |
| Chewing gum in class[b] | 2 | 0 | 0 | 0 | ... | ... | ... | ... | ... | ... |
| Addressing teacher by first name | 2 | 0 | 0 | 0 | 0 | 0 | 0 | 0 | 0 | 0 |
| Boy entering girl's bathroom | 1 | 0 | 2 | 1 | 1 | 2 | 0 | 3 | 0 | 0 |
| Eating lunch with fingers | 0 | 5 | 0 | 5 | 0 | 8 | 0 | 8 | 0 | 9 |
| Eating in class[e] | ... | ... | ... | ... | 1 | 0 | 1 | 0 | 0 | 0 |
| Talking without raising hand[e] | ... | ... | ... | ... | 2 | 0 | 1 | 0 | 0 | 0 |
| Personal: | | | | | | | | | | |
| Watching TV on a sunny day[b] | 1 | 13 | 0 | 16 | ... | ... | ... | ... | ... | ... |
| Keeping correspondence private | 1 | 12 | 0 | 12 | 0 | 13 | 0 | 13 | 0 | 13 |
| Interacting with forbidden friend | 0 | 12 | 0 | 13 | 0 | 13 | 0 | 13 | 0 | 13 |
| Boy wearing long hair | 0 | 13 | 0 | 12 | 0 | 15 | 0 | 15 | 0 | 13 |
| Smoking at home[e] | ... | ... | ... | ... | 0 | 12 | 0 | 12 | 0 | 12 |
| Refusing to join recreation group[e] | ... | ... | ... | ... | 0 | 12 | 0 | 12 | 0 | 13 |

[a] Eight subjects would be expected to sort an action as "wrong even in absence of rule" or "should be person's business" by chance; $p < .05$ or greater when 12 or more subjects sort an action in a given category; $p < .01$ or greater when 14 or more subjects sort an action in a given category using $\chi^2$ goodness-of-fit test.
[b] Actions sorted by subjects in grades 2 and 5, but not grades 8, 11, or college.
[e] Actions sorted by subjects in grades 8, 11, and college, but not grades 2 or 5.

agreement. Occasionally, however, there will be instances in which a given rule or law is ambiguously tied to the maintenance of societal regularity. In such cases there will be inter-individual disagreement over whether engaging in the act should be considered a personal matter. An example of this sort appeared in the present study. Eating messy foods (such as lasagna) with one's hands in a formal restaurant was classified by some subjects as conventional and by others as personal. Those considering it a conventional matter saw the act as disrupting the normal decorum and functioning of a social group. Those seeing it as a personal matter suggested that it only affected the messy eater, who may have had a personal preference for that style of eating, and had virtually nothing to do with the normal operation of the restaurant.

Though instances of overlap between the moral and personal are less likely, an example of such overlap is indicated in recent research (Smetana, Note 3) on women's reasoning about abortion, which suggests that decisions to undergo an abortion depend in many instances on whether the woman sees abortion as a personal or moral issue. Smetana reports that many women who opt for abortions do so because they interpret the fetus to be an extension of their own bodies rather than an independent human life. The decision to abort is viewed by such women as a personal matter in which they are exercising control over their own bodies rather than harming another person. Interestingly, a number of these women indicated that once a fetus reached a given stage of development (e.g., 3-months gestation), it attained status as a human life. At that point, these women reasoned, abortion should not occur since the act now involved the taking of a human life (moral issue).

Such instances of overlap among domains illustrate the complex nature of social cognition. However, they are not in contradiction with the position presented here. Instead they are viewed as raising questions best answered by investigations of how aspects of differing social domains are coordinated and/or confused with each other. As a heuristic device, this study investigated relatively unambiguous examples of actions in each domain to permit an analysis of the proposition that individuals do, in fact, classify a set of social actions as personal matters. It remains for further research to adequately address how instances of overlap among the various domains are conceptualized.

## Reference Notes

1. Nucci, L., & Nucci, M. S. Social interactions and the development of moral and societal concepts. Paper presented at the meeting of the Society for Research in Child Development, San Francisco, April, 1979.
2. Nucci, L. Social development: personal, conventional and moral concepts. Unpublished doctoral dissertation, University of California, Santa Cruz, 1977.
3. Smetana, J. Personal and moral concepts: a study of women's reasoning and decision-making regarding abortion. Unpublished doctoral dissertation, University of California, Santa Cruz, 1978.

## References

Damon, W. Early conceptions of positive justice as related to the development of logical operations. *Child Development*, 1975, **46**, 301–312.

Nucci, L., & Turiel, E. Social interactions and the development of social concepts in preschool children. *Child Development*, 1978, **49**, 400–407.

Turiel, E. The development of concepts of social structure. In J. Glick & A. Clarke-Stewart (Eds.), *Personality and social development*. Vol. 1. New York: Gardner, 1978. (a)

Turiel, E. Social regulations and domains of social concepts. In W. Damon (Ed.), *New Directions for Child Development*. Vol. 1: *Social Cognition*. San Francisco: Jossey-Bass, 1978. (b)

Weston, D., & Turiel, E. Act-rule relations: children's concepts of social rules. *Developmental Psychology*, 1980, **16**, 417–424.

Winer, B. J. *Statistical principles in experimental design* (2d ed.). New York: McGraw-Hill, 1971.

*Moral development proceeds in three phases:*
*rule attunement, social sensitivity, and self-awareness.*

# a socioanalytic theory
# of moral development

robert hogan
john a. johnson
nicholas p. emler

The space limitations of most journals require that authors provide only a cursory account of the theoretical context for their ideas. The purpose of this chapter is to present, for the first time, our perspective on moral development in a way that will clarify its theoretical foundations. The chapter is organized in four sections. The first develops definitions. The second section outlines the metatheory—the assumptions and presuppositions that support the model. The theory itself is presented in the third section, and the final section briefly reviews some implications of the theory that might not be obvious from a statement of its principal claims.

### introduction and definitions

Before the 1900s psychology and philosophy were nearly synonymous. The rise of behaviorism and logical positivism during the 1920s, however, drove a wedge between them. The positivist movement argued that "real" sci-

We are grateful to William Damon for inviting us to devote a chapter exclusively to the conceptual issues surrounding our theoretical model. And we thank Joyce Hogan and Carolyn Johnson for their helpful comments on this chapter.

*New Directions for Child Development, 2, 1978*

1

ence avoids speculation and restricts itself to what is immediately observable or to logical deductions from statements about the observable. Psychology enthusiastically adopted this positivism philosophy (Boring, 1950), with the result that the study of moral development became disreputable — morality, after all, involves concepts that are in principle unobservable.

Soon other philosophers began to argue that positivism was misguided. Margenau (1950) and Collingwood (1940) showed how all science requires metaphysical presuppositions; Pepper (1942) argued that all knowledge is essentially metaphorical; Hanson (1961) and Feyerabend (1965) showed how objective observations can be and usually are theory-laden. As the intellectual climate changed, the study of value-related psychological phenomena again became legitimate in the 1960s.

Positivism, nevertheless, continues to influence contemporary psychology, specifically in the degree to which philosophy is banished from psychological curricula. Their positivist-inspired educations often leave psychologists ill equipped to discover, evaluate, or justify their unconscious intellectual commitments — see, for example, Bem's (1970) discussion of "zero-order beliefs." Because the moral-development literature abounds with theoretical arguments whose presuppositions are unspecified, making meaningful comparisons among them is impossible. Failure to clarify one's implicit philosophical stance leads to conceptual confusion; failure to examine one's biases leads to the trivialization and politicization of knowledge (Emler and Hogan, forthcoming).

*Relativism, Absolutism, and Relative Absolutism.* There are four core issues implicit in every competent theory of moral development; these issues are largely matters of definition. The first concerns the moral relativism/moral absolutism dichotomy, which, on closer analysis, turns into a split among relativism, absolutism, and relative absolutism. *Moral relativism* maintains that there are no defensible grounds for preferring one set of moral values to another. Certain sociologists take this view by stressing the arbitrary nature of social institutions. Thus Berger and Luckmann (1967) refer to the socialization process as a "confidence trick" (p. 135). Anthropologist Ruth Benedict (1959) insists that cultures often adopt and even glorify values which serve no purpose. Finally, behavioristic social learning theorists (such as Aronfreed, 1968, and Bandura, 1969) focus on the mechanisms of socialization to the exclusion of the purposes socialized values serve; thus, they become relativists by default. Bandura (1969), for example, claims that the values one adopts "toward individualism, equalitarianism, theism," and so on, depend upon one's idiosyncratic social learning history (p. 614); this view (that the values one holds are a product of chance circumstances) implies that values serve no purpose and cannot therefore be justified.

Moral relativism appears to be supported by anthropological evidence showing that values do indeed vary from culture to culture. Moral relativism also remains implicit in many contemporary social theories with behavioristic origins. Nonetheless, sophisticated anthropologists (Herskovits, 1972; Kluckhohn and Strodtbeck, 1961) have argued that extreme moral relativism is untenable for several reasons. First, the existence of cultural universals — such as religion, language, family groups, incest taboos, prohibitions on gratuitous cruelty—indicates that cultural institutions are neither arbitrary nor idiosyncratic. Second, the variations one observes in values across cultures are not random; rather, they are predictable, given the ecology and history of each culture. Finally, nearly everyone, including moral relativists, has intuitions about the wrongness of genocide, torture, and slavery, yet moral relativism provides no grounds for criticizing these practices. On the other hand, moral absolutism and relative moral absolutism suggest grounds in terms of which such practices can be criticized.

*Moral absolutism* assumes that by careful thought one can discover timeless, universal moral principles applicable to all mankind. The values of any culture or person are justified only to the extent that they correspond to these moral principles. Currently popular universal moral principles include the sacredness of human life and a notion of justice defined as the equal preservation of everyone's rights. Cognitive-developmental theory is the primary example of moral absolutism in contemporary psychology. Moral absolutism is an important counterfoil to the simplicities of moral relativism. Still, it contains simplicities of its own. Because absolutism attempts to provide final solutions when in fact there are none, it suffers from two major shortcomings. The first is that even the most careful moral philosophers cannot agree on a set of universal moral principles, and those principles endorsed by cognitive-developmental theory reflect distinctive social-class and political biases (see Emler and Hogan, forthcoming). The second problem is that even if humans could get universal consensus on what is moral, it does not follow that they ought to act that way; knowledge of what is can never tell people what ought to be.

Our perspective, which we call *relative moral absolutism,* has the following tenets: Certain behaviors are essential for group living and the survival of culture. These are necessary for the existence of any social group and are therefore universal. There are other behaviors that if unchecked would destroy any society. The morality of a culture therefore includes rules that make such behaviors either mandatory or forbidden. At a deep level all viable cultures share the same set of rules—rules about lying, cheating, stealing, incest, and so on. Each culture also has rules that reflect what people have to do to survive in their unique ecological circumstances. There are two points to be noted about this perspective. First, there is no ultimate justification for those moral rules shared by all ongoing social groups; the rules are justified only by the fact that they make social life possible. This justification is not trivial, however, since social living is the key to man's evolutionary success. If the rules are ignored, social living is impossible. If a person seriously does not care about the survival of his or her culture, then that person would not be immoral in an absolute sense—but that person would be either criminal or insane. Second, the moral rules that make social living possible only tell us what kinds of behavior were necessary for survival in the past; they may not be valid for the future. Moreover, the conditions under which any social group lives may change. Thus cultures must always be open to the possibilities for change and innovation.

*Morality.* The second major issue is the definition of morality itself.

We regard it as a set of (usually codified) rules that defines a network of reciprocal rights and obligations, prohibits gross acts of malevolence, and specifies the range of persons to whom the rules apply. This definition means that morality has to do with rules, moral behavior has to do with conduct oriented toward these rules (obeying, disobeying, justifying, and criticizing them), and the rules may not extend to everyone. Moral relativists argue that these rules are perfectly arbitrary. Absolutists maintain that these rules are related only conditionally to morality; true morality is defined by a set of universal principles, discoverable by the use of reason and/or moral intuition, which is then used to evaluate and criticize the existing rules of a culture. Our view, in contrast with the preceding two, is that the rules are important not in themselves but because they serve to legitimize, sanction, and promote certain behaviors that are essential to the operation and survival of culture. Whether or not these rules are "truly moral" is a debatable point—but one for which a sound argument can be made (Gert, 1970). Their philosophical status aside, these rules are what most people mean by the word *morality*.

*Morality and Authority.* A third theme running through discussions of moral development is the problem of authority: What are the reasons for and the sources of our obligation to follow the rules of our society? This is one of those implicit, hidden issues about which moral development theorists rarely make their assumptions clear. It is important first to distinguish the question of why people follow the rules—a psychological problem—from the question of how the rules are justified—the logical/philosophical problem of authority. Again there are three views here. The first is the utilitarian or social-contract view: People follow the rules for rational reasons—because they believe it is in their best interests to do so, because they can only enjoy the benefits of civilization by following the rules. They justify the rules in terms of their collective best interests and their mutual agreement to live by a common set of laws or rules. The second view is the higher-law position; here, people follow the rules only if these correspond to their personal views of justice and the preservation of human rights. The reason for following the rules and the manner in which these are justified are the same—the rules correspond to people's conscious view of what a rational morality should look like. When public rules do not correspond to their private views of morality and justice, these laws lose their legitimacy, and people no longer need follow them. Thus, in this case, the sources of moral authority lie in the operation of reason and the dictates of personal conscience.

The third view, a classic statement of which can be found in Weber (1946), suggests there are at least three sets of reasons why people follow the rules. First, most people comply most of the time because they believe they want to and because they perceive their government as legitimate. When or if they no longer perceive this leadership as legitimate, they may discover the second reason for their compliance—that they have no choice, because their compliance will be ensured by force. Third, people comply for unconscious reasons: They need order, guidance, and direction, and fear its absence. Concerning the question of how the rules are justified, this third view distinguishes between morality and authority (which exist in a constant state of tension) and regards force as the ultimate source of authority in society. In every social group, power will be concentrated in the hands of the political leadership; if one refuses to comply with the rules long enough, force will be used to bring about compliance. Thus, according to this position, it is a myth to think that one's compliance is voluntary (because it serves one's long-range interests or is consistent with one's private view of morality). The reasons one uses to rationalize his or her compliance are often unrelated to the true causes of that compliance.

*Development.* When we come to the fourth core issue, defining development, we again find three prevailing definitions. For social-learning theorists, development consists of acquiring specific behavior patterns. These behaviors are not acquired in any particular order, and the end point of development is defined by a repertoire of behaviors common to most adults. From the cognitive-developmental standpoint, development proceeds in terms of a series of intellectual stages, each more complex but adaptively more adequate than the one that preceded it. Development is therefore defined as the achievement of increasingly more complex and adequate modes of thought. The sequence of stages is assumed to be invariant, and the end of development is achievement of the highest stage in the sequence. The socioanalytic view, like cognitive-developmental theory, adopts a quasi-biological model of development, but with certain important differences. First, there are no stages defined by qualitatively distinct modes of thought; there are only developmental periods or phases characterized by the unique psychological problems found in each phase of growth. Second, development is a never-ending process of trying to adjust internal conditions to external demands (that is, to adapt). These adjustments are necessary because the environment as well as the person is continually changing. But since change is the only certainty, any accommodation made will only be temporary. Finally, according to socioanalytic theory, the person's moral development ends in moral maturity, but this is largely an ideal state rather than something that is practically attainable.

### metatheoretical assumptions

In the preceding section we tried to show how our definitions of certain key words differ from those employed by other major theoretical perspectives on moral development. In this section we want to show how our theoretical assumptions are different.

*The Evolutionary Basis of Morality.* Socioanalytic theory differs from other perspectives first of all in its ties to evolutionary theory and evolutionary ethics as developed by Charles Darwin and Herbert Spencer and more recently by Donald Campbell (1975), Erik Erikson (1950), and C. H. Waddington (1967). Here, moral behavior is assumed to be a solution to the problems of survival that confronted our ancestors nearly four million years ago. The relative defenselessness of early man (lack of fighting teeth, nails, or horns), coupled with the dangers of living on the open African savannah (Washburn, 1961), made group living and cooperation essential for survival.

**6**

Group living was synonymous with the evolution of culture—defined in terms of language, family structure, patterns of leadership and authority, division of labor, tools, and other technology. Thus, the distinctive feature of man's evolution is his group-living, culture-bearing tendencies. Groups that on the whole were more structured and cohesive, and that had superior technology, would have had greater reproductive success. Culture also includes rules and values that support those behaviors that proved to be evolutionarily adaptive; thus the process of transmitting culture across human generations is fundamental to human survival.

*Individualism and Communalism.* These speculations about human evolution lead to the second set of assumptions that characterize socioanalytic theory. Every other theory of socialization and moral development in psychology can be described as a form of individualism (see Hogan, 1975b). The essence of individualism is a particular view of the relation between the person and his or her society. Specifically, individualism assumes that each child's nature is fundamentally transformed during the socialization process. This transformation is necessary because each child's natural or presocialized tendencies are incompatible with the demands of adult society as transmitted in the socialization process. In this view deviancy is normal and conformity must be explained. From a socioanalytic perspective, the individualism of contemporary psychology is highly implausible. Given the central role culture played in human evolution, it is more sensible to assume a deep compatibility between each child's natural tendencies and the demands of adult society; thus conformity is normal and deviancy must be explained. Not only is conformity to culture normal, but the internalization of culture is essential to the normal development of personality. Man has a deep, organic need for his culture, and the feeling of belonging to and participating in a viable, ongoing group gives substance to personality and meaning to life (Berger and Kellner, 1964; Turner, 1975).

*Human Motivation.* A third distinctive feature of socioanalytic theory is its view of human motivation. Although it is currently unfashionable in developmental psychology to talk about motivation, we assume that, as a result of man's particular evolutionary history, three broad motives underlie social behavior. These hypothetical motives or drives give rise to three separate classes of behavior that are essential for cooperative group living. The first of these is a need for social attention and approval. Much social behavior is designed to maximize positive attention and approval or to minimize social criticism (Lovejoy, 1961). The net effect of this motivational tendency is to produce the affiliative behavior that preserves the cohesiveness of social groups.

The second hypothetical instinct is a need for structure, predictability, and order. This need produces the tendency to turn repeated interactions (the morning coffee, the evening meal, baby's bath) into rituals; it also produces the tendency to codify, classify, and legislate and to organize groups into functional roles (sex roles, work roles, leadership roles, and so on). These tendencies toward ritualization, codification, and organization make social living predictable and more efficient.

Finally, we assume people have a need for aggressive self-expression, which results in competitive tendencies, status seeking, self-aggrandizement, and dominance behavior. These tendencies produce status hierarchies (pecking orders) in children as young as four or five, and these hierarchies, with their associated group leadership roles, make social living even more predictable. Thus, these tendencies both reinforce hierarchical order and ensure a steady supply of effective leadership to the group.

Three final points about this view of motivation should be mentioned. First, the effects of these motivational tendencies are interlocking and complementary, producing, within a group, cohesiveness, predictability, and efficient use of human resources. All the distinctive features of human social organization can be derived from these motivational assumptions; however, these hypothetical motives give us no clue to the actual contents of any culture, which will of course be determined by the culture's history and the specific local conditions to which it must adapt.

The second point is that the needs for attention and for competitive self-expression result in contradictory behaviors — that is, affiliation and competition. This suggests a deep conflict is built into human nature so that, although we are a group-living species, interpersonal relations are inherently conflictful; social existence is invariably marked by struggles for status, competition for scarce resources, jealousy, and rivalry, as well as affiliation and cooperation.

Third, the operation of these hypothetical motives is chiefly unconscious. This assumption contradicts the rationalist trend in modern psychology, perhaps best exemplified by cognitive-developmental theory. According to this theory, social behavior is guided by a conscious rational attempt to cope with the moral conflicts which accompany interpersonal relations. We are suggesting on the contrary that our social conduct is largely determined by unconscious motives outside our rational control — needs for attention, predictability, and status.

*Morality, Personality, and Culture.* Our final set of theoretical assumptions concerns the role of moral socialization in the development of personality and the evolution of culture. Every human group inhabits a concrete and specific geographic environment (the Sahara desert, the Arctic, the steppes of central Asia) that defines the material conditions of its existence. If the group is to survive, it must develop and sustain a culture that allows it to exploit the resources available in its particular environment. One important aspect of this culture is the accumulated technology that determines how these resources can be exploited. Another is a set of values that orients the members of the culture appropriately to their environment; thus farmers must be dependable, farsighted, acquisitive, and willing to stay in one place. Nomadic hunters, on the other hand, must be entrepreneurial, somewhat restless, and nonacquisitive. A third aspect of culture is a set of child-rearing practices that serves to transmit whatever technological wisdom the group has evolved, together with the values necessary to apply that wisdom effectively. Thus we have a feedback loop consisting of environmental demands, the cultural resources developed in response to these demands, and child-rearing practices which provide for cultural transmission and development of the character type best suited to the environmental demands. The members of a single culture or social class will share a common set of values; for the concept of modal personality (Inkeles and Levinson, 1954) we would substitute the notion of a modal character type.

### the theory

Two structures form the basis of human personality. The first of these, character structure, reflects the accommodations one has made to the demands of one's parents, the expectations of one's peers, and the promptings of one's inner demon by late adolescence. The second major aspect of personality, role structure, consists of the strategies of self-presentation and styles of value expression that appear in one's dealings with other people. Character structure includes one's attitudes toward the rules of the social game; role structure provides one's unique style of playing the social game. Character structure evolves early, is relatively unconscious, stable, and enduring. Role structure evolves later, is relatively conscious, responsive to situational demands, and therefore changeable. In socioanalytic theory, moral development is equivalent to the evolution of character structure.

*Rule Attunement.* Character structure evolves through three phases in response to three different but overlapping sets of problems that confront each developing individual. The first requirement each child faces is rapid assimilation of its culture—including, most crucially, language—so as to enhance its chances of survival. Because human infants lack both the instincts and the physical capacities necessary to survive by themselves, they are, compared to the young in other species, unusually helpless. Consequently, young children are probably predisposed to accept adult authority and to defer to tribal lore regarding natural hazards and dangers, dietary customs, food gathering, tool making, and religious observances. In an era of permissive child rearing it is important to point out that aspects of this first phase of development are deeply authoritarian. In the process of teaching a child language, for example, normal parents do not negotiate with their children about the names of common objects; they merely tell the child what a thing is called. And so it is with other aspects of the socialization process. Only children who are educable, who are able to follow effortlessly the demands, requests, and instructions of adults, will be able to assimilate their culture and survive.

The developmental precursors of educability are relatively well understood. With Bowlby (1969), we believe the development of a secure attachment relationship between each child and its caretakers is the most important event in that child's development. A successful attachment seems to require parents who love their child and are sensitive to its needs. Obviously, parents who are frequently egocentric, self-absorbed, imperceptive, depressed, anxious, or merely worried will foster a less than optimal attachment bond. Since people are all occasionally self-absorbed, depressed, anxious, and so on, even the best-intentioned parents will act in ways that disrupt the attachment

relationship. Whereas Bowlby implies that unambivalent attachment relationships are attainable, we feel they are an ideal rarely achieved in reality.
We would further qualify attachment theory by arguing that rule attunement
depends on limit setting and parental authoritativeness as well as warmth and
sensitivity.

Stayton, Hogan, and Ainsworth (1971) present evidence that clearly
supports these conjectures. In a sample of eleven-month-old children, those
infants who, by an independent measure, were classified as well attached were
also willing to comply with maternal directives; the other children were essentially noncompliant. Variations along the dimensions of parental warmth and
restrictiveness suggest four kinds of rule attunement by the time children
reach nursery school age. Children whose parents were warm and restrictive
make an effortless accommodation to adult authority. A second group with
warm, permissive parents tend to be self-confident and self-assured but un-
concerned with rule following because they feel their transgressions will be
overlooked; in ordinary language such children are called spoiled. A third
group, whose parents were cold but restrictive, tend to be angry, anxious, and
sullenly compliant. Finally, the most delinquent children tend to have parents
who are cold and permissive; such children are hostile and rule defying. This
typology works well as a first approximation, but it obviously ignores genetic
factors underlying the disposition to comply with rules. We feel these genetic
factors will in the long run be of great theoretical importance (see Mednick
and Christiansen, 1977).

*Social Sensitivity.* The second problem faced by every developing child
involves learning to get along in the peer group and extended family. Many
theories of social development regard children as egocentric until some time
between ages ten and twelve, when intellectual maturity is supposed to break
down their natural egocentrism (Piaget, 1965). Our view, however, is that
children are sociocentric at birth and that peer interaction is impeded by
social incompetence rather than egocentrism. The surprisingly complex patterns of verbal interaction found among children as young as three and a half
years simply would not occur if the egocentrism hypothesis were true (Garvey
and Hogan, 1973). The speed and facility of the transition to peer interaction, however, depends on the quality of the earlier attachment relationship (Lieberman, 1977).

In their roles as tutors, adults tell children what they should or should
not do. Very little instruction of this type goes on in the peer group, where
successful interaction requires that children be sensitive to each other's (often
implicit) social expectations. The evolution of social sensitivity or empathy is
the key process during this second phase of development. Individual differences in social sensitivity seem largely to be a function of earlier attachment
bonds, intelligence, and unspecified genetic factors.

Once developed, social sensitivity can compensate for failures during
the first phase of development (Kurtines and Hogan, 1972). This is not surprising; group cooperation is so vital to human survival that it is no doubt
overdetermined. Empathy can be thought of as a backup mechanism which
ensures moderate levels of rule compliance even in unsocialized individuals.

Rule attunement is associated with following the letter of the law; empathy, however, permits a child to think in terms of the spirit of the law. This capacity provides a means by which contradictions in the rules can be resolved — that is, by appealing to the principle(s) guiding the activity rather than the rules structuring it.

Cognitive-developmental theorists maintain that peer interaction produces the concept of fairness in children (Piaget, 1965; Rawls, 1971), which subsequently turns into the concept of justice in adulthood. According to these writers, the idea of fairness arises out of the experience of cooperation, turn taking, sharing, and considerateness in the peer group. Moreover, these natural and desirable features of peer experience are inhibited when adults intervene in children's play. We would like to suggest, in contrast, that what children actually encounter in the peer group when adults are not around is bullying, exploitation, and persecution. Turn taking and cooperation occur primarily because adults intervene and force children to share, take turns, and "play fair." The concept of justice, in this analysis, is largely produced by the injustice one suffers at the hands of older and larger peers in childhood.

To summarize this discussion, there are two distinguishable aspects of social sensitivity that develop during the approximate age range of four to sixteen. The first is a capacity for social interaction; this is a matter of acquiring social skills, of being able to take the role of the other, to read others' implicit intentions, feelings, needs, and expectations. The second is an appreciation of a general principle for regulating interaction with others, a principle variously called reciprocity, fairness, turn taking, and justice.

*Autonomy.* The third challenge facing every developing individual after age fourteen to sixteen is one of establishing a life and family of one's own. This involves the concept of autonomy (Durkheim, 1961). Autonomous behavior also corresponds to what we normally think of as "moral behavior." That is, persons who conform to authority or the social pressures of peers are often regarded as conventional and not very heroic in moral stature. Many psychologists believe that truly moral conduct often contradicts conventional law and social pressure. Thus autonomy is often defined so as to stress this element of nonconformity in the concept. For example, in cognitive-developmental theory, principled moral thinking is believed to derive from one's personal views of justice, which may often contradict the established rules of society. In our view, however, autonomous moral behavior is not autonomous with regard to collective rules and values. It is, rather, the autonomous defense of what one sees as highest in one's culture, despite the demands of family, peers, and conventional authority. Socrates choosing to drink the hemlock poison provides a timeless example of autonomous behavior. He drank the poison not to please the corrupt authorities who had condemned him, and despite the pleas of his friends; he drank it because he felt it was consistent with the ideals of Athenian citizenship to do so.

The next question concerns the psychological mechanisms leading to autonomy. The critical mechanism underlying autonomy, we believe, is self-awareness. This includes a conscious appreciation of (1) the motives for one's actions; (2) the relativity of one's own values and principles; (3) the limitations of all human philosophies; and (4) the message of Ecclesiastes — that the race is not to the swift nor the battle to the strong but rather that life is unpredictable, unjust, and without any clearly visible meaning. Self-awareness has two consequences. On the one hand it produces a sense of inner detachment and role distance (Goffman, 1959), the capacity for what some Oriental philosophers call wu-wei, or actionless action (Waley, 1958), and a distrust of violent passions or enthusiasms because one knows from experience the nonrational sources of these emotions. On the other hand, self-awareness can produce an enlightened commitment to the values and conventional evaluative standards of one's society. This is so because one realizes that no values can be justified in an absolute sense, that there must be values in any case, and the existing values are usually no more or less valid than any others.

The developmental processes fostering autonomy are not as well understood as they might be. Baumrind (1971) provides persuasive evidence for the role of modeling in the development of autonomy: Autonomous school children have been exposed to autonomous adult models (usually their parents). Beyond modeling, we believe any experience that encourages introspection, role distance, and perspective on one's self is important. This would include travel, a wide range of social experience (pleasant as well as unpleasant), and parents or caretakers who encourage or require children to engage in self-monitoring and introspection.

We can distinguish three kinds of nonautonomous moral conduct, which we call moral realism, moral enthusiasm, and zealotry. These behavior patterns reflect lack of self-awareness and can have disastrous consequences. Moral realism is a function of high rule attunement, low social sensitivity, and low self-awareness. This pattern of dispositions produces an unconscious overaccommodation to authority and institutionalized rules. Moral realists make good bureaucrats and police; but rule following as an end in itself can be detrimental to the welfare of a society in those cases where the rules are unjust or dysfunctional. Moral enthusiasm is a function of high rule attunement, high social sensitivity, and low self-awareness. Moral enthusiasts are conventionally moral and well-intentioned, but they have no internal moral gyroscope. As a consequence of their lack of perspective, they rush from one moral cause to another — this week saving the whales, next week banning the bomb. Their very enthusiasm reduces their effectiveness. Zealotry is a function of hostility toward authority (low rule attunement), sensitivity to injustice (high social sensitivity), and low self-awareness. Zealots are the urban guerillas and terrorists who seek aggressive confrontations with authority in the name of social justice.

In short, moral development, defined as the evolution of character structure, proceeds through three phases, called rule attunement, social sensitivity, and self-awareness. During the first phase children must learn to live with authority; during the second, they learn to live with other people; and in the third they must learn to live with themselves. There are characteristic developmental processes and problems associated with each phase. People differ in terms of how successfully they master the problems associated with each phase; consequently, as a result of his or her developmental history, each person has a relatively unique moral orientation.

*Evidence.* Three central concepts of this theory have been operationally defined in terms of objective personality scales for socialization (rule attunement), empathy (social sensitivity), and autonomy (self-awareness). These measures are scorable from the California Psychological Inventory (CPI) (Gough, 1975) and can be used with subjects as young as junior high school age. It would be inappropriate to review here the evidence for the theory based on these measures. Suffice it to say that these measures have repeatedly been shown to predict various kinds and degrees of delinquent behavior, presocial conduct, and level or quality of moral reasoning (Haier, 1977; Hogan, 1975a; Tsujimoto and Nardi, forthcoming). Thus socialization, empathy, and autonomy are deeply implicated in conventional rule following/rule violation and in predisposing toward certain forms of moral reasoning.

The theory also provides a useful way to conceptualize guilt—the emotional consequence of rule violation. According to the theory, guilt responses should fall into four classes: (1) impunitive responses where there is no guilt; (2) guilt over the disapproval of authority figures; (3) guilt about disappointing others; and (4) guilt about not living up to personal standards of conduct. Hogan and Beehler (1978) asked 104 adult men and women about their guilt experiences. Two of their findings are relevant here. First, with no prior training, raters could sort all responses into the four above-mentioned categories with 78 percent agreement. Second, younger subjects (late adolescents) generally felt guilty about disruptions in relations with parents and peers, whereas older subjects (job-holding adults and parents) generally felt guilty about not meeting responsibilities. Both findings support the analysis of guilt derived from socioanalytic theory.

## summary

There are three major developmental problems, rule attunement (socialization), social sensitivity (empathy), and self-awareness (autonomy) which are worked out in different ways throughout the life cycle. Rule attunement begins in attachment. Adolescents who are attuned to rules are educable—they can be coached, taught, advised, and depended on. Well-socialized adolescents do well in athletics, in peer relations (Hogan, forthcoming), and in their studies (Holland, 1959). Finally, their unambivalent accommodation to authority ensures that their morality in adulthood will be consistent with the requirements of conventional religious orientations.

Social sensitivity also begins in secure attachment. Socially sensitive adolescents are other-directed, socially acute, tactful, understanding, and perceptive (Hogan, 1969). In adulthood these people are concerned with fairness, justice, equity, civil rights, and other traditional ethical issues (Hogan and Dickstein, 1972).

Autonomy begins in attachment as well. Autonomous adolescents are inner-directed, task oriented, and more concerned with adult than peer approval. As adults they are autonomous and self-aware and live according to their own self-chosen principles of conduct, principles which (recalling Socrates) are consistent with the values and ideals of their culture.

## implications and speculations

In this final section we will highlight five issues that were implicit in the foregoing discussion and require further elaboration.

*Differences from Earlier Versions.* The present discussion differs from earlier published versions of the same theory in three important aspects. No mention has been made so far of the Ethics of Personal Conscience/Ethics of Social Responsibility dimension of moral judgment. The reason for this will be clarified below. A second difference is the role assigned to religion in the development of character structure. Earlier versions of the theory explained autonomy in terms of "ideological maturity"—the capacity to rationalize one's goals, values, and interests in terms of a metaphysical world view. Religions are ready sources of world views and therefore could provide the basis for ideological maturity and, hence, autonomy. We no longer believe this analysis. Our present view is that religion has less to do with autonomy and more to do with a healthy accommodation to authority and the demands of society in adulthood; that is, being religious in the conventional sense implies no self-chosen commitment. It reflects instead an unquestioning acceptance of the legitimacy of all the routines, customs, traditions, values, and rules of one's society, of which church attendance is one aspect. We now conceptualize autonomy in much the same way that Kierkegaard defined authentic Christianity. Persons who are authentic have arrived at Christian (or any other) values through a process of intense and agonizing introspection; their religiosity, however, bears almost no relationship to organized religion, which they regard as a perfidious abomination. Like Kierkegaard, we also believe that few people develop true self-awareness and autonomy.

*Personality and Moral Development.* The second point is one we have made before but is so important that it deserves special reemphasis. There is a strong tendency in contemporary psychology to treat moral development as if it were a specialized topic in developmental or social psychology (see Brown and Herrnstein, 1975; Lamb, 1978). In so doing the topic is decontextualized, misconstrued, and, in our judgment, trivialized. Moral development is properly considered within the context of personality development as a whole. The principle function of morality is to link the individual to his or her society or culture; there is a distinct tendency to lose sight of this function when moral development is studied in the abstract as an isolated phenomenon.

*Ethics of Conscience* vs. *Ethics of Responsibility.* Our third point, related to the foregoing, concerns the role of the Ethics of Personal Conscience/Ethics of Social Responsibility continuum in moral development. Hogan (1970) developed the Survey of Ethical Attitudes (SEA) to assess individual differences along the continuum defined by these two perspectives. Persons who adopt the Ethics of Conscience are idealistic reformers who love their brother man, dislike rules, and regard unjust social institutions as the major source of injustice in the world. Persons who chose the Ethics of Responsibility are pragmatic, factual, and conservative; they distrust other people and believe social institutions, rules, and laws are necessary to keep their wayward impulses under control.

Subsequent work with this scale has led us to reconceptualize the meaning of the dimension in the following way. Tomkins (1965) describes what he calls an ideological polarity in Western thought. The polarity consists of the (New Testament) view on one hand that man is an end in himself, intrinsically valuable, and if given the opportunity, man will develop his innate potential and worth. The other pole consists of the (Old Testament) view that man has no intrinsic value but rather achieves value by living up to or aspiring toward certain external standards of excellence. Tomkins goes on to show how this ideological polarity runs through mathematics, the philosophy of science, metaphysics, epistemology, the general theory of value, political theory, jurisprudence, aesthetics, educational theory, psychology, psychiatry, and child development. Consider these two examples provided by Tomkins (p. 86):

| *New Testament* | *Old Testament* |
| --- | --- |
| "And ye Fathers provoke not your children to wrath lest they be discouraged." — Eph. 6:2 and 3 | "He that curseth Father or Mother let him die the death." — Lev. 20:9 |

The two quotations reflect remarkably different attitudes toward child rearing, paralleling Tomkins' ideological polarity.

We believe that the Ethics of Conscience/Ethics of Responsibility dichotomy reflects the same ideological polarity that Tomkins has identified; in moral reasoning this comes down to a series of mini-polarities, including contrasts between mercy and justice, liberalism and conservatism, rule avoiding and rule following. But more importantly, we believe these ideological polarities reflect the presence of two broad *personality syndromes* that are equally represented in most human groups. The nature of these two types is given by the following contrasting terms: hysteric vs. paranoid; health-souled vs. sick-souled; socioemotional orientation vs. task orientation; passionate-spontaneous vs. rational-reflective.

Our point regarding the SEA can be simply stated as follows. There are two broad personality syndromes to be found in every human group. These two s    romes entail dramatically contrasting views of human nature; these view  of human nature will be reflected in the moral judgments and moral reasoning of the persons who hold them. The SEA is a robust but somewhat inefficient measure of these two personality syndromes. The research on the SEA, finally, provides one more example of how personality theory and moral development are inextricably linked.

*Delinquency and Cultural Decay.* The fourth point concerns a possible misconception that our heavy emphasis on evolutionary theory may have fostered. In view of the stress on how moral development is overdetermined and how culture evolves in response to environmental demands, the reader may wonder why, according to this theory, individuals go bad or civilizations fail. In fact the theory has explicit answers to both these questions.

Individual failures in moral development (delinquency) begin with poor attachment bonds between an infant and its caretakers. This produces insecurity, hostility, and low rule attunement. Disturbances in the attachment bond spill over into the next phase of development, disrupting peer relations and further isolating the child. By adolescence such children are socially isolated, insecure, hostile to authority, and insensitive to social expectations and to the rights of others — in short they are potential criminals.

Social systems or culture also fail when the process of socialization/moral development goes awry, as it may do in three ways. First, the environmental conditions to which a culture is adapted may change, requiring the culture to produce a new modal character type; but changes in institutionalized child-rearing practices occur very slowly, if at all. The fate of the Plains Indians of North America reflects this kind of externally caused failure — a nomadic culture, adapted to a migratory life style on the open plains, was forced into a farmlike existence on reservations with predictable and disastrous consequences.

A second condition for the failure of social systems occurs when the feedback loop between environmental demands and cultural responses is broken. Currently, for example, the technology of advanced Western societies buffers individuals from the demands of the environment. This buffering makes it unclear what kinds of values, skills, and character types are necessary to respond to the environment. When the world's supply of cheap energy is finally exhausted, there is bound to be a painful transition period as the Western technological societies begin to move back into realistic alignment with nature.

The failure of a social system may also be generated internally by the factionalism that is an inevitable feature of human societies. The status hierarchies and division-of-labor characteristic of culture are, at the same time, a source of internal division and strife that undermine group solidarity and unified purpose. Thus, through forces latent in human nature, culture can self-destruct.

*Real and Ideal Views of Moral Maturity.* Our last point concerns the contrast between ideal definitions of moral conduct and moral maturity and the levels of moral maturity that one can realistically expect to encounter in the world. Over time, human action becomes more self-conscious and self-controlled. In phylogenetic terms, we have evolved, over the course of several million years, from creatures impelled largely by instincts to creatures capable (at least in principle) of some conscious control of our actions. In ontogenetic terms, each person evolves from an initial presocialized state through the period of rule attunement, where actions are almost instinctually regulated by the letter of the law, through the period of social sensitivity, where actions are regulated by the spirit of the law, and then, one hopes, onto the period of self-awareness, where actions are under full conscious control.

Part of what it means to be self-aware (autonomous) is to realize that the motives for one's actions are never fully conscious, that it is always possible

**16**

to be self-deceived about the "true" causes of one's behavior. And this, consequently, implies that is is unrealistic to expect very many people to be "truly
moral" very much of the time. In fact, authentic moral conduct may be a rare
event, precisely because it requires absolute self-understanding—the necessary psychological condition for freedom. And freedom is the necessary pre-
condition for moral action. To put the argument in a nutshell, in order for an
act to be moral, it must be the product of free choice; it cannot be determined. The only free actor is one who is fully self-aware. But absolute self-
awareness is, in daily reality, unattainable. So then is truly moral conduct.

Truly moral conduct is thus an ideal, and it is unrealistic to hope that
many people will ever behave in a moral fashion defined in ideal terms. Thus,
the most we can hope for is that people will avoid deliberately doing evil, that
they will comply with the conventional norms of civil conduct, and that they
will consider the consequences of their actions for the general welfare. Even
this limited aspiration may be too ambitious.

## references

Aronfreed, J. *Conduct and Conscience: The Socialization of Internalized Control over
Behavior.* New York: Academic Press, 1968.

Bandura, A. *Principles of Behavior Modification.* New York: Holt, Rinehart and
Winston, 1969.

Baumrind, D. "Current Patterns of Parental Authority." *Developmental Psychology,*
1971, *4*(1), Pt. 2, 1-103.

Bem, D. J. *Beliefs, Attitudes, and Human Affairs.* Belmont, Calif.: Brooks/Cole, 1970.

Benedict, R. *Patterns of Culture.* Boston: Houghton Mifflin, 1959.

Berger, P. L., and Kellner, P. "Marriage and the Construction of Reality." *Diogenes,*
1964, *46*, 1-23.

Berger, P. L., and Luckmann, T. *The Social Construction of Reality.* New York: Doubleday Anchor, 1967.

Boring, E. G. *A History of Experimental Psychology.* (2nd ed.) New York: Appleton-
Century-Crofts, 1950.

Bowlby, J. *Attachment and Loss.* Vol. 1. New York: Basic Books, 1969.

Brown, R., and Herrnstein, R. J. *Psychology.* Boston: Little, Brown, 1975.

Campbell, D. T. "On the Conflicts Between Biological and Social Evolution and Between Psychology and Moral Tradition." *American Psychologist,* 1975, *30*, 1103-
1126.

Collingwood, R. G. *An Essay on Metaphysics.* Oxford: Oxford University Press, 1940.

Durkheim, E. *Moral Education: A Study in the Theory and Application of the Sociology of Education.* New York: Free Press, 1961.

Emler, N. P., and Hogan, R. "Ideological Biases in Social Psychology." *Social Research,* forthcoming.

Erikson, E. H. *Childhood and Society.* New York: Norton, 1950.

Feyerabend, P. "Problems in Empiricism." In R. G. Colodny (Ed.), *Beyond the Edge
of Certainty.* Englewood Cliffs, N.J.: Prentice-Hall, 1965.

Garvey, C. J., and Hogan, R. "Social Speech and Social Interaction: Egocentrism Revisited." *Child Development,* 1973, *44*, 562-568.

Gert, B. *The Moral Rules.* New York: Harper & Row, 1970.

Goffman, E. *The Presentation of Self in Everyday Life.* New York: Doubleday Anchor,
1959.

Gough, H. G. *Manual: The California Psychological Inventory.* (rev. ed.) Palo Alto,
Calif.: Consulting Psychologists Press, 1975.

Haier, R. J. "Moral Reasoning and Moral Character: Relationships Between the Kohlberg and the Hogan Models." *Psychological Reports,* 1977, *40,* 215-226.

Hanson, N. R. *Patterns of Discovery.* Cambridge: Syndics of the Cambridge University Press, 1961.

Herskovits, M. *Cultural Relativism.* F. H. Herskovits (Ed.). New York: Random House, 1972.

Hogan, R. "Development of an Empathy Scale." *Journal of Consulting and Clinical Psychology,* 1970, *35,* 205-212.

Hogan, R. "Moral Development and Personality." In D. J. DePalma and J. M. Foley (Eds.), *Moral Development: Current Theory and Research.* Hillsdale, N.J.: Erlbaum Associates, 1975a.

Hogan, R. "Theoretical Egocentrism and the Problem of Compliance." *American Psychologist,* 1975b, *30,* 533-540.

Hogan, R. "The Gifted Adolescent." In J. Adelson (Ed.), *Handbook of Adolescent Psychology.* New York: Wiley, forthcoming.

Hogan, R., and Beehler, M. G. "A Study of Guilt." Paper presented at the First Annual Meeting of the Southwest Society for Research in Child Development, Dallas, 1978.

Hogan, R., and Dickstein, E. "Moral Judgment and Perceptions of Injustice." *Journal of Personality and Social Psychology,* 1972, *23,* 409-413.

Holland, J. L. "The Prediction of College Grades from the California Psychological Inventory and the Scholastic Aptitude Test." *Journal of Educational Psychology,* 1959, *50,* 135-142.

Inkeles, A., and Levinson, D. J. "The Study of Modal Personality and Sociocultural Systems." In G. Lindzey (Ed.), *Handbook of Social Psychology.* Vol. 2. Reading, Pa.: Addison-Wesley, 1954.

Kluckhohn, F. R., and Strodtbeck, F. L. *Variation in Value Orientations.* Evanston, Ill.: Row, Peterson, 1961.

Kurtines, W., and Hogan, R. "Sources of Conformity in Unsocialized College Students. *Journal of Abnormal Psychology,* 1972, *80,* 49-51.

Lamb, M. E. (Ed.). *Social and Personality Development.* New York: Holt, Rinehart and Winston, 1978.

Lieberman, A. F. "Preschoolers' Competence with a Peer: Relations with Attachment and Peer Experience." *Child Development,* 1977, *48,* 1277-1287.

Lovejoy, A. O. *Reflections on Human Nature.* Baltimore: Johns Hopkins University Press, 1961.

Margenau, H. *The Nature of Physical Reality: A Philosophy of Modern Physics.* New York: McGraw-Hill, 1950.

Mednick, S. A., and Christiansen, K. O. (Eds.). *Biosocial Basis of Criminal Behavior.* New York: Halsted Press, 1977.

Nardi, P. M. "Moral Socialization: An Empirical Analysis of the Hogan Model." Paper presented at the Seventy-Second Annual Meeting of the American Sociological Association, Chicago, 1977.

Pepper, S. *World Hypotheses.* Berkeley: University of California Press, 1942.

Piaget, J. *The Moral Judgment of the Child.* New York: Free Press, 1965.

Rawls, J. *A Theory of Justice.* Cambridge, Mass.: Belknap Press 1971.

Stayton, D., Hogan, R., and Ainsworth, M. D. S. "Infa · Obedience and Maternal Behavior: The Origins of Socialization Reconsidered   *Child Development,* 1971, *42,* 1057-1069.

Tomkins, S. S. "Affect and the Psychology of Knowledge." In S. S. Tomkins and C. E. Izard (Eds.), *Affect, Cognition, and Personality: Empirica Studies.* New York: Springer, 1965.

Tsujimoto, R., and Nardi, A. "A Comparison of Koh berg's and Hogan's Theories of Moral Development. *Sociometry,* forthcoming.

**18**

Turner, J. "Social Comparison and Social Identity: Some Prospects for Intergroup Behavior. *European Journal of Social Psychology*, 1975, *5*, 5-34.

Waddington, C. H. *The Ethical Animal.* Chicago: University of Chicago Press, 1967.

Waley, A. *The Way and Its Power.* New York: Grove Press, 1958.

Washburn, S. L. (Ed.). *Social Life of Early Man.* New York: Wenner-Gren Foundation for Anthropological Research, 1961.

Weber, M. "Politics as a Vocation." In H. H. Gerth and C. W. Mills (Eds. and Trans.), *From Max Weber: Essays in Sociology.* New York: Oxford University Press, 1946.

*Robert Hogan is professor of psychology at the John Hopkins University.*

*John Johnson is a graduate student in psychology at the John Hopkins University.*

*Nicholas Emler is an assistant professor at the University of Dundee.*

*320*

# CHAPTER 12

# Research on Piaget's Theory of Moral Development

## Piaget's Theory of Moral Judgment Development

In *The Moral Judgment of the Child* (1932) Piaget relates a conversation he had with a 7-year-old boy, Stor, about playing marbles:

Stor tells us that children played at marbles before Noah's ark. "How did they play?— *Like we played.*" . . . Stor invents a new game in the shape of a triangle. . . . "Is it as fair a game as the [other game] you showed me?—*No.*—Why?—*Because it isn't a square.* —And if everyone played that way, even the big children, would it be fair?—*No.*—Why not? *Because it isn't a square*" (p. 60).

Stor, interviewed here for his thinking about the rules of a game, was one of scores of Swiss children that Piaget and his Genevan associates queried a half-century ago in a pioneering effort to discover how children reason about rules and transgressions, right and wrong. The book on moral judgment (Piaget, 1932) which resulted from that effort has since stimulated a spate of studies on children's moral thinking and helped to establish the cognitive-

developmental approach (see Kohlberg, Chap. 2, 1969b) as a major theoretical framework for conceptualizing the moral growth of the child as well as related facets of social development, such as the capacity for friendship and love (Lickona, 1974). This approach views all children as moving through a series of stages or patterns of thought which are qualitatively different from each other, constructed by the individual through his own active experience, and the same in sequence for all persons and all cultures.

Piaget began his search for stages in moral development with the notion that the core of morality is twofold, based on (1) respect for the rules of the social order, and (2) a sense of justice—a concept of the rights of persons that stems from considerations of equality, social contract, and reciprocity in human relations. In order to identify the nature of change in these two broad facets of morality, Piaget used the flexible "clinical interview" technique to try to strike beneath the surface content of children's statements at the underlying structure or qualitative aspects of their spontaneous moral reasoning. He typically began his interviews by reading the child a story or pair of stories about transgressions or some other moral events involving children, and then proceeded to probe the child's thinking about whatever dimension of moral thought the stories were designed to elicit. For example, the child might be asked to explain who was naughtier—a well-meaning boy who accidentally gave wrong directions to a man who then got lost, or a boy who deliberately gave wrong directions to a man who found his way anyhow. In this fashion, Piaget questioned 5- to 13-year-old children[1] about various moral matters such as where rules come from, whether a rule can be changed, what a fair punishment is, what defines a lie, how rewards should be distributed, why it's wrong to cheat, and whether it's ever right to disobey an adult.

Through these conversations with children, Piaget identified what he believed to be two major stages of moral development. The developmentally earlier stage he alternately called *heteronomous morality, moral realism,* or a *morality of constraint*; the later stage he called a *morality of cooperation.* These two stages differ on nine dimensions—the left pole defining constraint, the right cooperation. These dimensions are:

1. Absolutism of moral perspective, as opposed to awareness of differing viewpoints
2. Conception of rules as unchangeable, as opposed to a view of rules as flexible
3. Belief in inevitable punishment, "immanent justice," for wrongdoing, as opposed to a naturalistic conception of punishment
4. "Objective responsibility" in judging blame, as opposed to consideration of the actor's intentions
5. Definition of moral wrongness in terms of what is forbidden or punished, as opposed to what violates the spirit of cooperation
6. Belief in arbitrary or expiatory punishment, as opposed to belief in restitution or reciprocity-based punishment
7. Approval of authority's punishment of peer aggression, as opposed to approval

of eye-for-an-eye retaliation by the victim
8. Approval of arbitrary, unequal distribution of goods or rewards by authority, as opposed to insistence on equal distribution
9. Definition of duty as obedience to authority, as opposed to allegiance to the principle of equality or concern for the welfare of others (adapted from Kohlberg, 1968b).

Piaget believes that the young child's morality of constraint is the product of two interacting factors: cognitive immaturity and unilateral emotional respect for adults. The first is the more fundamental source; Piaget sees moral realism as one expression of a generally immature cognitive organization which is both egocentric and "realistic." In this view, egocentrism, the child's broad failure to distinguish between aspects of the self and aspects of the external world, prevents him from taking the viewpoint of others in social situations. Realism, a consequence of egocentrism, refers to the child's confusion of subjective and objective aspects of experience. In the moral realm this confusion causes him to externalize moral rules and treat them as immutable absolutes, rather than as flexible instruments of human purposes and values.

Manifestation of the contrasting moralities of constraint and cooperation typically coexist in the same child, Piaget (1932) observed; he concludes that the two moral stages are best conceived as overlapping thought processes, the more mature of which "gradually succeeds in dominating the first" (p. 133). The child's progress to cooperative morality is a process of developing the *capacity* to function at the higher level. A morally mature child can, but does not necessarily, apply the principles of autonomous cooperation in his moral judgment.

Piaget (1932) holds that all children make the transition from a morality of constraint to a morality of cooperation, unless their development is retarded by deprivation of opportunities for reciprocal social interaction. Piaget (1932) maintains that under conditions of mutual respect and equality in social interchange, the developing mind cannot help coming to regard the principle of cooperation as "an immanent condition of social relationships" (p. 198). At this advanced level of development, morality is seen not as the will of authority, but as a system of modifiable rules expressing common rights and obligations among equals, a system essential to the intact functioning of any social unit.

## The Validity of Piagetian Moral Judgments as Developmental Dimensions

### MORAL DIMENSIONS RELATED TO THE DEVELOPMENT OF COGNITIVE DIFFERENTIATION

In defining moral development in terms of general cognitive growth as well as in terms of an emotional shift in orientation of respect, Piaget identifies four moral judgment dimensions which bear a clear relation to his conception of overall cognitive development as a process of progressive differentiation between the subjective and external aspects of experience. These dimensions (defined by their immature poles) are (1) absolutism of moral perspective, (2) concept of rules as unchangeable, (3) belief in immanent justice, and (4) evaluation of responsibility in terms of consequences. What does the research show regarding these four judgmental dimensions?

*Absolutism of moral perspective versus awareness of different viewpoints.* Several studies (e.g., Pinard & Laurendeau, 1970) have replicated Piaget's finding (Piaget & Inhelder, 1956) that the child under 6 years of age is egocentric in his perceptions of the physical world, believing, for example, that someone standing opposite him has the same view of a model mountain that he has. This kind of egocentrism, Piaget says, also prevails in the moral thinking of young children, who believe that there is only one viewpoint, held by everyone, on whether an act is right or wrong.

Absolutism of moral perspective (Dimension 1) and its developmental decline were demonstrated clearly in the responses of different-aged children who were told or read a story about a lazy schoolboy named Frank (E. Lerner, 1937b). Frank's teacher, to make him work harder, had forbidden his classmates to help him or play with him; but a boy named Paul broke the teacher's rule and helped Frank anyway. The experimenter asked the children whether they thought the friendly classmate was right or wrong for helping, whether Paul himself thought he was right or wrong, what the lazy boy Frank thinks, what the teacher thinks, and so on. At age 6, most children said that everyone in the story would think the same as they did. By age 9, most children recognized that different characters would have different views of the situation.

Similarly, Feffer and Gourevitch (1960) found marked improvement with age on a test of role taking which requires a child to make up a story and retell it from the viewpoint of each of the characters. Older children were able to shift perspective and to coordinate successive retellings of the story with previous ones. Children also show increases with age in the ability to be self-critical (Kohlberg, 1963b), a trend consistent with the developing child's abandonment of an egocentric, single-perspective view of his experience.

*Conception of rules as unchangeable versus conception of rules as flexible.* Piaget maintains that the failure of egocentric thinking to distinguish in the natural arena between the psychological and the physical (for example, between dreams and real events) is paralleled by a confusion of these two realms in moral judgment. Thus, young children view moral rules as being permanent regularities, like physical laws (Dimension 2)—an attitude that becomes even more rigid, Piaget believes, because of the child's deep respect for the adult authority which created the rules.

Research by Epstein (1965) has confirmed Piaget's findings on rule rigidity during early childhood, but has not supported Piaget's analysis of the attitudinal underpinnings of this rigidity. Consistent with Piaget's hypothesis, Epstein found that only 25 percent of 4-year-olds believed that the rules of a game could be changed, and none believed a school rule or law could be changed, whereas by age 7, a majority of children said that it was possible to change all three types of rules. A closer look at Epstein's results, however, calls into question Piaget's interpretation that young children's inflexibility springs from a full consciousness of rules as the sacred creations of authority. Epstein found five steps between the ages of 4 and 7 in children's awareness and understanding of rules that formed a scale of difficulty such that a child who "passed" a given step had to also have passed all the earlier steps in the sequence. Almost all the youngest children (4 years) had not yet mastered the second step (can give an example of a prohibited or prescribed activity) or even the first (understands that certain activities are prohibited or required). How, then, can a young child orient to rules as fixed and unchangeable if he has not yet really developed a concept of a rule?

An answer to this puzzle is suggested by another five-step scale which Epstein (1965) identifies as describing the development between ages 4 and 7 of the child's thinking about the issue of changing rules. The five developmental steps are as follows:

1. The child can respond to a description of "changing a rule" as some kind of departure from established practice.

2. The child can distinguish between changing a rule and breaking a rule; and the child recognizes that changing a rule is better than breaking it.
3. The child states that it is possible for a child in a game or the children and the teacher in a class to change a rule.
4. The child discriminates between some rule changes which would be "fair" and some which would not be, because they would be harmful or discriminatory.
5. The child has some sense of the necessity of majority consent for rule change in a game or the law, and for the teacher's consideration of the children's viewpoint and rights in changing classroom rules.

What Epstein's findings suggest is that "insofar as the young child does claim that the rule is unchangeable, it is largely because he does not distinguish between changing and breaking a rule" (Kohlberg, 1968b, p. 122). If, however, the children had a conception of rule change as distinct from rule breaking—as most of the 5-year-olds in Epstein's bright laboratory school sample did—then they were quite likely to say that the rules of a game *could* be changed. Jacqueline, aged 5 was typical.

*Can you ever change a rule in this game?*
Some times we give them a hint of which color it is.
*Are they fair rules when you change them?*
My mother lets me change the rules if I want.
*What about your friends?*
My friends let me do it. Sometimes they change rules.
*Are they good rules when they change them?*
I think so (quoted in Kohlberg, 1968b, p. 124).

Jacqueline said, however, that a classroom rule couldn't be changed by children ("It's not allowed"), nor could a law ("The police won't let you"). But "grownups," she said, "can change the real, real rules." Teachers can change the rules in the classroom, except the ones the principal makes, "because the principal would throw them out of the school."

Epstein's interviews (1965) indicate, then, that a child's judgment of a rule's changeability depends on his perception of where the power lies. Once he has grasped that changing a rule is different from violating it (Step 2 in the scale), he is ready to understand that the rules of a game among equals can be changed (Step 3). This flexibility is not immediately generalized, however; subordinates in an authority structure are not allowed to change rules. This analysis of immature thinking about rules differs from Piaget's interpretation (1932) that young children believe that "rules are sacred and unchangeable because they partake of parental or divine authority" (p. 48). The young child's reasoning appears from Epstein's research to be determined less by reverential respect than by his assessment of who's in charge.

The rule rigidity that Piaget observed in young Swiss children, illustrated by the interview with Stor at the beginning of this chapter, may have been due to their having not yet reached Step 2 in the rule comprehension scale: knowing the difference between changing and breaking a rule. In another manifestation of poor cognitive differentiation, some of Epstein's subjects (1965) seemed unable even to distinguish breaking a rule from breaking a physical object. In general, then, Epstein's interviews show Piaget to be correct in identifying cognitive immaturity as a source of the young child's inflexibility about rules and in identifying increasing flexibility toward rules as a developmental change in the child's conception of the social-moral order.

*Belief in immanent justice versus naturalistic concept of justice.* Another moral judgment dimension with a clear cognitive component is the child's belief about consequences for wrongdoing (Dimension 3). Because the young child does not distinguish between violating a social rule and

violating a physical law, Piaget (1932) reasons that the child expects the physical universe to aid in maintaining the moral order. Consequently, young children who are told a story about a boy who steals money and runs across an old wooden bridge say that the bridge will collapse because the boy stole, but would not collapse had he not stolen (Piaget, 1932). As another illustration of this view of justice, Piaget (1932) cites the reactions of children who look upon nightmares as punishments for the bad things they did during the day.

A substantial body of research, spanning several continents (Europe, Africa, and North America) and different social classes, has replicated Piaget's own finding that belief in automatic, or "immanent," justice exists early in development and gives way gradually to the belief that punishment for misdeeds in a social phenomenon, like the transgression itself, and therefore not necessarily inevitable (Caruso, 1943; Dennis, 1943; Grinder, 1964; Jahoda, 1958; R. C. Johnson, 1962; E. Lerner, 1937a; Liu, 1950; MacRae, 1954; Medinnus, 1959; Najarian-Svajian, 1966). The exceptions to this trend, however, have been cited (M. L. Hoffman, 1970b) as evidence against Piaget's claim that his stage sequences are universal. Curdin (1966), for example, found a curvilinear relation between age and immanent justice, with 8-year-olds being more mature than both younger and older children. Medinnus's finding (1959) of decreasing immanent justice with age for one story but increasing immanent justice for another story suggests that situation-specific factors may override general developmental tendencies in determining the child's judgment.

The power of culture to retard or even reverse Piagetian moral judgments has been brought into focus by Havighurst and Neugarten's study (1955) of ten American Indian groups. In four of these groups, the researchers found no age decline in belief in immanent justice, and in six groups they found *increases* to as high as 85 percent of 12- to 18-year-olds. Kohlberg (1968b), in reexamining these data, finds "some evidence (not clear-cut) for a natural childhood developmental trend toward naturalistic interpretation of misfortune, followed by an adolescent 'regression' to the adult cultural belief in immanent justice" (p. 87). Similarly, Curdin (1966) has explained his finding that immanent justice first declined and then rose in his sample of American boys by citing his subjects' growing awareness of their religion's fundamentalist belief that sin is always punished. Even if one maintains that the initial childhood tendency away from immanent justice is a universal feature of moral development, these studies underscore the point that development occurs in a particular sociocultural context, which over the long run may alter the "natural" or typical course of growth.

Personality as well as culture has been shown to affect the belief that retribution is inevitably visited upon the wrongdoer. Hart (1962), for example, discovered that men hospitalized for mental illness (but not women) held to a more primitive concept of justice on Piagetian stories than normal subjects; this finding suggests that regression to earlier levels on Piaget moral judgment dimensions may occur in adulthood and stem from idiosyncratic factors within the person as well as from external influences in the acculturation process.

*Objective versus subjective concept of responsibility.* How do young children evaluate the badness of what they believe to be a moral offense? Piaget (1932) has found that they judge actions in terms of observable physical aspects and consequences rather than in terms of the actor's intent (Dimension 4), presumably because they do not yet differentiate the subjective domain from things that are external and physical. A harmless but implausible exaggeration ("A little boy said he saw a dog as big as a cow") is therefore considered a naughtier "lie" than a deliberate deceit that deviates less from probable reality ("A girl told her mother she got good grades in school when she didn't"). In assessing blame for negative material consequences, the young child judges as worse the person who has done more damage, regardless of motives. Around the age of 7, intentions become more important to the child than consequences; in Piaget's terms, the child's concept of responsibility becomes subjective rather than objective. The developmental trend toward increasing intentionality, found in different countries (Switzerland, Great Britain, Belgium, the United States, Taiwan, and Israel) and in different social classes, is perhaps the best documented of all Piaget's moral judgment dimensions (Armsby, 1971; Boehm, 1962; Boehm & Nass, 1962; Caruso, 1943; Cowan, Langer, Heavenrich, & Nathanson, 1969; Dworkin, 1966; Grinder, 1964; R. C. Johnson, 1962; Kohlberg, Havighurst, & Neugarten, 1967; R. L. Krebs, 1965; Kugelmass & Breznitz, 1967; Lerner, 1937a; Lickona, 1967, 1971; MacRae, 1954; Medinnus, 1962; Nass, 1964; Whiteman, 1964).

A refinement of the global objective-to-subjective shift described by Piaget comes from a study by R. L. Krebs (1965). Using picture stories with children 4 to 7, Krebs elucidated three substages in the transition from consequence-centered judgment to full subjective responsibility. The child progresses from (1) recognizing intentions when consequences are equal to (2) recognizing intentions when consequences are weighed against them ("Breaking one cup when you're stealing jam is worse than breaking eight cups while you're helping your mother") to (3) recognizing that intentions can make an act with bad consequences good ("Helping his mother was good even though he broke a lot of cups").

My own research (Lickona, 1971, 1973) has examined sensitivity to intentions in the realm of lying. First-graders from both middle- and lower-class backgrounds almost invariably were found to say that a plausible intentional deception was worse than an implausible unmalicious exaggeration—at an age when Piaget's Swiss children (1932) tended to say just the opposite. Thus a boy who told his father he had a headache in order to get out of helping to shovel snow was considered naughtier by my American first-graders than a boy who got so excited that he said a kneehigh snowfall was way over his head. Intentionality declined sharply, however, when innocent mistruths carried observable negative consequences. Only 51 percent of the time did children orient to intentions when they compared a boy who unsuccessfully tried to trick his sister by telling her the wrong time with a boy who unwittingly told his brother the wrong time, causing him to miss the bus. The results indicated that these two kinds of lying items formed an order of difficulty; all children who were intentional in judging honest misstatements with negative consequences were also intentional in judging harmless exaggerations, but not vice versa. A parallel relationship was found for lying items and items depicting material damage. About half of the children who showed intentionality on lying stories such as the one about telling the wrong time gave no intentional responses at all to damage stories about dropped cups or spilt paint. These findings provide another illustration of the interaction between the structural tendency of the child's thinking and the situation being considered. Moral judgment clearly is formed by both content and structure.

A major cross-cultural investigation of intentionality was carried out by Kohlberg, Havighurst, and Neugarten (1967). They asked members of thirteen different Indian and Atayal tribes who was worse— a child who broke five bowls by accident while carrying them for his mother or a child who broke one bowl while playing with it after having been told not to. In eleven groups, there was a clear trend to-

ward intentionality; in one group the trend fell short of becoming the majority answer of late adolescents; in another, there was a regression toward a consequences orientation during the years 13 to 18. Even in these last two "deviant" tribal cultures, however, the change during the childhood years 6 to 11 was toward greater intentionality. This tendency provides evidence of a natural or universal trend in early development which is subsequently obscured by countervailing cultural forces. These data parallel the previously cited cultural departures from the typical developmental pattern for immanent justice.

A significant modification of Piaget's conception of intentionality is indicated in Kohlberg's longitudinal research (1968b) on the development of reasoning about moral responsibility. Beyond the "mature" intentionality depicted by Piaget is a level that Kohlberg characterizes as an orientation to categorical rules, in which the person judges an action by its conformity to a rule regardless of intentions or consequences: "Stealing is stealing, no matter what your motives, and obeying your mother is still obedience even if you break five cups in the process." Beyond this categorical level is another stage at which the individual recognizes that a good motive can modify disapproval of a transgression, but also believes that in general a good end does not justify a bad means: "I don't blame [Heinz] for stealing the drug to save his wife: I can see why he did it, but you can't have everyone stealing whenever they get desperate."

The fact that a categorical or literalistic orientation to rules appears late rather than early in the developmental sequence casts doubt on Piaget's belief that young children focus on the consequences of an act rather than on its spirit because they have a letter-of-the-law concern for rules. R. L. Krebs's study (1965) indicates that the reverse is true: Children are consequence-centered *until they* have a concept of respect for rules. He found that passing a test of "internality," which measured children's ability to judge the rightness of an act apart from whether it was rewarded or punished, was a prerequisite for passing Piaget's test of intentionality.

## OTHER PIAGETIAN MORAL JUDGMENT DIMENSIONS

Studies of the five other Piagetian dimensions defined in the first section of this chapter—while not as extensive as research on the four dimensions just reviewed—permit at least tentative conclusions about whether these other dimensions define genuine developmental trends in moral thinking. Harrower (1934) and Medinnus (1962) have replicated Piaget's finding (1932) that as children grow older they focus less on punishment and prohibitions and more on trust and fairness in explaining why it is wrong to lie or cheat. (Dimension 5). Further evidence of the tendency toward greater independence from external sanctions in moral judgment comes from research in which subjects were required to evaluate situations where children were punished by an adult for doing something good or rewarded for doing something bad (R. L. Krebs, 1965; R. L. Krebs, Brener, & Kohlberg, 1967). By age 7 a majority of children could say, for example, that a boy did a good thing by obediently watching his baby brother, even though the boy got spanked when his mother returned.

The next four judgmental dimensions (6 to 9) are presented by Piaget as reflecting the developing child's increasing awareness of reciprocity as the organizing principle of social relations—an awareness that Piaget holds to be at the heart of the child's affective shift from unilateral respect for authority toward mutual respect among equals. One manifestation of this shift, Piaget believes, is the change which occurs in the child's concept of what is appropriate punishment (Dimension 6) for misdeeds such as lying, damaging another's property, refusing to help out, or betraying a peer. Several studies (Boehm,

1962; Boehm & Nass, 1962; Harrower, 1934; R. C. Johnson, 1962; MacRae, 1954) have found that from about age 7 on children increasingly reject arbitrary or expiatory punishments (such as spankings), which bear no intrinsic relation to the offense, in favor of reciprocity-based punishments, which do to the culprit as he did to others, allow the offender to suffer the natural adverse consequences of his offense, or require him to make active restitution. A cross-cultural investigation (Boehm, 1957), however, found that a majority of Swiss children, whose teachers and parents stress respect for authority, preferred adult-administered expiatory punishment for bloodying the nose of a classmate at an age when most American children opted for directly apologizing to the injured peer.

Piaget (1932) has also sought to tap orientation to reciprocity by asking children, "If anyone punches you, what should you do?" He found that children "maintain with a conviction that grows with their years [6 to 12] that it is strictly fair to give back the blows one has received" (p. 302)—a trend that is followed in adolescence by a realization that "there can be reciprocity only in well-doing" (Dimension 7). Durkin (1959a, 1959b, 1959c; 1961) was unable to replicate this developmental pattern for American children, finding instead that approval of nonretaliatory responses was dominant at all ages and that junior and senior high school children as well as elementary school children typically recommended telling an authority rather than dealing directly with a peer aggressor. R. L. Krebs (1965), measuring reciprocity orientation somewhat differently, found a clear increase between ages 4 and 7 in reciprocity-based explanations (for example, "You wouldn't like somebody to do that to you") of why it is bad to aggress against a peer.

Piaget's last two moral judgment dimensions (8 and 9) define reciprocity in terms of the child's allegiance to the principle of equality as opposed to unquestioning submission to authority. With development, Piaget (1932) found, children come to regard equal distribution of goods as more important than the need to punish wrongdoing (Dimension 8); thus, older children tend to say that a mother was unfair to give more cake to her obedient little girl than to her disobedient daughter. Finally, children are with age increasingly prone to place equality and the concern for the welfare of peers that arises from equal relations above obedience to adult authority (Dimension 9). Thus, older children are more likely than younger ones to say that a child should not obey a command to do work alone that should be shared by several children (Piaget, 1932), that a child should not submit to an adult's demand to tattle on a sibling or friend (MacRae, 1954; Piaget, 1932), and that a child is justified in stealing a bag of apples from a supermarket for a poor and hungry friend (Grinder, 1964). Boehm (1957) and Nass (1964) found that increasing age was also accompanied by a greater tendency to prefer advice on a problem from a talented peer rather than from an adult described as having no competence in the problem area. This last age trend appears to lack universality, however, since most Swiss children continue into adolescence to insist that teachers and parents always give the best advice—even in the face of evidence to the contrary (Boehm, 1957).

In a critique of Piaget's theory, Kohlberg (1968b) has argued that the judgment dimensions that emphasize "peer conformity versus adult conformity" lack the clear cognitive basis of other Piagetian moral judgments; hence the difficulty in replicating age trends. "There is nothing rational," Kohlberg (1968b) maintains, "about orientation toward peers as opposed to authority" (p. 92). Piaget was not, however, seeking to measure orientation toward peers so much as orientation toward reciprocity and equality as the basis for determining what is right and just. Inconsistencies in the research findings may be due

more to weaknesses in the judgmental dimensions which Piaget used to measure this changing orientation than to his theoretical conception of rational morality. As discussed in Chapter 2, Kohlberg's own research seems to show clearly that the concepts of reciprocity and equality stand at the rational center of mature moral thought.

## Piaget's Moral Judgments as Stages: The Issue of Consistency

In defining moral development as a "process that is repeated for each new set of rules" (1932, p. 109), Piaget states that a child can be morally autonomous in his thinking about the rules of a game, but heteronomous in his thinking about lying or justice. Although Piaget's theory thereby rejects the notion of completely unitary stages, it calls for a certain consistency on the part of the child, since his various moral judgments are presumed to be the spontaneous products of a general cognitive and emotional disposition rather than learned responses acquired in separate situations. What is the evidence that the different facets of a child's moral thinking form a reasonably consistent pattern, that is, a "stage" of development?

Such a pattern of judgmental uniformity is hard to find in the existing data. Boehm and Nass (1962), in an investigation of children's thinking about lying, justice, authority, and responsibility, found that developmental differences for the *same* child from one type of story to the next were as great or greater than differences between age levels or between social-class groups. They concluded that "stage" of conscience development varies with the specific situation involved. R. C. Johnson's correlational study (1962) of 809 midwestern children in grades 5 through 11 found moderate consistency within a given area of judgment such as intentionality, but only low positive correlations (ranging from zero to .34) between different judgmental areas such as intentionality and belief in the efficacy of severe punishment. These results, providing only slender evidence of a general unifying factor in moral judgment, were essentially replicated by Harris (1970) in a study of 100 white and 100 black children in grades 4 to 6. Intercorrelations among five Piagetian judgmental dimensions ranged from .12 to .44, about the same as the modest correlations Hartshorne and May (1928) found among their various behavioral tests of honesty (see Burton, Chap. 10).

MacRae (1954) did a cluster analysis of Piagetian moral judgments, holding age constant. Rather than a single general factor, he found four relatively independent factors, which he identified as (1) sensitivity to intentions, (2) concept of punishment, (3) ability to take another's perspective, and (4) attitude toward deviating from the norms of authority. It makes no empirical sense, MacRae concluded, to treat questions dealing with these different aspects of moral development as measuring a single underlying stage such as "moral realism."

In the face of such data, one might speculate that inconsistencies in judgments about different areas of morality would sort themselves out with time. The research, however, uncovers no visible age trends toward greater consistency across different judgmental domains; the correlation between some pairs of Piaget dimensions has actually been found to decline between the ages of 11 and 17 (R. C. Johnson, 1962). Another way to try to make sense out of the data on the consistency issue would be to reconceptualize moral thought as reflecting a family of separate dimensions, each with its own developmental timetable. Correlational studies such as MacRae's and Johnson's have in fact found good consistency *within* judgmental areas such as justice concept, responsibility evaluations, and moral perspective taking. Likewise, Durkin's studies (1959a, 1959b) of Piaget justice concepts found that children, as they grow older, recommend nonretaliatory responses to social offenses with increasing regularity.

But even the existing evidence that children respond consistently within a particular area of judgment seems to pale by comparison with the mounting evidence of within-area variability. Lickona (1971) found only a low positive correlation (.25) between intentionality on stories contrasting different degrees of material damage and intentionality on stories contrasting deliberate lies with honest mistakes or exaggerations. Several other studies of intentionality have shown that varying the format (picture versus verbal stories, forced-choice versus open-ended) and the story content (simple versus complex situations, minor versus severe negative consequences) causes the level of judgment to fluctuate accordingly (Armsby, 1971; Caruso, 1943; Costanzo, Coie, Grument, & Farnill, 1973; R. L. Krebs, 1965). Armsby (1971), for example, found that 6-year-olds tend to judge in terms of motives if blame is to be assessed, but have difficulty judging in terms of motives when stories require comparison of positive rather than negative outcomes. Magowan and Lee (1970) demonstrated that stories assessing immanent justice tended to elicit high-level answers when the story was based on conditions familiar to the subject, and low-level responses when the story was based on situations taken from foreign cultures. Just the reverse was found in a study of beliefs of Navajo mountain children (aged 6 to 18 years) about the changeability of rules; they showed "immature" judgment for a situation close to home (rules of Navajo games could not be changed) and "mature" judgment for a more culturally remote situation (rules of American games could be changed) (Havighurst & Neugarten, 1955). There is obviously no simple rule of thumb for calculating the outcome of the complex interplay between culture and development (see also Lickona, Chap. 1).

In addition to lacking a strong foundation of empirical consistency, Piaget's moral judgments fail as stages by another criterion as well. As Kohlberg (1968b) points out, they do not, as Piaget's logical stages do (Piaget & Inhelder, 1969) specify a definite development going on in a delimited time period (for example, from age 5 to 8). A Piagetian dimension such as intentionality shows regular quantitative increases beginning at 5 to 6 years of age (Caruso, 1943; R. L. Krebs, 1965) and extending at least as late as 17 years (Kugelmass & Breznitz, 1967). If the individual's moral growth from ages 5 to 8 and his growth during adolescence can be characterized equally well in terms of increasing intentionality, then such a dimension cannot be considered part of a stage that defines a particular period of development.

It has been argued (Kohlberg, 1968b) that the problem with Piaget's theory of moral stages is not that stage patterns do not exist, but that Piaget's forced-choice stories (requiring the child, for example, to say which of two characters is naughtier) do not elicit the free, open-ended responses needed to get at the underlying thought structure that defines a stage. Because of the forced-choice methodology, Kohlberg (1969b) maintains, many of Piaget's dimensions "are really matters of content rather than cognitive form" (p. 375); that is, they describe *what* children believe, which is variable, rather than *how they reason* about moral beliefs, which is theoretically universal. Consequently, Piaget's dimensions do not show the properties, such as intercorrelation, which characterize components of "true structural stages." R. C. Johnson (1962) cites another problem with the classical Piagetian story items, namely, that their relatively low reliability of about .60 (children often change their minds about the same story) limits the size of the intercorrelations that can appear between different areas of judgment.

Whatever the reasons, the available research does not reveal a clear clustering of Piagetian moral judgments. This lack, coupled with the gradual, drawn-out changes in these judgments, leads to the conclusion that the various features of heteronomous and autonomous morality are best viewed as relatively distinct developmental dimensions, showing steady age increases under most circumstances, rather than as closely knit stages of moral thought.

## Field Research on Piaget's Theory of the Causation of Moral Judgment Development

In addition to documenting how children's moral thought changes as they grow older, much of Piaget's *The Moral Judgment of the Child* (1932) is an effort to explain *why* it changes. Piaget theorizes that three factors account for moral development: general intellectual growth, the experience of social equality with peers, and liberation from the coercive constraint of adult authority. But his own work does not attempt to test this explanation. A good deal of subsequent research, however, bears directly or indirectly on his theory of developmental change.

### GENERAL COGNITIVE DEVELOPMENT AND MORAL JUDGMENT CHANGE

The validity of Piaget's argument that the child's level of moral development is anchored to his general level of cognitive functioning is suggested by a well-documented positive relationship between IQ and moral judgment maturity (Abel, 1941; Boehm, 1962; Durkin, 1959a; R. C. Johnson, 1962; MacRae, 1954). The contribution of intelligence to moral reasoning is also quite clearly demonstrated by R. L. Krebs's finding (1965) that moral judgment differences between kindergarten and first-grade children disappeared when children of the same mental age were compared. Similarly, Boehm (1967) found that retarded adolescents aged 16 to 21 scored at the same level as younger normal children of equivalent mental age on dimensions of intentionality and peer reciprocity.

Further evidence of the relation between cognitive and moral development comes from an interesting longitudinal study by Pringle and Gooch (1965) of children during the years 11 to 15. These investigators found that mental age rather than chronological age was the best predictor of response to the task, "Make a list of the most wicked things anyone could do." At 11 years of age, 100 percent of "bright" children mentioned murder, compared with 81 percent and 57 percent of the "average" and "dull" children, respectively. Many of the dull 11-year-olds were still at the level of listing trivial or exotic offenses such as "swearing," "smoking," "ripping someone's eyes out." By age 15 these same low-intelligence children had progressed to the point of listing offenses of a conventional-legal nature (such as stealing), while bright children by 15 had advanced to listing acts of personal or social injustice such as letting someone down, racial discrimination, or starting a war. Bright 15-year-olds mentioned acts of this latter category much more often than did their average or dull agemates, or than they themselves had when they were 11. Shifts in children's conceptions of evil appear from these data to be tied to changes in their general level of intellectual development.

Other research, however, suggests that it is not simply IQ or mental age which accounts for moral judgment maturity. Kohlberg (1968b) cites the example of a morally immature 9-year-old boy with an IQ of 128 who, in a fashion characteristic of younger children, defined moral wrongness in terms of whether the person got caught and punished by the police, and the value of life in terms of how much furniture a person owned. MacRae (1950) found that high-IQ children believed *more* strongly in immanent justice than low-IQ children, though the former were superior

in terms of Piaget's hierarchy on measures of intentionality and attitude toward punishment.

The problem with conventional IQ measures in the context of Piaget's theory, however, is that they do not measure intellectual functioning as he defines it, and are therefore inadequate as a test of his notion that logical and moral progress go hand in hand. A better test would be to correlate Piagetian developmental measures of logical thinking with Piagetian moral judgment measures. Kohlberg (1968b) has done this, and reports positive correlations between consideration of a person's motives (subjective responsibility) and conception of a dream as a subjective event, between moral reciprocity (one good turn deserves another) and logical reciprocity (one physical change can compensate for another), and between maturity of moral judgment and physical conservation (something can remain the same in spite of apparent change), all with IQ controlled. Another investigation (Stuart, 1967) using a Piaget-based measure of cognitive development found that among 7- to 13-year-old children, "high decentraters" (facile at taking another's spatial and social perspective) were much more likely than "low decentraters" to show mature judgment on stories tapping intentionality, although the former group showed no superiority on immanent justice items. Lee (1971), in a study of 195 boys aged 5 to 17, found that as children mastered Piaget's concrete logical operations, they gave fewer authority-based moral judgments and more reciprocity-based responses. She also found that progress in adolescence to Piaget's highest intellectual stage, formal operational thinking, was predictive of the development of "societal, idealistic moral modes of conceptualization." Similarly, Kohlberg and Gilligan (1971) have reported evidence that the formal operational ability to consider many possibilities is prerequisite to the moral awareness of the multiplicity and relativity of values, and a recent study (Tomlinson-Keasey & Keasey, 1974) of logical problem-solving and moral reasoning in sixth-grade girls and college women found that only formal operational thinkers could reason at principled moral levels.

Since Piaget (1932) sees a connection between moral judgment and moral behavior—the function of the judgmental principle of cooperation being "to lead the child to the practice of reciprocity" (p. 71)—studies of moral behavior can also be used to evaluate his explanation of developmental change. Several investigations have suggested a link between declining cognitive egocentrism and increasing maturity of moral conduct. Rosenhan (1969a) reports "a large increment in the incidence of altruism from ages 6 to 7, much larger than that in the years that precede or follow those ages" (p. 9), and points out that this behavioral change occurs at the age when Piaget says the child is moving out of egocentrism toward the general capacity to experience the world from the viewpoint of another. Ugurel-Semin's study (1952) of sharing found a marked increase in children's generosity at about the same age, and a dominance of egocentric reactions in younger, more selfish subjects. Many of the youngest children believed that their partner did not want the extra nut in a pile of nine or were unable to see any way of dividing the odd number except to give the extra nut to themselves.

M. L. Hoffman and Saltzstein's study (1967) of childrearing disclosed that disciplinary techniques that reduced egocentrism by focusing the child's attention on the needs of others are associated with advanced moral development on a variety of behavioral and judgmental indices. Experimental evidence of the importance of perspective taking in cooperation comes from Chittenden's success (1942) in training initially domineering and self-centered children to anticipate and reconcile the reactions of doll characters in imaginary social conflict situations. Most 5-year-olds trained over several weeks subsequently showed a clear increase in cooperative preschool behavior.

## EXPERIENCE OF SOCIAL EQUALITY WITH PEERS

The core of Piaget's theory (1932) of moral development is its emphasis on equalitarian peer interaction as the principal source of the awareness that the ethic of cooperation is the basis of harmonious social relationships. Investigators of Piaget's theory have translated this emphasis into the prediction that peer-group participation will be positively related to moral maturity.

The data on the peer participation hypothesis are mixed. On the negative side, Kugelmass and Breznitz (1967) found that Israeli kibbutz children, reared in a peer group with great emphasis on peer-group morality, were no more sensitive to the intentions of others than Israeli children reared in conventional family settings. R. L. Krebs (1965) found no differences in intentionality between popular 6-year-old children with reciprocal friendships and socially isolated children matched with their popular classmates for chronological and mental age. In a study of young adolescents, Porteus and Johnson (1965) found no relation between popularity ("He or she makes a good friend") and maturity on a moral measure combining Piaget items on intentionality, immanent justice, and severity of punishment. Dilling (1967) found a low, nonsignificant relationship between a sociometric measure of acceptance by peers and two variants of internalized conscience ("humanistic" and "conventional"), assessed in terms of attitude toward norm violations. Finally, E. Lerner (1937b) concluded from his research that peers can have a negative effect on even the older child's moral judgment, very much like the effect of adult constraint, when peer majority opinion runs counter to the principles of co-operation and fairness.

In contrast to this negative evidence, a variety of studies lend support to Piaget's theory that peer social interaction promotes moral development. Some of the findings, which are suggestive rather than conclusive, come from behavioral research. Ugurel-Semin's study (1952) of sharing found a negative relationship between selfish behavior and family size, the most selfish children coming from small families. Kibbutz children, while not superior on a specific judgmental dimension such as intentionality (for which only a "necessary minimum" of positive peer interaction may be required), display a marked and early sensitivity to the moral norms of their peer group, a strong sharing orientation, and a relative absence of such antisocial behaviors as stealing (Spiro, 1958). In a study of honesty, Einhorn (1971) has found a negative relation among 8-year-old children, but not among 5-year-olds, between cheating on a competitive task and the variables of peer-group cohesiveness and social experience (as inferred from sociometric data). Einhorn views this finding as confirming Piaget's theory that group ties and social interaction lead to moral autonomy at age 8, but not at age 5.

Judgmental data also support the peer participation hypothesis. Using Kohlberg's moral judgment interview, Keasey (1971) found that higher stages of moral reasoning were positively associated with social participation as measured by teacher and peer ratings of popularity and leadership and by self-reports of membership in social organizations. Performance on Piaget moral judgment tests, though unrelated to participation in scouting or Sunday school, has been found to be positively influenced by attendance at ungraded classrooms combining children of different ages, a condition which can be construed as an enrichment of the social environment (Whiteman, 1964). Especially intriguing is Nass's finding (1964) that a class of congenitally deaf children achieved inde-pendence of adult judgment on Piaget stories somewhat sooner than hearing children, and were far ahead of their hearing agemates in developing a concept of atonement in terms of peer reconciliation rather than adult punishment. A plausible interpretation is that greater peer solidarity of the deaf children, stemming from their common handicap and school experience, accelerated their progress on related moral dimensions. Equally interesting is the finding that deaf children were two years *behind* their hearing peers in learning to evaluate others according to their motives, awareness of which is presumably diminished by reduced verbal communication. Different judgmental dimensions such as intentionality and attitude toward punishment are apparently differently affected by the same experience. If this is so, then peer experiences, positive or negative, should not be expected to have a uniform effect on all areas of moral judgment development.

Combined data from two separate studies of childrearing by M. L. Hoffman (1960) and M. L. Hoffman and Saltzstein (1967) point to the importance of peer relations in moral development. In the earlier study, M. L. Hoffman (1960) found a strong association between a mother's use of coercive or punitive power assertion as a disciplinary technique and her child's adjustment with his peers in nursery school. Mothers high on power assertion had children who were themselves power-assertive with other children, hostile toward playmates, and resistant to peer influence. In the later study, M. L. Hoffman and Saltzstein (1967) found that seventh-grade children of power-assertive parents tended to be relatively retarded on measures of guilt, acceptance of responsibility, and internalization of moral principles. Quite possibly, the link between a mother's early coercive behavior and an older child's lagging moral development is the disruption of the positive peer relationships that Piaget regards as vital to moral growth. This interpretation gains credibility in the light of Dilling's finding (1967) that an external conscience orientation, characterized by fear of punishment as opposed to internalized values, was associated with low peer acceptance among fifth and sixth grade children.

The effects on moral judgment of institutionalization (a form of deprivation of social interaction) were examined in a study (Abel, 1941) comparing three groups of retarded girls aged 15 to 21 and matched for mental age. The first group lived in the community and attended a trade adjustment school, while the second group had been institutionalized for one year and the third for five years. On Piaget intentionality stories only 31 percent of the community-based group gave immature consequence-centered judgments, compared with 53 percent of the one-year institutionalized group and 63 percent of the five-year group. The differences were even greater on immanent justice stories. Kohlberg (1968b) interprets these findings as suggesting that marked social deprivation of a general sort does lead to retardation of Piaget moral judgments, even though reduced peer-group interaction (as in the case of sociometric isolates) does not. Reduced peer interaction *is* reflected, however, in Kohlberg's moral stages, with socially participating children being more advanced than peer isolates (Kohlberg, 1968b). This finding suggests that peer experience is important, but that Piagetian moral judgment dimensions are not adequately sensitive to variations in peer experience. As with the consistency issue discussed earlier, Piaget's general theoretical conception of moral development appears to be stronger than the methodology he used to measure it. Even with this limitation, though, the data seem to substantiate Piaget's notion that peer interchange plays a role in the development of mature moral thinking.

An important qualification of the discussion of peer interaction is that Piaget does not maintain that only a child's agemates can provide the experience of social equality necessary for moral develop-ment. He simply observes that peers are typically the most common source of such experience for children. Piaget emphasizes, however, that an adult can choose to relinquish his unilateral authority and interact with the child on the basis of mutual trust and respect. Piaget (1932) states that if a parent gives the child "a feeling of equality by laying stress on one's own obligations and deficiencies" (p. 137) and "preaches by example rather than precept, he exercises an enormous influence" (p. 319) on the child's progress toward moral maturity. This affirmation of the value of nonauthoritarian childrearing is the bridge between Piaget's discussion of equalitarian peer interaction and his conception of a third source of moral growth, namely, increasing independence of the constraining effects of adult authority.

### INDEPENDENCE OF ADULT CONSTRAINT

Increasing independence of adult constraint is conceived by Piaget to be both a cause and an effect of the child's growing allegiance to a mature morality of cooperation, just as the decline of cognitive egocentrism is seen as both cause and effect of increasing peer cooperation. Piaget does not convert this idea into specific predictions of behavior, but other researchers have derived two testable hypotheses from his discussion of independence:

1. The child's maturity of moral judgment should correlate positively with judgmental and behavioral independence of or flexibility toward authority-based norms.

2. Parental encouragement of independence by, for example, democratic childrearing practices should relate positively to maturity of moral thought in the child, while parental authoritarianism should relate negatively.

The first independence hypothesis finds some support in Abel's finding (1941) that institutionalized adolescent girls who were rebellious against authority and consequently continually punished scored much higher on an intentionality measure than passive, obedient girls, who were rarely punished. This finding suggests that the individual's *perception* of authority rather than his experience of constraint per se relates to moral judgment. Kohlberg (1963a) likewise found that a lack of deference to adult authority accompanied advance on his moral judgment scale to a reciprocity-oriented morality.

A surprisingly different pattern of associations, however, emerges from studies by Boehm (1962) and Boehm and Nass (1962), in which many children who were mature in their moral judgments about lying and responsibility nevertheless gave immature responses to stories requiring a choice between peer reciprocity and submission to adult authority. Moreover, Boehm discovered that while her middle-class children were clearly superior to lower-class subjects (with IQ controlled) on stories measuring intentionality, the reverse was true for stories measuring independence from adults. On the latter, lower-class children were significantly more advanced. This same pattern of social-class variation showed up in MacRae's investigation (1954) of Piaget's theory and undercuts earlier conclusions (Harrower, 1934; E. Lerner, 1937b) that the upper- or middle-class child, presumably enjoying greater parental permissiveness, is uniformly more advanced in moral thinking than his lower-class counterpart. The fact that middle-class children are superior on one dimension but inferior on another also points up again the impracticality of conceptualizing cognitive-moral development as a global advance with even progress on all fronts.

The second independence hypothesis, focusing on "democratic childrearing" as an antecedent of mature independent judgment, is supported by Boehm's previously mentioned finding (1957) that American children become peer-oriented and adult-independent considerably sooner than Swiss children, who are reportedly encouraged to regard adults as omnipotent and omniscient. R. C. Johnson (1962) has gone one step further than Boehm and actually measured parental attitudes on scales of *dominativeness, possessiveness,* and *ignoringness.* These attitudes correlated only infrequently with five Piaget moral judgment dimensions, but then usually in the theoretical direction; parents high on dominativeness, for example, had children who were rated immature on judgments about punishment. Interestingly, extreme ratings of parental attitudes on either end of the three scales related negatively to mature judgment, suggesting that the relationship between parental permissiveness and some aspects of moral development may be curvilinear.

A key study by MacRae (1954) dealt with both independence hypotheses and suggested a fruitful reformulation of the independence issue. He found that neither the extent of parental effort to control the child's behavior nor the child's compliance with parents' demands (an inverse behavioral measure of independence) correlated significantly with Piagetian measures of intentionality, punishment concept, or perspective shifting. MacRae did find, however, a significant negative correlation between the variables of parental control and childish compliance, on the one hand, and the child's willingness, on the other hand, to approve of acts violating norms of obedience or truth telling when those norms conflicted with other moral values such as loyalty. In MacRae's study (1954), children who were either less regulated by their parents or less compliant with existing regulations were more likely to approve norm violations.

One way to make sense out of MacRae's findings would be to classify Piaget's moral judgment dimensions into two distinct categories: The first category includes dimensions such as perspective shifting and concepts about punishment and responsibility which do *not* involve definitions of what would be right and wrong for a child *to do.* Such cognitions appear from MacRae's study to be unrelated to the parent's authoritarianism or to the child's behavioral independence of the parent, and from Boehm's studies (1962; Boehm & Nass, 1962) to be unrelated to his judgmental independence of adults. The second category of judgments deal with what would be good and bad for a child to do—whether good behavior consists in accommodation to an adult-imposed morality or in following cooperative principles which may or may not conform to the conventions of authority.

The development of moral priorities in this second category of judgment is more "emotional" than the development of judgments in the first category. This greater emotionality arises because parental authority is quite capable of generating anxiety about judgments regarding rule deviations. This line of reasoning would anticipate MacRae's finding (1954) that highly controlling parents tend to have convention-bound children. This analysis also dovetails with M. L. Hoffman's finding (1960) that the children of parents who relied upon love withdrawal, an anxiety-arousing technique, internalized conventional moral rules quite readily but applied them much more rigidly than children of parents who relied more upon reasoning in dealing with their children's transgressions.

The above twofold classification of moral judgments makes it possible to deal with some research findings that have been troublesome for Piaget's theory. In the context of this scheme, for example, no problem is posed by Liu's finding (1950) that Chinese-American children, despite strong filial piety, are ahead of white American children in developing a subjective concept of responsibility. The Chinese child's criterion for assessing moral responsibility falls into the first category of judgments, which does not require him to be independent of adults.

To summarize, the first independence hypothesis predicts a positive relationship between the child's independence of au-

thority and his maturity of moral judgment. The research has supported the prediction for some measures of independence and some dimensions of moral judgment, but not for others. The second independence hypothesis predicts a negative correlation between parents' authoritarianism and the child's judgmental maturity. The research confirmed this prediction only for judgments about departures from conventional norms.

For all three hypothesized causes of moral change—cognitive development, experience of social equality, and increased independence of adult constraint—the research reviewed thus far has been correlational rather than experimental. The most that can be said on the basis of these naturalistic data is that the factors identified by Piaget as sources of moral growth have typically been found to correlate with mature judgment on one or another of his dimensions. The evidence is strongest for the role of cognitive development, mixed but generally supportive regarding the contribution of peer experience, and weakest with respect to the role of freedom from the constraining influence of adult authority. In search of further clarification of the nature of moral development, let us now turn to experimental investigations that have directly manipulated potential antecedents of moral judgment change.

## Experimental Modifications of Piagetian Moral Judgments

Can the child's moral judgment on Piaget's dimensions be experimentally changed? An affirmative answer comes from six tests of the responsiveness of Piaget's moral judgments to a variety of experimental ingenuities (Bandura & McDonald, 1963; Cowan et al., 1969; Crowley, 1968; Dworkin, 1966; Lickona, 1967, 1971, 1973). These experimental efforts, however, have been narrowly focused; all of them have dealt with only one of the nine Piagetian dimensions: the child's attention to motives versus consequences in evaluating another's responsibility for an action (Dimension 4).

The very first investigation of this nature took the form of a challenge to Piaget from the rival, social-learning theory of moral development, which views moral judgments as modifiable products of observation learning rather than as manifestations of irreversible developmental tendencies. Bandura and McDonald (1963) demonstrated that 5- to 11-year-old children could be influenced to change their responsibility judgments in the direction of a model who gave responses that contradicted the child's pretest orientation. Initially intentional children and initially consequence-centered children both made a 30-percent shift in the opposite direction after hearing the experimenter reinforce an adult model for answers that were contrary to those of the subject. These changes held up during an intentionality posttest with no model present, and were cited as evidence that "the developmental sequence proposed by Piaget is by no means invariant . . . because the so-called developmental stages were readily altered" (Bandura & McDonald, 1963, pp. 207, 209). Following this frontal assault on Piaget's theory, the rationale, procedures, data analysis, and conclusions of Bandura and McDonald's investigation became the target of critical scrutiny by several writers (Cowan et al., 1969; Dworkin, 1966; Lickona, 1969; Turiel, 1966). Among other things, Bandura and McDonald were criticized for failing to report data on the reasons children gave for their judgments, and for inadequately assessing whether overt judgmental changes reflected merely short-term conformity or lasting change in moral orientation.

Using a design that attempted to correct the deficiencies of the Bandura and McDonald study, Cowan et al. (1969) found that lower-class subjects showed just as much model-induced change as had Bandura and McDonald's upper middle-class population. Cowan and his co-workers also found, however, that children who were "pure cases"—either 100 percent objective or subjective on the intentionality pretest—changed less during training than subjects with mixed pretest performances. Most significantly, these investigators found that on a second posttest two weeks after training, "trained-up" (initially objective) children showed even greater intentionality than they had on the immediate posttest. In distinct contrast, the "trained-down" (initially subjective) children began to return to their pretraining orientation toward intentions. This finding can be taken as evidence of a natural developmental direction (objective to subjective) which training-down had reversed only superficially and temporarily. LeFurgy and Woloshin (1969), employing Kohlberg-type dilemmas rather than Piagetian stories, likewise found that morally relativistic seventh- and eighth-graders trained downward returned gradually to their pre-experimental level over a 100-day period, whereas initially rigid subjects trained upward toward relativism maintained their large experimental gains.

Dworkin (1966) criticized Bandura and McDonald for confounding the variables of "modeling cues" and "cognitive information." He sought to separate these by devising an *imitation only* condition, (model simply names the naughtier of two story characters), a *cognitive information* condition (model also provides justification for naming response), and an *imitation plus reinforcement* condition (experimenter verbally reinforces the model and the child for desired naming response). He found that the cognitive information condition produced a 50 percent increase in intentional judgments, which was more than double the gains under the other two conditions and still in evidence four weeks later.

Crowley (1968), in the most intensive Piagetian moral judgment acceleration study thus far conducted, carried out small-group rather than individual training with first-graders in sessions that totaled three hours over a two-week period. He found that simply labeling for the child which story character was naughtier and giving prizes for intentional responses produced the same dramatic rise in intentionality, a stable 80 percent gain, as did labeling plus discussion of why the ill-intentioned character was worse. Crowley attributed the effectiveness of both his experimental conditions to their heightening the salience of intentions by using "simple" training stories which varied motives while holding damage constant. However, his simultaneous use of extrinsic rewards and corrective feedback, in addition to labeling, makes it impossible to isolate the contributions of the several training influences.

A training study of my own (Lickona, 1967) found that only 20 percent of initially objective children became subjective after having been cast in the role of the well-meaning offender in a hypothetical story about the subject and a friend. Most of these first- and third-graders who ignored motives in judging others did the very same thing when judging themselves. Intention-based responsibility judgments obviously require more than mere access to the viewpoint of the well-meaning offender, since these children remained consequence-oriented even though the subjective viewpoint of the "good child" in the story was their own.

Since none of the previous training studies directly investigated Piaget's ideas about why moral judgment changes, I attempted to put his hypotheses to an experimental test by providing judgmentally immature children (objective in their responsibility judgments) with the experiences presumed by Piaget to stimulate development (Lickona, 1971, 1973). These experiences were translated into three training conditions: (1) *decentering*, using stories with accompanying cartoon sequences (Figure 12.1) to help children differentiate motives from consequences and hold both in mind at once; (2) *peer interaction*, involving face-to-face debate between an objective subject and an al-

ready subjective peer in order to break down the former's egocentrism and increase sensitivity to another's viewpoint; and (3) *adult conflict*, exposing children to adults who repeatedly and assertively contradicted each other and themselves in their story judgments in order to reduce monolithic adult constraint on the child's moral thinking. A fourth, non-Piagetian condition, *didactic training*, was included as a theoretical foil, and consisted of simply telling the child straight out that a judgment based on intentions was right, and explaining why this was so.

All four experimental conditions generated substantial training-phase increases in intentional judgments among first- and second-grade subjects, and all but adult conflict gains were maintained during posttesting one month later (see Figure 12.2). Decentering training stimulated an overall 32 percent pretest-to-posttest increase, but over a third of the children in this group showed no change at all. Some even explicitly acknowledged the good intentions of a character while still convicting him of being the guiltier culprit—a finding that substantiates the suggestion of my earlier study (Lickona, 1967) that a subjective responsibility concept depends on the child's *valuing* intentions as well as being aware of them. The clash of viewpoints between objective and subjective children in the peer interaction condition was followed by a 60 percent gain in subjectivity for initially objective children, but no regression whatever for initially subjective children. The fact that change under this condition followed what Piaget sees as the natural direction of development suggests that downward training effects in previous studies were most likely no more than subjects' outward accommodation to the standard of authority (the adult model).

The results of adult conflict training were puzzling. Most children in this group increased their intentional responses during training, but gains were stable for only half of the subjects. Of the 16 children, 5 actually showed a net "loss" and gave sig-

Good Intentions
(Helping mother with dishes)

Bad Intentions
(Sneaking jam)

JOHN

REGGIE

JAM

JOHN

REGGIE

Large negative consequences
(8 broken cups)

Small negative consequences
(1 broken cup)

**Figure 12.1.** Sketches used in intentionality training (Lickona, 1971) to promote decentering of attention to include both the intentions and damage of story characters (*drawings by Cheryl Lickona*).

nificantly fewer subjective responses on the posttest than they had given on the pretest. This regressive tendency appears to parallel Langer's finding (1969) that some children trained in "class inclusion" became more primitive in their classification behavior after being given an impossible problem designed to facilitate understanding that a whole class is greater than any of its component subclasses. Children seem to differ in their tolerance of the affective disequilibrium created by input the cannot readily assimilate to what they already know and understand.

The result in my study that is most difficult for Piaget's theory to assimilate is

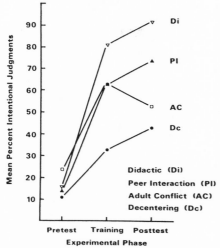

**Figure 12.2.** Pretest, training, and posttest percentages of intentional judgments on Piagetian responsibility stories for four experimental groups (Lickona, 1971).

the 76 percent gain under authoritative didactic training, which also produced the only significant generalization of trained intentionality to posttest stories about children's lies. These impressive gains could be interpreted as showing that Piaget underestimates the power of language to stimulate disequilibrium and cognitive reorganization in children. Kohnstamm (1970), for one, has taken Piaget to task for his "assumption that as soon as the adult starts speaking, the child stops his active handling and operational thinking and becomes a passive machine, waiting for the atomistic S-R connections to be stamped in" (p. 371). Or the didactic-training gains could be taken to mean that children simply learned what to say (content) but did not acquire a deeper grasp of reasons (structure), and that a didactic lesson in *objective* responsibility could easily reverse this surface learning. The latter interpretation implies that as a general procedure, all experimentally induced changes in moral judgment should be subjected to tests of "resistance to extinction" such as those used to determine the durability of trained logical operations such as conservation (Smedslund, 1961).

On the whole, the moral judgment training research leaves one with the feeling that the sources of change that Piaget speaks about, such as peer interaction and broad cognitive growth, do not lend themselves to being telescoped into a brief experimental session. Even though Piagetian antecedents may be quite important over the course of development, they seem doomed to fare badly in short-term experiments when compared to straightforward modeling or didactic methods. Longitudinal training research, with varied and long-range follow-ups to test both permanence and generalization of change, is perhaps the only legitimate way to conduct an experimental test of a developmental theory.

## Conclusion

At the end of this tour through the Piagetian moral judgment literature the reader may feel that—contrary to the honored axiom of scholarship—more research is not needed. His intuition is probably sound. All of the evidence may not be in, but there is enough from a generation of testing Piaget's theory to render a verdict on at least the broad outlines of his conception of moral judgment growth.

Moral judgment, as depicted by Piaget, is indisputably developmental; it changes with age and experience. Piaget has demonstrated that the young child, in his conscience as in his logic, cannot be viewed as an adult in miniature, lacking only an adequate dose of indoctrination. It is at the same time evident that children's moral judgments do not exist in a social or cultural vacuum; however spontaneous they may be in their origins, they are very much subject to direct and indirect social influence both in their rate of development and, at least for some judgmental dimensions, in the shape they take in adulthood. The available research also shows plainly that the child's moral thought, as it unfolds in Piagetian interviews, is not all of a piece but more of a patchwork of diverse parts.

The findings also suggest that while Piaget's analysis of the cognitive basis of moral judgment is well founded, his speculations about its affective side are on shaky ground. Young children do not, as their parents or teachers can wearily attest, stand in awe of the authority of adults or the rules they repeatedly set forth. When a preschool boy flushes the father doll down the toilet, as Kohlberg (1968b) observes, it is hard to view his action as consistent with a sense of heteronomous respect for the patriarchial father. Rather, the research (R. L. Krebs, Brener, & Kohlberg, 1967) indicates that loyalty to and genuine respect for personal authority, like respect for rules, is something that children must *develop* during the early school years (ages 4 to 7) and something that accompanies *advance*, not immaturity, on moral dimensions such as judging the rightness of an action apart from its external consequences. The child's early obedience orientation in moral thinking appears to be based less on respect for the moral status of adults than on simple recognition of their superior power.

Moral judgment also appears to mature more slowly than Piaget's theory leads us to believe. Using Piaget-type stories with 11- to 18-year-olds representing a variety of personality and subcultural types, Loughran (1967) concluded that "adolescents arrive at Piaget's level of mature autonomous judgment between 12 and 17 years, not between 11 and 12 as Piaget says" (p. 89). Kohlberg's longitudinal research (see Chap. 2) has led to the postulation of three stages *beyond* the relatively simple "Golden Rule morality" that constitutes Piaget's highest, autonomous-cooperative stage—indicating that the latter is "yet far from the morality of mutual respect and social contract which is shared by both humanitarian liberals and bureaucratic constitutionalists" (Kohlberg, 1968b, p. 139). And if Kohlberg's authority-independent but still self-centered Stage 2 morality is a universal step in development, then Piaget also errs at the lower end of the moral ladder by omitting this intermediate second stage and presenting children as moving directly from a Stage 1 obedience orientation to a Stage 3 morality based on concern for the approval and welfare of others.

A comparison of Piaget's two-stage theory with Kohlberg's highly refined six-stage moral sequence makes it clear that an early, groundbreaking cognitive-developmental theory has been subsumed and supplanted by a later, more comprehensive theory in the same tradition. It is not surprising that moral judgment research tends increasingly to be done within Kohlberg's framework. Kohlberg and his colleagues are, however, continuing what Piaget largely began with his gentle inquisitions of Swiss children some forty years ago: the charting of developmental changes in thinking about moral issues, the search for sequential and universal stages, and the effort to understand how conceptions of morality are bound inextricably to the overall growth of the human mind.

Chapter 4

# Moral Stages and the Development of Faith

## JAMES FOWLER

## INTRODUCTION

In 1974 Lawrence Kohlberg published an article entitled "Education, Moral Development and Faith."[1] Originally an address to the National Catholic Educational Association, this paper represents a rather direct statement of the central themes of Kohlbergian "faith." It expresses Kohlberg's commitment to a Platonic understanding of justice as the central and unitary moral virtue.[2] It states his claim that justice is a naturalistic virtue, emerging in children (at differing rates and with differing points of final equilibration) in all cultures as a result of their interaction with other persons and with social institutions. It affirms that the capacity for discerning the requirements of justice has an ontogenetic history, recapitulated at varying rates in individuals and their societies, but essentially common to all persons. It claims that moral education can be pursued in public schools without reference to the contents of students' particular beliefs, attitudes, or values. To fulfill this possibility, public education must meet the following imperatives: according to Kohlberg, (1) justice must be embodied in the *modus operandi* of the school; (2) moral thinking must be stimulated by attention to real and hypothetical moral dilemmas; and (3) students must be exposed to moral arguments on these issues one stage beyond their own. If these significant conditions are met, Kohlberg believes, growth in individuals' capacity to discern the requirements of justice should occur. Further, if the social environment encourages children and youth to take the personal and social perspectives of others, the expansion of moral imagination eventually required for principled moral reasoning will be nurtured.

Underlying these elements of Kohlbergian faith is a conception of moral development which Kohlberg appropriated from J. Mark Baldwin, John Dewey, Jean Piaget, and others. This tradition rejects theories of moral development centering in the teaching of multiple virtues or moral ideals. Instead, it argues that moral judgment and action arise out of a person's way of constructing (knowing) situations requiring moral choice. The key to moral development, and therefore to moral education, lies in the cognitive operations by which persons "know" their social environments. Moral development requires progress in the ability accurately to take the perspectives of others, their needs and rights, and to see one's own claims and obligations with similar balance, detachment, and accuracy. Following the path of cognitive development more generally, moral judgment—cognitive operations as applied to questions of rightness, goodness, obligation, duty, and responsibility—also exhibits a developmental trajectory.

Kohlberg's stage theory sets forth the developmental trajectory he finds in persons' moral thinking. Claiming both empirical validation and logical-philosophical justification for the stage sequence,[3] Kohlberg has provided a powerful heuristic model against which to examine patterns of moral reasoning in individuals and groups.

"Education, Moral Development and Faith"either assumes or explicitly restates most of the elements of the Kohlbergian faith I have just enumerated. But it also does more. Kohlberg begins the article in an interesting way:

While moral development has a larger context including faith, it is possible to have a public moral education which has a foundation independent of religion. We believe that the public school should engage in moral education and that the moral basis of such education centers on universal principles of justice, not broader religious and personal values.[4]

The references to "faith," "religion," and "broader religious and personal values" signal an agenda to which Kohlberg returns later in the article.

In a section headed "Moral Development and Education as Centered on Justice," he points to Socrates and Martin Luther King, Jr. as great moral teachers whose lives and teachings manifested their centering commitments to principles of justice. For Kohlberg, the principle of justice held by both these men derived from their considering "social justice, or the nature of an ideal society."[5] The principle of justice, this suggests, is a transcendent ideal, a universal norm arising from the vision of a just society. With this point Kohlberg circles back to the themes promised in his opening sentences:

> We have stressed so far the place of universal principles of human justice as central to moral development, principles which can be defined and justified without reference to a specific religious tradition. We need now to note that while Socrates and Martin Luther King died for principles of human justice, they were also deeply religious men. What, then, is the relation of the development of religious faith to the development of moral principles?[6]

At this juncture in his 1974 text, Kohlberg introduces the fledgling work on stages of faith development of his then Harvard colleague James Fowler, myself. He quoted an early version of our stage theory *in extenso,* but without any attention to what we mean by "faith." In order to discuss some of the relations between moral development and faith, and between stages of moral judgment and possible stages in faith, let me present an introduction to the focus of our work in its present form.

## THE FOCUS ON FAITH

I begin with three brief case synopses.
Case Number 1:

> A woman in her mid-twenties tells her story. "The years from seventeen to twenty-two were my lost years, the years I searched and tried everything, but

accomplished nothing. I tried sex, illicit drugs, Eastern religions, the occult, everything. I filled myself with vain knowledge, but gained nothing as far as my real spiritual hunger was concerned." At twenty-two, eight months after "an extraordinary experience on L.S.D.," and after having two persons close to her witness to the lordship of Jesus Christ, she accepted him as her Lord. Her story of the next five years resembles those of many in her generation: movement from one new Christian, true church movement to another; submission to the often conflicting authority of self-appointed Christian elders and to the disciplines of neo-Christian group life. She suffered the psychological violence inflicted by newly converted folk who, in radically denying their own pasts and affirming their new beings in Christ, projected much of the horror and guilt of what they denied in themselves onto others. Her odyssey carried her through at least four such groups before she found one led by mature Christians. At the encouragement of one ill-prepared leader, she had married a man she hardly knew, and for two years "submitted" to horrendous marital anarchy and degradation. Through it all, she affirms, "The Lord never left me bereft. He was leading me, teaching me, shaping me." Though raw and hurting, her faith in the Lord more than ever occupies the center of her efforts to discern what she should do next and to know how to think of herself. "I just pray that the Lord will show me the ministry he has for me."

## Case Number 2:

A small-town merchant pours six long days a week into the management of his clothing store. A kind man with a friendly and helpful attitude, his business flourishes. He belongs to a local church and contributes generously. He belongs to a local civic association and gives modestly of his time to its projects. He is a respected member of the town's Chamber of Commerce, and is admired as a progressive force in the refurbishing of Main Street. One day his son, intending it as a joke, gives the attentive observer a frightening clue: "Daddy," he says, "doesn't have a thing except Mama that he wouldn't sell if the price were right!" And this was true. It would be too extreme to speak of money in his case as a fetish, but clearly his son had named the center of the father's value system. And the other involvements and extensions of self—even to the extent of caring financially for an alcoholic brother—served this central devotion to enlarging his "estate."

## Case Number 3:

The fourth of ten children born to an Irish-Italian marriage, Jack grew up in "the Projects." "There were so many of us boys that people never knew our first names. They just called us 'Seely' (not the real name). My voice sounded so much like my brothers that sometimes even I got confused." Under the influence of the Sisters in parochial school he became, during his late childhood and early adolescence, a faithful churchgoer. "One year," he said, "I made mass every day and did two novenas, which was hard. I got up early every day and went over there; I never sat on the bench, but always stayed on my knees. I felt like I was one of Jesus' special kids. I liked it, and I kind of made a bargain that I would do all this for him if he would sort of straighten my dad's drinking out a little bit. He would go out on Friday, Saturday, and Sunday nights and come back drunk. Sometimes he beat mother when they argued." At the end of his seventh grade year Sister called him up to the front of the room and publicly recognized him as the only boy who had been faithful in attending mass daily throughout the spring. "She should'na done that," he said. "They got me then, the bullies. They gave me a hard time for the next two years. I quit going to church. But I guess it was just as well. The old man didn't ease up on the drinking. In fact, he started going out on Thursday nights too!" Today, near thirty, still out of church, he lives in a nice but confining low-cost private housing project. Every thirty seconds during most of the day the large jets taking off or landing at the nearby airport shake the windows in their apartment. He and his wife lead the Tenants Association in its struggle against rent-gouging landlords. They have helped organize tenant groups all over their part of the city, and, for their troubles, have two separate $1 million suits against them initiated by landlord associations. His $12,000 per year job and her nightly work as a waitress keep them both very busy. "Blacks and poor white people need to get together here. We've been pitted against each other, to *their* advantage, for too long. I don't know much theory; I can't talk about Hegel and philosophy, and I don't know Marx too good. But I do know my class and I know we're getting stepped on. Me and my wife want to give everything we got to giving poor folks a break. And while we do it, we gotta remember that there are people under us too, people worse off. We may be in the alley fighting, but down below in the cellar somewhere they are fighting for a chance to breathe, too. We gotta be careful not to step on them."

These are vignettes on faith; windows into the organizing images and value patterns by which people live. The stories let us in on their life wagers. They give us access to the ways three persons are pouring out their life energies—spending and being spent in the service of valued projects, in light of which their own value and worth as persons seek confirmation.

In this way of thinking, faith need not be approached as necessarily a religious matter. Nor need it be thought of as doctrinal belief or assent. Rather, faith becomes the designation for a way of leaning into life. It points to a way of making sense of one's existence. It denotes a way giving order and coherence to the force-field of life. It speaks of the investment of life-grounding trust and of life-orienting commitment.

Now let us look at these matters a little more systematically. This way of approaching faith means to imply that this phenomenon is a human universal. That is to say, as members of a species burdened with consciousness and self-consciousness, and with freedom to name and organize the phenomenal world, we nowhere can escape the task of forming tacit or explicit coherent images of our action-worlds. We are born into fields of forces impinging upon us from all sides. The development of perception means a profound limiting and selection of the *sensa* to which we can consciously or unconsciously attend. The development of cognition—understood here in its broadest sense—means the construction of operations of thought and valuing in accordance with which the *sensa* to which we attend are organized and formed. Composition and interpretation of meanings, then, are the inescapable burdens of our species. Consciously or unconsciously, in this process, we invest trust in powerful images which unify our experience, and which order it in accordance with interpretations that serve our acknowledgment of centers of value and power.

We encounter this force-field of life in the presence of others. From the beginning others *mediate* in our interaction with the conditions of our existence. Somatic contact, gestures, words, rituals from other persons—all serve to link us with aspects of the surrounding environment. And before we can think with words or symbols, primitive images or pre-images of felt "sense" begin to form in us. Therefore we must think of even our earliest steps toward interpretation and meaning as shared, as social.

Reflection on this social character of even our earliest moves toward construction of meaning points to another important feature of faith. Our investment of reliance upon, or trust in, interpretative images does not occur apart from our investment of reliance upon or trust in the significant others who are companions or mediators in our acts of meaning construction. Faith involves, from the beginning, our participation in what we may call tacit, covenantal, fiduciary relationships. Put another way, our interpretations of and responses to events which disclose the conditions of our existence are formed in the company of co-interpreters and co-respondents whom we trust and to whom we are loyal. Faith is a relational matter. As we relate to the conditions of our existence with acts of interpretative commitment, we do so as persons also related to and co-involved with companions whom we trust and to whom we are loyal. This means that the interpretative images by which we make sense of the conditions of our lives inevitably implicate our companions. It also means, reciprocally, that our experiences with these companions in interpretation have decisive impact on the forming and re-forming of our interpretative images and for the values and powers they serve.

Let us designate those images by which we holistically grasp the conditions of our existence with the name *images of the ultimate environment*. And let us point out that such images of the ultimate environment derive their unity and their principle of coherence from a center (or centers) of value and power to which persons of faith are attracted with conviction. Faith then, is a matter of composing an image of the ultimate environment, through the commitment of self to a center (or centers) of value and power giving it coherence. We do this in interaction with communities of co-interpreters and co-commitants. And our commitments so made with the interpretative impacts they carry, become occasions for the re-ordering of our loves and the re-directing of our spending and being spent.

We have intended in these paragraphs on faith to present it as a dynamic phenomenon. Faith is an ongoing process. It is a way of being and of leaning into life. Crises, disclosure-events, the fulfillment or failure of hopes, betrayals and experiences of fidelity in the force-field of life continually impact a person's image of the ultimate environment and his or her commitment to the value- or power-center(s) sustaining it. Conversion or re-conversion in small or large ways can be precipitated without conscious desire or intent. Confusion, doubt, and the conflicts of double or multiple pulls to commitment represent inherent dynamics of faith. And for most of us our controlling image of the ultimate environment is likely to be as much an aspiration to worthy and true faith as it is an accomplished and integrated reality of faith. Competing master images of the ultimate environment contend for loyalty in societies and cultures, and within individual human breasts.

Let us try to bring this introductory characterization of faith into summary focus. Faith, we may say, is

—a disposition of the total self toward the ultimate environment
—in which trust and loyalty are invested in a center or centers of value and power
—which order and give coherence to the force-field of life, *and*
—which support and sustain (or qualify and relativize) our mundane or everyday commitments and trusts
—combining to give orientation, courage, meaning, and hope to our lives, and
—to unite us into communities of shared interpretation, loyalty, and trust.[7]

## FAITH AND MORAL REASONING

Before we go on to the matters of stages of faith in relation to stages of moral reasoning we should examine some conceptual and phenomenal relations between faith and moral reasoning. I am claiming that we human beings necessarily engage in constructing frames of meaning for our lives, and that we do this, with others, by making tacit and/or explicit commitments to value-and-power centers which promise to sustain our lives and meanings. This activity I call faith. Faith is a valuing and a committing; it is axiological and volitional. But it is also a knowing—a composing, a construing, an interpreting. Faith, like moral judgment, has an important epistemological dimension.[8]

Kohlberg recognizes this in the latter parts of "Education, Moral Development and Faith." There he introduces—for the only time in published form that I am aware of—reference to a metaphorical, nonmoral "stage 7." He introduces this intriguing notion after having reiterated his belief that moral principles can be formulated and justified without reliance upon faith or religion. He says:

In some sense, however, to ultimately live up to moral principles requires faith. For this reason, we believe, the ultimate exemplars of stage 6 morality also appear to be men of faith. . . . I believe then, like Kant, that ultimate moral principles, stage 6 morality, can and should be formulated and justified on grounds of autonomous moral rationality. Such morality, however, "requires" an ultimate stage of faith and moves men toward it. The faith orientation required by universal moral principles I call stage 7, though at this point the term is only a metaphor. This faith orientation does not basically change the definition of universal principles of human justice found at stage 6, but it integrates them with a perspective on life's ultimate meaning.[9]

In other writings Kohlberg has held that the critical question, "Why be moral?" is answered from within the logic of stages one through five. In "Moral Stages and Moralization," for example, he includes a chart which provides one of the most recent accounts of stage specific "reasons for doing right."[10] At stage 1 the person "does right" in order to avoid punishment and because of the superior power of authorities. At stage 3, one is moral because of "the need to be a good person in your own eyes and those of others. . . . " Adherence to the requirements of justice at stage 5 derives from "a sense of obligation to law because of one's social contract to make and abide by laws for the welfare of all and for the protection of all peoples' rights."[11] Kohlberg nowhere claims that these motivational factors *exhaustively* account for persons' adherence to the requirements of right or justice. But clearly he wants to avoid any suggestion that moral judgments are essentially dependent upon the particular contents of a person's or group's values, attitudes, world view, or religious orientation.

At stage 6, however, Kohlberg sees no rationale inherent in universal moral principles by which to answer the question, "Why be moral?" The answer to this question at stage 6, he has often said in public discussions, is always a religious answer. In "Education, Moral Development and Faith," he puts it this way:

> I have argued that the answer to the question, "Why be moral?" at this level entails the question, "Why live?" (and the parallel question, "How face death?") so that ultimate moral maturity requires a mature solution to the question of the meaning of life. This, in turn, is hardly a moral question per se, it is an ontological or religious one.[12]

"Solutions" to these ontological or religious questions, Kohlberg points out, cannot be reached on purely logical or rational grounds.

They represent ways of seeing the human situation in relation to a more transcending framework of meaning and value. In Kohlberg's language:

> The characteristic of all these stage 7 solutions is that they involve contemplative experience of a nondualistic variety. The logic of such experience is sometimes expressed in theistic terms of union with God but it need not be. Its essential is the sense of being a part of the whole of life and the adoption of a cosmic, as opposed to a universal humanistic "stage 6" perspective.[13]

He turns then to an example of stage 7 faith constituted by the Stoic, mystical resignation of the *Meditations of Marcus Aurelius.*

In private, and in a brief published statement,[14] I have expressed my agreement with Kohlberg in his claim that moral stage 6 implies an accompanying faith vision and faith commitment. I am glad for his recognition that commitment to principled morality is part of a more comprehensive stance or disposition toward the ultimate conditions of our lives. But this recognition, I contend, does not go far enough. The question, "Why be moral?" cannot be answered adequately within the terms of *any* of Kohlberg's stages without reference to a person's commitments to a wider frame of meaning and value. There is a faith context—as I characterize the term faith—informing and supporting a person's consistent adherence to justice, the right or the good, as discerned through the logic of *any* of the stages of moral reasoning.

Let us consider a few examples. In stage 1, Kohlberg tells us, the child's reason for doing good is to avoid punishment and to be rewarded. Also there is deference—presumably a mixture of fear and respect—for the superior physical power of authorities. I am inclined to believe Kohlberg is right as regards the epistemology of moral judgment at this stage. Children do determine what is right by reference to the punishment and reward responses of parents or parentlike adults. But surely the issue of why the child wants to be good, or is interested at all, requires us to go further. My own research with children leads me to suggest that because of ties of dependence and affection, and because of the preoperational child's imitative interest in adult behaviors and values, there is already forming by stage 1 what I call a rudimentary loyalty to the *child's construction* of her or his family's "ethos of goodness." For punishment and reward to make any sense to the child, and for it to contribute to moral growth, it must be linked to a framework of shared meaning and value, no matter how primitively construed by the child. Otherwise we have no way to account for the generalization of experiences of punishment and reward into "improved behavior" across the board, or for the child's countless adoptions of desirable behavior patterns for which there have been no specific occasions of positive or negative sanction. Moral decision or choice for the preschool and early school child, I am arguing, is already beginning to be lodged in a framework of meaning and value, and is part of the child's way of participating in the faith ethos of his or her family or family surrogate.

At moral stage 2, Kohlberg tells us, persons are moral "To serve one's own needs or interests in a world where you have to recognize that other people have their interests too."[15] Stage 2's instrumental hedonism, with its reciprocity of perspectives and its recognition of others' claims, represents the child's first constructions of "fairness." Surely with these insights Kohlberg contributes something extremely valuable to our understanding of the epistemology underlying the child's conception of fairness. But as an account of why the child becomes committed to fairness as a normative principle, it is plainly incomplete. It sheds very little light on why the child feels that some ligament of the universe has been torn if he or she, or a friend, or even a stranger, is treated unfairly. Here again, I submit that the child's adherence to fairness as a valued and respected norm bespeaks a broader frame of meaning and value through which the child finds coherence in life and maintains a sense of worthy membership in a valued group.

In other writings[16] I have followed theologian H. Richard Niebuhr and philosopher Josiah Royce in claiming that any lasting human relation or association has a fiduciary or faith structure. By this I mean initially that as selves we maintain our identities through relations of reciprocal trust in and loyalty to significant others. Our mutual investments of trust and loyalty with these others, however, are deepened, stabilized, and prevented from having to bear more moral weight than they can sustain, by our shared trusts and loyalties to centers of value and power of more transcendent worth.

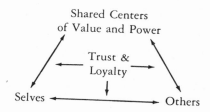

Kohlberg's stages of moral judgment, *especially* through stage 4 and the conventional level, are inexplicable as regards moral motivation and accountability apart from a self's valued membership in groups or communities joined by commitments to meaning frames centering in shared values and images of power.[17]

The stages of faith development to which I now wish to turn, represent our effort to describe a series of stagelike "styles" in which persons participate in the activity of meaning-making and in communities of shared meaning and value. From this perspective, faith stages are to be understood as formal (i.e., content-free) descriptions of the operations of knowing and valuing underlying a person's composing and maintenance of a meaning-value perspective. As such, a faith stage includes and contextualizes a form of moral reasoning such as that characterized in the corresponding Kohlberg stage. After examining the overview of faith stages, we will look briefly at some theoretically predicted and empirically determined relations between the faith stages and stages of moral reasoning.

## STAGES OF FAITH

We are going to examine here stages of faith development as we have identified them in the course of seven years of research. Our research procedure has been described in detail elsewhere.[18] Briefly, we employ a semiclinical, open-ended interview of one to three hours (somewhat briefer with children) in which the respondent is asked to share aspects of his or her life history and to express in detail his or her feelings and attitudes regarding a cluster of universal life-issues with which faith must deal. (The list of issues: death and afterlife; the limits of knowledge; causation and effectance in personal and historical life; evil and suffering; freedom and determinism; power and agency; meaning of life; ideal manhood or womanhood; the future; grounding of ethical and moral imperatives; communal identifications and belongings; bases of guilt and shame; central loyalties and commitments; locus of transcendent beauty, value, or power; objects of reverence or awe; grounds of terror or dread; sin and violation; religious experiences, beliefs, and practices; specific meaningful religious symbols.) This list is uniformly pursued in each interview. Respondents are encouraged to share concrete experiences and crises out of their own lives, and to address the faith issues experientially whenever possible. Though respondents often voluntarily answer in specifically religious terms, religion as an issue and context is not explicitly introduced until the last one-third of the interview. An effort is made to test espoused beliefs, values, and attitudes against self-reports of performance and choice in actual situations.

These interviews are then transcribed. Analysis for structural features is carried out by trained scorers. The formulations of position and outlook in relation to the faith issues are regarded as the *contents* of the person's faith. A thematic or content analysis can be carried out and systematized in order to understand the person's faith or belief system. Structural analysis, however, aims to go "under" the content elements to "liberate" the deeper structural operations of knowing and valuing which underlie, ground, and organize the thematic content.

We have conducted and analyzed about 380 interviews of the type just described. The sample has been cross-sectionally balanced for age from four to eighty. It includes slightly more females than males, includes Protestants, Catholics, Jews, atheists, and agnostics (in representative numbers), several Western adherents of Eastern traditions, and has a reasonable range of educational, social class, and ethnic variations. We have begun to follow a select longitudinal sample at five-year intervals, but have only limited longitudinal data so far. We have not conducted cross-cultural investigations. Therefore the stage descriptions we offer here must still be considered as provisional.

In this context, what do we mean by the term "stage"? In contemporary usage this word has a lot of meanings. Here we intend by it the following: *one of a sequence of formally describable "styles" of composing an ultimate environment, of committing the self to centers of value and power, of symbolizing and expressing those commitments, and of relating them to the valued perspectives of others.* We speak of stages rather than of types because we believe that the stage sequence we have identified is invariant. That is, we believe the stages come in the order presented here and that persons do not skip over a stage. Please notice that we say "formally describable." This means that a stage is not defined by a particular *content* of belief or valuing. Rather, a stage is a particular *way* or organizing, composing, or of giving form to the contents of beliefs or values. Stage descriptions focus on the *how* of faith rather than on the *what* or the content of faith.

Stages are not "there" like a set of stair-steps to climb up. To make a transition from one stage to another is to undergo the often painful process of giving up one's familiar and comfortable ways of making meaning and sustaining commitment. Transition means a kind of coming apart as well as a new construction. Periods of transition can be protracted over several years.

Let me make one other potentially confusing matter clear. Many stage theories, such as Erikson's "Eight Ages of the Life Cycle,"[19] tie the movement from one stage to another directly to chronological age and biological maturation. Particularly in the earlier stages which, for Erikson, are most directly psycho-sexual stages, maturation sets the pace and precipitates the movement from one stage to another. Our stages, like Piaget's and Kohlberg's, are dependent upon age and maturation in that these factors provide some of the *necessary* conditions for stage transition. But they are not *sufficient* conditions. Other factors, such as the richness and stimulation of the environment, the availability of models of the next "place," and

"catch" a subject as to correct a test-taking set to choose items on the person's encounter with crises or dilemmas which shake up his or her faith outlook, play significant roles in determining the rate and timing of stage changes. To show what this means, it is not too unusual to find normal persons who are chronologically and biologically adult, but whose patterns of faith can best be described by our stage 2. This is a stage that typically arises during the years from seven to eleven. We are suggesting that "normal" persons may equilibrate or arrest in faith growth at any of these stages from the second stage on. Certain factors in maturation must occur before the school child is ready for transition to stage 3, but maturation and age, by themselves, do not guarantee readiness for the next stage.

Now we are ready to examine an overview of this sequence of stages. The description of each stage will include a general characterization. This will be followed by a somewhat more detailed elaboration. Then, briefly, we will suggest some of the signs of transition to the next stage.[20]

## Undifferentiated Faith

The preconceptual, largely prelinguistic stage in which the infant unconsciously forms a disposition toward its world.

Trust, courage, hope, and love are fused in an undifferentiated way and contend with sensed threats of abandonment, inconsistencies, and deprivations in the infant's environment. Though really a prestage, and largely inaccessible to empirical inquiry of the kind we pursue, the quality of mutuality and the strength of trust, autonomy, hope, and courage (or their opposites) developed in this phase, underlie (or undermine) all that comes later in faith development.

Transition to stage 1 begins with the convergence of thought and language, opening up the use of symbols in speech and ritual play.

## Stage 1. Intuitive-Projective Faith

The fantasy-filled, imitative phase in which the child can be powerfully and permanently influenced by the examples, moods, actions, and language of the visible faith of primal adults.

The stage most typical of the child of three to seven, it is marked by a relative fluidity of thought patterns. The child is continually encountering novelties for which no stable operations of knowing have been formed. The imaginative processes underlying fantasy are unrestrained and uninhibited by logical thought. In league with forms of knowing dominated by perception, imagination in this stage is extremely productive of long-lasting images and feelings (positive and negative) which later, more stable and self-reflective valuing and thinking will have to order and sort out. This is the stage of first self-awareness. The "self-aware" child is egocentric as regards the perspectives of others. Here we find the first awarenesses of death and sex, and of the strong taboos by which cultures and families insulate those powerful areas.

The emergence of "concrete operational" thinking underlies the transition to stage 2. Affectively, the resolution of Oedipal issues or their submersion in latency are important accompanying factors. At the heart of the transition is the child's growing concern to *know* how things are and to clarify for himself or herself the bases of distinctions between what is real and what only "seems to be."

## Stage 2. Mythic-Literal Faith

The stage in which the person begins to take on for himself or herself the stories, beliefs, and observances which symbolize belonging to his or her community. Beliefs are appropriated with literal interpretations, as are moral rules and attitudes. Symbols are taken as one-dimensional and literal in meaning.

In this stage the rise of "concrete operations" leads to the curbing and ordering of the previous stage's imaginative composing of the world. The episodic quality of intuitive-projective faith gives way to a more linear, narrative construction of coherence and meaning. Story becomes the major way of giving unity and value to experience. This is the faith stage of the school child (though we sometimes find its structures dominant in adolescents and in adults). Marked by increased accuracy in taking the perspective of other persons, stage 2 composes a world based on reciprocal fairness and an immanent justice based on reciprocity. The actors in its cosmic stories are full-fledged anthropomorphic "personalities." Those in this stage can be affected deeply and powerfully by symbolic and dramatic materials, and can describe in endlessly detailed narrative what has occurred. Stage 2 does not, however, step back from the flow of its stories to formulate reflective, conceptual meanings. For this stage the meaning is both carried and "trapped" in the narrative.

The implicit clash or contradictions of stories leads to reflection on meanings. The transition to "formal operational" thought makes such reflection possible and necessary. Previous literalism breaks down; new "cognitive conceit" (Elkind) leads to disillusionment with previous teachers and teachings. Conflicts between authoritative stories (i.e., Genesis on creation vs. evolutionary theory) must be faced. The emergence of mutual interpersonal perspective-taking ("I see you seeing me; I see me as you see me; I see you seeing me seeing you") creates the need for a more personal relationship with the unifying power of the ultimate environment.

## Stage 3. Synthetic-Conventional Faith

The person's experience of the world now extends beyond the family. A number of spheres demand attention: family, school or work, peers, street society and media, and perhaps religion. Faith must provide a coherent orientation in the midst of that more complex and diverse range of involvements. Faith must synthesize values and information; it must provide a basis for identity and outlook.

Stage 3 typically has its rise and ascendancy in adolescence, but for many adults it becomes a permanent equilibration. It structures the ultimate environment in interpersonal terms. Its images of unifying value and power derive from the extension of qualities experienced in personal relationships. It is a "conformist" stage in the sense that it is acutely tuned to the expectations and judgments of significant others, and as yet does not have a sure enough grasp on its own identity and autonomous judgment to construct and maintain an independent perspective. While beliefs and values are deeply felt, they typically are tacitly held—the person "dwells" in them and the meaning world they mediate. But there has not been occasion to reflectively step outside them so as to examine them explicitly or systematically. At stage 3 a person has an "ideology," a more or less consistent clustering of values and beliefs, but he or she has not objectified it for examination, and in a sense is unaware of having it. Differences of outlook with others are experienced as differences in "kind" of person. Authority is located in the incumbents of traditional authority-roles (if perceived as personally worthy) or in the consensus of a valued, face-to-face group.

Factors contributing to the breakdown of stage 3 and to readiness for transition may include any one or more of the following: serious clashes or contradictions between valued authority sources; marked changes, by officially sanctioned leaders, of policies or practices previously deemed sacred and unbreachable (e.g., in the Catholic church, changing the mass from Latin to the vernacular, or no longer requiring abstinence from meat on Friday); the encounter with experiences or perspectives that lead to critical reflection on how one's beliefs and values have formed and changed, and on how "relative" they are to one's particular group or background.

## Stage 4. Individuative-Reflective Faith

The movement from stage 3 to stage 4 is particularly critical, for it is in this transition that the late adolescent or adult must begin to take seriously the burden of responsibility for his or her own commitments, lifestyle, beliefs, and attitudes. Where genuine movement toward stage 4 is underway, the person must face certain unavoidable tensions: individuality vs. being defined by a group or group membership; subjectivity and the power of one's strongly felt but unexamined feelings vs. objectivity and the requirement of critical reflection; self-fulfillment or self-actualization as a primary concern vs. service to and being for others; the question of being committed to the relative vs. struggle with the possibility of an absolute.

> This stage most appropriately takes form in young adulthood (but let us remember that many adults do *not* construct it and that for a significant group it emerges only in the mid-thirties or forties). This stage is marked by a double development. The self, previously sustained in its identity and faith compositions by an interpersonal circle of significant others, now claims an identity no longer defined by the composite of one's roles or meanings to others. To sustain that new identity it composes a meaning frame conscious of its own boundaries and inner connections, and aware of itself as a "worldview." Self (identity) and outlook (worldview) are differentiated from those of others, and become acknowledged factors in the reactions, interpretations, and judgments one makes on the actions of the self and others. The self expresses its intuitions

of coherence in an ultimate environment in terms of an explicit system of
meanings. Stage 4 typically translates symbols into conceptual meanings. This
is a "demythologizing" stage. The self is likely to attend minimally to unconscious factors influencing its judgments and behaviors.

Restless with the self-images and outlook maintained by stage 4,
the person ready for transition finds him/herself attending to what
may feel like anarchic and disturbing inner voices. Elements from a
childish past, images and energies from a deeper self, a gnawing sense
of the sterility and flatness of the meanings one serves—any or all of
these may signal readiness for something new. Stories, symbols,
myths paradoxes from one's own or other traditions may insist on
breaking in upon the neatness of the previous faith. Disillusionment
with one's compromises, and recognition that life is more complex
than stage 4's logic of clear distinctions and abstract concepts can comprehend, press one toward a more dialectical and multileveled approach to life-truth.

## Stage 5. Paradoxical-Consolidative Faith

This stage involves the integration into self and outlook of much
that was suppressed or evaded in the interest of stage 4's self-
certainty and conscious cognitive and affective adaptation to reality.
This stage develops a "second naivete" (Ricoeur) in which symbolic
power is reunited with conceptual meanings. Here there must also
be a new reclaiming and reworking of one's past. There must be an
opening to the voices of one's "deeper self." Importantly, this involves a critical recognition of one's *social* unconscious—the myths,
ideal images, and prejudices built deeply into the self-system by
virtue of one's being nurtured within a particular social class, religious tradition, ethnic group, or the like.

> Unusual before midlife, stage 5 knows the sacrament of defeat and the reality
> of irrevocable commitments and acts. What the previous stage struggled to
> clarify, in terms of the boundaries of self and outlook, this stage now makes
> porous and permeable. Alive to paradox and the truth in apparent contradic-
> tions, this stage strives to unify opposites in mind and experience. It generates
> and maintains vulnerability to the strange truths of those who are "other."

> Ready for closeness to that which is different and threatening to self and outlook (including new depths of experience in spirituality and religious revelation), this stage's commitment to justice is freed from the confines of tribe, class, religious community, or nation. And with the seriousness that can arise when life is more than half over, this stage is ready to spend and be spent for the cause of conserving and cultivating the possibility of others' generating identity and meaning.

Stage 5 can appreciate symbols, myths and rituals (its own and others') because it has been grasped, in some measure, by the depth of reality to which they refer. It also sees the divisions of the human family vividly because it has been apprehended by the possibility (and imperative) of an inclusive community of being. But this stage remains divided. It lives and acts between an untransformed world and a transforming vision and loyalties. In some few cases this division yields to the call of the radical actualization that we call stage 6.

## Stage 6. Universalizing Faith

This stage is exceedingly rare. The persons best described by this stage have generated faith compositions in which their felt sense of an ultimate environment is inclusive of all being. They become incarnators and actualizers of the spirit of a fulfilled human community.

> They are "contagious" in the sense that they create zones of liberation from the social, political, economic, and ideological shackles we place and endure on human futurity. Living with felt participation in a power that unifies and transforms the world, universalizers are often experienced as subversive of the structures (including religious structures) by which we sustain our individual and corporate survival, security, and significance. Many persons in this stage die at the hands of those whom they hope to change. Universalizers are often more honored and revered after death than during their lives. The rare persons who may be described by this stage have a special grace that makes them seem more lucid, more simple, and yet somehow more fully human than the rest of us. Their community is universal in extent. Particularities are cherished because they are vessels of the universal, and are thereby valuable apart from any utilitarian considerations. Life is both loved and held to loosely. Such persons are ready for fellowship with persons at any of the other stages and from any other faith tradition.

# MORAL STAGES AND THE DEVELOPMENT OF FAITH

As I conceive them, the faith stages are more comprehensive constructs than are the Kohlberg stages of moral reasoning. A faith
stage is meant to integrate operations of knowing and valuing which
underlie and give form to the contents of a person's system of
meaning. As such, faith stages represent modes of knowing, commitment, and action, in which thought and emotion, rationality and passionality, are held together. This does not mean, as some
critics have suggested, that faith is an irrational or a'rational matter.[21] It does mean, however, that the logic of faith is more comprehensive than the logic of rational certainty characterizing
Piaget's and Kohlberg's cognitive theories. Faith employs images
and ontological intuitions. It relies on historical and present experiences of disclosure and "revelation." Faith works with elements of
religious, philosophical, and ideological traditions. The culture of
myths, symbols, and ritual are part of its media. These elements
faith interrogates by means of rational operations testing for sense
and consistency. The resulting "logic of conviction" (as I have called
it elsewhere)[22] is open to ongoing tests for existential validity,
generalizable truth, and reflective equilibrium. To recognize that
the logic of conviction has this dialectical character in no way rend-
ers it a'rational or irrational. This recognition simply reminds us
that a logic of rational certainty alone cannot resolve ontological and
axiological questions.

Kohlberg's only published response to the stage theory of faith
development in "Education, Moral Development and Faith" seems
uncertain as to how to regard the relation of faith stages to stages of
moral reasoning. In some passages he writes as though faith and
moral judgment stages are two comparable strands of a larger developmental process, such as ego. In other passages he seems to recognize the kind of claim I make here, that faith stages are broader
constructs aiming to comprehend and contextualize stages of moral
judgment. Finally the choice between these options is less important for him than the issues of whether moral judgment stages
precede faith stages (both logically and chronologically) in de-

velopment, and whether faith stage development is *caused* by moral stage change rather than vice versa. Kohlberg—because of his deep concern for the foundations of a nonsectarian approach to moral education in the public schools of the United States—wants to demonstrate that moral reason requires faith rather than that morality derives from faith. In his words,

We may then expect a parallel development of faith stages and moral stages. The critical question, both psychologically and philosophically, is whether moral development precedes (and causes) faith development or vice versa. The data on this question is not yet available. We hypothesize, however, that development to a given moral stage precedes development to the parallel faith stage. Psychologically I believe that it takes a long time to work out a moral stage in terms of its elaboration as an organized pattern of belief and feeling about the cosmos which Fowler calls a faith stage. Philosophically I incline to Kant's solution that faith is grounded on moral reason because moral reason "requires" faith rather than that moral reason is grounded on faith. . . . Universal moral principles cannot be derived from faith because not all men's faith is, or can be, the same.

Moral principles, then, do not require faith for their formulation or for their justification. In some sense, however, to ultimately live up to moral principles requires faith.[23]

Consistant with my understanding of faith stages as the more comprehensive constructs, inclusive of moral judgment making, and drawing on our interview data, my associates and I have distinguished seven structural "aspects" of each faith stage. I have tried to suggest in my longer writings how these aspects undergo transformations from stage to stage.[24] Among these aspects I have included the patterns of cognitive development as identified by Piaget. I have included the stagelike levels of social-perspective taking as researched by Robert Selman.[25] Kohlberg's stages of moral reasoning have been included, showing the broad parallels he predicted, and which we have found, between moral and faith stages. In addition to these three aspects, we have distinguished four others in the integrated operations of a faith stage. They are: (1) the locus of authority, (2) the bounds of social awareness, (3) the form of world coherence, and (4) the role of symbols.[26] In Table 1 we suggest the correspondences we find between these aspects in the faith stages.

Notice that our data supports Kohlberg's prediction that there

## TABLE 1: FAITH STAGES BY ASPECTS
### (FROM "FAITH AND STRUCTURING OF MEANING")

| Aspect Stage | Form of Logic (Piaget) | Role-Taking (Selman) | Form of Moral Judgment (Kohlberg) | Bounds of Social Awareness | Locus of Authority | Form of World Coherence | Role of Symbols |
|---|---|---|---|---|---|---|---|
| 0 | | | | | Undifferentiated combination of basic trust, organismic courage, premonitory hope with admixtures of their opposites—preconceptual, prelinguistic mutuality. | | |
| 1 | Preoperational. | Rudimentary empathy (egocentric). | Punishment—reward. | Family, primal others. | Attachment/dependence relationships. Size, power, visible symbols of authority. | Episodic. | Magical-numinous. |
| 2 | Concrete operational. | Simple Perspective taking. | Instrumental hedonism (reciprocal fairness). | "Those like us" (in familial, ethnic, racial, class and religious terms). | Incumbents of authority roles, salience increased by personal relatedness. | Narrative-dramatic. | One-dimensional; literal. |
| 3 | Early formal operations. | Mutual Interpersonal. | Interpersonal expectations and concordance. | Composite of groups in which one has interpersonal relationships. | Consensus of valued groups and in personally worthy representatives of belief-value traditions. | Tacit system, felt meanings symbolically mediated, globally held. | Symbols multi-dimensional; evocative power inheres in symbol. |

152

| | | | | | | |
|---|---|---|---|---|---|---|
| 4 | Formal Operation. (Dichotomizing) | Mutual with self-selected group or class (social). | Societal perspective; Reflective Relativism or class-biased universalism. | Ideologically compatible communities with congruence to self-chosen norms and insights. | One's own judgment as informed by a self-ratified ideological perspective. Authorities and norms must be congruent with this. | Explicit system, conceptually mediated, clarity about boundaries and inner connections of system. | Symbols separated from symbolized. Translated (reduced) to ideations. Evocative power inheres in *meaning* conveyed by symbols. |
| 5 | Formal operations. (Dialectical) | Mutual with groups, classes and traditions "other" than one's own. | Prior to society, principled higher law (universal and critical). | Extends beyond class norms and interests. Disciplined ideological vulnerability to "truths" and "claims" of out-groups and other traditions. | Dialectical joining of judgment-experience processes with reflective claims of others and of various expressions of cumulative human wisdom. | Multisystemic symbolic and conceptual mediation. | Postcritical rejoining of irreducible symbolic power and ideational meaning. Evocative power inherent in the reality in and beyond symbol *and* in the power of unconscious processes in the self. |
| 6 | Formal operations. (Synthetic) | Mutual, with the commonwealth of being. | Loyalty to being. | Identification with the species. Trans-narcissistic love of being. | In a personal judgment informed by the experiences and truths of previous stages, purified of egoic striving, and linked by disciplined intuition to the principle of being. | Unitive actuality felt and participated unity of "One beyond the many." | Evocative power of symbols actualized through unification of reality mediated by symbols and the self. |

153

will be a close parallel between moral and faith stages. Variations come around stages 3 and 4, however. Up to and through faith stage 3, the parallels are exact. Some faith stage 3s, however (usually men), are best described by moral stage 4. Most faith stage 4s are best described by a position which Kohlberg, for a time, would have called moral "stage 4½," a transitional position exhibiting a relativistic outlook.[27] These persons take account of the need for occasional departures from law or the rules governing systemically defined roles in the service of the "greater good." However, they lack a consistently principled basis for shaping and justifying actions on these occasions. We call this position "reflective relativism" or "class-biased universalism." The latter reference is to persons who recognize higher law principles and claims, but in applying them fall into a pattern of distorting the interests and well-being of other persons and groups by assimilating them to their own, resulting in a kind of moral pseudo-stage 5.

This latter point indicates that moral stage 5, as an intellectual or cognitive construct, is possible at faith stage 4. But a moral stage 5 which integrates and forms a person's consistent moral action appears to be unlikely apart from a faith stage 5. Faith stage 5, we believe, can exhibit either moral stages 5 or 6 with authentic comprehension. Our data on faith stage 5 is far more limited than our studies of faith stages 3, 3(4), 4(3), and 4; therefore, our claims about the relations between faith and moral stages 5 and 6 are more speculative than our claims about the middle stages.

Considerably more detailed data, testing the issue of precedence and cause of development between moral judgment and faith stages, are found in the doctoral dissertation completed by Eugene J. Mischey at the University of Toronto, in 1976.[28] "Faith Development and Its Relationship to Moral Reasoning and Identity Status in Young Adults" is the title of this study. Mischey used the Fowler faith development interview and scoring procedures. He tested for identity status with Marcia's (1966) interview format. In addition he administered Kohlberg's moral dilemmas in a written form, Faulkner and Dejong's Religiosity Scale, and Rotter's Internal-External Locus of Control Scale. His subjects were 30 young adults between the ages of 20 and 35. While we must observe some caution about the adequacy of relying upon pencil and paper measurement of response to Kohlberg's moral dilemmas, Mischey's findings about the relations between faith and moral stages of his respondents are quite interesting. Of the 30 subjects, only 4 showed a level of moral judgment more developed than their faith stage. Interestingly, these 4 were not randomly distributed throughout the sample, but were clustered together in the group Mischey scored as faith stage 3(2). Each of the four scored this way showed a somewhat more fully developed moral judgment stage than faith stage. Nine of his respondents, this time representing faith stages 3, 4(3), 4, and 4(5), showed directly parallel development in faith and moral stages. Surprisingly, 17 of his subjects reflected faith stages more developed than their moral stages.

Most striking in this study are Mischey's findings about the relations between the faith and moral stages and the identity status of his respondents. The 4 subjects whose moral stages exceeded their faith stages in development were the lowest of the sample on both stage scales. In addition, all 4 reflected a *diffuse* pattern of identity. Of those who showed either direct stage parallels (9) or more developed faith stages (17), 4 were described as "mixed" in identity status and 7 showed characteristics of identity "foreclosure." The remaining 15, the most developed by both faith and moral measures, all reflected Marcia's "identity achieved" status. This represents an important independent corroboration of the faith theory's findings about faith stage 4 and individuating identity. It also provides significant light on the question of precedence in faith and moral growth, and concerning the "causes" of the development. Mischey summarizes these implications:

If the present sample of young adults can be considered "random" to the extent that it is not "deviant" in any form or fashion, then it seems that Kohlberg's contention that development to a given moral stage precedes development to the parallel faith stage is open to question. It seems ironical that not *one* individual, who has achieved an identity for himself, tends to score higher on morality than on faith. Consequently it is imperative to ask whether it is truly possible that this sample of individuals fails to provide at least *one* example of where an identity-achieved person is found to be in the process of "working out a moral stage in terms of its elaboration as an organized pattern of belief and feeling about the cosmos which Fowler calls a faith stage." In terms of Kohlberg's perspective it would stand to reason that the present sample should exemplify individuals scoring higher in moral reasoning and in the midst of formulating a parallel faith stage since, as he notes, the faith element is a wider, more comprehensive system of constructs requiring more time and experience; this latter situation would then predicate a lower faith score. The results of the present study, however, show no evidence to validate such an assumption.[29]

Mischey himself acknowledges that while his data provide a basis for questioning Kohlberg's theoretical prediction that moral stages will precede faith stages, and in some sense "cause" them, much more research on these issues is needed. Of most significance is his relation of moral and faith stage to identity formation. Mischey's work supports my claim, made earlier, that forms of moral judgment at each stage are anchored in and supported by the larger frames of meaning and value we call faith. Mischey's work suggests that in young adults who have exercised some choice about the kind of persons they intend to be—and have formed ways of seeing the world and leaning into life that express those intentions—forms of moral judgment which are congruent with these value and belief choices then emerge. He writes:

... (T)he present results indicate that ontological issues and perspectives are an integral part of the "developing personality" and that these perspectives significantly contribute to the structuring of one's moral reasoning and behavior. . . . (I)t seems that an individual initially seeks out answers to questions surrounding his existence as a human being and the general purpose of his life before he realizes the *need* to be ethically responsible in society. It seems that if individuals do not find answers or, at the very least, do not come to some general understanding of ontologically based questions, then the incentive or motivation to be morally inclined may be placed in a precarious position. . . . [30]

Clark Power, a research associate of both Kohlberg and Fowler, undertood a careful study of 21 protocols which included both faith and moral dilemma interviews.[31] Power's careful paper delineates the separable but integrally related domains of morality and faith as they appear in these interviews. His sample included Jews,

Catholics, Protestants, and Orthodox (Eastern) representatives, as well as agnostics and atheists. Ten females and 11 males were included, and the interviews were distributed from stages 1–5. Power was only incidentally interested in the question of precedence. He found "a hundred percent agreement between the major faith stage and the major moral stage through stage three. At stage four I found moral stage four only with faith stage four, but moral five with both [faith] stages four and five."[32] Power's paper represents an original clarification of the interrelatedness of moral and faith stages, but is too substantive and nuanced for brief summary. For our purposes his conclusions about the moral and faith domains can be presented and placed alongside those of Mischey.

Referring to faith as a kind of relatedness of human beings to the ultimate conditions of our existence, Power speaks of six functions faith plays in supporting and informing moral judgment. First, faith constitutes an "onlook"—a way of seeing, a mode of interpreting a moral situation. "An onlook can provide an interpretation of a situation which can motivate action."[33] Second, faith represents a sense of commitment. The experience of one's contingency or finitude gives rise, Power argues, to a renewed sense of purpose: "I must be here to do something." Third, faith impacts ethical sensitivity. As Power puts it, "If the order of the universe is sensed as being lawful or loving then we feel that we should conform our spirit so as to be at one with all that is." (I might point out that conversely, and in a less benign sense, a faith vision that sees the universe as ultimately indifferent or hostile would also have powerful determinative impact on moral judgment.) Fourth, faith can offer "the reassurance that ethical actions in an unjust world are not fruitless, that they (may) have some eternal or eschatological significance."[34] Faith requires a complementarity with being, which relativizes the tendency of persons to center their meanings in themselves. Finally, Power suggests, faith functions "to support human action especially in the ambiguities of life when one cannot control or predict the outcomes of one's actions."[35] As a summary of his claims Power writes,

The role of faith in relation to moral judgment would seem to be that of providing the very condition for the possibility of making any moral judgment. That is,
in every moral judgment there is an implicit future judgment that the activity of
moral judging is in fact necessary.... It is the very ground to our ethical
judgment which I hold to be the province of faith.[36]

## CONCLUSION

Kohlberg has so far opted not to develop a theory of the moral self
or of the development of virtue.[37] He has aimed instead to restore
that dimension of the natural law tradition which affirms that there
is a rational core to moral decision making and action, and that this
rational core is universal. Further, he has had a passionate commitment to the development of an approach to moral education which
avoids dependence upon specific religious or ideological traditions
which could not meet the constitutional requirements regarding separation of church and state. While Kohlberg has been clear that his
developmental stages focus upon and are limited to the structures of
moral reasoning, he has frequently—especially in connection with
his educational writings—propounded a commitment to justice as
the unitary virtue (or comprehensive value) in a faith-like moral
ideology. His writing about "stage 7" is, in a sense, his owning of a
faith vision which sustains and is the culmination of the moral stage
sequence.

The faith development theory conceptually and empirically offers
a way of broadening Kohlberg's account of moral development. I
have suggested here that each moral judgment stage implies and
requires anchorage in a more extensive framework of belief and
value. We have examined the research of Mischey and Power which
corroborates and extends this claim. Our stage theory attempts to
describe this sequence of structural approaches to the forming and
maintenance of faith visions in formal, non-content-specific terms. I
hope Kohlberg and his followers will consider whether the faith
theory opens a way to expand the focus of moral development research without jettisoning its heuristic power. I hope those Kohlberg
critics who find his research and educational approaches too nar-

rowly cognitive[38] may see in the faith stages a more adequate, though still formally descriptive and normative, model for investigating and sponsoring moral development.

# NOTES

1. In *Journal of Moral Education,* Vol. 4, No. 1, pp. 5–16. Cited hereafter as Kohlberg, 1974.

2. See also Kohlberg, "Education for Justice: A Modern Statement of the Platonic View," in Nancy F. and Theodore R. Sizer, Eds., *Moral Education.* Cambridge, Mass.: Harvard University Press, 1970, pp. 57.–83.

3. See Kohlberg, "From Is to Ought: How to Commit the Naturalistic Fallacy and Get Away with It in the Study of Moral Development," in T. Mischel, Ed., *Cognitive Development and Epistemology.* New York: Academic Press, 1971, pp. 151–284.

4. Kohlberg, 1974, p. 5.

5. Ibid., p. 10.

6. Ibid., p. 11.

7. For other, more detailed discussions of our understanding of faith, see Fowler, "Stages in Faith: The Structural-Developmental Perspective," in Thomas Hennessy, Ed., *Values and Moral Development.* New York: Paulist Press, 1976, pp. 173–179, and Fowler and Keen, *Life Maps: Conversations on the Journey of Faith,* Waco, Texas: Word Books, 1978, pp. 14–25.

8. See Fowler, "Faith and the Structuring of Meaning," to be published by Silver Burdett as part of a Symposium on Moral and Faith Development in 1980, James W. Fowler, Ed.

9. Kohlberg, 1974, p. 14.

10. In Thomas Lickona, Ed., *Moral Development and Behavior.* New York: Holt, Rinehart and Winston, 1976, pp. 34–35.

11. Ibid.

12. Kohlberg, 1974, pp. 14–15.

13. Ibid. p. 15.

14. See Fowler, "Stages in Faith: The Structural Developmental Perspective," in Hennessy, op.cit., pp. 207–211.

15. Kohlberg in Lickona, op.cit., pp. 34–35.

16. Fowler in *Life Maps* and "Faith and the Structuring of Meaning."

17. See Fowler, *To See the Kingdom: The Theological Vision of H. Richard Niebuhr.* Nashville, Tenn.: Abingdon Press, 1974, especially Ch. 5.

18. Fowler, "Stages in Faith: The Structural Developmental Perspective," in Hennessey, op.cit., pp. 179–183.

19. Erik H. Erikson, *Childhood and Society* (Second Ed.). New York: WW Norton, 1963, Ch. 7.

20. For more detailed accounts of the structural features of the stages and for examples from interviews, see *Life Maps,* pp. 39–95.

21. See the critical perspective of Ernest Wallwork in this volume.

22. See"Faith and the Structuring of Meaning."

23. Kohlberg, 1974, p. 14.

24. *Life Maps;* "Stages in Faith . . . "

25. Robert L. Selman, "The Developmental Conceptions of Interpersonal Relations." Publication of the Harvard-Judge Baker Social Reasoning Project, December, 1974, Vols. I and II. See also Selman, "Social-Cognitive Understanding," in T. Lickona, Ed., *Moral Development and Behavior.* New York: Holt, Rinehart and Winston, 1976, pp. 299–316.

26. For explications of these categories see *Life Maps* and "Faith and the Structuring of Meaning."

27. Kohlberg, "Continuities in Childhood and Adult Moral Development Revisited," in P. B. Baltes and K. W. Schaie, Eds., *Life-Span Developmental Psychology: Personality and Socialization.* New York: Academic Press, 1973, pp. 179–204.

28. Eugene J. Mischey, *Faith Development and Its Relationship to Moral Reasoning and Identity Status in Young Adults.* Unpublished doctoral dissertation, Department of Educational Theory, University of Toronto, 1976.

29. Ibid., pp. 227–28.

30. Ibid., p. 235.

31. Clark Power, Unpublished and untitled paper prepared for presentation at the American Psychological Association Convention, Section 36, San Francisco, August 26, 1977.

32. Power, p. 4.

33. Ibid., p. 47.

34. Ibid.

35. Ibid.

36. Ibid., pp. 47–48.

37. See indications of the promising ways in which he could move in these directions in "Stage and Sequence: The Cognitive-Developmental Approach to Socialization," in David A. Goslin, Ed., *Handbook of Socialization Theory and Research,* Chicago: Rand-McNally, 1969, pp. 347–480. See especially parts 5–10, pp. 397–433.

38. The most helpful of these constructive critiques are those by Paul J. Philibert, "Kohlberg's Use of Virtue," in *International Philosophical Quarterly,* Vol. 15, No. 4, 1975, pp. 455–479; and Andre Guindon, "Moral Development: Form, Content and Self. A Critique of Kohlberg's Sequence." Unpublished paper, 1978.

*Religious judgment is the way in which an individual reconstructs his or her experience from the point of view of a personal relationship with an Ultimate (God). Religious development is concerned with the age-related, meaning-making qualities of this reconstruction.*

# The Development of Religious Judgment

*Fritz K. Oser*

## The Developmental Frame in the Study of Religious Judgment

Religion as experienced, institutional religion, and religion as defined by theologians and philosophers differ considerably from one another. In this chapter, I focus on the first sense of religion: questions of how individuals experience religion and use religion to create meaning and find direction. My answers to these questions are framed in terms of the development of religious judgment and what underlies that development, namely, transformations in the way individuals define their relationships to God or some Ultimate Being in concrete situations. (The term God or Gods refers to one or more personalized Ultimate Beings and is related to the revelations of particular religions, whereas the term Ultimate Being refers to a less narrow description of a divine being to which an individual feels committed. In this chapter, both terms are used interchangeably. The term Divine Reality would be the least precise notion.)

Only a few efforts have attempted to address the issues of religious experience and meaning making (for an overview, see Meadow and Kahoe, 1984). For example, there have been applications of the Piagetian model of logical development to religious contents (Elkind, 1964a, 1964b, 1970, 1971; Goldman, 1964), attempts to conceptualize religious development as a combination of self, morality, logic, and meaning-making processes (Fowler, 1974, 1976, 1981, this volume; Power, 1988), and studies aimed at understanding

I thank Wolfgang Althof, Anton A. Bucher, K. Helmut Reich, and W. George Scarlett for their suggestions, constructive critiques, and translational help.

NEW DIRECTIONS FOR CHILD DEVELOPMENT, no. 52, Summer 1991 © Jossey-Bass Inc., Publishers

the development of ontological categories (Broughton, 1978, 1980a, 1980b; Fetz, 1982, 1985). Apart from these approaches, there have been few investigations directed at building up a theory about the development of an individual's constructions and reconstructions of religious experiences and beliefs. For this reason, many of us in the field of religious development are attempting to formulate a new paradigm of religious development, using a structural concept of discontinuous, stagelike development and the classical semiclinical interview method as our primary research strategy.

What do we mean by religious judgment? We do not mean judgment based simply on dogmas or religious traditions. Nor do we mean judgment based on any content or descriptive notion such as "God is almighty." Rather, we mean reasoning that relates reality as experienced to something beyond reality and that serves to provide meaning and direction beyond learned content. Such reasoning may occur at any time but is especially likely in times of crisis, as in the following example:

> A boy from a junior high school suffered a serious motorcycle accident that left him with a broken spine and the loss of any ability to walk. His classmates asked their teacher to help them sort out questions arising from the accident, in particular, the question of how God could have let this happen. Some spoke of chance, not God, governing destiny. Others argued that God still governs but in ways that are often unfathomable. For awhile the teacher did not intervene. Then, after several students expressed fear of losing their faith, the teacher shared his belief that a strong faith can only emerge when engaging the world as it really is: full of conflict, injustice, sickness, and death.

What happened in this situation? The students were forced to rethink their individual relationships to God because those relationships provided them with a crucial means to make sense of a particular tragedy. In short, their assessment of the accident involved religious judgments made in the light of their conceptions of how God and they are related. In other words, they interpreted a contingency situation by engaging their religious deep structures of reflection. These "contingency" situations, or at least perceived contingency situations, constitute, in Aristotelian terminology, a fact, a state of affairs, or a process that does not exist or happen necessarily or logically. It could also be in the opposite direction or not at all; there does not exist any rational argument for why it is as it is and is not in some other way. But not only contingency situations call for religious judgment. Sometimes situations are such that individuals are deeply touched by a particular event or are led to reflect on general goals in their lives. These deep structures inform their religious knowledge, their religious attachment, and their religious feelings. Religious judgments represent a form or quality of acts of balancing different value elements against each other, struggling for faith, rehearsing and rejecting solutions, and building up religious "views" of the world's ontological and cultural unevenness.

This example also illustrates how religious judgment is a construction and capacity that can change and develop with age. In the students' collective judgment there was a disequilibrium, a sense of something being out of balance. But this was not the case in what the teacher had to say. A developmental theory of religious judgment thus states that, as in the prior example, an individual relates his or her experience to an Ultimate Being (God), and that this is done *in qualitatively different ways during the life cycle, depending on the developmental stage.* In concrete situations, this connection is expressed through religious discourse and prayer, religious interpretation of events, religious texts and signs, and participation in religious or religiously conceived ceremonies. The individual's understanding of all these activities is filtered and shaped by his or her given stage structure, which is more or less intense or explicit, more or less autonomous, more or less balanced as far as religious expression is concerned, and more or less reversible with respect to the criteria discussed shortly here.

How can we describe this reconstructive religious capacity more thoroughly? How can we identify qualitatively different forms of religious reasoning that are developmentally connected to one another? From a first set of data resulting from interviews with individuals of different ages about their religious meaning making, my colleagues and I extracted seven polar dimensions that emerged in all of the interviews. Moreover, we found similar dimensions when consulting the most important studies on the nature of religion, such as those of Eliade (1957) and Durkheim (1915), and when reviewing the history of theology.

As discussed shortly, we used these seven dimensions to construct religious dilemmas and the respective probe questions for interview purposes. We found that an individual must balance these dimensions and relate them to each other in order to render the religious construction of a particular life situation, or, in other words, to produce a religious judgment.

The first polar dimension is *freedom versus dependence.* An individual's feeling of having been cast into this world and the experience of his or her natural limits are often rationalized by a notion of dependence on the Ultimate Being's decision making. Persons ask themselves to which extent God (the Ultimate Being) might let them have their own way and to which extent obedience is demanded. Religious judgment typically shows an awareness of both dependence and freedom (with respect of God's will), but developmental differences are marked when analyzed for stage characteristics. At a lower stage, in religiously significant situations, individuals tend to see the dependence as immediate; and conversely, they also see individual freedom as given directly by the Ultimate Being. The higher the stage, the more both types of experience are seen as mutually determined (and mutually dependent): Freedom is achieved via experiences of dependence, and we are dependent because we know that it is the connection to God that gives us freedom. Thus, the "will of God" is internally related to the free will of human beings.

The second polar dimension is *transcendence versus immanence*. Again, at the lower stages of development, one pole is in focus to the exclusion of the other, or the two poles are experienced as opposites: either God intervenes directly or he does not, either he is inside or outside of our world. At higher stages, transcendence is experienced as emerging indirectly, through a person's good actions, style, listening, interpreting, and commitments to the welfare of others, so that eventually immanence becomes a necessary priority for transcendence, and vice versa.

The third polar dimension is *hope versus absurdity*. At first, situations determine whether or not an individual feels hope; questions about whether life is absurd or full of hope simply do not exist. But with development come such questions, which are initially answered by pitting one pole against the other. Eventually, the two are understood in terms of each other: Hope supersedes absurdity, but the experience of absurdity remains a necessary (though not sufficient) condition for hope.

The fourth polar dimension is functional *transparency versus opacity*. This dimension refers to how individuals understand God's will, how they judge or read the "signs." At lower stages, either pole is acceptable in particular situations. With development, one pole is acceptable in particular situations, and one pole is accepted over the other: Either an event reveals God's will and action or God's will remains inscrutable. At the highest stages, individuals create a tension between what seems a "sign" (transparency) coming from what is essentially mysterious. We see, but "through a glass darkly."

The fifth polar dimension is *faith (trust) versus fear (mistrust)*. The message may be "Trust in the Lord" while the primary experience is fear and loneliness in face of sickness, suffering, and death. At lower stages, these poles are unequilibrated: Faith does not allow for fear, nor fear for faith. With development, however, strong faith, or deeply felt trust, comes especially through having feared, through coping with life's vicissitudes and "dark nights of the soul."

The sixth and seventh polar dimensions are *the holy versus the profane* and *eternity versus ephemerity*, respectively. Again, at lower stages of development, individuals focus on only one pole while rejecting or ignoring the other. And at intermediate stages, the poles are understood as highly separate and exclusive, for example, feeling we have to abandon any idea of holiness in the world once we confront its profanity. At higher stages, the holy and eternity are seen in the most profane and ephemeral events or actions.

It is how these polar elements are coordinated that constitutes a person's religious deep structure. It is this deep structure that explains how individuals judge particular events, sermons, and religious texts. And it is the development of religious deep structure that constitutes the focus of the theory of religious judgment articulated in this chapter.

# Measuring the Development of Religious Judgment

A religious judgment is made consciously; in contrast, an individual is usually unaware of the deep structure on which it is based. So, measurement and evaluation of a religious judgment require an interpretation of what it reveals about the underlying structure. But before discussing the way my colleagues and I interpreted judgments in order to reveal underlying structure, I need to say something about how we find out about such judgments in the first place.

**Religious Dilemmas.** Religious judgments occur spontaneously in a variety of situations: in prayer, meditation, religious celebration, and crisis. But these situations are difficult to study for a variety of reasons, especially ethical ones. So, my research group followed the Piaget-Kohlberg research paradigm and elicited religious judgments from hypothetical dilemmas dealing with religiously significant problems of a reasonably universal nature.

The most widely used dilemma describes a situation in which Paul, a young medical doctor, sits in a plane about to crash. Out of desperation, he promises to dedicate his life to the sick and poor in Third World countries if he survives the crash. He does survive and then struggles with whether or not to keep his promise. A second dilemma describes a situation similar to Job's: A judge who has led a good and responsible life finds himself in misery and pain, asking why a just man has to suffer so much. This dilemma poses questions about God's justice, will, and power. And a third dilemma deals with whether certain events (for example, winning the lottery) occur solely by chance or whether they can be attributed to a divine plan. These three dilemmas were selected out of a total of twelve because they, more than the others, evoked strong reactions and because they could be understood by individuals from a variety of cultures and religious traditions (with, of course, some changes made in content as we went from one culture to another).

In semiclinical interviews, our subjects were asked what they would do if they were the actors in the stories, and why. Responses to these questions and follow-up questions revealed the subjects' religious deep structures and demonstrated that the structure of religious thought is independent of its content.

**Stages of Religious Judgment.** On the basis of extensive empirical study using these dilemmas to elicit religious judgments, we have been able to discern five qualitatively different forms of religious judgment. In the process of theory building, that is, of identifying major features of possible developmental stages, we followed the approach of interlinking and mutual bootstrapping between theory and empirical investigation. A helix led from initial data to an intuitive theoretical model, then back to the data in order to modify and extend the model, and so on. The five stages defined below form a sequence. The model satisfies the criteria for a developmental theory as usually employed in the cognitive-developmental paradigm: (1) The stages of religious judgment are defined by operational structures differing not only in quantitative respects (number of elements) but also in qualitative respects (organization of elements). (2) The stages form structured wholes. (3) Their sequence follows an invariant developmental logic (empirically, no skipping of stages). (4) The sequence follows the law of hierarchical integration of the elements (the relations between the elements at a former stage become transformed and better integrated at the next higher stage). I introduce each stage with a brief synopsis (Table 1) before giving more details. But a sufficiently detailed description of the stages would require more space than is available here. The following outline thus presents only the most important features of each stage.

At *Stage 1*, the Ultimate Being is conceived as all-powerful, intervening directly in the world and in individuals' fates. The Ultimate Being is pro-

## Table 1. Stages of Religious Judgment

| Stage | Description |
| --- | --- |
| Stage 1 | Orientation of religious heteronomy (*deus ex machina*). God (the Ultimate Being) is understood as active, intervening unexpectedly in the world. The human being is conceived as reactive; he or she is guided because the Ultimate Being is provided with power, with the possibility to make things happen. |
| Stage 2 | Orientation of *do et des*, 'give so that you may receive.' God (the Ultimate Being) is still viewed as being always external and as an all-powerful being who may either punish or reward. However, the Ultimate Being can be influenced by good deeds, promises, and vows. The human being can exert a prophylactic influence (restricted autonomy, first form of rationalization). |
| Stage 3 | Orientation of ego autonomy and one sided self-responsibility (deism). The influence of the Ultimate Being is consciously reduced. Transcendence and immanence are separated from one another. The human being is solipsistically autonomous, responsible for his or her own life and for secular matters. The Ultimate Being, if its existence is accepted, has its own domain of hidden responsibility. |
| Stage 4 | Mediated autonomy and salvation plan. God (the Ultimate Being) is mediated with the immanence, as a cipher of the "self" per se. Multiple forms of religiosity are apparent, all accepting a divine plan that brings things to a good end. Social engagement becomes a religious form of life. |
| Stage 5 | Orientation to religious intersubjectivity and autonomy, universal and unconditional religiosity. The individual's religious reasoning displays a complete and equilibrated coordination of the seven polar dimensions. Religion is more a working model than a security concept. The person feels that he or she has always been unconditionally related to the Ultimate Being: *unio mystica*, *boddhi*, and similar impressions. |

vided with absolute power; it may protect or destroy, send something hurtful or joyful, dispense health or sickness. Often, it is assumed that God made all things, even mountains or big buildings, and caused all events, such as plane crashes. In addition to this artificialism (interpreting the origin of things as a concrete fabrication by an all-powerful divine being), children at this stage often show an anthropomorphic representation of God. The Ultimate Being's will must always and unreservedly be fulfilled; if not, the relationship breaks, and the Ultimate Being inflicts sanctions on the disobedient person. On the other hand, the individual's opportunities to influence the Ultimate Being are viewed as minimal. In the religious judgment interviews, this line of reasoning showed up when subjects stated, in response to the plane crash dilemma, that Paul has to fulfill his promise to God in order to avoid punishment, such as an accident or a stomach ulcer, directly sent by God.

At *Stage 2*, a major structural transformation is evidenced in a dramatic change regarding the conception of the relationship between the individual and the Ultimate Being. This stage can best be characterized by the Latin saying *do et des*, 'give so that you may receive,' just as the Romans sacrificed to the God of the winds in order to survive journeys on the Mediterranean Sea. At this stage, the individual is convinced that God's will and mood can be influenced by prayers, by good deeds, and by adherence to religious rules and customs. If one cares about the Ultimate Being and passes the tests it sends, the Ultimate Being will act like a trusting and loving father or mother, and the individual will be happy, healthy, and successful. In the Paul dilemma interview, subjects at this stage argued that Paul has to go to the Third World because God has done something good for him. If Paul refused to keep his promise, God would become angry and refuse to help him in the next situation of danger. Likewise, it could be reasoned (opposite content of choice but same structure) that Paul does not have to leave his hometown if he is willing to do a lot of good deeds for the poor and the sick, and if he gives a lot of money to relief organizations engaged in the Third World.

But what is going to happen if such good behavior is not rewarded, if the just person must suffer while the Ultimate Being does not lift a finger and wraps itself in silence? In the long run, such experiences are not compatible with the main orientation of Stage 2. The deep structure of religious reasoning has to be broken and transformed in order to cope with situations that do not fit the "tit-for-tat" view of the relationship. Henceforth, the individual feels responsible for his or her own life and destiny.

At *Stage 3*, reasoning can be characterized as "deistic" because the Ultimate Being is conceived as being apart from and outside of the world. The idea of a God in charge of all the details of human existence and nature is abandoned. Rather, it is assumed that God has a particular realm of action. In individual and social matters, an individual's will is crucial;

God's will cannot be known or is not directed to secular matters. This form of religious consciousness is widespread, particularly among adolescents. Evidently, there is a broader developmental foundation for an attitude claiming the separation of domains. Adolescents are in search of their identity; they demand ego autonomy, and often they rebel against external control, objecting to dependence on their parents as well as to the authority of religious institutions with their "antiquated" notions of life style and proper religiosity. The following statements regarding Paul's dilemma are characteristic of this stage: "Paul has to decide alone; I can't see God's will in his fate; all depends on his own will."

It is not surprising that we often find atheistic attitudes at this stage of development. Most of the time, they are explained by the subjects themselves as being caused by disillusionment: "God didn't help in situations of pain and anxiety; he didn't show up when I begged entreatingly. He tolerates unspeakable misery and injustice in the world. Obviously, he does not exist at all." However, we often find an attitude representing the opposite content, namely, an attitude in which autonomy of the self is abandoned, and God is viewed as the only authority to be "served." Examples of this attitude are the so-called youth religions or "cults." Thus, Stage 3 shows a particular imbalance of two autonomous realms, the immanent and the transcendent.

From having tested autonomy (or rejection of autonomy), individuals may come to a new realization about both the necessity and the limits of autonomy. At *Stage 4*, individuals recognize that their freedom and lives cannot originate and give meaning solely within themselves. Rather, in a global sense freedom and life have been made possible and meaningful through an Ultimate Being. Henceforth, God or the Ultimate Being is considered the bearing ground of the world and of each individual's existence. Now, an indirect, mediated relationship with God emerges. Individuals see themselves as free and responsible, but freedom now is tied to the Ultimate Being who gives and sustains freedom. Individuals at this stage often speak of a divine plan underlying and giving meaning to life's events, life's ups and downs. In the Paul dilemma, persons at this stage typically answer that it is God's will that Paul decide himself, but only after carefully considering what is the most responsible course of action.

*Stage 5* reasoning is the most difficult to describe, in part because we found so few examples in our research but also because such reasoning can appear to run counter to what are often taken to be norms for maturity and health. At Stage 5, God or the Ultimate Being informs and inhabits each moment and commitment, however profane and insignificant. The Ultimate Being is realized through human action, wherever there is care and love. Freedom and dependence, transcendence and immanence, all of the polar dimensions become equilibrated to produce a way of being that can at times seem strange and marvelous. The self appears both more and

less than what it was at lower stages. Individuals at this stage seem uncon-
cerned with personal security, and yet they seem the most secure of all.
Freedom now is found in utter commitment and obedience, which to
others appears as a loss of freedom. Wealth becomes poverty, and poverty
wealth. Even sickness and suffering can be valued because of the opportunities they offer for feeling closer to what is Ultimate. An example of a
Stage 5 response to the Paul dilemma is the following: "Paul should not go
if that would mean his life would simply be his fulfilling the promise he
made on the airplane. Whether he goes or stays is not so important; what
is important is that he fulfill the larger promise to live, whatever that may
mean in the many, many challenges he will find."

Taking these stages together, we see a growing need for autonomy and
a deepening appreciation for the unity or "partnership" of opposites. From
"the Ultimate Being does it," to "the Ultimate Being does it, if . . .," to "the
Ultimate Being and humankind do . . .," and, finally, to "humankind does
through an Ultimate Being's doing, which functions through humankind's
doing" is a long road and a struggle because each new stage brings losses
as well as gains.

The growth from one stage to the other is only possible if a number of
conditions are met. Within this developmental sequence, the function—
namely, belief—remains the same, but the structure must go through a
process of disequilibration and subsequent restructuring. Here are the main
conditions of growth: First, the individual feels that the old structure does
not adequately help to explain situations that call for meaning making.
There comes the time when most people understand that "making deals"
with God does not work in the long run; what's more, the notion of "dealing" in itself begins to be questioned. For example, people typically are
responsible for organizing a sufficient water supply and cannot resort to
praying for rain instead of building irrigation systems. Second, there must
be a subjective need for autonomy toward and within the connection to
the supernatural. Third, it must be possible for the individual to reconstruct
the given structural level and apply new elements of reasoning to many
situations in order to differentiate and integrate the new mode of thinking.
The point of departure for each structural transformation is a rejection of
the old reasoning structure: "For a long time I believed that God punishes
us for bad doings; nowadays I don't believe in that anymore. God is not
punishing us; rather, we punish ourselves for bad doings." This typical
statement describes the transformation that begins with the rejection of an
inadequate or "dangerous" thought system that once was important to the
individual. In this sense, rejecting an old structure means building an
atheistic view of it. And, as illustrated in the following section, without the
development of a new structure, the individual would remain within this
kind of atheistic view that is defined by the rejection of former conceptions
of God and the relationship between human being and Ultimate Being.

## Empirical Studies

The following discussion focuses on validation studies of the developmental model of religious judgment, studies of conditions underlying development of religious judgment, cross-cultural studies, and studies comparing religious judgment and other domains of development (for example, moral judgment).

**Validation Studies.** The first study aimed at validating our developmental model of religious judgment was conducted in Grenchen, a middle-sized industrial town in Switzerland: 112 subjects, half females, ages seven to seventy-five, were interviewed using the three standard dilemmas described earlier. Figure 1 shows that the hypothesized age trend was supported for ages seven through twenty-five.

**Figure 1. Age Trends in the Development of Religious Judgment**

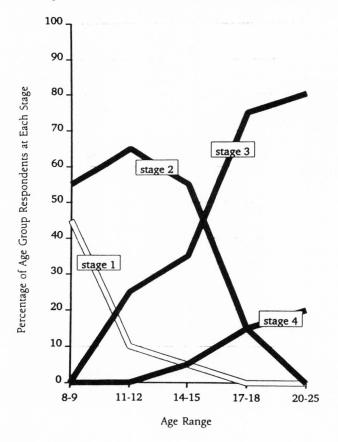

*Source:* Oser and Gmünder, 1968, p. 175.

In contrast, the trend did not continue past early adulthood. Rather, in late adulthood there appeared to be a regression to lower stages. The results pertaining to our older subjects were difficult to interpret. First, the sample of subjects between ages sixty-five and seventy-five was very small, so it was difficult to detect trends in the small data base, and the results may be subject to sampling error. Second, since this was a cross-sectional study, the data may reflect cohort effects. And third, the scores for older subjects may well be a function of the way older people are sometimes treated (mistreated) rather than a function of their age. (This issue is discussed more thoroughly in Oser, 1990.)

The results of the Grenchen study do not show significant differences between Roman Catholic and Protestant subjects. However, there are significant effects for socioeconomic status: Persons with higher socioeconomic status were more likely to perform at higher levels of religious judgment. Gender effects are mixed: Boys scored highest in stage development during the primary school years, girls during adolescence. In adulthood, this gender difference disappeared. Finally, a clear and positive correlation was found between stage of religious judgment and "interest in religious affairs."

In 1988, we began a longitudinal study to further validate the model. The preliminary findings of this study lend additional support to the hypothesized order of stages. As a variant on the longitudinal approach, we also have been conducting biographical studies. Brachel and Oser (1984) interviewed fifty adults about their own religious development. Most were well aware of the transformations that had taken place in their lives, and many offered specific descriptions of their previous thinking that correspond to our lower stages. Contrary to our expectations, these subjects attributed changes in their religious thinking to normal changes in the course of life rather than to critical life events such as personal crises.

In a second group of biographical studies, Bucher (1985), Brumlik (1985), and Hager (1986) analyzed the religious development of Rainer Maria Rilke, Martin Buber, and Johann Henrich Pestalozzi, respectively—all persons famous for both their work and their spirituality. Overall, the stage model of the development of religious judgment aptly described the religious (spiritual) development of these three people, indicating the usefulness of the model for analyzing written material as well as material gleaned from interviews and observations. This method may prove especially valuable in articulating the terminal point of religious development.

**Studies of Conditions Underlying Development.** To identify conditions underlying the development of religious judgment, we conducted an intervention study with two groups of adolescents, fourteen years of age, from the Swiss village of Malters. In the first treatment group, religious judgment was stimulated through discussions of religiously significant issues: Teachers confronted students with higher levels of responses to the issues than the levels reached by fourteen-year-olds. In the second treatment group, the same method was combined with variations in the content of the issues presented and with discussion about the nature of religious reflection. A control group of fourteen-year-olds received conventional religious instruction, where the emphasis was on providing information rather than on stimulating judgment. After three months of intervention, the treatment groups showed significant increases in level of religious judgment, whereas the control group did not. In another interventional study, Caldwell and Berkowitz (1986) showed that both moral and religious stimulation leads to significant maturational effects on religious judgment, whereas religious stimulation does not enhance ability for moral reasoning.

The context of religious development has been investigated by Niggli (1988). This author found that parents who supported, encouraged, and provided positive feedback for their children's religious judgments fostered religious development, whereas parents who did the opposite (for example, criticized and discouraged religious judgments) retarded that development.

A similar result was found by Klaghofer and Oser (1987). The findings of their study suggest that it is not the developmental status of parental religious judgment but rather the presence versus absence of a positive educational and open religious climate in the family that influences the growth of religious reasoning in children. Such results show us that the development of religious judgment depends on features of communication and social interaction experienced in religious and general education. For this reason, the context alone and the "religious capital" of the family alone (such as religious habits, religious discussions, and participation in religious events) are not sufficient conditions for stimulation of religious development. Only if both variables are integrated and embedded in a positive and communicative style of life and education can children and adolescents move toward higher and more autonomous stages of religious judgment. This finding has at least one important implication for religious institutions: Apparently, they lessen their chances of surviving as guiding and meaningful enterprises if they indoctrinate people by using only their inner "religious capital" and if they do not tolerate and even stimulate religious autonomy. The more these institutions encapsulate themselves in the claims of orthodoxy, the more individual religious development is hindered and even undermined. We do not yet have sufficient empirical data to back this hypothesis, but we expect to find relevant material in our longitudinal study.

**Cross-Cultural Studies.** Dick (1982) has carried out a number of studies supporting our assumption that the stage model of religious judgment applies cross-culturally. In samples of Hindus and Jains from Rajasthan, India, Mahayana Buddhists from near the Tibetan border, and a Christian group practicing ancestor worship from Rwanda, Africa, Dick found the same structures of religious judgment and, with one exception, the expected age trends. This was particularly interesting in the case of the

**Figure 2. Stages of Religious Judgment for
Members of a Traditional Religion (Bantu Cult) and
Members of a Christian Missionary Group in Rwanda, by Age**

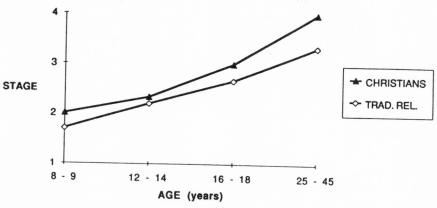

*Source:* Dick, 1982.

group from Rwanda because their theology does not allow for the possibility of God punishing someone who does not keep a promise. Yet, the younger subjects argued exactly this way. Figure 2 shows the Rwanda findings.

**Religious Judgment and Other Domains of Development.** There has been considerable interest in understanding the relationship between moral and religious judgment. However, research has not provided a clear picture of the relationship. For example, it is widely assumed that the development of religious judgment lags behind that of moral judgment (as measured by Kohlberg's stage model), and yet studies by Gut (1984) and others provide mixed results with respect to this assumption. A more sophisticated model is required (Oser and Reich, 1990b).

It is not surprising that the development of religious judgment has been shown to parallel changes and developments in children's worldviews. For example, Fetz, Reich, and Valentin (1989) found that lower stages of religious judgment were highly correlated with archaic views of the world, for example, heaven and earth relate to one another as top to bottom, and with views of the world's creation consistent with Piaget's concept of artificialism, for example, God made the world, even the buildings in it, much as a craftsman makes a piece of furniture.

## Religious and Atheistic Development

We would understand the process of religious development better if we understood the gains and losses that accompany this development. The whole research program described above (and especially the intervention studies) is based on and justified by the idea that the development of religious judgment can and should be stimulated, particularly when it has been delayed. Increases in the ability for religious reasoning lead subjects to a higher religious autonomy, enabling them to be independently religious in a pluralistic world, even within increasingly centralistic religious institutions. However, we must not forget that such development is necessarily purchased through losses. The losses involve old sources of security: a parental image of God, religious dogmas, even faith in a divine plan. The gains are deeper knowledge, wisdom, and direction for living. From rather fixed ways of "being religious," we see individuals developing more open ways of thought so that "to be religious means to question passionately the meaning of life and to be open for answers even if they trouble us. Such a position makes religion something universally human, even if this is not the usual meaning of the word religion" (Tillich, 1958).

In terms of religious consciousness, the child who has abandoned Stage 1 and reached Stage 2 thinking has lost his or her naive notion of security warranted by an all-powerful Divine Being who guides him or her through the vicissitudes of life; what has been gained, on the other side, is the autonomy of feeling able to influence the Ultimate Being. The subject also has lost the immediacy of an animistic, artificialistic, and magical worldview, that is, the "first naiveté," but he or she has gained a more enlightened worldview. (The terms "first naiveté" and "second naiveté" invoke Ricoeur's concept of the development of symbolic interpretation. The "first naiveté" sees the symbol as if it were reality; the "second naiveté" dares to question the truth behind the symbol. See Ricoeur, 1980.) Even at higher stages, religious development necessarily includes losses. When a person's thinking is transformed from Stage 4 to Stage 5, the security of a salvation plan (Stage 4) gets lost, but the full immediacy of powerful religious experience is recovered. Theologically, the Ultimate Being is realized in such symbol-laden events as an embrace, a reconciling gesture, and a solution to conflict. Here, the subject has reached the so-called "second naiveté" that cannot be obtained without losses, ruptures, and often hurtful experiences. There also are losses at the medium stages of religious development. Especially in transcending Stage 2 thinking, people often lose their faith in God and become atheists or, at least, religiously indifferent. This leads to one of the issues raised in the introduction to this section: When talking about those persons, can we still call their reasoning "religious"? As an expansion of my earlier reply to critics (Oser, 1988a), I here want to state some considerations on atheistic thought within religious development.

The following thoughts are based on a recent interview study we conducted with subjects who explicitly declared their atheism. Preliminary results suggest that we have to distinguish four types of atheists: (1) Some people designate themselves as atheists when they do not believe anymore in what they believed before. This self-description seems to be transitional, so this type can be called "developmental atheists." (2) Some individuals call themselves atheists because they have quit as members of a church or other religious institution. In these cases, we could use the term "social or ecclesiastical atheists." (3) In other cases, individuals have thoroughly worked through their former beliefs, at whatever stage they are, and henceforth they deny any existence of a divine Ultimate Being. Instead, their worldviews may be variations of existential philosophy, Marxism, and the like. This type can be called "philosophical atheists." (4) Some individuals are characterized by an absolute absence of interest in religious affairs. Often they also lack concern for existential questions such as "What is the meaning of human life?" and "What is the destiny of humanity in the immense and incomprehensible universe?" Given that many societies foster superficial, hedonistic, and indifferent attitudes, and given that the major message of mass media is that knowledge can be split up in easy-to-use portions and that there is no such thing as universal truth, it can be expected that the societal context prevents many people from asking fundamental questions (Döbert, 1978) and, thus, that this type of atheism is widespread. Nonreligiosity of this kind can, however, go together well with mystical attitudes or quasi-religious forms of irrationality (from astrology to occultism). This fourth type can thus be called "easy atheists."

In the study on which this preliminary typology is based we interviewed subjects with respect not only to the standard religious dilemma situations but also to biographical events and transitions, focusing, for instance, on experiences with the Church and religious education. Instead of giving a detailed outline of results, I restrict discussion here to two findings.

First, as mentioned, developmental atheists are characterized by the rejection of belief systems to which they earlier adhered. Let us suppose that an individual has moved from Stage 2 to Stage 3. In order to make that step, he or she must deny the representation of God typical of Stage 2, including the notion that God rewards or punishes through concrete actions. Before the person has constructed a new representation of God, he or she necessarily develops an atheistic notion, essentially, an image of God that cannot support or establish a religious identity. Consequently, we can assume that certain phases of atheism are necessary, caused by religious development itself.

A special form of atheism occurs at the Stage 3 crossing. Here it seems that subjects who reject religious concepts and institutions are more likely to stay at Stage 3 than are others. For example, Schweitzer and Bucher (1989) show that in their sample of thirty-six adolescents and adults, among the twelve who reasoned at the Stage 3 level, nine rejected religiosity or Church-oriented thinking. In this sample, all subjects who totally rejected religiosity were scored at Stage 3.

Second, most of the individuals in our sample who understood themselves as atheists showed some idea of an Ultimate Reality when interviewed about religious dilemmas or contingency situations and when confronted with fundamental questions concerning the meaning of human existence. Frequently, the most important feature in the atheistic attitude of these subjects was that they solved the dilemmas and answered such questions without reference to a representation of God as it is understood by churches or other religious institutions. Most of the subjects in a study by Achermann (1981) were not rejecting faith per se but rather the Church as an institution, religious customs, the secular power of religions, and so on. Other atheists, with a more elaborated view, put something else in the place of such representations of God and referred, instead, to some other entities that henceforth performed the equivalent function. For example, a young woman denied the existence of the Christian God but articulated the idea that all things depend on nature, and that we have to worship nature for this reason. She did not know that also within the Christian tradition there exists a tradition of devotion to nature. Other, and most serious, atheists referred to social ideals that more or less can be pursued by political engagement. Achermann (1981) constructed a stage theory of the development of atheistic thinking that suggests a progression from (materialistic) determinism to belief in a global changeability of social affairs. From the point of view of religious socialization, most atheists (83 percent) felt that religious education never helped them to deal with relevant or critical life events (see Buggle, 1990).

## Question of Universality

The issue of atheism is deeply connected to the question of universality of the stages of religious judgment. This question refers not only to the cross-cultural validity of the stage scheme but also to the viability of the notion of a religious "mother structure" that cannot be reduced to some other kind of thought structure, such as the structure of moral reasoning. By this definition, a religious mother structure is a kind of subjective *theologia naturalis* (natural theology), a capacity to deal with the seven polar dimensions in life situations in a subjectively necessary way. In this sense, we can assume that each individual is religious. This assumption, however, is a very global supposition calling for certain distinctions.

First, I believe that there is a religious mother structure that is represented in the way individuals relate the Ultimate Reality to their own thinking and acting. The ontological and anthropological conditions, on the one hand, are given by the way subjects experience contingency, weakness, surprise, change, and limits in life. The culture-specific content in different societies, on the other hand, influences the mother structure and is given by religious traditions and by the culture's symbols, rites, and typical interpretations. Depending on the forms of religious socialization, which may change from generation to generation, and on subjects' sensitivity to religiously relevant experiences and questions, contextual factors shape the mother structure, which itself defines the quality of the respective stage of religious development.

Second, a distinction must be made with respect to what we call negative religious judgment, for example, "I do not believe in God because if there was a God, he would help the poor, or there would be more justice in the world." The negative form of stating a judgment corresponds to the positive form, that is, it is based on the same organization of elements. The same elements, for example, the notion that God's actions are manifested in concrete, observable events can be utilized to apologetically assume or to deny God's existence. Even at the highest stage of development and for the most sophisticated people, there is a daily challenge to make sense of life and a daily temptation to focus on secular interpretations of events.

Third, a cultural distinction is needed to properly frame the universality of the developmental stage hierarchy. Although our cross-cultural data showed age-related development across samples, the rates of growth clearly depended on cultural and religious contextual factors. Development is faster in modern ("enlightened") societies than in traditional societies, especially in those traditional societies characterized by orthodoxy. In the latter, individuals conceive of religious rules as rigidly as they do moral rules, whereas in enlightened societies liberally educated individuals tend to see religious rules as matters of personal decision making.

Fourth, a distinction must be made with respect to the universality of stage-typical reasoning. From our perspective, only Stage 5 reasoning can be fully universal and at the same time serve to establish a firm religious identity. At this stage, the central features of revelation are understood as the common essence of all religions, however different their belief systems may be. For this reason Stage 5 thinkers can be perceived as the most promising hope for religious peace in the world.

## Multidirectionality of Religiosity and Limits of Theory

Interviews with the subjects at different ages about the courses of their lives showed that variations in context or setting have an enormous influence on the development of religious judgment. Persons at Stage 3 who grew up in a traditional religious setting frequently rejected the standards of this setting, starting from denial of a personalized divine transcendence in attempting to build their own identities. On the other hand, people at the same stage who grew up in a cold, rational setting, frequently followed mystical tracks, for example, showed some kind of New Age religiosity or joined religious groups with a strong reference to a religious leader and to a personal transcendence. Thus, the courses of individual development strongly depend on biographical circumstances (Brachel and Oser, 1984).

Clearly, we do not yet know enough about the multidirectionality of religious development. We shall have to elaborate our theory on the basis of further research, probably in such a way that religious symbols, religious acts, religious justifications, and religious relationships to the Ultimate Being are seen as embedding and differentiating the structural core of stages of religious development. Additionally, we shall have to improve our understanding of the developmental process. For instance, it can be expected that there are focal points of development: During certain time periods, subjects develop more in one domain of thinking (for example, social cognition) than in others (for example, moral or religious reasoning). These focal points have to be identified in order to understand cross-domain influences.

While we are well aware of the limits of our theory of religious development, some of them are an unavoidable consequence of inherent features of theory building within developmental psychology. A structural-developmental theory cannot give sufficient information about the necessary and optimal educational situations that stimulate religious development. Our theory does not say anything about theological models representing the fifth stage. Nor does it explain the sociological and motivational conditions for religious growth or stagnation. But it does address the logic of religious autonomy, the profound relationships people have with God, the conceptions individuals at different levels of judgment have about the relationship between science and religion, the religious understanding of texts, rites, and cults (Bucher, 1990), and the possibility of being free and religious at the same time in a modern, enlightened society. Our goal is to show that one can be religious, rational, and oriented to a lasting meaning (*re-ligere*) and still be free, committed, and self-guided. So while it is important to see the limitations of a theory, some of them will have to be accepted as necessary and maybe even insurmountable. In general, a theory that claims to explain all will not explain much. As such, a theory's explanatory power depends on its limitations in scope.

## References

Achermann, M. "Kognitive Argumentationsfiguren des religiösen Urteils bei Atheisten" [Cognitive argumentation patterns of religious judgment among atheists]. Lizentiatsarbeit (unpublished thesis), Pädagogisches Institut der Universität Fribourg, Fribourg, Switzerland, 1981.

Brachel, H. U., von, and Oser, F. *Kritische Lebensereignisse und religiöse Struktur-transformationen* [Critical life events and transformation of religious structures]. Bericht zur Erziehungswissenschaft, nr. 43 [Report on educational research, no. 43]. Fribourg, Switzerland: Pädagogisches Institut der Universität Fribourg, 1984.

Broughton, J. M. "The Development of the Concepts of Self, Mind, Reality, and

Knowledge." In W. Damon (ed.), *Social Cognition*. New Directions for Child Development, no. 1. San Francisco: Jossey-Bass, 1978.

Broughton, J. M. "Genetic Metaphysics: The Developmental Psychology of Mind-Body Concepts." In R. W. Rieber (ed.), *Body and Mind*. Orlando, Fla.: Academic Press, 1980a.

Broughton, J. M. "Psychology and the History of the Self: From Substance to Function." In R. W. Rieber and K. Salzinger (eds.), *Psychology: Theoretical-Historical Perspectives*. Orlando, Fla.: Academic Press, 1980b.

Brumlik, M. "Die religiöse Entwicklung von Martin Buber" [The religious development of Martin Buber]. Unpublished manuscript, Pädagogisches Institut der Universität Fribourg, Fribourg, Switzerland, 1985.

Bucher, A. A. *Die religiöse Entwicklung des Dichters Rainer Maria Rilke* [The religious development of the poet Rainer Maria Rilke]. Bericht zur Erziehungswissenschaft, nr. 52 [Report on educational research, no. 52]. Fribourg, Switzerland: Pädagogisches Institut der Universität Fribourg, 1985.

Bucher, A. A. *Gleichnisse verstehen lernen: Strukturgenetische Untersuchungen zur Rezeption synoptischer Parabeln* [Learning to understand parables: Research, from a structural-genetic perspective, into the reception of synoptic parables]. Fribourg, Switzerland: Universitätsverlag, 1990.

Buggle, F. "Wie sehen dezidierte Atheisten ihre eigene religiöse Sozialisation, ihre Ablösung von der Kirche und Religion und ihre aktuelle Befindlichkeit? Ergebnisse einer empirischen Untersuchung" [How do decided atheists see their religious socialization, their separation from church and religion, and their present well-being? Results of an empirical study]. Colloquium paper presented at the Pädagogische Institut der Universität Fribourg, Fribourg, Switzerland, 1990.

Caldwell, J. A., and Berkowitz, M. W. "The Development of Religious and Moral Thinking in a Religious Education Program." Paper presented at the annual meeting of the American Educational Research Association, San Francisco, April 16-20, 1986. (German translation in *Unterrichtswissenschaft*, 1986, *15*, 157-176.)

Dick, A. "Drei transkulturelle Erhebungen des religiösen Urteils, eine Pilotstudie" [Three transcultural inquiries into religious judgment: A pilot study]. Lizentiatsarbeit (unpublished thesis), Pädagogisches Institut der Universität Fribourg, Fribourg, Switzerland, 1982.

Döbert, R. "Sinnstiftung ohne Sinnsystem?" [Meaning making without a meaning system?]. In W. Fischer and W. Marhold (eds.), *Religionssoziologie als Wissenssoziologie* [Sociology of religion as sociology of knowledge]. Stuttgart, Germany: Kohlhammer, 1978.

Durkheim, E. *Les formes élémentaires de la vie religieuse*. Paris: Presses Universitaires de France, 1915. *The Elementary Forms of the Religious Life*. London: Allen & Unwin, 1968.

Eliade, M. *Das Heilige und das Profane*. Reinbek bei Hamburg, Germany: Rowohet, 1957. *The Sacred and the Profane: The Nature of Religion*. San Diego, Calif.: Harcourt Brace Jovanovich, 1959.

Elkind, D. "The Child's Conception of His Religious Identity." *Lumen Vitae*, 1964a, *19*, 635-646.

Elkind, D. "Piaget's Semiclinical Interview and the Study of Spontaneous Religion." *Journal for the Scientific Study of Religion*, 1964b, *4*, 40-47.

Elkind, D. "The Origin of Religion in the Child." *Review of Religious Research*, 1970, *12*, 35-42.

Elkind, D. "The Development of Religious Understanding in Children and Adolescents." In M. P. Strommen (ed.), *Research on Religious Development: A Comprehensive Handbook*. New York: Hawthorn, 1971.

Fetz, R. L. "Naturdenken beim Kind und bei Aristoteles. Fragen einer genetischen Ontologie" [Natural thought of children and as seen by Aristotle: Questions of a genetic ontology]. *Tijdschrift voor Filosofie* [Journal of philosophy], 1982, *44* (3), 473–513.

Fetz, R. L. "Die Himmelssymbolik in Menschheitsgeschichte und individueller Entwicklung" [The symbolism of heaven in human history and individual development]. In A. Zweig (ed.), *Zur Entstehung von Symbolen* [On the genesis of symbols]. Symposium der Gesellschaft für Symbolforschung [Symposium of the Society for the Study of Symbols]. Vol. 2. Bern, Switzerland: Lang, 1985.

Fetz, R. L., Reich, K. H., and Valentin, P. "'Cosmogony' According to Children and Adolescents: An Empirical Study of Developmental Steps." In J. M. van der Lans and J. A. van Belzen (eds.), *Proceedings of the Fourth Symposium on the Psychology of Religion in Europe*. Nijmegen, The Netherlands: Department of Cultural Psychology and Psychology of Religion, University of Nijmegen, 1989.

Fowler, J. W. *To See the Kingdom*. Nashville, Tenn.: Abingdon, 1974.

Fowler, J. W. "Stages in Faith: The Structural-Developmental Approach." In T. C. Hennessy (ed.), *Values and Moral Development*. New York: Paulist Press, 1976.

Fowler, J. W. *Stages of Faith: The Psychology of Human Development and the Quest for Meaning*. New York: Harper & Row, 1981.

Goldman, R. *Religious Thinking from Childhood to Adolescence*. Boston: Routledge & Kegan Paul, 1964.

Gut, U. "Zur Validierung des Stufenkonzepts mittels des Kriteriums 'Moralisches Urteil'" [On the validation of the stage concept using the criterion 'moral judgment']. In F. K. Oser and P. Gmünder (eds.), *Der Mensch—Stufen seiner religiösen: Ein strukturgenetischer Ansatz*. [The human being—Stages of his or her religious development: A structural-genetic approach]. Zurich, Switzerland: Benziger, 1984.

Hager, F. "Die religiöse Entwicklung von Johann Heinrich Pestalozzi" [The religious development of Johann Heinrich Pestalozzi]. Unpublished manuscript, Pädagogisches Institut der Universität Fribourg, Fribourg, Switzerland, 1986.

Klaghofer, R., and Oser, F. K. "Dimensionen und Erfassung des religiösen Familienklimas" [The dimensions and perception of the religious family climate]. *Unterrichtswissenschaft*, 1987, *15* (2), 190–206.

Meadow, M. J., and Kahoe, R. D. *Psychology of Religion: Religion in Individual Lives*. New York: Harper & Row, 1984.

Niggli, A. *Familie und religiöse Erziehung in unserer Zeit. Eine empirische Studie über elterliche Erziehungspraktiken und religiöse Merkmale bei Erzogenen* [Family and religious education in our time: An empirical study on parental educational approaches and the religious characteristics of the learners]. Bern, Switzerland: Lang, 1988.

Oser, F. K. "Genese und Logik der Entwicklung des religiösen Bewuesstseins: Eine Entgegnung auf Kritiken." In K. E. Nipkow, F. Schweitzer, and J. W. Fowler (eds.), *Glaubensentwicklung und Erziehung*. Gütersloh, Germany: Gerd Mohn, 1988. "Toward a Logic of Religious Development: A Reply to My Critics." In J. W. Fowler, K. E. Nipkow, and F. Schweitzer (eds.), *Stages of Faith and Religious Development: An Intercontinental Debate*. New York: Crossroads, 1991.

Oser, F. K. *Religiöse Entwicklung im Erwachsenenalter* [Religious development in adulthood]. Bericht zur Erziehungswissenschaft, nr. 88 [Report on educational research, no. 88]. Fribourg, Switzerland: Pädagogisches Institut der Universität Fribourg, 1990.

Oser, F. K., and Gmünder, P. (eds.). *Der Mensch—Stufen seiner religiösen Entwicklung. Ein strukturgenetischer Ansatz* [The human being—Stages of his or her religious development: A structural-genetic approach]. (2nd ed.) Gütersloh, Germany:

Gerd Mohn, 1988. (English translation to be published by Religious Education Press, Birmingham, Ala.)

Oser, F. K., and Reich, K. H. *Entwicklung und Religiosität* [Development and religiousness]. Bericht zur Erziehungswissenschaft, nr. 85 [Report on educational research, no. 85]. Fribourg, Switzerland: Pädagogisches Institut der Universität Fribourg, 1990a.

Oser, F. K., and Reich, K. H. "Moral Judgment, Religious Judgment, Worldview, and Logical Thought: A Review of Their Relationship." *British Journal of Religious Education*, 1990b, *12*, 94-101, 172-183.

Power, C. "Harte oder weiche Stufen der Entwicklung des Glaubens und des religiosen Urteils? Eine Piagetsche Kritik." In K. E. Nipkow, F. Schweitzer, and J. W. Fowler (eds.), *Glaubensentwicklung und Erziehung*. Gütersloh, Germany: Gerd Mohn, 1988. "Development of Faith and of Religious Judgment: Hard or Soft Stages?" In J. W. Fowler, K. E. Nipkow, and F. Schweitzer (eds.), *Stages of Faith and Religious Development: An Intercontinental Debate*. New York: Crossroads, 1991.

Ricoeur, P. *Essays on Biblical Interpretation*. (L. S. Mudge, ed.) Philadelphia: Fortress Press, 1980.

Schweitzer, F., and Bucher, A. A. "Schwierigkeiten mit Religion. Zur subjektiven Wahrnehmung religiöser Entwicklung" [Difficulties with religion: On the subjective perception of religious development]. In A. A. Bucher and K. H. Reich (eds.), *Entwicklung von Religionsität. Grundlagen—Theorieprobleme—Praktische Anwendung* [Development of religiousness: Conceptual foundation—Problems of theory—Practical application]. Fribourg, Switzerland: Universitätsverlag Fribourg, 1989.

Tillich, P. "The Lost Dimension in Religion." *Saturday Evening Post*, 1958 (50).

*Fritz K. Oser is professor of educational psychology and chair of the Pedagogical Institute, University of Fribourg, Fribourg, Switzerland.*

# ACKNOWLEDGMENTS

Blatt, Moshe M. and Lawrence Kohlberg. "The Effects of Classroom Moral Discussion upon Children's Level of Moral Judgment." *Journal of Moral Education* 4 (1975): 129–61. Reprinted with the permission of Carfax Publishing Co. Courtesy of Yale University Sterling Memorial Library.

Rest, James R. "The Hierarchical Nature of Moral Judgment: A Study of Patterns of Comprehension and Preference of Moral Stages." *Journal of Personality* 41 (1973): 86–109. Copyright Duke University Press 1973. Reprinted with the permission of the publisher. Courtesy of Yale University Sterling Memorial Library.

Rest, James, Elliot Turiel, and Lawrence Kohlberg. "Level of Moral Development as a Determinant of Preference and Comprehension of Moral Judgments Made by Others." *Journal of Personality* 37 (1969): 225–52. Copyright Duke University Press 1969. Reprinted with the permission of the publisher. Courtesy of Yale University Sterling Memorial Library.

Selman, Robert L. "The Relation of Role Taking to the Development of Moral Judgment in Children." *Child Development* 42 (1971): 79–91. Reprinted with the permission of the Society for Research in Child Development. Courtesy of Yale University Sterling Memorial Library.

Candee, Dan. "Structure and Choice in Moral Reasoning." *Journal of Personality and Social Psychology* 34 (1976): 1293–301. Copyright 1976 by the American Psychological Association, Inc. Reprinted by permission. Courtesy of the editor.

Krebs, Dennis and Alli Rosenwald. "Moral Reasoning and Moral Behavior in Conventional Adults." *Merrill-Palmer Quarterly* 23 (1977): 77–87. Reprinted with the permission of the Merrill-Palmer Institute. Courtesy of Yale University Seeley G. Mudd Library.

Blasi, Augusto. "Bridging Moral Cognition and Moral Action: A Critical Review of the Literature." *Psychological Bulletin* 88

(1980): 1–45. Copyright 1980 by the American Psychological Association. Reprinted by permission. Courtesy of Yale University Medical Library.

Blasi, Augusto. "Moral Identity: Its Role in Moral Functioning." In William M. Kurtines and Jacob L. Gewirtz, eds., *Morality, Moral Behavior, and Moral Development* (New York: John Wiley & Sons, 1984): 128–39. Reprinted by permission of John Wiley & Sons, Inc. Courtesy of Yale University Cross Campus Library.

Denney, Nancy Wadsworth and Diane M. Duffy. "Possible Environmental Causes of Stages in Moral Reasoning." *Journal of Genetic Psychology* 125 (1974): 277–83. Reprinted with the permission of Heldref Publications. Courtesy of Yale University Seeley G. Mudd Library.

Damon, William. "Fair Distribution and Sharing: The Development of Positive Justice." In William Damon, ed., *The Social World of the Child* (San Francisco, CA: Jossey-Bass Inc., Publishers, 1979): 71–136. Reprinted with the permission of William Damon. Courtesy of Yale University Cross Campus Library.

Turiel, Elliot. "The Development of Social-Conventional and Moral Concepts." In Myra Windmiller, Nadine Lambert, and Elliot Turiel, eds., *Moral Development and Socialization* (Boston, MA: Allyn and Bacon, Inc., 1980): 69–106. Reprinted with the permission of Allyn and Bacon, Inc. Courtesy of Yale University Sterling Memorial Library.

Nucci, Larry. "Conceptions of Personal Issues: A Domain Distinct from Moral or Societal Concepts." *Child Development* 52 (1981): 114–21. Reprinted with the permission of the Society for Research in Child Development. Courtesy of Yale University Sterling Memorial Library.

Hogan, Robert, John A. Johnson, and Nicholas P. Emler. "A Socioanalytic Theory of Moral Development." In William Damon, ed., *Moral Development: New Directions for Child Development* (San Francisco, CA: Jossey-Bass Inc., Publishers, 1978): 1–18. Reprinted with the permission of Jossey-Bass Inc., Publishers. Courtesy of Yale University Cross Campus Library.

Lickona, Thomas. "Research on Piaget's Theory of Moral Development." In Thomas Lickona, ed., *Moral Development and Behavior: Theory, Research, and Social Issues* (New York: Holt, Rinehart and Winston, 1976): 219–40. Reprinted with the permission of Thomas Lickona, copyright holder. Courtesy of Yale University Cross Campus Library.

Fowler, James. "Moral Stages and the Development of Faith." In Brenda Munsey, ed., *Moral Development, Moral Education, and Kohlberg* (Birmingham, AL: Religious Education Press, 1980): 130–60. Reprinted with the permission of Religious Education Press. Courtesy of Yale University Divinity Library.

Oser, Fritz K. "The Development of Religious Judgment." In *New Directions for Child Development* (San Francisco, CA: Jossey-Bass Inc., Publishers, 1991): 5–25. Reprinted with the permission of Jossey-Bass Inc., Publishers. Courtesy of the editor.